Shoot to Sell
Make Money Producing Special Interest Videos

Shoot to Sell
Make Money Producing Special Interest Videos

Rick Smith and Kim Miller

Focal Press
Taylor & Francis Group

NEW YORK AND LONDON

First published 2013

by Focal Press
70 Blanchard Road, Suite 402
Burlington, MA 01803
781-313-8808

Simultaneously published in the UK
by Focal Press
2 Park Square, Milton Park, Abingdon, Oxon OX14 4RN

Focal Press is an imprint of the Taylor & Francis Group, an informa business.

Library of Congress Cataloging-in-Publication Data
Smith, Rick, 1952-
  Shoot to sell : make money producing special interest videos / Rick Smith and Kim Miller.
     pages cm
  Includes bibliographical references and index.
  ISBN 978-0-240-82376-8 (pbk. : alk. paper) 1. Video recording. 2. Video recordings--Production and direction. 3. Motion pictures--Plots, themes, etc. 4. Photography--Business methods. 5. Photographs--Marketing. I. Miller, Kim, 1958- II. Title.
  TR850.S57 2013
  777.068'8--dc23
                                                                                    2012032834
ISBN: [9780240823768] (pbk)
ISBN: [9780240824772] (ebk)

Typeset in Times LT Std
by MPS Limited, Chennai, India
www.adi-mps.com

Contents

Part I
Video Publishing Business

Introduction   3

1. Special Interest Videos and the World of Video Publishing

2. Types of Special Interest Videos

3. Choosing a Successful Topic

4. Researching Your Topic

Part II
Pre-Production

Part III
Production and Post-Production

Part IV
Getting It Ready for Sale

Part V
Marketing

Disclaimer

This book is written solely for educational purposes and is designed to give helpful information regarding the subject matter covered. It is sold with the understanding that the publisher and authors are not offering it as legal, financial, or other professional services advice. If legal or other assistance is required, the services of a qualified professional should be sought.

While the best efforts have been used in making this book as accurate as possible, the authors and publisher make no representations or warranties of any kind and assume no liabilities of any kind with respect to the accuracy or completeness of the contents nor responsibility to any person or entity with respect to loss or damage caused, or alleged to be caused, directly or indirectly by the information or programs contained within this book. The authors and publisher specifically disclaim any implied warranties of merchantability or fitness of use for a particular purpose. No warranty may be created or extended by sales or promotional materials. Every company is different and the advice and strategies contained herein may not be suitable for your situation.

This text should be used only as a general guide and not as the definitive source of information on producing special interest videos. It is not the purpose of this book to provide all the information on every conceivable business and marketing method that is available to readers, but to explain how the authors organize and run their video publishing business. It is up to the reader to supplement this information with other texts and resources. Available materials may be found on the web, in libraries, bookstores, and from other sources. Some are listed in the Resources section of this book. The fact that an organization or website is referred to in this work as a citation and/or a potential source of further information does not mean the authors or the publisher endorses the information the organization or website may provide or recommendations it may make. Further, readers should be aware the internet websites listed in this work may have changed or disappeared between when this work was written, and when it is read.

Welcome to the world of video publishing and the special interest video (SIV) industry. This book is for anyone interested in producing and selling their own videos. Whether you're an experienced filmmaker or simply someone with a desire to produce a video, you've come to the right place.

One of the first things you should do is get a notebook. We'll be asking you to think about and write down a lot of ideas. Keep your notebook handy and as you're reading this book, take the time to write down questions, ideas, and processes that occur to you. You also should have on hand manila file folders because as you go through the processes we recommend, you'll be collecting a lot of written material to use for inspiration and marketing ideas.

We applaud your enthusiasm but want to stress that this is not a "get rich quick" scheme. It is a business and like any business you will have to put work into it, plan well and have the determination to succeed. Everyone we know who has been successful in this industry has worked hard at it, occasionally taken their lumps, learned from their mistakes and continued to improve. While it is work, it's creatively and financially rewarding. We wouldn't trade it for anything.

We'll share with you the things we've learned that work and help you avoid the mistakes we've made. You'll read case studies of people we know who are successfully selling SIVs. For some of them it's a full-time business; for others it is an important additional source of income but it's not the only thing they do. That's a message we want you to get. You can start out producing one video, learn the ropes, and decide if this is for you. Later you may decide to make it a career or just keep it as a supplement to something else you are doing.

This is not meant to be a course in video production, although we will cover the basics of equipment and enough production techniques to give you a good start. There are lots of books, videos, and resources available for learning video production and we encourage you to seek them out if you want to dig deeper into that topic. We're going to focus more on a vital part of the business that you won't find a lot of resources on—producing and marketing a special interest video.

If you want to make money then you need to start with a good marketing plan because SIV success is about producing what you *can* sell, rather than attempting to sell what you can produce. Marketing decisions need to be made at *each* step of the product development process *before* you have a finished video for sale because marketing is much more than figuring out a way to promote your video once it is complete.

You should be thinking about marketing from idea conception to delivering your video into the hands of your customer. Some of the activities that we will be covering and questions you will be answering throughout this book include:

Business Development—How you'll structure your business, how you'll fund your video, what your budget will be, etc.

Product Development—What you will produce, what it will look like, who will be involved, are you the expert on the topic, and will you have partners?

Market Research—Is it a viable topic? Who will buy it, where are the buyers, and how can you reach them profitably?

Competitor Analysis—What other videos and programs are you competing against? How are they priced, how are they promoted, and can you find your own unique niche?
Production Strategies—What style of production will it be and how will you approach production efficiently and professionally?
Pricing Strategy—How will you price it?
Distribution and eCommerce Strategies—How will you get it to your customers? How will you get paid?
Marketing Strategies—What are the best ways of letting your potential customers know about your video and how to create desire to purchase it?

WHY ALL THE TALK ABOUT MARKETING?

Can you shoot a video before you have a marketing plan? Of course you can, but then you may find out too late that your market was too small, your cost of production too high, your price was wrong, or your market too difficult and expensive to reach. Trust us … this we have learned from personal experience! You'll be more successful if you plan and research each one of these activities before producing your video and we'll show you how to do that.

On the other hand, we don't want you to have paralysis of analysis either. Just follow the steps we lay out for you, do due diligence with an objective eye, and then take your best shot. If you miss the mark a bit you can sharpen your axe and go at it again next time with renewed energy and new skills. If you hit it out of the ballpark the first time, and it does happen, we want to know about it.

Our approach to our video publishing business is to create multiple streams of income. We don't count on a single video to retire on. Rather, we want to have a lot of products on the market at different stages in the sales cycle, each one adding to our overall income. That's the model we're suggesting you follow, too.

DON'T GO IT ALONE

Very few people who read this book will have all the skills needed to go it alone so don't worry about that. You don't want to do everything yourself anyway. That's not running a business, that's just creating a job for yourself. You want to leverage your time and talents by surrounding yourself with people who can boost you up the ladder of success.

We tell you about seeking partners who are the experts in your video topic, or if you're the subject expert we talk about hiring a production company. We talk a lot about marketing but if copywriting and web design are not your thing, by all means get some help. We tell you how to do that inexpensively, too.

One of our concerns while writing this is that the pace of change is so rapid that the specific equipment, software, or websites we mention today may not exist in a few years. That's bound to happen, so we've built a companion website at www.shoot-to-sell.com where we'll keep you current on the latest trends, make specific recommendations, offer equipment reviews, and do everything we can to provide the information you need to succeed.

Rick Smith and Kim Miller

Acknowledgments

We have a lot of people to thank for helping us make this book a reality. Ron Dexter (www.rondexter.com), a friend and mentor of mine, helped by allowing us to draw from his decades of film production experience. We want to also thank Joe Clokey, Rich Ferguson, Dave Sheahan, Jessica Swanson, Alan Berg, Gail Bottomley, and Mike Deiure for allowing us to interview them for our case studies.

We are grateful to Larry Jordan, our peer reviewer, for helping us stay focused and on track throughout writing this book.

Thanks also to our friends Thomas Roberts and Perry Lawrence for endorsing our initial proposal for the book and for moral support.

Finally, we want to thank Elinor Actipis who found us through Twitter and opened the door for us to have this opportunity, our editor Dennis McGonagle, and Melissa Sandford, our project manager, our copy editor Liz Dawn, our proofreader Simon Bailey, and our production editor Denise Power who helped walk us through this exciting new process of getting a book from our brains to the pages.

A Few Housekeeping Notes before We Start

First and foremost, this book was written by two people: Rick Smith and Kim Miller. We discovered that it was too confusing to write it in both our voices even though we did both write it, so it is written from my perspective (Rick). However, there is no way this book could have or would have been written without Kim's knowledge, motivation, and determination to see it through. In fact, if it wasn't for her astute use of Twitter the connections would have never been made for us to write this in the first place. So, a huge thank you and acknowledgment is due to Kim.

You will see us use the word camera and camcorder interchangeably. Since this book is about shooting videos, if you see the word "camera" just assume we are talking about a video camera, and that includes a digital SLR, your smartphone, pocket camera, basically anything that records video.

We alternately use the terms shooting, taping, and filming. They mean the same thing—recording to video.

We refer to search engines often. We may say Google since it is the largest search engine but unless we're specifically referencing a Google tool, if you prefer Yahoo, Bing, Ask, AOL Search, AltaVista, Gigablast, or other search engines, feel free to substitute those.

When talking about how well a website shows up in search engines you'll see me use the term page rank a lot in this book. I use it for the sake of simplicity. This phrase is used almost universally but in fact Google owns the trademark and patent for the word PageRank®. Technically, other search engines use a different phrase. For example, Yahoo's official word for it is Yahoo! Web Rank®.

You will see us use the words online and offline in this book. When we use them we are referencing marketing activities that happen on and off of the internet. Those terms can mean something different in the world of high-end editing.

Also when we talk about studio, we're referring to an indoor environment set up for filming that is relatively sound proof. It can be in your home or a rented space. Unless we're specifically talking about making a feature-length film, we don't mean a movie studio company.

Lastly, because we live and work in the United States of America, when we refer to laws and regulations in this book, we are talking about those in the U.S. If you live in another country, they may not be the same. You have to research the laws where you live and how they apply in your situation.

Part I

Video Publishing Business

I used to have a "real job." I was head of a university media production department. Like many people, I got up early, dressed for work, put in my time, came home, and did it again the next day. And the next ... for 22 years. In that job I had a lot of friends, made good money, won a bunch of national awards, and supported my family. I enjoyed the work and the steady paycheck, but I longed to be my own boss. For some reason, I always felt that my life was not really mine. As it turned out, neither was that job.

My wife Kim was also good at her job, but she was unhappy. She had to get up so early to commute 45 minutes to be at work at 7:30 a.m., and then process paperwork all day. She used to get so blue on Sunday nights that just thinking about going to work the next day would make her sick. She's a creative person and her job in human resources was stifling her spirit. She was a square peg in a round hole, a bad fit and a waste of talent.

Now we get up when we feel like it, usually by 6:00 a.m. or earlier *by choice* because we're so excited to get back to our work. We set our own schedules, pursue creative projects of our choosing, are constantly learning, travel a lot, and have an incredible amount of freedom to live our lives the way we want to. Our work is stimulating, challenging, and rewarding. It feels more like play than work. I've never been happier.

The thing that allows us to do this now is our home business producing and marketing special interest videos (I'm generally going to refer to them in this book as "SIVs"). Our commute consists of going upstairs to make coffee and turn on the computer, often to find that we've made sales while we slept. Our business never closes and our "store" is worldwide.

Does this sound like something you've been dreaming of? If so, then this book is for you. If you yearn for the freedom I just described, if you're an entrepreneurial person just waiting for an outlet for your creativity, or if you're an expert on a topic and you want to share your knowledge with a wider audience, you will love what this book is going to teach you.

Did you notice that in the previous sentence I didn't specifically say if you're a filmmaker or videographer? I did that for a reason.

Having a background in video or filmmaking is an asset in the SIV business but it is not a requirement, as you'll see when you read further.

Here's how I, Rick Smith, got into this business. I started working at Visual Education Productions (VEP) at California Polytechnic State University in San Luis Obispo, California, way back in 1976, right out of college. VEP was a unique quasi-commercial operation that produced and sold classroom educational materials to agriculture teachers all around the United States.

I had just graduated from the University of Central Florida with a degree in photography and so started out as a photographer. I loved shooting slides to a script, editing them, recording a narrator, mixing sound and adding music, then marketing them and seeing the final product sell over and over, all around the country, for years.

This was prior to the first consumer VHS machines and the technology of the day was films and sound filmstrips. By 1980 VHS machines were beginning to show up in classrooms and so we began producing videos, which was even more fun. I was hooked.

I enjoyed several years doing every possible production role and soon became director of the program. "Director" was an administrative title and I actually spent most of my time budgeting, planning, reporting, and managing personnel. Direct mail marketing of our products became the focus of my job and I discovered that I was quite adept at it; I liked copywriting, design, list selection, analysis … pretty much all of it. I missed being involved in the creative side of production but I learned a lot of sound business and marketing principles that help me today.

In 1997 the university suddenly closed the program. Bang, gone! My entire career had been spent in VEP so my work experience was quite specific: I knew how to produce and market educational videos. There were no similar job opportunities available to me in that area and I really had to think about what to do next with my life.

One of the key lessons I took away from that job was that you can package visual information and people will pay you for it, and pay pretty good prices, too. Another lesson was that I never again wanted to work for an organization that could chop my job on a whim. I saw how vulnerable you are when you work for someone else.

I took stock of my situation and realized that I was itching to get behind the camera again. I also knew that I had the business skills to run a successful business and that's when I started my own video production company. Because the loss of my job came on the heels of a divorce (I've since married Kim, my business partner and co-author of this book), I had practically no financial resources to start with but I didn't let that stop me. In my mind, I burned the bridge behind me. There was no way but forward.

At first I did work for clients because I needed to pay the bills, and that was good experience, but I always had plans to get back into video publishing. I started slowly switching from client work to producing videos to sell and today it is rare that I do any client work, and that's the way I like it.

Over time I saw that this business was perfect for many people but they just didn't even know that it existed. I see opportunities everywhere; in fact there are far more today than ever before and there will be even more in the future. This is an industry just beginning a huge growth phase that will last for decades and now is the perfect time to get on board.

The more we meet and talk with authors, entrepreneurs, coaches, video and film producers, and experts on any subject, the more Kim and I feel the need to take the lead and show others how they can be successful SIV producers.

Teaching others how to create and market special interest videos has became a driving passion for us and we've taken steps to put that passion into action. We blog extensively on the subject at www.howtosellyourvideos.com and produced two videos on this topic, *Make Money Selling Your Videos* and *My Secrets Of Producing Special Interest Videos*, which you'll find at that website. We have formed the Special Interest Video Organization (www.specialinterest-video.org) and the Special Interest Video Academy (www.sivacademy.com). You are invited to visit us at all of those sites, plus the free companion site to this book at www.shoot-to-sell.com.

A WORD TO FILMMAKERS

The affordability of digital cameras and editing systems has spawned a generation of independent filmmakers. Our hats are off to these creative artists. They are producing some great entertainment. Most don't have a chance of getting picked up by big distributors, but here's the good news. The marketing techniques we'll cover in this book also apply to independent films. You can take the reins and market and distribute your films yourself. There are many cases of filmmakers producing good movies on budgets under $10,000 who are making profits by selling their films using the strategies and tactics we'll cover.

Ready to get started? Let's begin with an introduction to what SIVs are and who buys them.

Chapter 1

Special Interest Videos and the World of Video Publishing

Chapter Objectives
- Understand what special interest videos (SIVs) are.
- Learn who produces SIVs.
- Get a better idea of who buys SIVs.
- See the financial potential of producing SIVs.

What do exercise videos, documentaries, and computer tutorials have in common? They are all special interest videos!

I personally don't care for the term "special interest videos," but I've struggled to find a better way to describe them and I always come back to that. Take the phrase apart and it is actually an accurate description. They are simply videos that appeal to a special interest. In fact, that's the name Amazon and Netflix use to describe this broad category.

SIVs are usually differentiated from the movie and pure entertainment category like the book publishing industry differentiates non-fiction books from novels. Other terms you will see used to describe these types of programs include educational, instructional, non-fiction, or how-to videos. Call them what you like, for the sake of brevity we'll stick with SIVs.

SIV topics can include histories, documentaries, nature programs, "kidvid," safety, health, tutorials, travel, cooking, training, biographies, and much, much more. If there is something someone wants to know about a specific topic and the best way of explaining or showing it is through a video, that's a special interest video.

WHO PRODUCES SPECIAL INTEREST VIDEOS?

I want to stress again that this is not a get rich quick business. If that's what you're looking for then you're going to be disappointed. This is a real business and it's going to take work and dedication, just like any other business.

That said, it is something that people of even quite modest means can get into. It isn't just large production companies with big budgets making these types of videos. For every large company, there are thousands of regular people like you and me, with small budgets and simple gear, producing profitable videos on all types of topics. In fact, many people are making and selling videos they produced without a camera, using only their computer. We introduce you to a couple of them in this book.

SIVs present a huge opportunity for coaches, speakers, or experts in a subject who want to take their special skill or knowledge, turn it into a video, and sell it. Making a video is easier and faster for most people than writing a book and can have more impact. Instead of training one-on-one, you could reach thousands of people around the world! Imagine how many people's lives you can influence and change in this manner.

There are many examples of people making fortunes in SIVs. Jane Fonda and Suzanne Somers blazed a trail in the home exercise video market, a path taken up by their contemporary counterparts like Jillian Michaels and Tracy Anderson. The late Stephen Covey, Tony Robbins, Robert Kiyosaki, Brian Tracy, and scores of famous trainers and coaches have produced videos that are viewed millions of times all around the world. This business model is still highly profitable today with people like Suze Orman not only making a mark on television but selling SIVs as well.

But don't think you need to be famous or a celebrity to make a successful special interest video.

Cole Mathews is the son of my former office manager. He took an early interest in video production and extreme sports, skateboarding competitions specifically, and he now travels the world producing videos on these events. He gets to indulge in his favorite activities and make a good living while he's doing it. There are some teenage video entrepreneurs making successful SIVs by taping skateboarding, surfing, and BMX events, activities they love. Age is no barrier. Not having millions to invest isn't either.

We have other filmmaker and non-videographer friends and associates successfully making and selling videos on diving, ocean kayaking, horse training, internet marketing, exercise, magic, dating, poker, real estate, and more.

My point is that almost any topic is fair game and almost everyone has the potential to produce one. If you have a hobby or burning interest in a subject, chances are there are other people who share your interest and they are your potential customers.

So you see, what falls under the category of "special interest videos" is almost limitless. The ability to produce one, no matter your age, financial situation, or lack of video knowledge, is within your reach.

Of course not everyone will be as financially successful as Jane Fonda or Tony Robbins, making millions off of their videos. However, what would an additional $500, $1,000, or more per month mean in your life? That could buy you a new car, cover your mortgage payment, fund your children's college accounts, pay for that trip of a lifetime, or build up your retirement savings.

If you turn what you know into a video that sells moderately well, it is quite possible to make that much or far more. For us, sales of our SIVs allow us to say no to client work we don't want, get our weekends back, focus on higher paying corporate clients, and of course, produce and sell more of our own video titles!

How would that additional income change your life?

WHAT IS THE MARKET FOR SPECIAL INTEREST VIDEOS?

Before we talk about who buys SIVs, you need to understand the concept of a niche because determining what niche you intend to sell in plays a large part in determining how much money you'll make. One of my favorite sayings is, "there are riches in niches." It comes down to knowing your market and going after it with laser focus.

In the marketing world and as defined in www.thefreedictionary.com, a niche is a special area of demand for a product or service.

For example, golf is such a broad topic that I wouldn't call it a niche. Whereas "female golfers over age 50" is much more narrowly defined, and that is a niche. Can you see how much easier it would be to produce a video that appealed to that specific target market?

When I say there are "riches in niches," what I mean is you need to produce your video with the needs of a specific market in mind. The more targeted your video is to a particular group of people (niche audience), the better your chances of reaching and selling to them. This is an important point that we will again discuss in the chapter on choosing a topic to produce.

For example, the videos I produced about producing and marketing special interest videos are in themselves special interest videos targeted to a fairly narrow niche: people who want to produce and sell special interest videos. *You* are obviously interested in this topic or you wouldn't be reading this book, but this is a subject that will fly under the radar of most people. "Special interest video producers" is a niche.

The niches in which Stephen Covey, Wayne Dyer, and Jillian Michaels produced their videos are some of the most commercially successful special interest video categories: self-help and fitness. In fact they are so large, I would use the word genre to describe them rather than niche. Other top-selling genres are sports and children's video (also called "kidvid"); dance, business, and sex videos are close behind. Your best bet is to choose a topic that appeals to a niche within these large genres so that you are more clearly targeting a specific interest.

However, SIVs don't have to be big, exciting topics in these genres to be successful. You don't have to stoop to producing pornography either. (Personally I wouldn't recommend that if you want to keep your reputation.)

In fact, all of the aforementioned multi-million dollar areas are also highly saturated and fiercely competitive. If you are a small producer on a limited budget, it will be much harder to be seen in these markets and convince people to buy your video over the well-known brands that are so established. Focusing on a more specific niche is a much better way to start out. "Niche it down," we say.

The first video we produced at VEP, around 1981, was *The Elements of Pruning*. It was a simple program about why and how to prune shrubs and trees. Now that doesn't sound very exciting, does it? And it wasn't, unless you happened to want to learn how to prune trees and shrubs. Then it was the perfect product to satisfy your special interest! In fact, we sold thousands of them at an average cost of $100 each.

It pleases me to know that that video is still selling today for the company that now owns that title, over 30 years later, at a now *reduced* price of $80 per copy. That simple video production has earned hundreds of thousands of dollars over its lifetime and it's still going strong. Pruning practices aren't likely to change much, so it'll probably sell for many more years.

My close friend and fellow filmmaker, Joe Clokey, is passionate about horticulture and environmental concerns. He has created scores of videos on those topics. He sells these 20–25-minute videos through his company, San Luis Video Publishing, to schools and universities worldwide at a typical price of $120 each. These aren't Hollywood-quality productions but they are well made and are appropriate for the market they are intended for, which is primarily horticulture and agriculture teachers.

Joe's videos are relatively inexpensive to produce and most will have a sales life of more than ten years. They sell for premium prices because they are so specific and because there is little competition in that niche. Schools are used to paying higher prices for instructional videos because of the nature of how they are shown, i.e., in a classroom to a group of students. This is another important difference in producing special interest video titles as opposed to mass market movie titles that you see at discount stores for under $10; they can sell for higher prices due to the nature and market for which they are made.

Aside from making a good income from his videos, Joe is doing something with his skills that he feels is important. His business earns over $300,000 per year from titles that are mostly 10 years old or older, with relatively little effort on his part. He started working for me on a student video project almost 25 years ago and loved the work so much he made it a career. You'll meet him later.

Another friend, Jim Harrigan, also started his SIV publishing career as a student at the university. He produced a video for our department as his senior project. In fact, he's the on-camera host in that video I told you about, *The Elements of Pruning*. He followed that up with a bunch of horticulture videos before getting into producing medical training videos over 20 years ago and has made an excellent income from them. His titles sell for $300 to $400 each!

Don't fall into the following trap though ...

Let's take a moment to look at the other side of the coin. I have seen enthusiastic entrepreneurs lose their shirts by producing a video that they could not sell or that cost them so much that they never had a chance of breaking even. They didn't do their homework before starting. They let their enthusiasm for a subject take control before they did their research. This is a hard lesson to learn, believe me, but it is very important for you to get this point. I have seen people make some very expensive mistakes because they didn't do their research. I've been one of these guilty people.

We're going to discuss how to choose topics with a high chance of financial success and how to research your potential market and their willingness to buy your video in the following chapters.

WHO BUYS SPECIAL INTEREST VIDEOS?

A logical question you may have about now is who buys SIVs? Who would be your likely customers?

Customers come in all types, from schools, organizations, and companies that buy them for training, to individuals buying them to learn something new or polish a skill. Keep in mind, no matter how big the purchasing organization is, a *person* will be making the decision to purchase your video. That knowledge comes in very handy in your marketing efforts as I will explain.

Here are some samples of the types of customers to whom I have personally sold SIVs:

Armed Forces	Junior High Schools
Assisted Living Centers	Long-Term Care Facilities
Bookstores	Museums
Clubs	Non-Profit Organizations
Community Colleges	Pre-Schools
Disneyland	Prisons (they use them for job training)
Elementary Schools	Public Libraries
Gift Shops	School Libraries
High Schools	Sea World
Historical Societies	Small Business Owners
Hobby Shops	Specialty High Schools
Hobbyists in All Areas	Specialty Libraries (e.g., medical, agricultural, law)
Homeschoolers	The Capitol Mall
Hospitals	Trade Schools
Individuals	Training Departments for Corporations
Insurance Companies	Universities (both private and public)

These customers came from over 25 different countries. This list isn't complete and it doesn't include distributors who buy from us and then resell to even wider markets. We'll come back to this list later when we talk about doing research and marketing your videos.

I personally buy SIVs all the time. When I need to learn something about a video post-production topic I'm not familiar with I turn to www.larryjordan.biz, www.lynda.com or any number of specialty video publishers. I've also spent lots of money on tutorials to improve my guitar playing. I used to fly airplanes but it has been a number of years since I was pilot in command, so now I'm looking at pilot training videos to refresh my skills and knowledge. Kim and I also like to rent or check out videos on history, travel, and cooking from the library. And remember, the library has to buy these videos from someone, so why not you?

I'll bet you've bought SIVs too, although you may not have realized it or called them by that name. Did your teacher use videos to teach a subject? Have you downloaded cooking videos, software tutorials, or videos from live or taped events? Those are all SIVs too.

With the arrival of technology that can provide high quality video online to the rapidly expanding base of mobile users with smartphones and tablets, in addition to computers and TVs, the demand for content is growing exponentially. This is an excellent time for creative videographers, filmmakers, experts, and entrepreneurs to enter the special interest video production business to feed this hungry market.

OUR BUSINESS MODEL—"SHOOT IT ONCE, SELL IT FOR YEARS"™

Our business model is simple: you keep producing a stream of programs that have a long potential shelf life, sometimes as long as 15 to 20 years or more. We call these "evergreen" because they don't change or become obsolete quickly. The goal is to produce a body of programs that all contribute to your gross income. All of these streams of income feed into a flowing river. By producing multiple titles you even out the ups and downs of individual sales cycles, particularly if some of your titles sell more during one time of year, such as the Christmas gift season, than others.

The potential long shelf life of SIVs is a key benefit of the business. With a carefully chosen topic you can enjoy residual income from your work for many years, even decades. Imagine spending as little as a week or two producing a video that sells for 20 years. As I mentioned earlier, my first instructional video, *The Elements of Pruning*, produced in 1981, is still selling today at $80 to the school market.

We like to use the term "shoot it once, sell it for years"™ to describe this aspect of producing SIVs.

Kim left her secure university position in human resources to join me in my video business in 2003, producing her first video on—drum roll please—*The Properties of Soil*. Yep, that's right, it was about soil, how it's formed and how its properties are evaluated. The market was high school agriculture and horticulture classes, as well as beginning soil science classes. This is a very narrow niche and you probably think that's about as boring a topic as you could pick, right?

Here's what Kim has to say about that:

"I absolutely loved the process of creating it! It brought together all my creative and intellectual sides; researching, conceptualizing, scripting, storyboarding, working with people (the advisor, narrator, on-camera talent, etc.), shooting and editing. I'm also pleased to say that it started selling well as soon as it came out!"

Now, if a former human resources specialist with no previous video production experience can produce a profitable program like this her first time out, what's stopping you?

Kim and I are both creative types with degrees in art and we used our skills to take something as mundane as *The Properties of Soil* and turn it into a Telly Award winning video. I hired a composer to write an original soundtrack, we shot beautiful footage and it came out great. It was produced on a budget of $7,000 and to date the client we produced it for has sold over $100,000 of that video and it will continue to sell for years to come. Insight Media, one of their distributors, marks it up to $179 each, and they sell a lot of them.

When you think about it, how much competition do you think that video has? Probably none. How soon will it become outdated? Soil science doesn't change fast so the content will be relevant for decades to come. A long shelf life is guaranteed! That's a perfect example of an evergreen product and a brilliantly chosen niche video topic.

Our objective in choosing videos to produce is simple: choose a topic that will have a high chance of success and which will produce income for many years. Repeat the process over and over again.

HOW MUCH MONEY CAN YOU MAKE WITH SPECIAL INTEREST VIDEOS?

Let's get down to the dollars and cents of this business. The selling price of SIVs varies wildly, depending on the market.

I caution first-time producers to stay away from titles where you have to compete with Walmart prices. You don't want to be selling $10 DVDs because you'll never sell enough to make much money, especially if you are going through distributors who take 50 percent or more of the sales price. Take out your cost of goods and you're left with almost nothing.

Remember this is a business and you have to run it that way.

I produced a video with an expert car detailer a few years back. He kept insisting we try to get this video into Walmart, then we could just sit back and watch the money flow in. I explained to him that to compete we'd have to probably sell it for $3 to $4 to Walmart if their retail price will be $8.95 to $9.95, maybe even less. After taking out the cost of duplicating and packaging (approximately $1.25), and if I pay him a 20 percent royalty (which is very generous; in the book publishing industry, it averages 10 to 12 percent), he would be looking at making around $0.35 to $0.55 per DVD.

Now, you may say, if you sell millions of them, then that would be very profitable. True, but you probably wouldn't sell millions, and when you deal with large discount stores you encounter a different set of problems that may end up costing *you* thousands of dollars instead of making any money. Later on, you'll meet one of my friends and hear why he no longer sells to discount outlets.

There are cases where selling through a large retail outlet would be very profitable and I don't want to dissuade you from trying that, it's just not an easy route nor always the best choice. It's hard to get your video in front of a buyer and onto store shelves, and they'll take a huge discount for doing so. That's one way to go. We prefer hands-on involvement in the marketing process, not handing it over to someone to whom your product is just one more item to sell. We're all about internet sales and a large portion of this book is dedicated to that subject.

Now let's take a look at the income potential for SIVs.

Like I shared earlier when I talked about the school market, a typical SIV price is $100 to $150. A two-DVD set comprised of four 20-minute programs may sell for $350 to $400 on the high end. An average price in a specialty consumer market may be $29 to $49. Many more sell for $19.95 to the home market. These markets are much easier for the independent producer to get into and tap than national discount stores.

Let's do some math so you can see the potential.

Assume you have produced just one title and you sell one copy per day at $20 each. In one month that's 30 copies, earning $600. (There's that car payment.) In one year that's $7,200. In five years that adds up to $36,000.00.

$$30 \times \$20 = \$600/\text{month}$$
$$12 \times \$600 = \$7,200/\text{yr}$$
$$(5 \times 12) \times \$600 = \$36,000$$

That's not a lot yet, but hold on. What if over time you produced 10 titles and each one sells just one copy per day. At $20 each, that's $200 a day. In one month, $6,000. In one year, $72,000. Over five years those 10 videos selling one copy a day would net you $360,000. Now we're talking!

Just for fun let's boost that to $50 per title, selling one per day of 10 titles. Your annual income would be $182,500. That's pretty exciting to think about, isn't it?

$$(10 \times \$50) \times 30 = \$15,000/\text{month}$$
$$12 \times \$15,000 = \$180,000/\text{yr}$$
$$(5 \times 12) \times \$15,000 - \$900,000$$

Now, are those kind of sales really possible? Yes, but in all honesty you'll have to work for it.

Although there are producers who have met the right person at the right time and sold millions, for most of us, you can't expect that to happen. There's much more to it than sending it to Amazon or calling a few stores, sending out a few emails to other distributors or retail store buyers and expecting checks to come pouring in. Nor can you put up a website and expect people you think would want it to find it, then click on the Buy Button the minute they see what you have to offer.

I wish it was that easy, but it isn't. But what you will probably find, if you are passionate about making money with your videos, is that you will find it fun. Heck, you may discover a whole new talent or skill you didn't know you had and you'll meet some incredible people and future business partners along the way. That's what happened to us and how we came to be writing this book.

We are lucky in that we not only love video production, we also love marketing. For Kim, her passion for marketing wasn't there in the beginning. Now she's not only passionate about it, you could almost say she's obsessed with marketing, especially online marketing. We have found that, like anything else, if you put your shoulder into it you'll learn more, it'll get easier as you get better at it, and you'll make more money.

Our philosophy is that you have to be hands-on with marketing your products. Even if you turn it over to Amazon or a distributor, you're just one of many titles they have and you probably won't get the kind of sales you'd like (unless of course you're Al Gore). That's why we spend so much time in this book focusing on marketing.

If that causes you to groan, all I ask is that you stick with me. I'm not talking about door-to-door selling, or making cold calls, or spending thousands of dollars on advertising. I'm talking about direct marketing with a very big emphasis on using all the incredible and affordable internet and social media marketing tools at our disposal.

Like I said previously, Kim hated marketing. She somehow equated online marketing to scammy tactics. Once she saw that it was about building relationships and how people were really excited about and happy to buy the videos we produced, she got it. She really became thrilled when she saw her efforts turn into repeat customers and money in our bank account!

Now that you know what special interest videos are and the financial opportunities that are available to you, it's time to dig in and figure out what you want to produce. The first step in doing this is to pick your topic, research it, and then define and research your market and competition.

Action Steps

- Look back at the types of SIVs you have watched, purchased, or checked out at the library.
- Review the list of people and places that I've sold SIVs to and see if you can add more to the list.
- Run your own mathematical scenarios of your income potential.

Chapter 2

Types of Special Interest Videos

Chapter Objectives
- Understand the various types of SIVs that you can produce.
- Choose which type you'd like to pursue first.

If you have never operated a video camera or written a script, the thought of producing a special interest video can be bewildering. Don't let that discourage you from getting started. When you break it down into logical steps it becomes quite manageable.

We're going to explore the basic formats you can choose for your SIV, from the simplest possible approach to a fully scripted movie-style production.

You may be the hands-on, roll up your sleeves and get behind the camera type or maybe your goal is to just get it done quickly, in which case it may be wiser for you to hire a professional video production crew to shoot and edit your video.

Whatever you decide to do, you have a lot of choices about the format or style that will be best suited to your topic.

SPECIAL INTEREST VIDEO FORMATS

Let's review some of the options you have for producing your SIV. We'll start with the simplest approaches and work up to the more challenging formats.

You are There

This is as simple as it gets. I worked with a man a few years ago who was making a very good living selling videos of flowers. That was it, no story, just close-ups of beautiful flowers with relaxing music behind it. He also did one on streams; it was simply beautiful shots of water running in streams, again with a relaxing soundtrack. It was hypnotic to watch. Last I heard from him he was continuing to expand his titles and was doing very well.

Similarly, we met a man recently who has produced a video of wild birds in Florida. It's nicely edited footage of birds, mostly in flocks, feeding in natural settings. It has soothing music in the background. Bird watching is his hobby and he leads groups of people on cruises and arranges excursion tours to go bird watching. Talk about living your passion!

Many years ago my parents sent me a VHS tape called *Video Catnip*. It was just shots of birds in the wild. It didn't even have music, it was just video of birds flitting around in trees, shrubs, and on the ground. My cat absolutely loved it. I thought it was brilliant. I've seen videos of fireplaces burning that go on for hours; it turns a TV into a fireplace. And the same thing with aquarium videos: I've seen one that was just a single very long shot of the fish swimming in a beautiful aquarium. It turns your TV into an aquarium but you don't have to feed the fish.

Some people like to just look at things they love. I know of people who like to watch jets land. There's a place at the end of the Los Angeles International Airport runway where these people gather to watch planes land and take off. I've often considered making a video of that. There's no storyline, nothing to editorialize on, no opinion to express, just lots of shots of jets coming and going. There are fans of trains, big rig trucks, boats, ships, airplanes, Harley-Davidsons, etc., who would buy videos just showing a lot of these cherished items.

In the early 1990's, independent video producer Fred Levine hit a home run when he made a video of construction equipment at work called *Road Construction Ahead*. He was inspired to produce this video from watching his children's fascination with big machines. At the same time, he wanted to create videos for children that were not only educational but entertaining as well. Little boys, particularly, loved to just sit and watch big equipment at work. That video was a big success and launched many more titles outlining the simple concept of tapping into children's curiosity and showing them how things work. He sells his videos through many outlets and at his site, www.littlehardhats.com.

You never know what simple idea can be your big hit, so keep these types of productions in mind.

Recorded Seminars or Workshops

I've produced and sold several of these. This is when you simply record someone (or yourself) like an expert, author, professor, coach, or motivational speaker on a stage giving a talk or workshop. These are generally easy to do, with a few caveats.

The great thing about this format is that it is usually a one-take affair, meaning you turn the camera on, record the talk, turn the camera off, and you're done shooting. Editing can sometimes be as simple as trimming out bits here and there and adding titles. You can complete these very quickly.

By shooting these with more than one camera, which I almost always do, you increase the production value but also the complexity of editing them. One of the reasons I like to shoot everything with more than one camera is because I want a backup camera in case the main camera fails. You don't even have to use the footage from the second camera, but it is comforting to know it is there if you need it.

The other reason I like to shoot with a second camera is that I can get audience reaction shots to cover a bad shot, like the speaker standing in front of the light of the projector, with a better angle.

You often have no control over the lighting in these situations and possibly have no control over audio either. Also, a lot of speakers today use PowerPoint slide shows and it can be hard to get a good exposure for both the speaker and the slide show. In these situations I often ask for a copy of their slide show and then insert these slides in the editing phase. This takes more time and skill but produces a superior product.

In summary, this format is not that difficult to produce and it is a frequently used approach to SIVs. If you're the expert, you can hire a videographer to shoot it and put the final program together. This is such a common and profitable format that we've devoted an entire chapter to shooting seminar presentations.

Follow Along Videos

This is just what it sounds like. You follow someone with the camera as they demonstrate something. This is most likely a topic they know so thoroughly that they do not need a script; just mic them up, turn on the camera, stay out of their way, and let them show you their skill.

My best personal example of this is the video I produced on automobile detailing. I had no idea beforehand what he was going to demonstrate, but I knew he was an expert car detailer, that he did live workshops, and knew how to present his topic well. After we met up and I got a clear idea of what we'd shoot and the environment I had to work in, I put a wireless microphone on him, added some lights where needed, and just followed him around as he demonstrated to the camera how to detail a car, from start to finish. There was rarely a time when I asked for a second take, although I would take close-up shots of his hands doing certain things for cutaways.

This type of production can be simple. Other good examples of a follow along video would be a cooking show or a fishing program.

Educational or "How-To"

These can be produced in either of the formats described above or follow the more organized, scripted format I describe below.

I spent over 20 years producing professional educational films and videos for schools. Most of these were well-planned, scripted productions that usually took months to complete. They were often shot at multiple locations and over a period of time. They usually included graphics and animations to make concepts clear.

If you do decide to produce videos for classroom sales, make sure your topic has a place in school curriculums. No matter how wonderful your video may be, if there isn't a slot in the curriculum for it the teachers probably can't use it. They only have so many hours in each class and if it isn't a good fit then you've missed the mark. This is why knowing your target market, this one being teachers, is so important.

To be effective, an educational video has to have a clear purpose, specific learning outcomes, and be focused as narrowly on the topic as possible. Remember how we talked about niching down your market? Well, you should also niche down your topic. For classroom use, about 20 to 25 minutes is ideal. This allows time in a 50-minute class period to call roll, make announcements, introduce the video, show it, and do a little Q&A after viewing.

Of course the older the student and the more sophisticated the audience is, the deeper you can go into the information and the longer it can be. Educational or how-to videos geared to a consumer market can be longer, but 60 minutes is probably the maximum length you want to reach. Shorter is better.

Documentary

Documentary films (docs) and videos are non-fiction, meant to create a historical record of a person, event, or series of events. Certainly the definition of a documentary production is rapidly changing in the media-rich society in which we live, but at its essence it should be non-fiction, which begs the question: Are today's "reality shows" documentaries? Adding entertainment value and expressing an editorial opinion through creative staging, shooting and editing is widely accepted. Since this book is about generating income from SIVs, let's just assume that you are going to approach a documentary project with an eye to giving it sales appeal.

Docs can be simple or a long, complicated production lasting months or even years. I've seen a lot of beginning videographers say they are working on a documentary when really they have no plan other than to shoot a lot of footage and hope to make something out of it later. That's not a very good plan.

I've shot a lot of docs like this myself. Some turned out well and some did not. One thing I learned is that as the producer you really need to have a goal in mind and must often take charge of the situation to get the shots you want. Just being a fly on the wall with a camera isn't going to get you far.

Admittedly, sometimes a documentary is just that—you are documenting an event as it unfolds without trying to make anything more of it than that. An example of a simple documentary would be to tape the activities at an event such as an air show, sports event, or car rally. The more you work interviews and personal stories into it the better. Get your camera into the middle of things and get the energy of the situation.

Since you are doing this with the intention to sell it, you really have to make it entertaining. It needs to be coherent and tell a good story. You are the director, so direct! Don't just accept whatever an interviewee is saying if it isn't giving you the energy or going in the direction you want. Re-direct the question, dig deeper, and take control of the situation.

Scripted Production

This style is well suited to fiction and non-fiction alike. It is my favorite style of production and the one I am most familiar with. I find the more organized a production is, the less stressful it is in the production phase and I'm all for having less stress. The scripted production is particularly well suited to educational programs, and the more complex the topic, the more you want to thoroughly flesh out the content in a script first.

I'm a closet movie producer anyway. I love everything about planning, scripting, shooting, and editing this type of production. Although it may sound a little overwhelming in the beginning, there is a structure to this type of work that will almost certainly help you produce a superior SIV.

The heart of this type of production is the script and we'll be covering scripts and shot lists in a later chapter. A script is a roadmap that will ensure that you include all necessary information about your topic. You are creating the video on paper (or computer) before you ever shoot a frame of video. Elements to consider with a scripted production include reenactments, voice-over narration, on-camera narrator or host, interview, and the hybrid, which includes a combination of these.

If you plan on shooting this yourself but you've never done a large-scale video program before, don't make the mistake of attempting to make a lavish production your first time out. I want to emphasize that you should focus on presenting your topic in the most easily digestible form possible, without trying to add a lot of fancy shooting or editing—until you are ready and unless it is appropriate.

Screen Capture

Don't have a camera? Not a problem.

Many SIVs are presenting information on how to do something, often related to computers, software, and internet programs. Ponder for a moment how enormous the market is for information about how to use specific software or how to accomplish something on a computer. It is huge and will continue to be.

For example, if I want to learn how to do a special effect in my editing software I don't need to see anything but the computer screen as a voice talks me through the process. In some cases you may not even need any narration, just a visual demonstration. This type of production is made with a process called "screen capture" in which the actions on a computer screen are recorded by a software program on that computer. We call the final result a screencast.

Some very successful screencast videos are basically just slide shows using PowerPoint.

CHOOSE THE FORMAT THAT FITS YOUR PROJECT

There are many variations of these formats, so don't let this limit your thinking. If you stay in the SIV business for long you will probably work in all of these formats, which will give you the opportunity to decide for yourself which one works best for different projects. I like and use them all.

Action Step

- Know your options about types of SIVs and choose the format that best fits your project.

Choosing a Successful Topic

Chapter Objectives
- Discover where we recommend you first start in choosing a topic for your SIV.
- Learn the places and ways you can look and find ideas for a topic.

There are a lot of things to think through before you start shooting your video. Obviously, you want a topic that will be marketable and successful. Don't just follow your intuition and say "I know this will be a big hit." Trust me, I've done that more than once and it doesn't work. You need enthusiasm, yes, but you also need sound business sense.

In this chapter we're going to show you a lot of places and ways to find potential topics. We'll also share our stories and the stories of people we've met who have taken a hobby or skill in an area and turned it into a successful SIV. As you read, try to think how you can apply the same process to your life. Keep your notebook handy and make notes as you get ideas. Don't censor yourself at this point. Write down every idea that excites you. We'll learn to do research to find the most promising topics in the next chapter.

I wish I could give you a bullet-proof success formula but there are no guarantees. As with any business, there are always risks involved. You can minimize the financial risks by doing systematic research before you ever shoot a frame of video. You want to know if there is demand for your idea, if and how you can reach your potential market economically, and what competition you will be facing.

Now don't think that competition is necessarily a bad thing. If people are successfully selling similar titles that just proves that a profitable market already exists for this topic or they wouldn't be in business. The longer they've been doing it, the better the indication that this is a good niche or else there wouldn't be a consistent demand. Now your task is to find your own unique place in that market.

You also want to know how to reach your potential customers. You'll read many times in this book that I like to market to schools and institutions. Schools are very easy to reach. You can target teachers by state, by grade level and subject matter, even by whether they are new teachers or not, which gives you a very precise way to contact and communicate with them. This type of target-ability is rare and wonderful. You may not find it that easy of a target but you definitely want to produce your video for a specific market and you want to know in advance how you are going to reach it with your marketing message.

So to summarize, choosing a topic involves assessing the market potential, evaluating the competition, and judging the ease or difficulty of reaching that market. You also want to try to make it something you are passionate about.

PICK SOMETHING YOU ARE PASSIONATE ABOUT

One of the things I love about this business is that it allows me to use my video and marketing skills to indulge my other interests. I produce videos on topics that I am genuinely interested in and I recommend that you do the same. If you're passionate about a topic, like your favorite hobby, you'll put more energy into both producing it and marketing it. You'll know the language of the topic and be able to speak directly to others who enjoy that topic. You'll be working with people who share your interest. It's going to take a sustained effort to produce and successfully market your video so you might as well pick something you enjoy spending a lot of time with, because you will be!

For an example, I enjoy growing cacti and succulents. They are wildly exotic looking plants and are generally easy to keep, a feature that is required since my gardening habit is to ignore my plants for months at a time. Only the strong survive my horticultural practices, and that's basically cacti and succulents.

What got me started in this hobby was a filmstrip I made around 1980 about growing cacti and succulents. I became fascinated with them. I had a nice collection back then but over the years my interest waned and my collection died. When a horticulture professor friend of mine asked me to help his students produce a video on succulents a few years ago I jumped at the opportunity. This totally reinvigorated my dormant passion for growing these plants. Shooting these new videos got me into some fascinating locations such as the Huntington Botanical Gardens in Pasadena, The Getty Center and the Getty Villa in Los Angeles, and some gigantic wholesale cactus and succulent nurseries in Southern California. I loved it! As I got further into the videos my personal cactus collection grew and I joined the local cactus and succulent society, for whom I built and now maintain a website. That was a perfect marriage of a personal passion and a way to turn it into profit through video publishing.

Now we not only sell those videos to schools throughout the world, we have repackaged them and sell them to cacti and succulent clubs and to individual cacti and succulent enthusiasts through our website www.captivatingcacti.com and other retail outlets. Because I'm interested in this topic, marketing what I love is very enjoyable and the videos sell well as a result. As an added bonus, I got to write off all those fun trips on my income taxes—a huge side benefit of this business.

Are you seeing any connections with your own hobbies and interests? Here's another example. Several years ago I bought a white PT Cruiser that I just fell in love with. I wanted to learn to keep it looking great. I became a bit obsessed with keeping my car looking new. I started hanging out in car care forums and soon met up with that auto detailer I told you about earlier who was moderating several of these forums. We formed a partnership and I produced a video on car detailing. During the course of shooting I learned a ton of things I was doing wrong and what to do to take better care of my car. Not only did I get a great car detailing video to sell, my PT Cruiser still looks as good as the day I bought it.

When I have gone off-course and produced a video on something that I didn't care much about I have had a hard time putting the required effort into marketing it over the long haul and the sales have reflected that. Success in this business will require sustained effort, so pick something that will keep you interested. Every person we interviewed in our case studies said this was what keeps them motivated and carries them through challenging times.

Do you have a hobby or special interest such as fishing, photography, motorcycles, knitting, wood working, playing a musical instrument, building models, quilting, scrap booking, fishing, golf, or any sport ... anything that a large number of people are similarly interested in? That's a great place to start. Write those ideas down.

Hobbies are a rich source of ideas and probably something you or your subject matter expert are passionate about. One of my mentors, Bill Myers, recently produced a successful video titled *Metal Detecting on Florida Beaches,* a favorite hobby of his. He's also an avid video producer and so was able to combine two of his favorite activities: video and metal detecting (and probably being on the beach). Notice that he made it specific—*Metal Detecting on* Florida *Beaches.* He niched it down to a specific state. Do you think that will sell better to people in Florida than a video titled *Metal Detecting on Beaches*? You bet it will.

I met a man many years ago who enjoyed working on Harley-Davidsons. He started making videos on really basic things you could do yourself to maintain your motorcycle. When he tried selling them he found a very receptive market. He was just an ordinary guy who knew how to do basic motorcycle maintenance to save money and a lot of owners wanted to know what he knew and were willing to pay for his videos. In today's economy more people are wanting to know how to do maintenance things that can save them money. Can you think of a way you can take advantage of this?

I recently decided to re-learn how to play the guitar after a couple of decades away from it. I don't have time for lessons, so I buy tutorial videos so I can learn at my leisure. I found an excellent course on DVDs, *Learn & Master Guitar,* which sells for $250 and I bought it. This excellent course is very popular and I know the producer, Steve Krenz, has sold tens of thousands of sets. In fact, Gibson Guitar Corporation bought him out and re-branded it. I can only imagine how much money he made off of that deal.

Because I'm on several email lists, almost every day I get free tutorial samples and offers from a wide range of guitar courses, all very good. I'm always tempted to buy more and sometimes I do. I never knew there were so many options for online and DVD guitar lessons until I got interested in that topic. It's safe to say this is a niche that will never die.

Mike Deiure is one of those people successfully selling guitar lessons online. His story is one of passion, patience, and determination. Mike turned his talent and creativity into a successful video series.

Something to note about these competing guitar courses is that they each have their own niche. Some are about playing blues, others rock, folk, country, gospel, bluegrass ... electric, acoustic, finger picking, sweep picking ... beginning, intermediate, advanced ... they are all teaching guitar playing but the successful ones, like Mike's, have found their own unique place in the market. That's what you want to do, too.

Mike Deiure, Musician and Producer/Owner of Rock Guitar Power (www.rockguitarpower.com)

At the age of thirteen, Mike Deiure, like many young teens, became enamored with playing guitar, specifically rock guitar, having been heavily influenced by guitar greats such as Joe Satriani, Steve Vai, Zakk Wylde, and John Petrucci. He was so passionate about music that he started out in college studying classical guitar and later on switched to a Music Industry program.

I've always been involved with writing and recording my own music almost as soon as I started learning guitar, but it was around the time when I finished college in '02 that I became very busy recording and producing other musicians as a recording engineer and record producer. I wasn't looking to get a "job" as I was busy building a studio in my parent's basement, so I started teaching guitar as well. At first I was hired to teach at a couple of local music studios but soon branched out on my own.

Seven to eight years out of school, I was loving life, pursuing my craft of producing, recording and becoming a better guitar player through teaching. I was also refining my teaching techniques. And while I loved what I was doing, I was also working 6 days a week and getting burned out.

Then I had a revelation. There's only so much money I could bring in and people I could teach if I kept doing what I was doing. Even if I employed teaching staff, there was still a limit to who I could reach and what I could make. I could teach more people and make more money if I stopped selling my time.

He shared with us that after getting involved in a local marketing group and learning more about direct response marketing, he became interested in and very excited about creating a product he could sell. He decided to produce a DVD, *Rock Guitar Power*, with the help of his brother who was a videographer.

When it was finished, that was a big moment for me! I was able to say, "Here's my DVD! I'm done!" Well, that was awesome but the big fact was that nobody knew about it. I had to figure how to make this sell. That turned my focus to marketing and how to build my brand.

Having an older brother who was a videographer and who could lend his expertise, knowledge, and equipment to Mike's videos was a good kickstart but he soon took the reins on his own. While he wanted to project a professional image, he didn't want to rely on borrowed video equipment. It was also important he had an environment that he could set up and be able to be shooting in within minutes. After a lot of studying, testing, and tweaking, he soon figured out how to set up a nice studio and purchased a camera that worked for him.

I found I could set up a studio environment in my basement for less than $200. Lighting is very important and I found I could buy $15 portable work lights and cover them with a sheet of diffusion paper and that worked well. I now have a Kodak Zi8, a lavalier mic and colored gels. I discovered that with a nicely lit video environment you can get away with buying less professional stuff but still get a professional video feel.

Once he started getting better at delivering video programs, he wanted to find a way to deliver them quicker while keeping his costs down. Because Mike started out without a lot of money, he did most of the fulfillment (we'll cover this later) himself but soon found the process too cumbersome and dealing with payment processing a headache.

That's what led me online. With online video, my costs dropped significantly and became variable; I now only pay a fee when the product is sold. I use a program called Clickbank. They are a retailer of digital products and handle all the credit card processing.

From the beginning, Mike had big plans for a line of products, something we highly recommend you do. He knew at the onset that he wanted to build a brand so he was picky regarding the domain name and chose one that wouldn't constrain what he had to offer.

"Try to think big like that," he recommends,

Don't necessarily focus on a topic but a brand name that will allow you to release other programs in the same niche. After Rock Guitar Power *Volume 1 &* Rock Guitar Power *Volume 2, I created* Soloing and Lead Playing, *then came modes on guitar theory/ technique courses. Last year, after listening to my customers, I started a very successful series of video lessons on how to play your favorite rock songs.*

Marketing plays a large role in Mike's success. He shared many other nuggets of advice over our hour-long interview that we aren't able to share here but it is available on our site at www.shoot-to-sell.com. Mike is a great example of taking your passion and turning it into a successful video publishing business. Now that he's seen success, he's helping other people be successful online. He enjoys helping people with integrity-based products get a good start and be able to spread their message.

As he stresses,

This is a fun gig but it is work! Develop your products on what you're passionate about and that passion will get you through your failures and hard times. With the way technology and the internet is today, everything is open to make something happen so if you have an idea you're passionate about and it hasn't been done, do it because it's never been easier than now.

DON'T HAVE A TOPIC IDEA?

OK, so you're still interested in the SIV business model but you don't have a clue what kind of video you want to produce?

There are great sites on the internet where you can find topic ideas that have proven marketability. You're sure to get a great idea from them. Following are several suggestions.

Dummies.com is the publisher of the popular *Dummies Guide To* (fill in the blank) books. They've printed hundreds of books about a wide range of topics. You can be sure these topics are selling for them or they wouldn't be listed. When you go to their site, www.dummies.com, look at the categories on the left side of the page. These are broad topic areas that sell well for them and are a good guide to topics you might want to choose. Click any category to drill down to finer and finer niches. This should be a great source of inspiration.

If you look at the table of contents of a Dummies book you may see a chapter heading that is strong enough to be a video. Go to www.dummies.com/store.html and search in their book section for an interesting book title and click on the "title" to get further information. There you will see a tab for Table of Contents. Dummies.com is very generous in the amount of content they freely share with you so take advantage of that.

> A series of videos on a topic will sell better than a single title. Could you turn several of the chapters in the table of contents into individual videos? They don't have to be long but because they are related to each other and centered around the topic of the book they would make a logical "complete set" of videos. I have always found that a set of videos on a single topic, at a much higher price, will outsell a single video.

Using this same process, visit www.clickbank.com/marketplace.htm. Look at their categories on the left. Again, these are successful categories that are working for Clickbank and they will probably work for you. By clicking the individual categories you will be shown products within that category. These can get pretty specific but can also point you toward hot trends. ClickBank uses a measure called "gravity" to represent how well each product sells, based on how many sales have been made and how recent these sales were. Look at products with a gravity of 30+, because they have a proven track record of selling well.

You can also turn to www.google.com/trends, www.pulse.ebay.com, and Twitter trending topics to see what the hot topics of the day are.

A visit to your local public library's periodical section is also a good place to find topic ideas. Peruse the *New York Times*, *Wall Street Journal*, and other large newspapers. The best sections to look at are the business, home, and living sections where you can spot trends, new business ideas, hobbies, movements, and interesting people. Magazines are another great resource; start with those that capture your interest and dig through them. Make sure you take your notebook with you and write down the ideas that interest you most. Keep track of which periodical you find this information in because you want to find out the size of the publication's readership. This will be useful when you are researching your topic idea and its viability.

> Have you learned something special about a new camera, cell phone ... something new and technically complex? People will pay to know something that will save them time and effort. Such a video would have a short life span but it could sell a lot of copies fast as people try to learn the intricacies of that item.

As I shared previously, special interest videos don't have to be how-to or instructional programs. People like to be entertained and are willing to pay for simple documentaries, travelogues, and biographies. My current best-selling DVD is actually a very low budget oral history of a writer that I taped in Florida. In fact, he's my father and there was no budget. Check it out at www.patricksmithonline.com/sop.html. I did add some b-roll, but most of the footage is the author speaking to the camera, illustrated with old photographs animated in the Ken Burns style. That simple video won a top award at the Tupelo Film Festival and a Telly Award. To date, we've sold over 8,500 of them at prices from $20 to $95 each.

SIVs are the perfect way for public speakers, coaches, business consultants, and experts in any field to put their special knowledge into a video that can reach tens of thousands of people rather than a few at a time in person. Go to a Tony Robbins or Wayne Dyer seminar and watch what they sell at the back of the room. It's astounding! They can make more in an hour than many people make in a year. People are buying every kind of information product they offer.

There are a lot of experts and professionals speaking at seminars and events. Perhaps you can record one of these events (with their participation and approval) and quickly turn it into a profitable video. This is what we did with real estate agent and feng shui expert, Holly Ziegler. While we were planning a more scripted video with her to follow along with her best-selling book, Sell Your Home Faster with Feng Shui she asked us to tape one of her seminars. Instead of the more complex video production we initially had in mind, we decided to turn that seminar, followed by two more similar events, into a three-volume video series for her. We were able to do that in a more economical way and in a much shorter time frame and now have that on the market.

I met a man while shooting my cactus and succulents videos that is a superstar in the rarified world of succulents. He is highly regarded both academically and as a seller of the finest plants, specifically lithops. Succulent collectors worship him and treasure every word he writes. He's also somewhat eccentric. I approached him about making a video of his horticultural techniques but haven't yet convinced him to do it. His following may only be 5,000 people worldwide but they are rabid fans and many of them would buy a video by this man. Here is a small market filled with fanatical succulent collectors who spend money on their hobby no matter what the economy is doing. If only I could convince him to do it! Be on the lookout for people like that in your life.

I've spent a lot of time working with university professors, creating educational videos on their area of expertise. As I said, these often sell to schools at much higher prices than to the public. Many younger professors are happy to do this because it can qualify as publishing and may help them get tenure or progress in their career. Younger professors can often use the extra money, too. With professors we usually pay them an "honorarium" of $500 to $1,000 for their assistance, depending on their involvement, but they do not get royalties. Educators know what kind of curriculum materials are available to them so may have good suggestions about what you can produce to fill a need.

Do you know any professors, authors, coaches, or subject matter experts that you can talk to about this? They don't have to be famous or big stars, although that certainly helps. You'll be surprised at how willing most people are to participate in an instructional video. Look to your local college, community college, high school, speakers bureau, or chamber of commerce for recognized experts in their field.

I'm constantly coming up with new ideas on SIV topics that I'd like to produce. It's almost a curse! Once you start thinking this way it's hard to shut it off. Of course only a few ever actually get made but I feel you need to generate a lot of ideas to narrow them down to the jewels.

So start brainstorming. The following exercise will help.

GENERATING PROJECT IDEAS

1. What are your hobbies and interests? Would you like to make a video on that topic?
2. What do you enjoy talking about? Could you make a video about that?
3. Do you know a specific technique within this hobby? Is there a great product out there that you love and use all the time and people are always asking you how you use it? Make a video about the unique way you use it for your business or personal use. It doesn't have to be long, videos can be a short lesson on how to do one specific thing that a lot of other people may want to know.
4. What are my friends and family's hobbies and interests? We've received several great ideas from our parents (the idea for our current best-selling DVD came from my father), other family members and friends.
5. What problem can you solve, or what information or instruction can you provide? Don't be afraid to contact local schools—elementary schools, high schools, community colleges, universities, special schools—to see what instructional materials may be missing or needed within their curriculum.
6. What experts do you know? Do they teach and do they need supporting materials to sell?
7. What trends are you seeing in your industry magazines, the newspaper, online? What is grabbing your attention? How-to videos on some new gadget or technology may be desperately needed.
8. When you're networking—at a party, via internet forums, social networking sites, at business functions, masterminding events—what are people talking about? Focus on them and really listen to what they are saying and you will be surprised at how many people are experts on something but never thought of making a video about it. This happens to us all the time. Explain that you make niche videos for sale and you'll be amazed at the ideas people give you.
9. If you could produce your "dream video," what would it be? What's stopping you from doing it?

This is just a partial list of questions to ask yourself. The key here is to get your creative juices flowing. Take some time to think about these things and write your answers down.

After you've gone through the exercise you will undoubtedly have not just one but a number of ideas written down. That's great because now the work begins to determine if any of those have the potential to be a successful product. Once you get started the ideas will just flow, so watch out!

Here's a cautionary tip from our experience: resist the temptation to take on too many projects at once. Don't let your enthusiasm carry you away. You should focus on only one video project at a time, especially as you are getting started. Otherwise you'll scatter your energies and delay your success.

Action Steps

- Develop a list of your favorite topics, hobbies, and special interests to find potential topics for your SIV. We'll research those in the next chapter.
- Look at www.dummies.com, www.clickbank.com, and www.google.com/trends for ideas.

- Visit your library's periodical section or your local bookstore's magazine rack for ideas. Did you find similar titles already available? Read about them online or order a copy to check out your competition.
- Complete the Generating Project Ideas exercise.
- Take out a blank sheet of paper. Write down all the topic ideas you came up with in the exercise. Rank them in order of your own interest in them.
- Narrow your choice to three topics that you feel strongest about.

Researching Your Topic

Chapter Objectives
- Research to find existing, competing products.
- Define your video's purpose.
- Identify your ideal customer.
- Narrow down your niche.

So far you've learned what SIVs are and that just about any topic of interest to a sizable group of people is a potential subject for a SIV. We shared with you the stories of many people who took a hobby or skill and turned that into a video. We also looked at some places you can go to see the type of topics people are looking for.

We encouraged you to write down any ideas that occurred to you as you were reading this. Now it's time to start refining those ideas.

What you need to do next is determine your video's purpose, identify your ideal customer, figure out what and who your competition is, and narrow down your niche. This is going to take research.

When we say research, don't panic. You're not going to be writing a master's thesis here. This isn't formal like a school research paper, you just need an inquisitive nature, the ability to take notes, and an open mind. A lot of your research can be done from the comfort of your own home, or with a trip to a library, or the magazine rack at your local bookstore.

In fact, if this is an area where you just don't want to do the work, you can find someone to do it for you. You can hire a writer or researcher at an outsourcing site like www.odesk.com, www.elance.com, www.freelancer.com, www.guru.com, and www.vworker.com. Keep in mind though, they may not have as much knowledge about your topic or may not do as thorough of a job as you. Look over all the information they find and check out the sources and ideas they come up with *before* you put any time or money into your video.

What you are looking into first is the viability of your video, then you'll turn your sights on your competition.

What I find when I start researching is that your topic viability, competition, target market, distribution channels, etc. research will all overlap. You may click on a site with a similar video and realize that you've stumbled on a competing product and there is information on that website as to how they distribute, their pricing, their sales copy, sales funnel, compatible products to yours, etc. That will all be very helpful.

This sample checklist will help you stay organized. Type it into a word processing program, print several copies and take them with you to the library or bookstore:

- Topic _____
- Site/Source _____
- Video? Book? _____
- Price _____
- Distribution channel, i.e., where is it sold? Through Amazon? Another distributor?
  _____
- Links off of the site_____
- Complementary Products _____

RESEARCHING ON THE INTERNET

First off, Google is your friend. Simple as it sounds, I always start with a search on Google for videos on a topic I'm considering producing. I'm looking to see if videos already exist, what they are about, what they cost, how old they are, who's selling them, and if they are selling well.

So go to Google, Bing, Yahoo, or your favorite search engine and start searching for videos that exist on your topic. Be sure to click the "Videos" category (if they have one) to narrow your search down. While this may take you to many free video sharing sites, the information you find there will come in handy too. Make note of what you find. Try to find the date they were produced, by whom, and the price. Drill down to get as much information as possible.

If nothing but dated videos exist, then you may have found a need. For example, my 30+ year-old video on pruning definitely needs replacing. The clothes are dated, the image quality is nowhere as good as with today's cameras, and we didn't have the sophisticated character generation and graphics capability built in to the most basic non-linear editing (NLE) systems today. If someone produced a modern version with basically the same content, aimed at the same school market, they would have a high probability of success. (If this topic interests you, I just gave you a great idea!) Sometimes all you need to do is update a dated but successful video.

Be specific in your searching. I would search for something like "Growing Cactus Videos" "or "Video about Growing Cactus Plants." Since all cacti are succulents I'd also search using the word succulent as well as cacti and cactus. Be sure to include the word "video" because that will narrow your search. The more specific you get, such as "Growing Cactus Videos" rather than "Cactus Videos," the more you will eliminate things you don't want. If I simply search on "Cactus" it returns a lot of hits on a band called Cactus, so I want to eliminate those. You should also search using the word DVD instead of video. Keep track of all of your responses.

You will narrow your search further if you include the quotation marks surrounding your search terms. Also, if you are searching in Google, sign out of any Google products, i.e., YouTube, Gmail, GoogleDocs, etc. you may be in so you can see wider results.

Another great place to look is www.amazon.com. If videos already exist on your topic, chances are they're being sold on Amazon. The thing I love about Amazon is that you can read user reviews about a product. This can give you a clue about how good your competing products are and what their strengths and weaknesses are. Do people rate them highly? What do they like about them? What don't they like? Amazon will often give you a breakdown of the content, which can help you find your own unique angle on the topic.

It's always a good idea to search on YouTube to see if there are videos on your subject. Unfortunately, you will often find a lot of free videos on YouTube and other video sharing sites, like www.ehow.com. Although these free videos can compete with your product idea, don't let this discourage you right away. What you find on YouTube can often be a superficial treatment of a topic, poorly done, or just plain inaccurate. You usually get what you pay for. This is not always the case, but sometimes. Plus, they are not being actively promoted like yours will be. The more unique your topic is, the less likely that someone will be giving something similar away for free online. That should encourage you to work hard to find a unique niche or approach to your topic.

If your research turns up books on the topic that too can be valuable information. Checking out some of these books may give you ideas about how to structure a video. Their table of contents could be a topical outline for you. If you see that books on the topic sell well on www.amazon.com, you know there is interest in the topic.

Follow up your leads from the search engines and then go offline and look at books, magazines, and trade journals on your topic. Look in the back where they have classified and small space ads. Are there any for videos for sale on your topic?

As you're doing this research you want to make note of the prices people are charging, the length of the video, titles, and shipping costs.

Use Google Alerts

Remember what I said about Google being your friend? You can put google searches on auto-pilot to do automated research for you with Google Alerts.

Google Alerts is a free service that will search for you. You can find it at www.google.com/alerts. Once you sign up you can choose a query. Then you will receive "alerts" via email of the latest relevant Google results (news, blogs, video, discussions, books, or all categories) based on your choice. You can choose whether you want just the best results or all results and whether you want to receive them as they happen, once a day, or once a week. You can have as many alerts as you want and this robot researcher will do the work for you. This is a very powerful research tool and you should be using it.

You can use Google Alerts to do many types of research such as monitoring a developing news story, keeping current on a competitor or industry, getting notified if and when others are talking about you or your product. Yes, set up an alert on your own name and product to make sure nothing negative is being spread to tarnish your reputation.

Once you're signed up for Google Alerts, just enter in the topics you've been considering producing a video on and schedule how often you want to be notified. You will soon get a good sense of what information is out there already on the topic and if you can add something new to the niche.

In fact, you don't even have to create the alert to get information. Just filling in the search query box will immediately return the results for the day in a column on the right side of the page. Using it this way is a very fast way to get research results.

For example, you may be interested in doing a cooking video series on vegan desserts. You sign up to be alerted to the words "vegan desserts" and see there are a lot of people talking about the topic. Then you can click on the website links provided to get a better sense of the buzz around the topic and what type of information is already available.

You may also discover that there is not much activity around that query. That gives you good feedback as well. Maybe you didn't choose the best search term or perhaps this topic or niche is not as hot an area as you thought it would be, since people aren't talking about it. Now you can decide if your time and effort producing a video would be better spent on other topics. Not every idea is going to pan out.

You may also find very similar videos or products such as yours being offered. Again, this gives you a good indication of the type of competition you face. If you are still excited about this topic, then you need to position yourself differently from them and decide what unique angle you are bringing to the marketplace.

Other Internet Research Tools

Another good source of free research is www.google.com/trends which I mentioned in the last chapter. You can enter a word and see articles that have appeared about that particular topic. You can see if interest is growing, shrinking, or is cyclical.

For example, let's enter the word "Christmas." You can see a wave beginning every year starting in October and maxing out in December, then dropping flat. "Easter" shows the same dramatic spike in April. This also gives you good information about your marketing cycle. "Weddings" shows a big spike in spring and summer and a dramatic drop in winter, as you would expect. "Car wash" shows a peak of interest in the spring and early summer and a drop in late summer and early fall.

Look at Apple's iPad on www.google.com/trends. You can see there was no interest at all before it appeared in 2010, and interest has grown substantially since then. This is now a hot topic!

Be sure to use Google trends to look for cycles that may influence your marketing plans.

Another good place to research is eBay pulse. Go to pulse.ebay.com and you'll see how many people are looking for a specific item or topic, giving you a good idea of the demand. You see an overall snapshot of the most popular searches and you can drill down by category.

There are a few more places to check to see how much a product on your topic is or is not in demand.

One of those is www.ezinearticles.com. In the search box type in the *name of your product* and click *search*. This will bring up a list of articles and you can just pick on any one you choose. At the top of the page you'll see how many articles have been contributed about that topic. This is a gauge of popularity.

Go to the bottom of the page of one of the stories and you can see how many views the story has had. If you find articles there that have had anywhere from 3,000 views and up then it's a pretty good bet there are lots of people interested in that topic. Bookmark these articles for future investigation for the pre-production phase of your video project.

Another good source is Yahoo Answers at www.answers.yahoo.com. Search for questions that your video could solve. If you see that there are a lot of questions your video could solve then you have probably picked a good topic.

You also want to find out if the people answering those questions are leaving links to products in their answers. If they are then you know the competition is going to be stiff but you also know that others are finding this a viable market, which is good.

 If there are no links to products in the answers, you may have good success making sales just by leaving links to your video sales page when you leave an answer in Yahoo Answers.

Other online places to research are social media sites such as Facebook, Google+, LinkedIn, Twitter, and social bookmarking sites such as Delicious Reddit, and StumbleUpon. Look for the search bar and enter your topic words.

Most of the sites I mentioned have settings in them where you can be alerted when someone is talking about a certain topic. If they don't, you can find other programs such as SocialOomph (www.socialoomph.com) that will do it for you. Doing this will make your searches much more manageable.

This is not a complete list of research tools but should get you well on your way. New sites to help you research are cropping up every day. Check our companion website at www.shoot-to-sell.com where we'll be posting articles about new research tools and how to use them.

RESEARCHING AT THE LIBRARY

As I mentioned previously, your public library's periodical section is a great resource of current information and a gauge of trends and interests. The *Readers' Guide to Periodical Literature* lists magazine articles organized by article subject. The way you access these volumes will be through the Research Librarian. Many of these resources are available online but only accessible through institutional credentials.

You can also get an idea of the size of the markets these magazines and newspapers reach by looking at publications such as *Ulrich's International Periodicals Directory*, which lists thousands of magazines, and the *Oxbridge Directory of Newsletters*. Similarly, *Standard Rate and Data Service (SRDS)* lists media rates and information on more than 100,000 U.S. and international publications, newspapers, and broadcast media. This can help you find publications on your topic that you didn't know about.

Another good resource is *The Encyclopedia of Associations* which lists over 151,000 nonprofit membership organizations worldwide along with their membership make-up, publications, and circulation. What you are searching for are how many magazines and newsletters focus on your topic (a good sign that their readers are finding it relevant) and the content and number of videos and information products they advertise. This will give you an idea of how large a market this topic has and how you can reach this market. These specialized publications may not be available at your local public library. You may have to visit an academic library to find a copy or request an inter-library loan.

Moving along now, let's assume you now have some topic ideas and through your research you have determined that this is something that a lot of people are interested in. What do you do next?

RESEARCHING YOUR MARKET FIRST

The thing you don't want to do is produce a video first and then go out and look for buyers. It's the other way around if you want to make money. You want to produce a video or information product for an audience that's ready and waiting to buy it. The first step in doing this is to identify your video's purpose. Then, second, you need to find a target market that will benefit from it.

Find Your Video's Purpose

Say what? That might sound like a strange statement but put yourself in your customer's shoes. Your customers don't want your video for the thrill of owning it; they want the information in it to do *something* for them. It should solve a problem, teach a new skill, help them improve in some area, help them make more money, or avoid some form of pain or stress—you need to be clear on what it will do for them. This will also be important when crafting your marketing message.

If you're in business to make money then you need to sell what people *want* and what they will *buy*, not what you think they *need*. You can't decide in your mind what people need and try to force it on them if they're not ready.

This is an important point I can't stress enough. You have to take your ego out of this process and focus on what customers are telling you they want. *Want* is the operative word here. Yes, people should buy what they need but they don't buy that way. Take the diet pill industry. It's booming because even though people really need to eat better and exercise, that isn't really what they want, they want a quick fix, a magic pill. This doesn't mean that you have to sell them some hocus pocus or snake oil, it's that you have to figure out how to deliver what they *need* in such a way that they feel they are getting what they *want*. If your video doesn't do that, you won't sell many and you won't really give your customers what they need after all is said and done.

If your video doesn't sell, you shouldn't blame the customer for not being smart enough to see your genius or too dense to feel your passion or understand your approach. They don't care about any of that. You only have yourself to blame for not determining specifically what they want and giving it to them in the first place.

An additional key sales concept is to make sure you're marketing to people who have the resources to buy what you're selling. I want to buy a multi-million dollar estate at the beach. Do I need one? No. If I could afford one, would I buy it? Yes! However, if I went to an open house and was approached by the agent, she could talk until she's blue in the face but I wouldn't buy it because I can't. I'm not what they call a "qualified buyer" in marketing lingo. You want to find qualified buyers for your videos so you don't waste your valuable time and resources marketing to people who cannot or will not buy. Finding out who those people are is where you need to focus next.

You'll see us mention many times in this book that we like to produce videos for schools. We like marketing to schools because they are easy to identify and contact. You can target teachers by grade level and subject matter.

An important point before producing videos for schools is identifying a need for your product. If it doesn't fit into the curriculum there is little chance of success. How do you know if there is a place in the curriculum for it?

We market to Florida schools a lot, so let's use them as an example. Florida calls its educational standards the Sunshine State Standards. If I do a Google search on "Florida School Standards" I'll see the Florida Department of Education Sunshine State Standards. You could do a similar search on other states (e.g., Ohio School Standards, etc.). Also search under academic standards or frameworks.

I see links for both the "Common Core" standards and the Sunshine State Standards. The Common Core standards are learning outcomes shared among states, whereas the Sunshine State Standards apply just to Florida schools. The goal of the Common Core standards is to ensure that students are receiving a high quality education consistently, from state to state. They do not replace an individual state's standards.

Each state's site is different but there are similarities. You can select a subject area, usually a grade level, and see the things that the student will study. If there is no place for your video idea, better slow down and do more research.

It is also a good idea to contact teachers in the grade level you are considering producing for to get their opinion of your video idea. Of course you will also research existing products that may be serving that market.

Several states have a process where you can submit a product for consideration of formal adoption into the curriculum. Having your product formally adopted will result in more sales but can be an arduous process, especially for an independent producer with only one product. We typically market directly to the teachers or media librarians.

By digging through the standards you may be able to refine your idea to better fill a need. Spend significant time researching standards and following threads if you are considering marketing to schools.

Define Your Target Market

You need to clearly identify who your market is, what they will buy, and how to speak to them in ways they can relate to, regarding both your video topic and you the marketer. The rapport this builds between you and your prospective buyers will ultimately lead to sales. We'll be talking more about this when we get to marketing but I wanted to share with you here why it's so important to find out at the outset if you have a viable target market before you produce your video.

Your goal is to identify a profitable market. Not just a market of enthusiasts or fans—*a market of buyers*.

I've seen plenty of times that a segment of people express an interest in a topic but just won't spend money on it, even if they can afford to. It's just not something they spend money on.

For example, I once produced a very good video on farm tractor safety for an agricultural insurance company. My client loved it. However, when we tried to sell it to farmers so they could train their employees to not kill themselves, we often heard something along these lines: "I've been a farmer for xx years. I've never had a tractor accident and I don't need any training and neither do my guys." They may have never had any formal training but they did not want any, either.

The truth is, fatal farm tractor accidents account for the most accidents in the entire agriculture industry and new employees certainly *do* need training. There are many ways you can maim and kill yourself on a tractor. I've collected over one hundred news reports about experienced farmers being injured and killed in tractor accidents, but you couldn't convince farmers of that. They wouldn't part with their money to buy that video.

Once you have your list of potential topics you'll need to now take the time to brainstorm and come up with every person, group, business, or organization that you think would want to watch and buy your video. Yes, we're going to "profile" your people to come up with what I like to call "an ideal customer."

Be specific and think outside the box. For example, if your topic is how to keep your plants from getting eaten by deer, write down all the people and groups that struggle with this problem that you know how to solve, like nurseries, home gardeners, corporate landscape maintenance companies, etc. Obviously these are not people living in city apartment buildings. How about other places that would be interested in sharing information on this problem like libraries, plant societies, master gardener programs, horticulture teachers, etc? The point of this exercise is to do two things: determine if you can identify your ideal customers and find out how to reach them. In doing so, you'll also get a very good idea of how they'll want the material presented to them.

Identify Your Ideal Customer

Because potential customers come in all sizes, shapes, and spending profiles— and because ideal customers don't come with their profiles taped to their heads—your challenge is to first identify which ones are the most likely to become your best customers and then to figure out how to reach and attract them.

Unless your time, production, and marketing dollars have no limit, the best use of those resources is to target the people most likely to buy your videos at the least cost and effort to you.

Identifying customers and using targeted marketing and advertising strategies delivers a much greater payoff than just peppering the internet or expensive print ads with your product and hoping to attract someone who will purchase *after* you produced your video.

Here are a few questions to ask as you create a picture of this person and how to reach him:

- Who do you think your best customers will be?
- Are they individuals or businesses?
- If they're individuals, what do they like? What don't they like? What are their needs and problems?
- How will those needs and problems be best addressed with your video?
- What's most important to your best customers?
- What's least important to them?
- How will you provide more of the former and less of the latter?
- What price is likely to attract them?
- Do they belong to organizations or attend events where you can reach them?
- Do mail or email lists of them exist?
- What publications do they read?
- What websites do they visit regularly?
- Do they visit online forums or social media sites?

- Do they have a common problem your video can solve?
- Do they have the disposable income to buy your video?
- What brings them joy?
- What are they worried about?
- What challenges do they face?
- What goals are they striving to attain?
- What experience thrills them?
- Where do they get their information?
- Who do they trust most?

Once you get going on this you'll probably come up with additional questions.

Now based on these questions, develop a written description of your ideal customer. Here's an example from a recent video project we completed.

My ideal customer is a new stay-at-home mom. Because she has decided to stay home, her income has been reduced. She's young and concerned about getting back in shape quickly. She would like the coaching and support of a personal trainer but she wants to work out at home and she doesn't have a lot of money to invest in home exercise equipment and has limited space for it. She needs to be able to work out at her convenience.

While the answers to the types of questions above are not always available, pondering them helps you form a clearer picture of who your customers are and to address their wants and how you might communicate with them. It doesn't mean that other people who don't exactly fit the profile would not be good customers for you, most likely they'll buy too, but it does help you craft a product as well as a message to a group of people who will think you are speaking directly to them. Your material and marketing message will be right on target.

Check Out Your Competition

Next you'll be looking for existing competitors. Like I shared earlier: having competing products is not always a bad thing. The "blue ocean" strategy where you look for a market without competition is attractive in theory, but more often a lack of competitors means a lack of buyers. If you search for videos specific to your topic area and don't find any it may not just be because nobody has thought of producing a video on that, but that they had and it failed or that they researched the viability of such a video and came up with no real market.

You are going to be looking for a few things in your competition. First, you'll want to make sure you aren't reinventing the wheel and producing a video that can't be differentiated from all the other similar videos out there. On the other hand, you want to work in areas or niches where others have had success selling videos.

Find out what slivers of your market *aren't* being served well. What's missing in the other offerings, good as they may be? What can you do that's different in a valuable way, in a way that better serves a slice of the market?

Innovation is great if you're innovating in the right direction. Instead of dreaming up a video no one has ever seen before, innovate *better ways to serve* a robust market.

NICHE IT DOWN

You have picked a topic area and identified your ideal customer. You've determined that there is good potential in producing a video in your topic. Now it's time to get even more specific. Remember when I said that there are "riches in niches?" It's true.

When you determine what needs aren't being met within your market and niche your topic down further, you might think you're reducing the size of your potential market too much. In actuality, you are going to make your marketing more efficient and improve your chance of sales. Your potential customers will feel you are speaking directly to their wants and needs, and resistance will be decreased.

So how do you niche your topic down? Instead of producing a video series on just vegetarian cooking you might niche it down to Thai vegetarian cooking or vegetarian dishes you can make in five minutes or less. It's like putting a spotting scope on a rifle. Your aim will be more accurate.

You also need to niche down your expectations of the potential sales to this market. It is quite common for people, in their optimistic enthusiasm, to overestimate the number of customers who will buy their product. Be optimistic but realistic—you will rarely sell to a majority of any market, so make sure that there are a lot of buyers in this niche.

Since you will probably only sell to a small percentage of a niche it is to your advantage to pick a topic that would be of interest to a big or super niche. Those are like the categories you saw listed in www.dummies.com and www.clickbank.com. A super niche is still a niche, but it contains lots of proven buyers. Selling to 2 percent of a niche of 1,000 equals 20 sales. Selling to 2 percent of a niche of 1,000,000 means 20,000 sales. If you pick a big super niche, you only need a small share of the market to have a large enough customer base to be profitable. Depending on the product, you may find that you can sell fewer units but at a premium price point. Keep in mind though, a big niche probably means more competition.

Take for example markets driven by the basic human desires that never change. People are always looking for personal improvement, relationship help, status, or to make more money. They want to look cool, to feel safe and secure, to create better relationships with kids or spouses, to be better cooks, to lose weight, to be more attractive, and they spend a lot of money pursuing these goals. We always have wanted those things and we always will. These are huge, saturated markets. Your job is to figure out where the holes are in this market and go after them.

Along those lines, we just completed a six-week workout video series consisting of over 42 videos to help people get in shape, lose weight, and gain strength very fast without joining a gym or working with a personal trainer. This series appeals to weight loss, body toning, strength training, and the thing everyone wants—*fast results*. We have plenty of competition but are carving out our specific niche in the home health and weight loss market by targeting people who want to be coached but do it in their own home, at an affordable price, with minimal equipment.

I can't tell you how many people make up a profitable niche. It depends on the competition and the price and profit margin of your videos. Although big niches are a good idea, I also know that money can be made in small niches where there may be little or no competition. If you can identify and economically contact the people in that niche, and if your product is something they want and are able to buy, you may rule that niche. If so, you can likely ask a higher price because of the exclusivity. That's the case with my friend Joe who sells to high school horticulture teachers.

Stay in Your Niche

It takes time, energy, money, and concentration to pursue any market. If you produce videos in many different subject areas in a scattershot way, each one of those needs a significant amount of energy to successfully establish itself. If you produce videos in a vertical niche, i.e., all along the same topic area and for the same target market, then your chances of being successful are much greater.

A success formula we recommend is to produce a growing number of titles in a vertical niche so that you get repeat sales. It's ideal when each new title builds on the previous one so that the customer always needs the next title. If people like your first product they are going to want more and more. It is also easier and less expensive to sell to a previous customer you already have a relationship with than to find a new customer. Happy customers are the best referral systems you have.

TEST YOUR MARKET

We've explored a lot of ways to research your product and your market. There's still one more, very direct way to do this, which is to simply ask people what they think. You can do this by asking questions on forums, on Facebook, Twitter, and other social media platforms. You can also post surveys on Facebook. Talk to people face to face if possible. If you have a mailing list you can use online tools like SurveyMonkey to send surveys. Listen to what people say but don't go 100 percent by their answers. Some people will tell you what they think you want to hear but would not actually be buyers.

I know it's hard to do all of this research and testing when you are anxious to get going but believe me, it will pay off in the end. If your research says *Go* then you'll end up with a better product more tailored to the needs and wants of your target market, and that means more profit in your pocket.

Action Steps

- Research your topic idea using the places I suggested.
- As you research, focus on:
  - Determining your video's purpose—what problem will it solve?
  - Defining your target market.
  - Identifying your ideal customer.
  - Checking out competing products and what is missing in the topic.
  - Finding complementary products.
  - Making sure you are niching it down and staying in your niche.
  - Testing the market with surveys, questions on forums, and advertising.

Chapter 5

Finding a Partner

- Learn what type of partnership arrangements you can make.
- Understand what each role should be and what to look for in a partner.
- Learn how we recommend working with that person and the type of monetary arrangement that works best.

Unless your video is a "you are there" kind of video where you are looking around with a camera and working without a script or verbal content, you'll need someone (could be you) who knows something about your subject and someone (could also be you) who knows how to put the video together. Simple enough.

There are three general scenarios that you are likely to encounter regarding this.

1. *The best case is when you are both the expert on your topic area and are experienced enough to produce the video.*

    You are the whole ball of wax, a one-man band operation. You may hire additional production help but you are knowledgeable enough about the topic that you can write a script or perform on camera with authority, and can run a camera, and direct the entire production. This is our case when we produce videos about creating special interest videos, such as you'll find in our courses at www.sivacademy.com.

    I have several acquaintances in this business who fit this profile. Although it is a rare combination of talents, I like this situation best because you'll keep more of the profits this way.

    I realize that few readers of this book will be both subject experts and experienced video producers, let alone script writers, directors, camera operators, talent, and editors, and I strongly encourage you to seek help in areas where you are least proficient if you want to get your video produced and on the market quickly. You'll save yourself a lot of pain, time, and money.

2. *You, a video professional, partners with someone who is a subject matter expert who doesn't know how to produce a video but has the desire to produce one.*

    Believe it or not, this is a common situation for us.

    We meet a lot of potential partners at parties, seminars and workshops, networking events—almost everywhere we go. It seems like everybody is an expert in something.

Truly, almost everybody has ideas and knows more than the average person about something, but most of the time these ideas never go anywhere. I use the filter of experience to weed out the marginal projects and then do plenty of research on the promising ones before we go any further. However, I always have my radar turned on and am listening for opportunities.

A few years ago we produced a series of videos with a yoga instructor who knew how to use yoga to get rid of various pain points in the body. She was teaching small classes and had been asked by her students to make a video, but had never seriously thought of recording her techniques in a video and selling it until we met at a gallery reception. You could just see the wheels turning in her head when I told her that we could do that. Before long we formed a partnership in which we shot a series of seven videos covering her techniques for relieving pain in the neck, shoulders, hands and wrists, lower back, hips, feet and ankles through gentle movements.

She didn't know anything about the video production process and we didn't know anything about yoga. She just wanted to get her videos done. In about two months we had a nice series of videos for sale.

This kind of arrangement is good for videographers who want to get into the video publishing business but don't have a topic of their own that is burning to be produced. One way to handle this would be to trade equity in the video for your skills, meaning you shoot the production on spec and get paid as the video sells. The danger here is that you invest a lot of time but the product is poorly marketed and doesn't sell.

Our preference when working with a subject matter expert on a topic we're interested in having complete control over marketing, is to pay them a flat fee up front for their services, but they have no rights to residual income. This way we own the video ourselves. We are much more motivated to spend the time and effort to market a program if we're getting all the profits.

3. *In this scenario you're the expert/coach/speaker/professor/consultant who has a message to get out, who wants to produce a video but you don't know how.*

In this case you need to find a video producer or videographer who will do the production work for you. There are a couple of ways to approach this.

If you have the money you can just hire a qualified video production company and possibly a script writer and have it done. In this case you are truly acting in the role of producer. You would own the project outright, including all copyrights and distribution rights, if it is a work for hire. Just make sure you get that in writing. We've included a sample Work for Hire Agreement in Appendix A.

In the situation I described in point 2 above, my partner didn't want to pay what my full rate would be for a work for hire and since I believed the videos had good sales potential we traded our video production skills for a part ownership in the product.

If you don't have the money to pay a production company outright, this is a good arrangement if you can find someone who is an entrepreneur, who believes in your product, and is willing to barter.

Not every video producer is willing to work like this. They have bills to pay and families to feed and so may just want the cash. Plus, they may not have faith that your product will sell, and that's totally understandable. More often than not you will have to pay a production company up front rather than trading equity. If you can pay them a flat fee then you have 100 percent ownership in your product which will probably be the most profitable situation for you in the long run, assuming the product sells well.

WHAT TO LOOK FOR IN A SUBJECT MATTER EXPERT

Assuming you're the video producer, what should you look for in your subject matter partner? There are a number of things.

It goes without saying that they should have genuine knowledge in the subject. If it is something you know nothing about, you are relying on them to provide accurate information. Putting out a misleading or inaccurate video will come back to bite you. If you are marketing to a strong vertical niche you can ruin your reputation with one bad video and never gain the trust of that niche again.

It also helps if your subject matter partner has professional recognition for their expertise. Maybe they've written a book, been featured on CNN, host a radio show, publish a newsletter, are a respected authority of some kind, or even a celebrity. Having authority or celebrity power will definitely help sales because your potential customers will automatically assume that the product is good based on their reputation.

Many of the horticulture videos I produced were with university professors with Ph.D. degrees. When selling to schools it helped to say that a Ph.D. was the authority behind the content. It created instant credibility.

If I am trading equity, I also look for someone who will be an active partner in marketing the video. Many experts speak at large conferences and have the opportunity to sell products on the spot. We call this "back of the room" or "back of house" sales and they can be substantial. I've sold thousands of dollars' worth of videos in a few minutes this way. I've actually had people shoving credit cards at me faster than I could process them, and that is a great experience!

If your potential partner has a proven track record of getting in the public eye, this is a great asset. It is reassuring to know that your partner is also out there pushing the product within their own sphere of influence. It is ideal if they can speak at events, do radio interviews, be featured in newspaper and magazine articles, do guest spots on TV shows, contribute to related blogs, etc. Free publicity is a wonderful asset.

I've had this expectation disappoint me a few times. When I made my car detailing video my partner was very active in giving talks, writing articles, contributing to forums, etc. Shortly after I completed the video he decided to sell his car detailing business and go back to work for an employer that provided full benefits so that he had health insurance for his child. This really took the wind out of my sails. I still sell this video but it would do significantly better if he was still actively keeping his name in the public eye. There was no way I could have seen this coming, but I offer this as an example of something to watch out for. You want to know that your partner is in it for the long haul.

My friend, Holly, the real estate Feng Shui expert, was very much in demand as a speaker internationally. Her books were so highly regarded that the National Association of REALTORS® used them in certification courses. She was a successful realtor and loved public speaking. We'd load her up with inventory when she did a talk but we quickly learned that selling DVDs on consignment is a bookkeeping challenge and is not something we now do.

In the U.S., you have to file 1099s on royalty payments over $600 in a year just as you have to for contract work so make sure your partner has basic business tools in place to accurately track sales. Also keep what they owe you and what you owe them as separate transactions. If you don't have a bookkeeper get some sort of bookkeeping software like QuickBooks.

Those are a couple of examples of important lessons learned from some of our partner relationships. I have many successful partnerships too. My current partner on our workout video series is extremely ambitious. Dave Sheahan, whom you'll meet next, approached us with his idea. Our contribution to the relationship was shooting and editing the videos, plus providing supporting photos and graphics. He has taken over promoting them and is doing a fantastic job. He uses email blasts, forum participation, Facebook, webinars, personal appearances, and is building an affiliate network—everything you could ask for in a partner. I'd like to find many more like him.

Dave has set an example that we look for in any type of equity partner. We really prefer to own our productions outright, but if you do form a partnership look for a partner that brings the right strengths to the partnership.

Dave Sheahan, Founder of 6 Weeks to a Cover Model Body (www.6weekstoacovermodelbody.com) and the *Dave Sheahan Home Workout System* **(www.davesheahanhomeworkoutsystem.com)**

In 2009, after 19 years spent running several successful personal training centers, bootcamps, and fitness coaching, and managing a staff of 60, Dave Sheahan made the decision to move his business online. Not only did he want to make a lifestyle change, he also wanted to gain an international reputation and leverage his expertise to help people all over the world. Dave explains,

I started using video right away, sharing nutrition and fitness tips on YouTube, attaching them to emails, conducting webinars and livestreams with people all over the world, but I always had wanted to offer my 6 Weeks to a Cover Model Body program in a video format and make it available online. I knew having a video program was going to be a key component of my business. But I wanted to do it proper.

Dave's niche is what is called a super niche—in fact I would classify the fitness and health industry as more of a genre. While his potential market and audience is *huge*, so is the competition. Others he had marked as direct competitors, P90X and Insanity, had some pretty high quality videos that were already well established. But while he knew his program was unlike theirs in many ways and spoke to a different audience, he knew video quality was important if he was going to compete.

I had ideas but didn't know how to get it done. When I connected and partnered with you and Kim, who knew how to produce quality video, it was a dream come true! I had

been looking at all my options—buying equipment and doing everything myself, hiring a videographer and editing it myself, or hiring a video company to do it all for me—but I really didn't have the money to pay the rates I was finding, or have the skill and experience to operate a camera, or deal with audio and lighting, let alone editing. Then I met these two professionals in the U.S. that had exactly what I was looking for, understood what I wanted to do, and were willing to joint venture with me on the project. I wasn't looking for someone to do my marketing and sales, I wanted to handle that, but I needed someone who would produce a high quality program. I was willing to go to America to get it done!

That's true ... Dave lives in Ireland! He flew all the way over here for a few months last summer and we shot his entire 6-week program in eleven days! After we met and got to know him better, we saw how motivated he was, how hard he worked, and the reputation he had at that point. We also witnessed how comfortable he was speaking in front of people and saw that he had outlined his unique selling proposition, had done his research, and had a strong marketing foundation set in place. We decided to work with him on this project in exchange for a steady stream of future revenue.

Since Dave switched his business online, he had already developed several successful marketing methods that served him well. He strongly believes in attraction marketing; it serves as the foundation of his marketing strategy—he wants to educate, motivate, and inspire while he builds his brand and global reputation. Along with offering free webinars and access to live broadcasts, he also gives access to view some of his videos for free. All of these methods help his prospects to not only get a taste of how he can help them, but also gets them in his sales funnel. Once in there, his prospects receive daily emails packed full of tips and advice. He's also very actively engaged in social media marketing, specifically within Facebook and YouTube, to attract and connect with his audience. He explains,

Building relationships is crucial within my market because it's so large and I have to set myself apart. It's important because people really don't want to exercise, and they've often heard wrong information about fitness and nutrition, and feel transforming their body and health will be too difficult or too expensive. I use social media to build those relationships and address their concerns. I want them to get to know me as an expert, the source of the best information and the solution they've been looking for ... a program that will give them fast results that last.

So I share a lot of content! I've found that when you do, they think "He's sharing all this good stuff for free, just think what I'll get if I pay." Also when they know you and come to love you, then when you have a new product coming out, they'll get it because they know it'll be a high quality product.

I knew going in that to be successful in marketing my new online coaching system, I needed a lot of passion so I could overcome obstacles that would invariably happen. And they did. I've found it challenging to deal with the technical side of things in finding the right providers for hosting my videos. But the wonderful aspect of my online program is that it is now so easy to add to it.

He gave us these words of advice for those of you who feel a project like this is not doable.

As I share with my coaching clients and in my bootcamps, nothing worthwhile achieving is ever easy. When you're creating a product like this, you have to take steps. You can't get to the top of the stairs unless you take the first step and that leads you to the next step and

the next step and the next step. Using a visual image for you, it's pretty hard to jump up five steps of stairs—sometimes you have to go back a bit due to something not going right.

He continued,

Everyone is an expert in something. Pick something you're good at and passionate about, be clear on when and what and why, and set a date! Get focused. Have a clear vision and put it on paper. Then invest in getting the best production quality you can afford and if you can't do it yourself, find a partner with expertise you need. Look long term, take your time and don't rush into things. Decide what you're going to do, then do it to the best of your ability.

Think you can't find a partner to do this? Think again! Now you may not have to go to the extreme of finding a partner thousands of miles away, but with a clear direction and sound plan, it isn't as improbable as you think. You can find the rest of the interview at www.shoot-to-sell.com.

WHAT TO LOOK FOR IN A VIDEO PRODUCTION COMPANY

Your budget is going to play a role in selecting a company or individual video producer to help you. Today there are a lot of unemployed and self-employed video professionals available, so depending on your budget you may have several choices in your area.

Ideally you want a professional who has shot more than weddings, because that is not the type of work you'll likely be doing. If your video is a scripted production you want someone who is experienced in shooting to a script, like a videographer experienced with shooting corporate or commercial videos. In general, look for someone who can show samples of work that is similar to what you want to do.

If your video requires multiple cameras you obviously need someone with the required equipment. Most modern video cameras shoot in high definition and make excellent images, so you should expect this. If they are hauling around an equipment cart with old, worn-out equipment, that's a bad sign.

If you want to use a teleprompter, ask if they have or can provide one. A teleprompter is a device that scrolls your script as it is being read. When you watch the evening news, the anchor is reading from a teleprompter. Working with a teleprompter takes some practice but once you get used to using one it can really make a production more efficient. I love mine.

You should meet with your potential video company and talk about all aspects of your production to learn if they are a good fit and if they can work within your budget. They will most likely want to look at your script before they can give you a price, which is another reason to develop a script or at least a thorough outline early in the process.

It's a pretty competitive market now so look around. I know independent, beginning videographers who would shoot something for as little as $25 per hour, but a more professional person will likely charge $75 per hour and up to shoot, and a similar fee to edit. The more equipment they bring to the shoot, the more they will charge. One of my favorite assistants, an independent producer, comes fully loaded with audio and video gear and charges $80 per hour and is worth every penny. It's not just his gear I'm paying for, it's his experience.

Frankly, if a person is charging below market rates I'll question if their services are also sub-par.

FINANCIAL ARRANGEMENTS

You have to treat a partnership like a business, regardless of who you are dealing with. If you want to make money then you have to be realistic about what this project is going to cost, what the potential sales are, what the cost of marketing will be, the cost of inventory (whether digital or physical products), packaging, lost opportunity cost, liability, etc.

I like to use the book publishing industry's model as a starting point since it is a very similar industry. A book publisher will typically pay an author 10 to 12 percent of retail sales, with the percentage going up as sales increase, to a certain point, rarely exceeding 15 percent. Then they will have all kinds of limitations on wholesale sales.

People new to the publishing industry sometimes think the author is getting shafted at this rate, especially when you hear about million-dollar book advances, but you have to understand that the publisher is taking a big financial risk in the author by printing and marketing a book. Those large book advances are not given to most authors; they are given when a publisher feels strongly that they will sell thousands and thousands of books and make millions more with that investment.

Inventory sitting in a warehouse is money not working, so if the inventory isn't turning over quickly then they are losing money. If the book doesn't sell out then they'll have inventory to dispose of, often at a loss. They are carrying the financial risk and so must be compensated for that. The same holds true in the video publishing business.

If I'm funding the cost of production and marketing, I'll offer my technical advisor either a flat fee to buy them out or somewhere in the range of 10 to 20 percent equity in the production, depending on the depth of their involvement. That's a starting point and we negotiate from there.

If they are significantly involved in marketing, paying for the inventory and all expenses other than production, *and* if I have faith that they will do a good job of marketing the videos so that we will make money, I'll offer more. This leaves them a realistic profit margin so they can afford to spend money on marketing and product delivery, and provides financial motivation for them to promote the video. This is always negotiable and totally dependent on the project, the people involved, and the potential of the project.

My partners can buy inventory from me for their own sales at better rates than other distributors. There is no hard rule for this but I usually allow them to buy inventory at more than 50 percent off, but I price it so that I make a reasonable profit on their purchase.

CONTRACTS

Whatever you do regarding finances, get it in writing right up front. You should at least have a letter of understanding explaining the financial arrangements and mutual expectations before you begin work. Get it signed. It's really easy to put this off and proceed on faith but don't do it! I speak from too much experience in this area.

Be prudent but don't go nuts about it. I had a potential partner on a project a few years ago who went way overboard in trying to nail down every conceivable point in advance. He spent so much time and money preparing his marketing plan, drafting contracts, and getting ready to get started that he blew his entire budget (around $80,000 he borrowed) on lawyers, consultants, graphic designers, office space rental, furnishings, and living expenses. He had business cards printed for everybody even vaguely connected with the project well before he had a product. I later learned that he had a track record of "failure to launch" due to too much preparation and a lack of action. That's an extreme case of over-preparing and spending money foolishly.

Always get your partnership arrangement in writing, I started with one partner with a verbal understanding that she would get 25 percent (which I thought was generous) and she would help with marketing by doing public appearances. She was fine with this until, to my total dismay, after I had edited the programs she decided that she should be getting 80 percent since she was "the talent."

This arrangement went downhill when I reluctantly agreed to a 50/50 split. Because I was carrying all costs of marketing and distribution I was really getting about 25 percent of each sale. I had no incentive to spend time or money marketing just to hand most of the profits over to her, so the project never sold well. My biggest regret is that we didn't get our arrangement in writing at the beginning.

It helps to know in advance what kind of marketing you will be doing. Will the product be handed over to a distributor who will handle everything but take 40 to 50 percent off the top? Or will one of the partners be the key marketing agent? If so they should be compensated for that. Is there physical inventory (DVDs) and packaging to be created and paid for, and by whom? Who is paying for the website? Will there be printed brochures or advertisements to pay for? You need to get all of these details spelled out so you have realistic expectations of the costs involved for each party. Make that part of your agreement and get it signed.

Ultimately you want it to be a fair and equitable arrangement so that you both are successful and motivated to keep the business moving forward in the same direction.

In Appendix B, I have included a Sample Letter of Agreement we've used with a partner.

Note: the Work for Hire and Sample Letter of Agreement are provided just for your reference and should not be considered legal documents. Alter them and seek legal advice as you see fit.

Action Steps

- Decide if you need a partner and what type: videographer for hire, technical advisor, etc.
- If you hire a videographer for a flat fee, make sure they sign a Work for Hire agreement.
- Meet with your partner to discuss what is expected, and what financial arrangements should be made.
- Negotiate the terms and financial arrangements between all parties.
- Refer to the Sample Letters of Agreement and craft one all parties agree on.

Chapter 6

Budgeting
Know What Your Special Interest Video Will Cost to Produce

Chapter Objectives
- Learn how to plan your production budget.
- Understand when you should make a "Go/No-Go" decision based on the projected cost and a realistic projection of sales.

Have you been filling your notebook up with potential video titles, possible partners, notes about contracts and agreements? Good. You have to do all of that to lay a solid foundation for your SIV venture. We're about to explore the topic of budgets which is the bedrock upon which your video project will be built.

Developing a budget is probably not going to be one of your favorite tasks in this process, but it is definitely one of the most important. You have to know how much this is going to cost in order to project whether or not you'll make a profit. You'll also want to create a marketing budget, which we cover in Chapter 33.

Let me say from the start that I'm a penny pincher when creating videos on my own dime. I've shot short independent films with budgets up to $240,000 and I love projects like that, but that is definitely *not* what we're talking about here. When you're spending your own money you want to make the video as good as reasonably possible given your financial resources, intended audience, and potential sales. Your intention is to make money in this business and if you spend more than you make, you won't. It's that simple.

My SIV projects tend to involve five or fewer people, including director, camera operator, sound recorder, subject matter expert, script writer and editor. Kim or I usually serve in multiple roles, meaning there may only be two to four of us involved.

In general, the videos my company produces for sale cost under $5,000 out-of-pocket, depending on the location and circumstances. It is often much less, but this figure is deceiving. We can keep actual expenses down because Kim and I are capable of writing, shooting, editing, and doing basically everything. I'm not saying that we *should* do all of those things, but we can. The fact is, we should *not* do everything because it ties up too much of our time that's better spent elsewhere. And as the saying goes, time is money. In our case, while doing all of those roles ourselves isn't really costing us actual money, it is costing us in lost opportunities to pursue other business ventures that would bring us more income in the long term.

I tell you this to illustrate that when you are creating your budget you need to calculate the value of everyone's time as well as actual expenses, even if you are including your time as part of the partnership. This can be useful when you decide on how much value each partner is contributing, which can affect the equity each owns in the project.

It is also extremely important because you want to know the total value of a video project so that when you are projecting your sales you can determine if this is really a good investment. If your out-of-pocket expense is only $1,000 it might sound like a bargain, but if it takes three months to complete and your time is worth $12,000 you have to make at least $13,000 in order to break even.

KNOW YOUR AUDIENCE

Keep your intended audience in mind when developing your budget. You don't have to go overboard with locations, effects, or expensive stock footage if your video is a simple "how-to" program that is all close-up shots. Scale the production value to the subject and intended audience.

You may also find you don't even need to shoot any video at all providing your topic is one that would work well as a screencast movie, such as teaching a computer software program, internet marketing technique, or social media tool.

I've seen people make expensive mistakes in this area. One of my associates spent well over $50,000 developing a series of educational videos for a very small niche market. He was paying the producer by the month rather than a flat fee (he learned his lesson to never do that) and it was taking far too long and getting more expensive by the month.

Give your audience just what they need in terms of production quality and don't spend anything more. We're not talking about feature film productions here. That's a different thing with different objectives.

ANTICIPATING EXPENSES

Before you can develop your budget you need to spend some time visualizing your final production. Think about these things:

- Where will you shoot it and how long will it take?
- Will you have to pay for shooting permits?
- Do you need to hire a director, camera operator, crew, editor, and rent equipment?
- Will there be lodging, meals, and transportation expenses?
- Is there an on-camera host or is it all voice-over narration? What will that cost?
- Do you need props, sets, and materials and what will they cost?

These are all major expense areas. Write all of this down. You're going to have to forecast these expenses.

HOW I APPROACH A BUDGET

I always make at least a simple budget to forecast expected expenses, no matter what size the project is. The more complicated the project, the greater the detail I put into the budget. This also helps tremendously when you are working with a partner or outside funding source. All parties can then see what needs to be done and what all the players can bring to the table in their expenditures and role in the project.

I break budgeting down into three areas:

Pre-Production—This includes planning, travel to meetings, script development, location scouting, acquiring permits, and other expenses required before you can begin production.

Production—This includes all activities involved in shooting the video including the director, camera operators, actors, grips, assistants, equipment rental, consumables like tape or memory chips and batteries, travel, meals; basically all expenses involved once you start production.

Post-Production—This includes the editor, effects or graphic artist, special software, stock footage, music and sound effects, hard drives for storage and archiving, voice-over narrator, tape stock, DVDs, office expenses, and possibly the time of the director to look over the editing process.

I further break each of these down line by line into projected hours times cost-per-hour, unless the item is a flat fee. This makes it easier to build a rational best-guess budget. I also like to keep one column that is the projected budget and one that is the actual budget. As I go along I fill in the actual costs to see how far I'm deviating from the budget. Over time this will help you improve your forecasting accuracy.

For your reference, below are some typical fees for a professional video director, crew, and rental equipment. I'm not talking part-time hobbyists, but professionals. These costs are typical where I live in California. Your costs will vary. They'd be more in New York City and less in Missoula, Montana.

Typical (even low) standard industry fees:

- Producer Fee: $500–$1,000/Day (you may be the producer)
- Script Writer: $500–$2,000 Total
- Director Fee: $500–$1,200/Day
- Camera Operator: $500/Day
- 2nd Camera Operator: $400/Day
- Script/Continuity Assistant: $200–$400/Day
- Camera and Audio Equipment Rental: $150–$750/Day
- Key Grip + Assistant + Lighting Gear: $500–$1,000/Day
- Wardrobe: Estimated $20–$200/Day Per Character
- City Permits: $25–$1,000/Day (depending on the city, whether roads need to be closed, and other factors)
- Props/Furniture Rental: Estimated $100–$500
- Possible Set Construction: $50–$300
- Set Location Rental: $500–$1,000/Day

Typical post-production costs:

- Editor Fee: $500/Day
- Redundant Hard Disk Archive: $200 (for storing your program files)
- Visual Effects/Stock Footage $50–$500

Variable costs not included above:

- On-Camera or Voice-Over Talent
- Stock Music

- Travel and Lodging
- Vehicle Rental
- Catering (food)

You may not need all of these items but as you can see, there are a lot of things to consider and it can really add up fast. This doesn't include the cost of designing the packaging for your DVD, marketing it, inventory and fulfillment services.

In Appendix C is a very simple budget template that I use to quickly estimate the costs of a production. You can also download this template as a blank spreadsheet at www.shoot-to-sell.com.

This kind of budget gives me a quick look at the costs and is often all I need.

The biggest single expense is Location Field Production. This can vary greatly for each project. If I'm editing it myself, which I usually do, then post-production will not be an out-of-pocket expense except for effects and music I may purchase. The next largest expense is the script. If you or your partner write the script then you can save here.

If it's a more complex project you probably want to make a more detailed budget, such as breaking equipment rental out into separate line items for camera, audio, lighting, and grip equipment. You can find a more detailed budget template for download at www.shoot-to-sell.com.

Once you develop a budget, ask yourself these questions:

- Do you think you can make enough to break even?
- Can you do much better than that?
- Would your time be better spent elsewhere?
- Can you afford to do this project if you don't sell that much?
- Is this a wise investment of both your time and your money?

Once you know what your video is going to cost to create, you'll want to do a quick income projection. Here is a very simple way to calculate profit based on estimated sales:

Simple Income Projection	
Price Per Video	$50.00
Duplication/Delivery Cost Each	$1.25
Net Profit Per Unit Sold	$48.75
Unit Sales Per Month (Projection)	30
Monthly Profit	$1,462.50
Annual Profit	$15,550.00

Your price and actual sales will vary, so just use this as a way to create a quick forecast. This model is based on selling one unit per day at $50. This does not include your marketing expenses.

HOW TO AMORTIZE PRODUCTION EXPENSES

You have to account for the cost to produce your video somehow. The simple way to do this is to write it off as a business expense in the year it occurs. That's how we do it. My old university department had a more complex system where we would amortize the production expenses over a certain number of sales. For example, if it cost $5,000 to make, we might expense that $5,000 over the first 300 copies which makes them cost $16.67 each plus duplication cost of about $1.50, so our cost of goods was $18.17 per DVD for the first 300 copies. This prevented us having a lot of large expenses but lowered the profit margin until we made that projected number of sales. If you are highly productive this might be a good option; otherwise just write the expenses off as we do.

A FINAL WORD ABOUT BUDGETS

Your budget is your friend. Don't look at budget development as an odious task. It should always be one of the first things you do when considering a new project. By developing a detailed budget before you begin production you can decide if there are areas where you can cut back to make your video project more affordable.

Producing on a small budget can be challenging for sure, but try to see it as an opportunity to be creative. No budget for exotic location shooting? Look around your area and see what substitutions you can come up with. Is there a public garden, arboretum, museum, park, or impressive cityscape you can use as a backdrop (check for required shooting permits first)? Try to find an expensive looking background that you can use for free.

You will be surprised at what you have around you and how willing others are to work with you. When we were shooting for our succulent and cactus series, we saw a beautiful cactus garden featured in our Sunday paper. It was at a home near where we lived and they had published the owners' names. They were in the phone book and one call later, we were on our way to shoot their garden. They were tickled and more than happy to accommodate us. We regularly call on our friends, neighbors, and local businesses to shoot at their locations.

Don't have a studio? Maybe all you need is your garage or basement, an inexpensive photo backdrop and some work lights. That's what Mike Deiure set up in his home. The total investment in equipment was under $200 and it looks fantastic. On a weekly basis, he's in his studio, cranking out a new guitar lesson that he adds to his ever-growing catalog of titles.

Want to add production value without busting the budget? Add some shots from unusual angles, like from ground level or high up. Can you get on a rooftop or balcony to get an opening shot? Consider buying rights to stock footage for an impressive opening shot. We use and recommend companies like www.pond5.com for affordable stock video. You can also find buyout DVDs of stock images at www.footagefirm.com and many other places.

Do you need to record voice-over narration but don't have a sound booth? Put your narrator in a car parked in the garage with the windows rolled up (with the engine off, of course). Works great! Or put them in a closet full of clothes to deaden the sound. Use your imagination.

Here's my best tip for adding production value: work from a script. Don't wing it in the field; have a plan and a script so you know where you are going and what you need to do. We're covering the way we write and use scripts in a later chapter.

Whatever you do, don't design a video that takes more time or money than you have. There are only two possible outcomes for this situation:

1.   Your product will suffer because you'll have to cut corners to make it fit the budget, or:
2.   You will spend too much time and/or money and it won't be profitable.

Resist the temptation to let a good idea lead you down this path. As a video publisher, you have to treat this as a business and the bottom line in business is turning a profit. That is why we have you focus on research and looking at all the components first so that you can make a decision with your eyes open and come out with a successful product that will sell for years.

Action Steps

- Know your audience and plan your budget to be appropriate for what they need. Don't go overboard.
- List shooting locations and logistics costs such as entry fees, shooting permits, etc.
- Enter the projected costs, either a flat fee or hourly/day rates, into a spreadsheet such as the one provided in Appendix C.
- Estimate your time and assign a dollar figure to the hours you will put into this project. Your time is valuable and is part of the cost of doing business.
- Make a "Go/No-Go" decision based on the projected cost and a realistic projection of sales. Use your net profit figure, not gross sales, to make this decision.

Chapter 7

Funding Your Project

Chapter Objectives
- Become aware of how to pitch your project.
- Learn about crowdfunding sources like indiegogo (www.indiegogo.com).

Are you funding your video or are you looking for outside funding sources? If it's the latter, you'll most likely need not just a production budget but a business and/or marketing plan to demonstrate that you have thought your project out realistically all the way through from production to marketing and that you have a good idea of its earning potential. A potential funder may ask to see a script.

High budget movies are rarely if ever produced unless the distribution networks are in place first. Since movies are largely funded by investors, those investors want to know how the movie will be marketed and distributed so they can see how likely it is they'll make a profit. Your funders are going to want to see the same sort of proof of profitability.

You're realistically not going to get funding from a traditional source, like a bank. You can hit up relatives, max out your credit cards, take a loan against your house (not a good idea), or approach potential partners or investors. We're hopefully not talking a big budget here, at least not on your first production.

Here are some tips for pitching your project:

- Give a good description but realize that people are busy. Don't hand them a 30-page proposal. One or two pages is fine, along with a budget and income projections.
- Let your enthusiasm and passion show through without going overboard.
- If you have a celebrity or recognized expert connected with the project, say so.
- Mention other videos that have done well in this niche.
- Give a brief description of the need you have found and how your video will provide the solution.

If at this stage you have already developed a script, by all means be ready to share the script with them.

You may have to revise and resubmit your pitch to gain final approval. Once you get approval you must make sure that the final product matches what you proposed. If changes are needed, communicate that with your sponsors.

Crowdfunding

An innovative new avenue of funding has opened up for independent films and videos called crowdfunding which is the process of raising money to fund private enterprises. The money comes from networks of people who pool their money together, usually via the internet, to support private projects of people or organizations. A good example can be found at www.indiegogo.com. This is a service where you place the pitch (proposal) for your project online and people can contribute to your funding goal. There is no fee to put your fund-raising campaign online. Indiegogo charges 4 percent of the money you raise if you meet your goal and 9 percent of the money you raise if you don't. This is an international platform so you are basically placing your proposal in front of the entire world. Another crowdfunding source for video projects is Kickstarter (www.kickstarter.com).

I haven't tried crowdfunding myself but have read several articles about it. One of the key pieces of advice I've read repeatedly is to not try to raise your entire budget this way if it is a lot. Just try for a few thousand dollars and you're much more likely to succeed.

Indiegogo is connected to a distribution company called Distribber. This is a service that will distribute your file through a network of outlets including Amazon, Netflix, iTunes, Hulu, and cable/satellite/telco VOD services. You choose which of these you want your video on and there are fairly high fees associated with each one. You can read more at www.distribber.com.

Remember that you are not only funding the cost of production, but also your marketing and fulfillment costs like advertising, website development, duplication and packaging, distribution, whether online or otherwise. Be sure to factor in those costs into your overall funding requirements.

Again, we're advising you to start out with a simple project and a small budget, so you may not need to seek outside funding. Even if you're funding it on your own you still want to do the market research and develop a budget first. It's your money you're spending!

Action Steps

- Develop a production/marketing budget and marketing plan (see Chapter 33) to show potential funders.
- Write a project funding proposal using the tips provided.
- Pitch your project.
- Revise the pitch if necessary.
- Communicate any changes in the project with your funding sources.
- Investigate crowdfunding to see if it's a good option for you.

Part II

Pre-Production

Chapter 8

Pre-Production

Chapter Objectives

- Refine your project idea.
- Create an overall project schedule.

Pre-production is essentially what the name implies. It is everything that happens prior to beginning actual production of your film or video. It may not be the most exciting stage, unless you're the script writer, but it is perhaps the most critical step to producing a successful video. No matter if you are working with a team of others or producing it by yourself, time-consuming and expensive errors and omissions can be avoided by spending the necessary time to make a clear plan. Not only that, but if you are looking to others to help you fund your project, you'll need a strong outline or script and marketing plan before you approach them.

It is not unlike planning for a vacation. When you get ready for a trip, you not only make arrangements ahead of time, you also determine where it is you want to go, who you're going to travel with, how you're going to get there, where you'll stay, what you need to take, what activities you want to do, etc. You need to know what you are going to pack, then assemble and pack all of your clothes and toiletries. Advance planning makes the trip so much easier and more pleasant. Spontaneity results in more surprises and adrenaline, but that's not what you want in your video production.

By the end of the pre-production phase you will have written a script, obtained funding, hired your key cast and crew members, determined your shooting locations, built sets if necessary, decided on wardrobe issues, finalized a shooting schedule, coordinated everyone's call times, and obtained any required permissions.

That's the way it should happen. I want to share with you an example of how not to do it:

As I was writing this book, I was hired to make a video that was to go directly to YouTube. The purpose was just shock value, with no real story. When I first met with the clients, all they said they wanted was to have a toilet drop on a Chevrolet Corvette from a helicopter and then have the Corvette blow up. Admittedly, this didn't make any sense to me but the client insisted that's all they wanted. "We don't want this to be a Hollywood production," he stressed over and over again. When I asked why he wanted to do this the answer always was, "because we can." OK, fine, I can do that. There was no script, no plan, no storyline other than to shoot a helicopter dropping a toilet on a car and blowing it up. I'm not going to turn down a well-paying job even if I don't really get the point.

Knowing that we only had one chance to get it right (we could only blow the car up once) and having been in this business for many years, I came over-prepared. At one point we had four shooters and eight cameras filming.

I should have expected what happened next. When we got to the site on the first day of the shoot for the helicopter dropping the toilet on the Corvette scene, the client had some different ideas in mind. Remember, he had told me this "is not a Hollywood production." Well, now he had this idea to get a shot of him driving the car in, then one looking up in the sky and seeing the helicopter (ominous foreshadowing), then another shot of him running for his life from the car, and … you get my drift. We only had a quick half hour before the helicopter arrived to sketch out a shooting plan and get these additional shots. No pressure.

Now, had I known that it would turn into a "Hollywood production" as he called it, I would have prepared differently, with a storyboard and a plan.

Communications didn't flow smoothly between my camera crew and the person pushing the button to blow the car up, resulting in two key cameras not running at the most important moment. One of my camera operators was absolutely sick about missing the shot.

Because of my over-preparing with cameras I did get the shots I needed and it came out looking great. Not much of a storyline, but I delivered what they asked for.

When we were editing we found that to tell the story better it would have been nice to have some reaction shots from the client as he saw his car blown up, something we definitely would have done had we had a plan. However, with these last minute changes and little time to shoot before the helicopter arrived, we didn't get them.

A couple of weeks later the client had another idea, which was to wrap this whole video inside a dream sequence, which actually made it make more sense. So, we billed for another day's shoot and a few hours of editing time and turned it into a much better video. It was a stressful and inefficient way to work but we turned it around and got a nice video out of it.

The next project is supposed to be a short zombie movie shot in a deserted prison way out in the boondocks, which will involve very meticulous pre-planning and storyboarding. In this remote location we'll have to plan everything from food and drinks for the cast and crew to an electrical generator, costumes and makeup, even a portable toilet. There's no running around the corner to get some extra batteries or more sandwiches so we have to bring everything. I actually love this client's crazy ideas, but next time we will come properly prepared.

You don't want to produce your SIV that way. Before you get to the point of turning your cameras on you should have everything planned out. It will save you valuable time and be less stressful for everyone. You have to be flexible and deal with the unforeseen circumstances that you encounter, but it's better to be prepared.

Even if your videos are going to be screencast movies, they need to be planned and thought out. You don't want to start your screencast program and then have to search your desktop for the program or other documents you are going to refer to—especially if someone is going to pay for this. You'll look disorganized and sloppy.

TO BEGIN, START AT THE END

Ideally you shouldn't start your video until you've figured out your budget, marketing and distribution strategies. That way you have those aspects in mind as you are writing and producing your video.

Always be thinking of how you can take advantage of a situation to benefit your later marketing efforts. For example, it's much more efficient to plan and shoot promotional videos while you're on the set with cast and crew shooting the actual project. You might later decide you need something for the promo you didn't shoot and it is impossible to get it, especially if you shot at a remote location, disassembled your set, and destroyed your props, or your narrator is no longer available.

Plan to have someone take high quality still images during your production, especially close-up shots of processes you are demonstrating, and wide angle shots of the production team at work. These are great for PR, for packaging, and for your website. People love to see behind the scenes shots.

It's always a good idea to offer free sample videos. Since you have everything set up, you can shoot these types of videos easily. Use your on-camera talent while you have them to do a special intro for some sample videos. In fact, we now add to our production tasks the job of scripting, shooting, and producing separate promotion videos while shooting our SIV.

Think about these things and add them into your shooting schedule.

REFINE YOUR PROJECT IDEA

Before you can write a script or even your outline you must clearly define what is to be accomplished. This is especially important if you have partners in the project. You want to make sure you are all on the same page.

If you've been doing your action steps, by now you should have identified and researched a topic of interest. Now it's time to develop your project further by asking and answering the following questions in more depth. All of these questions and answers need to be written out in a more comprehensive manner. From there you will develop your outline, script and shooting schedule, subjects we'll cover in the following chapters.

- *When do you need to get your video done?*

This is one of the first questions to ask—that way you work backwards from that deadline to get your project schedule. This is your launch date, the day the video is announced as being available for purchase. From this overall project schedule you'll develop your production schedule. They are different schedules: the project schedule will encompass the entire plan from inception to sales, whereas the production schedule is only about producing the actual video(s) and will fall into the project schedule.

You set this due date to keep yourself on track. If you have arranged for a distributor to carry your video they may be planning to include it in an upcoming catalog, so be sure to meet any distribution schedules.

- *What are your goals for your video?*

This takes into account your video's purpose but it goes further to determine what you'll do with the video after it is completed. Don't just say "my goal is to make money." What is the intended outcome of your video? Will viewers learn a new skill, be entertained, learn about a foreign country, or what? What is the completed project going to "look" like?

- *Who is your audience?*

Knowing your audience is critical. Keep this audience in mind as you write your script and develop your marketing materials. Your video will fit their needs and speak their language much more accurately that way.

- *What specific topic(s) will you cover?*

The best path to take is to produce a video on a narrowly defined topic that is targeted to a specific audience that you have identified. A video covering a broad general topic will be harder to market because it is harder to identify and contact the potential market.

- *How many videos will you produce?*

Even if you only have one title in mind now, be thinking of how you can expand this topic into more videos. Try to do this early in the pre-production phase and you can enjoy an economy of scale when you go into production.

For example, if you have three or four highly related topics you can be shooting for all of them while you are at a location, maximizing your time and travel expenses. Going back to my videos on growing and propagating cacti and succulents, while visiting large wholesale greenhouses in Southern California I could be shooting for both videos at the same location, plus another video on greenhouse conditions and a fourth title on soil mixtures for succulents. This type of work would require you to be very organized, with specific shots lists for all four videos, but what a great way to leverage your time.

- *How long will they be?*

I generally aim for 20 to 30 minutes maximum. If it is a lot of material then it is better to break it into smaller videos. That also gives the series more value and higher potential profits.

Like I said, these are just some things you need to think about before you start writing. I've put together the following checklist of areas in which you'll have to make decisions before you start and throughout the project. Go through each one and determine the targeted date of completion. Put this into a spreadsheet or word processing document and feel free to add to it. (Don't worry if some of these terms are foreign to you, we'll be explaining them throughout this book.)

Pre-Production Checklist		Launch/Release Date	
Task	Completion Date		Completion Date
B-roll		Project Outline	
Cast/Talent/Narrator		Props/Materials/Supplies	
Crew		Releases/Permits	
Delivery		Sales Funnel	
Distribution Channel		Script	
Editing		Set	
Graphics/Images		Shot List	
Interview Questions		Software	
Landing Pages		Storyboard	
Locations		Video/Audio Equipment	
Packaging		Website	

SCHEDULE

You'll need to establish timelines for the entire project. You may have to do it as part of the proposal if you're pitching it to a sponsor. It's important that you set clear deadlines for the production and marketing phases. If your deadlines are missed, especially in the production phase, then this may increase the number of hours or days on a project, which will increase costs and delay your release date. Delaying your project may or may not be a costly or dire situation if you aren't trying to have your video ready for a specific event. But if you are relying on making it available for a seasonal sales cycle, like Christmas, or for a special event, it's vital to make sure you get it done on time and on budget.

Get a blank calendar or computer planning program and establish due dates starting with—you guessed it—the end in mind, the date you need your video available for sale, the launch/release date. Pick something realistic that you can stick to. I like to say that in video, what can go wrong probably will go wrong. Provide a cushion time between critical dates to allow for unforeseen circumstances. You also want to determine who is responsible for what.

Consider everything. For example, we shot our series of 42 workout videos with HD (High Definition) cameras, so we had the logistics of dealing with huge amounts of HD files from three cameras, all of which were using 32 GB SDHC (Secure Digital High Capacity) cards for storage. (If you are still using tape, this is not as much of an issue; you can capture that later, just make sure that you have enough tape.) To deal with my situation we shot two complete workout videos each morning for eleven days. We'd shoot one in the morning and then during lunch I went to my office, dumped the files to my hard drive and reformatted the cards for the afternoon's shoot. After transferring them I always checked to make sure the files were fine before reformatting the cards. Then I even backed those files up to another drive.

Every evening I did this again to transfer my afternoon's shoot and to prepare for the next morning. The time required for "data wrangling" (moving and organizing files) was about three hours per day and had to be factored into my schedule. Ideally I would have liked an extra week or two to shoot so it wouldn't have been so exhausting for all parties. Since Dave came from Ireland and had other commitments, this was not possible. If anything major had gone wrong to disrupt our tight shooting schedule it would have been a big problem.

So your project timeline in reverse may look something like the one we did for the *Dave Sheahan Home Workout System* (this is a simplified version for brevity):

Launch date—November 1 (Dave and team)
Sales pages up—October 30 (Dave and team)
Website completed—October 27 (Dave and team)
All videos loaded to server—October 23 (Rick, Kim, and Dave's team)
Videos compressed for upload—October 20 (Rick)
Editing completed—October 17 (Rick)
Editing begins—August 1 (Rick)
Shooting ends—July 30 (Rick, Kim, Dave, and crew)
Shooting begins—July 19 (Rick, Kim, Dave, and crew)
Prep location/set—July 18 (Rick, Kim, and crew)
Supplies/equipment purchased—July 12 (Rick and Kim)
Scout locations—July 5 (Rick)
Script complete—June 28 (Dave)

That was our project timeline and included everything from the beginning to the launch date. There wasn't a script in the formal sense because Dave knows this stuff inside and out and was basically leading the viewer through each day's exercises as he demonstrated them, but he did have the order of his routines planned and outlined and put on cue cards. If this had been a scripted project there would be more planning, outlining, and casting before the production began.

PROJECT MANAGEMENT TOOLS

I hope your first SIV is not too complex but even simple productions run better if you thoroughly plan them out. You'll be developing an outline, script and storyboard, shot list, prop list, and keeping track of lots of details. You should be sharing these things with key members of your production team. Thanks to great project management and file sharing programs you can use your computer to organize everything. For project management we use Microsoft Word and Excel or their free open source counterpart, OpenOffice (which can be downloaded off the web), extensively. GoogleDocs (www.docs.google.com) and www.dropbox.com are great for online planning and file sharing.

There are many project management tools available if you want more control. Some have free trials so you can see if they are right for you. Here are some you can use on the computer or even download to your smartphone or tablet to help you keep your information organized:

- www.teamlab.com
- www.market7.com
- www.37signals.com (Base camp)
- www.box.net
- www.pbworks.com
- www.workflowy.com
- www.evernote.com

Software comes and goes, so do a search online for yourself. You may find that Microsoft Office or OpenOffice is all you need. I use Workflowy every day and find Evernote very helpful, too. You can also look at the resources page on www.shoot-to-sell.com which we'll update with new organizational tools as we discover them.

Action Steps

- Refine your project idea by answering the questions listed.
- Create an overall project schedule from the Pre-Production Checklist.

Chapter 9

Outlining Your Project

Chapter Objectives
- Learn how to organize your video's content.
- Understand how to outline your project.

Preparing a video production is similar to writing a paper in some ways. You want to effectively present your ideas to your audience in a logical, organized order. Even if you do not plan to have a written shooting script it is vital to at least have an in-depth outline of the ideas you want to convey and the images you'll need to do this.

A strong, detailed outline is also the foundation for your script and storyboards. Yet creating a *visual* product is in many ways much different than writing a paper. The viewer will not be relying only on the words to help them "see" what is described but will be actually looking at something happening. This is why creating an audio/video script is such a good tool for organizing your ideas and content so that the images and audio you visualize will complement each other when the finished product is on the screen. The script will give you the blueprint to ensure that your video makes sense to the viewer.

After reading our suggestions, you may find another approach that works better for you. However you will be working, even if you are recording events beyond your control that can't be scripted such as seminars, rallies, social events, natural disasters, riots and demonstrations, etc., we highly recommend starting out with a well-outlined plan or script, keeping in mind that things will most likely change during the shooting process. You'll want to leave room for flexibility or even for another story to unfold.

A few years ago, we shot a "behind the scenes making of" video of an opera production. As the production unfolded, there were many interesting stories that happened along the way that we couldn't possibly have anticipated before we turned the camera on, such as the female lead losing her voice on the last performance! We were able to effectively weave these unexpected side stories into the final program and it gave it an interesting twist. However, we did have an outline of the basics we had to cover, interview questions the principals needed to answer, where we would shoot, what it would look like, etc. Had we not had the outline and a basic idea of what we were going to shoot, we would have never been on the lookout for the little stories that made the video more interesting and informative.

We like to start by listing the content we definitely want to cover, and then making a rough outline. An outline is a helpful tool to organize your research as well. You can sketch a general outline, touching on the main topics you wish to cover, then possibly hand it off to someone, possibly an assistant or a script writer, to do research.

Even if you are working with an expert as your technical advisor, it is still important to sketch out a plan. I've found that if you have a rough outline and script to present to a busy advisor as a starting point you have a greater chance of getting your project completed on schedule. Busy professors, writers, and speakers may have a hard time creating an outline or script for you, so laying the groundwork and letting them make executive decisions can be more effective.

When we created the video *The Properties of Soil*, we had a good script ready before we even approached the professor we wanted to work with. We had done our research and knew the key points he needed to cover. We wrote specific things we wanted him to say on-camera, particularly the opening and closing parts. Then we planned on shooting in the field with him where he would say things in his own words, depending on the situation at hand. If we hadn't done all the work beforehand instead of relying on him to create it from scratch, most likely we wouldn't have this video to sell today.

Even if you are shooting an expert on-camera you'll want to have some kind of outline to make sure you hit all of the key points. Everyone can make mistakes and I've seen some very smart people melt down in front of the camera. Remember, you are in charge and the quality and success of your video will hinge on how well the subject is approached and directed.

My theory about making an effective educational video is this:

1. Tell them what you are going to teach them.
2. Show the information as succinctly as possible, keeping in mind that today's viewers are very media savvy and have short attention spans.
3. Tell them what you just taught them. In other words, remind them what they should have learned. Breaking the information into bite-sized modules is a good idea.

If you organize your video like you would a composition it will naturally fall into topical chapters or sections. If it doesn't, try to arrange it that way. This will come in handy when you are marking your chapter selections if you are going to have your video available on DVDs. It will also be extremely helpful if you are going to offer your content as separate short videos like in an online course or membership program.

The movie industry calls these DVD segments "scenes." We call them chapters. Whatever you want to call them, they serve as an index and allow people to quickly get a good idea of what is covered by looking at the chapters or scenes page. This also helps them return to a specific point in the DVD they may want to revisit. *Hint*: Teachers really love this feature! You can have chapters even if you are delivering your video online, so really try to break the topic into distinct modules.

OUTLINE BASICS

Remember high school composition classes? You may groan but those skills you learned then will come in handy now.

Authors, coaches, teachers, and professional speakers most likely already do this in preparation for writing books or making presentations. It boils down to arranging your points from beginning to end in a logical order.

It's a simple formula; put down your main topics as alpha bullet points like so:

A. Main Topic 1
B. Main Topic 2
C. Main Topic 3

Then underneath each letter, bullet out the related sub-topics.

A. Main Topic 1
    1. Sub-Topic 1
    2. Sub-Topic 2
    3. Sub-Topic 3
B. Main Topic 2
    1. Sub-Topic 1
    2. Sub-Topic 2
    3. Sub-Topic 3
C. Main Topic 3
    1. Sub-Topic 1
    2. Sub-Topic 2
    3. Sub-Topic 3

From there you need to break your topic down further.

D. Main Topic 1
    1. Sub-Topic 1
        i) Detail 1
        ii) Detail 2
        iii) Detail 3
    2. Sub-Topic 2
        i) Detail 1
        II) Detail 2
        iii) Detail 3
    3. Sub-Topic 3
        i) Detail 1
        ii) Detail 2
        iii) Detail 3

You can also start with numbers first then the alphabet or old-style starting with roman numerals. However you choose to do it, have a system where you organize your topics, sub-topics, and further details into logical categories. Go into as much detail on each level as necessary but make the breaks logical. As you write your script you'll want to think of good transitions between the top levels of your outline.

If you use a word processing program like Microsoft Word, it is easy to format your information into a numbered outline.

Here is a sample from the outline we put together for one scene of our *Hooked on Succulents* video.

1) Propagating Succulents
    a) Introduce the section—Succulents are propagated by four methods:
        i) Propagating by seeds
            (1) Supplies needed
                (a) Plastic container
                (b) Succulent seeds
                (c) Cactus and succulent soil
                (d) Spray bottle filled with water
            (2) Procedure
                (a) Punch holes in the top of the container

        (b) Put soil in the container
        (c) Spread seeds evenly on top of the soil
        (d) Water lightly with a spray bottle
        (e) Close the lid
        (f) Place in a greenhouse or room with the temperature at___ degrees
        (g) Check on the seeds every___ weeks
        (h) Once succulents reach a height of 1–2 inches, they can be replanted in a larger pot
    ii) Propagating by plantlets
        (1) Supplies needed
           (a) Large succulent plant
           (b) Plug tray
           (c) Cactus and succulent soil
        (2) Procedure
           (a) Put soil in the container
           (b) Remove the succulent leaves from the larger plant
           (c) Gently push them into the soil compartment

This planning part of the pre-production process may sound just as tedious as the research we stressed upon you earlier but if you do a good job here it will make all of the following processes easier and is vital to having an efficient shooting schedule. If we had missed any step in this process while we were on location with all of the supplies on hand we would have had to go back and reshoot at considerable expense and bother.

A good outline will make scriptwriting far easier. The outline is the backbone of the script. Give this step the attention it deserves and you're being nice to your script writer and production crew.

Action Steps

- Make a list of all the points you want to cover in your video.
- Organize your subject into topical areas.
- Outline your content based on topics and sub-topics, detailing it as much as possible.

Chapter 10

Scripts, Storyboards, and Shot Lists

Chapter Objectives

- Learn how to format a simple audio/video script.
- Find out what's involved in developing a shot list.
- Learn what's involved in developing a storyboard.
- Understand what continuity is and why it's important.

A script, storyboard, and shot list (sometimes called a shooting script) are essential elements for planning your video production and will be discussed in detail in this chapter. We'll continue with arranging talent and coordinating crew, equipment considerations, and location logistics in the following chapter.

THE SCRIPT

The most important tool for a special interest video is the script. The outline we discussed in Chapter 9 is the foundation upon which the script is built. With your outline as a guide you can start visualizing what the viewer will be seeing on the screen and what they will be hearing. If you've done the work with the outline as we suggested, you most likely will have a really good idea of what your shots will look like by now.

We'll be using some terminology in this chapter so refer to the glossary if at any time you aren't sure what we're referring to. For example, don't confuse script and shot list. The script is the sequential content of your program and flows from beginning to end. By reading the script you can see the video unfold in your mind's eye. Each scene, narration block, or change in camera angle is numbered. We call these shot numbers.

A *shot list*, as we use the term, is a production tool that contains shot numbers from your script grouped into similar locations or camera angles to make shooting more efficient. The shot list is also sometimes referred to as a shooting script. We use the term shot list to avoid confusion between the similar sounding terms script and shooting script.

We like to use a simple audio/video script format, commonly referred to as an AV script, that lists the audio and video components together to tell the "story" or explain a process. Here's a simple example of an AV script format.

Shot #	Video Image	Audio/Narration
7	Close-up of kitten's face	This kitten is only a few hours old. You can see that her eyes have not opened yet.
8	Mother licking kitten	Her mother is giving her her first bath.

The AV script format is well suited to special interest videos and especially to instructional programs. It is typically set up in tables with three columns, as opposed to the one-column format used for dramatic feature films. There is a script template for you to look at in Appendix D. It is also available for download at www.shoot-to-sell.com.

The first column is for numbering your shots. Think of this as numbering each paragraph in an article. You create a new sequential number each time you change shots, camera angles, location, or speaking roles. Numbering each shot of your script will make it easier when you are grouping shots together in your shot list.

Column 2 is for a description of the shot. This is how you pre-visualize what the viewer will see as he listens to the audio. Describe in as much detail as necessary what the viewer will be seeing or what the camera will be doing. These can be written descriptions of the shot and/or simple drawings. We usually just use written descriptions because drawing out each pre-visualized scene is too time-consuming and we're already familiar with the content, but for tricky camera moves or complex scenes we may make drawings or develop a formal storyboard. If you are presenting your script to a potential funding source or client, drawings may help sell the concept.

Column 3 is for the narration and any other types of audio cues, like music or sound effects.

You may also want to add a column for notes as you're shooting. Below is an example from the *Choose Horticulture* video script I worked on with my friend Joe Clokey. You will note that at the time of production, we used the working title of *Careers in Horticulture*. Using working titles (or production titles), i.e., the temporary name you give your project during its development, is a common practice in video production.

SHOT #	VIDEO IMAGE	NARRATION TEXT
Shot 1	Main title graphic.	**Careers In Horticulture**
Shot 8	Students in science and horticulture labs at university	Let's take a look at some of the interesting people who work in this industry, people who have earned the title of Professional Horticulturist.
Shot 9	Title graphic over live action	**Wholesale Nursery Production**
Shot 10	Seed Company Subtitle graphic. Images of various production activities.	We all know that plants can be grown from seeds, but where do those seeds come from? This **wholesale seed production** company produces billions of flower seeds each year. Seed production offers plant breeders the chance to develop new or improved plant varieties. The lightweight seeds from such plants can then be distributed to customers all over the world.
Shot 11	Mike Smith interview	"This is a very colorful business with a lot of challenges, especially early in the Spring."

There are scriptwriting computer programs available such as Scripped Writer (www.scripped.com) or one we've used, Final Draft (www.finaldraft.com). Final Draft even has a special version, Final Draft AV, for writing AV-style scripts. However, for the types of videos we produce, we've found these programs to be overkill and an unnecessary expense. We use Microsoft Word or OpenOffice. You can also use other word processing programs or even a spreadsheet program like Microsoft Excel. GoogleDocs (docs.google.com) is free and has a spreadsheet program that is fine for AV scripts. It's also a great way to share your work online with an associate as you develop the script.

Get really detailed when writing your narration in the audio column because this is what your actors or narrator will say. It should sound natural, as if someone is talking to you, not like someone reading out of a textbook. You want to create natural transitions between frames and between "chapters" in the video. You may do this with the spoken words or with graphic transitions.

Be equally specific about your shot description or camera direction. The more specific you are, the easier it will be on your cast and crew when you start production. Camera direction encompasses camera angles, lens effects, lighting, graphics or illustrations. We will be discussing camera direction when we get into the actual production phase of your project.

Even if your production consists of simply turning on your camera and talking to your audience, planning what you want to say in advance will make a big difference in your delivery and will help relieve nervousness in front of the camera. If you aren't using a teleprompter, taping a bulleted list of topics that must be covered below the camera lens, like a cue card, will help make sure your narrator or speaker doesn't miss any important points.

WRITING THE SCRIPT—KNOW AND SPEAK TO YOUR AUDIENCE

Although your outline is a great starting point there is much more you need to consider when it comes to writing the script. As I said, writing for a camera is different than writing a research paper; since video is intended to be seen you have to think visually. The great advantage of video is that you don't have to rely on the written word to get your point across or to transition to a new idea or section of the video. As the saying goes, "a picture is worth a thousand words," and a few seconds of video can explain more than volumes of written words.

If you took your time to create a good outline, the pieces should fall into place as you write the script. You should also be able to spot weaknesses in your script where additional research is needed.

It's your job to understand the material in depth, simplify it and determine how to visually "translate" it to an audience.

You should know your audience and write and speak to their level. However, don't think you need the writing talent of a Francis Ford Coppola or the comedic genius of a Jon Stewart or a *Saturday Night Live* writer to write a script. As you write, think of metaphors, analogies, and stories that can be used to illustrate your points.

If you don't feel capable of writing a script yourself, then don't. There are many reasonably priced script writers or scriptwriting services available. It's better to hire someone and get your project moving than to be forever stuck at the scriptwriting stage. We've used eLance (www.elance.com) and oDesk (www.odesk.com) to hire script writers. We found good writers there at very reasonable rates. You can also do an online search on "script writers" or "scriptwriting service" and you'll find lots of options.

Look for people who have had experience writing educational and training video scripts. You also want to find a person who can do research. Look at their portfolios and references. A good script writer can write on any topic, so don't worry if they haven't written about your topic before, just look at the quality of their samples.

Once you hire them, you need to give them your outline and good direction on what your project is about. You may also prefer them to do the research and draw up an outline for your approval. Most likely you should also provide some resources for them to start their research, especially if they aren't that familiar with your topic. The more resources and direction you provide the more efficient they will be and that should save you money. You will still need to review, edit, and finalize your script before you shoot. Make sure they are citing their sources and not plagiarizing!

The script writers we've hired have saved us a lot of time by organizing our programs and researching and pulling all the pieces together but we always take the time to add our own touches to the script.

We've given you some resources at the end of this book, and also on the website www.shoot-to-sell.com to help you in the scriptwriting process.

Although teaching you *exactly* how to write a script is beyond the scope of this book, here are a few things to watch out for:

- *Write to a fifth grade level.*

No offense to your audience but attention spans are short so the information needs to be easily digestible. Keep in mind, you also have moving images to illustrate your content. "Show it, don't say it," is a goal to strive for.

How do you know what level you are writing to? Check out this free online writing level tester at www.writingtester.com.

- *Avoid overusing trendy jargon, lingo, and slang.*

This includes industry lingo if it is apt to change soon. This can alienate some viewers and will quickly "date" your video.

- *Make sure your script is grammatically correct.*

If you have someone write it for you, review and check their work. Don't rely on them to get it right! If this isn't your strength, get someone who is good in this area to check and review the script.

- *Double check all the correct pronunciations of words and, if needed, write the word phonetically.*

This is especially important if you will be using scientific terms or words from another language. For example, the succulent echeveria should be pronounced [ech-uh-vuh-ree-uh]. The town near where we live is San Luis Obispo and is pronounced [san loo-is uh-bis-poh]. Out of towners frequently mispronounce it as [san-louise-uh-bis-poh] which instantly says to locals that they don't live here. I like to use www.reference.com to search for word pronunciations because along with the phonetic interpretation, it also gives you an audio recording of how the word should sound. You don't want to take away from the credibility of your narration by mispronouncing words.

- *If you are using graphics to explain things it is especially important that you spell words correctly.*

Not only are misspelled words embarrassing, schools will return videos with misspellings.

- *Do not overuse simple transition phrases to switch between topics.*

Statements such as "On another subject … " or "Let's look at [new topic] now … " are often overused. If you are using text or graphics to introduce a new chapter, there is no need for this type of verbal transition. If you use verbal transitions, think how they can link the previous subject with the next so that it is a natural flow.

Here's an example from our car detailing video: "As I've shown you, using the correct cloths to wash and dry your car is essential in keeping scratches to your paint surface to a minimum. Next I'm going to show you how to further protect your car's finish by using sealants."

A script is meant to be heard, not read, and an essential step before you shoot your script is to read it aloud. It should sound natural, as if someone is speaking. Avoid script-writing that sounds academic or literary; it will not sound natural when spoken. Don't try to impress with big words or complex sentence structure. Seriously, write as if you are speaking to a fifth grader. As you review your script, note any redundancies and delete them. If you have phrases that are difficult for you to say, your narrator will also have a problem. Don't ask your narrator to say tongue twisters—rewrite!

Make sure that everybody involved with your project who has a say in the final product agrees that this script is what they want and expect.

Depending on the style of video you choose, you may or may not need to complete your script before you start shooting. For example, a how-to video with an off-camera narrator, such as the one we did on cacti, will have dialogue that should be written prior to any filming. In a case like that we were shooting to the script but didn't record the narration until we had all the footage assembled.

In our succulent video, we edited to what is called a "scratch track." This is a recording of the script but without trying to get it perfect. That way we could alter the dialog to better fit circumstances we encountered during shooting, such as specific plant specimens we obtained. When we were happy with the script alterations we recorded the final narration.

Documentaries or videos taken at an event won't need to be all written out in advance but the content should be transcribed and added to the final version of your script, technically called a post-shoot script, after the shooting.

Even though it may take more work, make your post-shoot script comprehensive and include the interviews, unscripted lectures, events, etc., that you shot in the script. These final scripts are basically transcriptions of your final video and are needed in the closed captioning and subtitling process.

CLOSED CAPTIONING

Most schools and government agencies are required by the Americans with Disabilities Act to provide closed captions (this includes web videos) with every video. If you market to schools or government agencies, not having closed captioning may keep them from purchasing, no matter how much they want your video. We have seen this trend increasing.

Although you can purchase software to do closed captioning in your editing process, there are services that are well worth the investment. The company we have used is Aberdeen Captioning (www.abercap.com). Aberdeen also provides subtitling as well. Another company that does both and is highly regarded is CPC (www.cpcweb.com). When we produced *Hooked on Succulents* and *Crazy about Cacti*, we used Aberdeen's closed captioning and subtitling services. It cost us $250 each for a 25-minute video. Since those videos sell to the school market at $125 retail, $74 wholesale, we made up those costs very quickly.

If you are marketing to schools you should make closed captioning and subtitling part of your post-production budget.

Another reason why we encourage you to incorporate everything into your post-shoot script is that this transcribed script can be made into an ebook or PDF file for sale, or it can be included to add value to your video.

Your script may be updated and rewritten several times between the shooting and editing phases of your video. That's OK. It's important to also be flexible and have backup plans if you aren't able to get the shot you thought you needed or the expert didn't use the exact wording you wished he had used.

STORYBOARDS AND SHOT LISTS

Two other valuable tools you can use in the shooting process are storyboards and shot lists. I like to use both since they help me in different ways. The storyboard helps communicate my thoughts to the other people I am working with and makes sure everyone understands the end result. Also, since you often will not shoot in chronological order from the script, the shot list helps you group your shots together for efficiency when shooting.

Storyboards

Sometimes the written description in the video column (column 2) of your AV script is all the storyboard you need. This is a written or verbal storyboard. Other times you may want to make a more detailed, traditional storyboard as a way to visualize your shots. A traditional storyboard is a visual depiction of what will take place in each shot. The video "story" is told in the form of sketches and written descriptions; it is like a very detailed comic strip.

Several years ago I was production manager and editor on a stop-motion, animated Christmas special called *Davey and Goliath's Snowboard Christmas*. Extensive, detailed storyboards were required for every shot so the animators knew exactly what the director wanted and as a way to ensure continuity from shot to shot. The production office walls were covered with hundreds of storyboards, each one meticulously drawn out. You could essentially "watch" the entire movie from beginning to end by looking at the storyboards. This kind of detailed storyboard requires patience and drawing talent but is not often necessary for SIV-type work.

Storyboards are especially useful when you want a videographer to shoot a scene in a specific way. It also helps your cast and crew understand the action of a scene. Sketching out a drawing, even if you use stick figures, helps tremendously in getting your visual

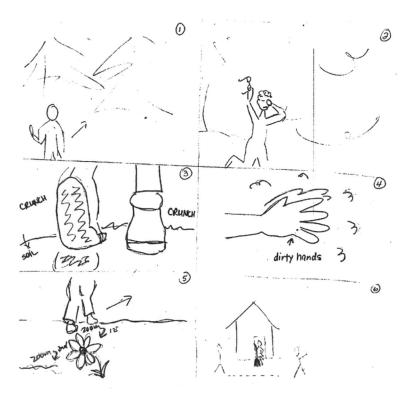

FIGURE 10.1   Storyboard

ideas across. Figure 10.1 gives you an example of a storyboard we did for the introduction to our *The Properties of Soil* video. Yes, it was rough (Kim drew these and she's even better than me at drawing) but the camera operator and actor were able to see exactly how I wanted the scene portrayed.

Storyboards can include details like camera angles, lighting, and action.

We have included two types of storyboard templates that you may want to use in Appendix E at the end of this book.

Shot Lists

A shot list is basically a written account of what a storyboard does visually. They are developed separately from the script so that you can group and film the shots together and out of order. This is done to make your shooting schedule more efficient.

Shooting out of order and with a shot list enables you to group shots by location, shooting angle, time of day, cast members, etc. Following the list allows you to make sure you get every shot as you check off each one after it is completed. For example, shots 1, 2, 5, 19, and 23 may share the same location, time of day, or camera angle.

While shooting out of the script order is the most efficient way to go, doing so adds a layer of complexity because you will need to ensure continuity between scenes. You've probably seen continuity issues in movies where the actor had a full glass of water in front of him then the next scene it's empty, then the next scene it's full again. Those are continuity errors. On more elaborate videos we'll have someone whose job is to ensure continuity between shots. Most feature films have this.

How do you put together a shot list? After you finish your script or storyboard, you will look at all of the shots to group the ones that will be shot in the same location, with the same props, the same angle, etc. Some scriptwriting software will do this for you. Here's an example from our *Hooked on Succulents* shoot.

SHOT #	VIDEO IMAGE	NOTES
	Camera A	
2	Split screen example of variety of species of cactus	
10	Shoot several smaller succulents	
22	Shoot with focus on the different textures	
23	Succulents under shade	
24	Pan from shady area to full sun	
35–39	Various shapes of succulents	
	Camera B	
3	Southwest Cactus Garden Split screen example of variety of species of cactus	
7	Cactus in full sun	

We have included a shot list template in Appendix F and it is also available as a download at www.shoot-to-sell.com.

While it seems shooting in this way will make your production more complicated, organizing it this way makes sense. Say you're shooting on location in a town a few hours away and you were only going to have your narrator or actor for a few hours. You have to shoot all your scenes with your narrator at once because it just wouldn't be reasonable to shoot your initial scenes, change locations, come back again, leave, shoot others, and then return to shoot the ending. That would cost too much and not be efficient so you will want to get the entire narrator part done in the few hours you have.

That is why you number each of your shots and should be as detailed as you need to be. This is where a script supervisor comes in handy. They ensure that, despite the production being shot out of script sequence, the video makes continuous verbal and visual sense. At the very least you may want to hire a detail-oriented person whose job is to deal solely with making sure you get every shot. You may think a job like this is only required on movie sets but even the simplest videos sometimes need it.

We have worked with directors and producers who did not work with a well thought-out plan and as a result we saw them spend unnecessary time and money, not to mention adding stress to their crew, talent, and themselves. We learned to hate the term, "fix it in post," meaning that it'll be dealt with in the post-production phase of editing. You can't always do that and even if you can it is so much better to get what you need the first time.

The script is just the starting point. After you have written the script and envisioned the shots, you will then need to plan the rest of your shoot. You will develop lists for prospective locations, supplies/props needed, shooting schedules that take into consideration seasons, time of day, etc., crew and talent call lists, among a few. Taking the time beforehand to plan for every detail will result in a more successful production phase.

Action Steps

- Using your project outline as a base, research and write your audio/video script.
- Hire a script writer or researcher if you don't feel comfortable with this process.
- Review and finalize your script.
- Develop a storyboard if needed.
- Go back through the script and storyboard to put together your shot list.
- Consider hiring someone in the script supervisor/continuity role.

Chapter 11

Coordinating the Shoot

Chapter Objectives

- Learn about the common types of "talent" you will want to use—on-camera narrator, voice-over narrator, or both.
- Discover the pros and cons of using professional versus amateur talent.
- Learn the roles of the production crew and what skills and experience to look for.
- Learn how to organize the shooting schedule.
- Learn what goes into scouting a location.

Now it's time to turn our attention to some other components of pre-production: coordinating and arranging talent, crew, props, supplies, wardrobe and makeup, and locations.

TALENT

Talent is an industry term to denote the people who will be in the video whether shown on camera or as voice-over with either speaking parts or not. Your talent may be your subject expert or it may be you who will be on camera, or maybe you want to hire a professional host or narrator. Regardless, when we say "talent" we mean on-camera talent.

Working with Narrators

Most non-fiction and educational videos involve narrators, either on-camera or as voice-over. There are a few decisions you will need to make regarding narrators. First, you need to determine if you want or need to have one.

If you are doing a how-to video and following the talent's activities as they explain a process, like I did with the car detailing expert, you won't need one. They, in fact, are the narrator. If you are going to use a lot of footage shot as b-roll or on location as I did in the cactus and succulent videos, then you'll need to add a voice-over narrator to explain what is happening.

If you decide your production needs a narrator, you'll have to decide if you'll hire a professional, if you want a male or female, if the person should be young or old, have an accent or not. You'll want to have someone represent your material in its best light so put some thought into this. Using a narrator who is obviously not a good match will detract from the impact of your video, so auditioning and casting is important.

Also, will this narrator be seen on-screen or be used as a voice-over? Having an on-camera narrator offers an advantage in that this person creates a rapport with the viewer and can give added interest. The trick is in hiring the right narrator for the job. Choosing the right narrator can make the message seem more authentic or sincere, like it's coming from an old friend.

Working with voice-over narrators is less complicated to shoot but it's still important to audition to get the right voice. The narrator in this instance is an unseen voice of authority. Since the viewer never sees the narrator, there is less of a personal connection.

Sometimes you can find the perfect voice for your product. Think of Tom Bodett and the Motel 6 ads (this may date me). See www.bodett.com/motel6commercials.htm for an example. Tom exudes a folksy, down-to-earth character that makes Motel 6 seem like a friend. They're going to keep the light on for us!

When we shot *Choose Horticulture* (about careers in horticulture), the producer hired a male high school student as a voice-over narrator. Since his targeted audience was going to be high school students, he felt they would relate more to a peer's voice. Also because this is a field that is perceived to be more female oriented, we hoped a male voice would encourage the guys to consider this field as well.

Voice-Over Narrator

In terms of dealing with technical production issues, this is one of the simplest forms of narrated video to produce. You can either edit to a pre-recorded narration track or edit your shots and place the narration over them, cutting it up and moving pieces around as necessary. The advantage of using voice-over narrators is that if you record them indoors you don't have to deal with the environmental challenges of wind, airplanes, traffic, barking dogs, etc., that you get when recording on-camera narrators on location. You also don't have to worry about wardrobe, makeup, lighting, camera angles, backgrounds, etc. It's just a lot simpler.

Although you can have anyone record a voice-over, one way to vastly improve the production quality is to hire a professional narrator. A professional voice will add so much to your production. A professional narrator or voice actor, as they are also called, knows how to modulate their voice so that your recording levels will be consistent yet interesting. A trained voice has a quality that lends polish to your video.

We hired Baxter Black, a famous National PBS radio personality, to narrate a video several years ago. We negotiated a fee that was far below his normal rate, although it was still a good portion of my budget. It was well worth it for the celebrity status he brought to the production. We also had original music composed and recorded for my soundtrack. We won a Telly Award for that production and I wouldn't doubt that the high quality of the soundtrack had something to do with it. His country gentleman voice was a perfect match for the subject of the video—the history of the College of Agriculture at Cal Poly.

I encourage you to consider hiring a professional narrator. It doesn't have to cost a lot and it will make a huge difference in your final production. There are many good places to find reasonably priced professional narrators online; just do a search for "professional voice-over narrator" and you'll find plenty. I've used two services; Voice Talent Now (www.voicetalentnow.com) and Voice123 (www.voice123.com). There is also www.voices.com you can look into.

Online services will usually provide a preview recording of each of their voice actors so that you can listen to their delivery and decide if that is the type of voice you want. This is an easy way to audition a voice, but if you want to hear how they'll sound reading your script you can send a page from your script and ask them to record a sample. You may have to pay a small fee but it's worth it in the long run.

I've hired narrators for as little as $50 to $100 for 30-second commercials, but you should expect to pay $500 and up for a longer production. I know some people who are having great results finding narrators on www.fiverr.com, an online marketplace of people selling their services, for just $5 for a 30-second commercial. I haven't tried them myself but many of them are getting very positive reviews. You can get some of these narrators to do longer scripts at great rates.

When you work with an online narrator they will do the recording in their own studio, which is typically a professional recording studio. The recording quality should be excellent. Some will have a way for you to listen in as they are recording so that you can stop them and ask them to read it a different way. Some will just send you a couple of recordings for you to choose from. When they are finished recording they will do any editing necessary and email the file to you. They'll ask you what format you want it in such as a WAV (Waveform Audio File Format) or AIFF (Audio Interchange File Format), and what sample rate, which is usually 48 kHz. I would choose AIFF and 48 kHz.

If you will be recording the voice-over narrator yourself then you will most likely not want to record it in the field. It will turn out better if you have a quiet, sound isolated place to do this. Don't have one? I am not above making my own little temporary sound studio with blankets and sleeping bags strategically draped over camera stands. Hey, it works. Or as I shared before, record them inside a well-upholstered car parked in a quiet spot. The viewer won't know how you did it, only that your audio sounds clean and professional.

On-Camera Narrator

In this style the narrator is shown on camera, speaking to the audience.

This is an effective presentation style but brings with it a lot more technical challenges. You have issues to deal with such as wardrobe, makeup, lighting, field audio, travel, etc. If you are shooting at an outside location, it is rare that you will shoot without sound issues like as air traffic, cars, wind, people, and other annoyances. You'll be amazed how noisy our environment is once you try to get a nice quiet shot. You can count on doing retakes due to interruptions from any of these.

Wind can be a real problem. Not only does wind make it difficult to get clean audio, you have visual problems like hair and clothing blowing around, and maybe fog, dust, or sand, etc. Depending on the shots you want you may need a microphone boom operator or expensive radio (wireless) mics. Also you may have the sun going in and out of clouds, creating continuity problems.

Not only that, your narrator, even if you hire a professional, will probably not nail his lines the first time so plan on shooting a lot of different takes.

I personally like the format of an on-camera narrator best but usually avoid it if I don't have sufficient budget and time to deal with the problems that come with it.

 If I had a choice I would choose a professional voice-over narrator over a non-professional on-camera narrator almost every time. Good audio is so important.

The Hybrid

I've made videos where you have an on-camera narrator introduce the program, maybe in just one shot, and the rest of the program is this person or even someone else doing voice-overs. It eliminates most of the problems I listed above. Maybe they are even shot in a studio so you have no environmental problems to deal with, making it nice and easy with a personal touch.

An effective variation of this is hearing an on-camera voice for the first few minutes, then there's a shot where you meet the narrator on camera, then it goes back to voice-over.

Working with Your Talent

If you are using a non-professional narrator, either on- or off-camera, you need to coach them. Have them take a few seconds before and after they speak. Watch the eyes as they tend to drop at the last word or glance somewhere at the wrong emphasis in the script. Also make sure any narrator you hire correctly pronounces technical words. Here is where adding the phonetic descriptions in your script is important. Make sure you know the correct pronunciation of all technical, foreign, or scientific terms.

A lavalier mic (also called a lapel mic) is usually attached to the front of a shirt or blouse, to a man's tie, or the lapel of a jacket. While it's a great way to get a natural-sounding voice, problems can arise if the person tends to talk with their hands or is not a professional actor and doesn't have experience working with this kind of mic.

Professional actors or others who are comfortable in front of a camera should have no problem with what you ask. However if you're dealing with an amateur or just a regular person, you should allow extra time to deal with him.

He may not be as aware of making distracting sounds like "em" or "uh," clicking his tongue, clearing his throat, starting each sentence the same way, or saying repetitive things like "like." Now if the viewer knows that this person is not a professional, some of that will be excused but it is better to pay attention to this and reshoot if necessary. Some of these habits are very difficult to control, but it's worth a try.

CREW

You may want or need to hire a crew to help you with the shooting. Although at the beginning I mentioned that you don't have to have the production values of a feature-length film, there may be occasions where you will want the help and expertise of grips, sound men, camera operators, lighting, etc.

Here are a few crew members you might want to hire:

- **Director**—An experienced director knows how to block shots, direct talent, and coordinate with lighting and audio professionals. The director has the overall "vision" of the production. A good director can make a big improvement in your video.
- **Videographer**—This person can also be known as director of photography (DP) or camera operator. This is the person who works with the director to achieve the look of the video.
- **Sound Tech or Audio Mixer**—This crew member is responsible for managing microphones and overseeing audio recording, whether through the camera or a separate recorder. They should monitor the sound through headphones. A good sound tech can solve a lot of audio problems on the shoot.

- **Script Supervisor**—This is someone who makes sure that you get all of the shots, oversees continuity between shots, and takes notes about each shot.
- **Grip**—Grips assist the camera operator and help move things, like light stands, dolly tracks, etc., around. They'll carry your gear and non-union grips will help with other duties like lighting and audio.
- **Gaffer or Lighting Tech**—This person manages lighting and electrical needs. He works with the director and DP to achieve a desired lighting design.

If you are doing this yourself, I would hire for the areas where you are the least experienced or don't have the equipment, or that you don't want to deal with. For me that is a sound guy; as I keep saying, high quality sound is one of the most important components and I place a high value on it. Fortunately I found a former PBS producer-turned-activist who happens to be a good friend. As a NYC film school graduate, he not only knows sound, he's a resourceful problem solver on location. I hire him every chance I get and it has always been a smart investment.

An under-appreciated role is the script supervisor. You are most likely to be wearing many hats on a shoot. It isn't that unusual for one person to be the director, camera operator, gaffer, sound recorder, and grip. These roles have different focuses. For instance, as the camera operator you are most likely concentrating on the actual shot, concerned about camera moves, lighting, audio, etc. When you're doing all of that, it's hard to keep track of the script and knowing if the lines were delivered properly.

Ideally you want to take time out after every shot to review what you did, look at your shot list, and take notes. You can't rely on your memory here. That's where a script supervisor earns their pay. I know this from first-hand experience.

Many times, when I'm behind the camera, Kim steps in to the role of script supervisor. It may be a thankless job at times but I've found that for all parties concerned, especially the editor and the producer who is responsible for delivering what the client wants, it's a very important job.

If you are not a detail-oriented person, have a poor memory, or hate taking notes, then you really need to hire someone like this. They also need to be assertive on a set. If they know a shot was missed or done incorrectly, then they have to speak up no matter if it means the shoot is going to run into the wee hours of the morning. Their insistence can save your project, your budget, and your reputation, so respect them for it. Although you may get a tired cast and crew grumping at you, it is well worth it in the end.

COORDINATING CAST AND CREW

Your talent or narrators should receive their script in advance. If the director and camera operator can meet and go over their storyboard and shot list in advance, it will make for a more prepared and productive shoot.

Issuing instructions, or "call sheets," with contact information (e.g., phone numbers), the schedule for the day, which scenes and script pages are being shot, and the address of the shoot location is a good practice. Everyone should receive these in advance.

On a small SIV this doesn't have to be a formal document but make sure everyone knows when and where to show up. It never hurts to confirm the day before. Everyone should have the phone number of the director or production coordinator in case of a problem. If you have a production coordinator or assistant, have them call everyone to confirm and to make sure that everyone has transportation. The call time means time to go to work or be ready to travel as a group to the set. It's not time to pour a cup of coffee and catch up on the gossip. If you want to socialize, come a bit early.

 One of the most important things you must do to ensure a smooth, enjoyable day's shooting: arrange for plenty of healthy food and beverages to be available!

Seriously, having nutritious food and refreshing drinks (not alcohol) on the set will go a long way toward keeping your little troupe alert and energetic. I've been on shoots where you can just see the energy drain out of people as the day goes on without refreshments. Don't just provide potato chips, donuts, and soda pop either. Make it something nutritious and have plenty of water on hand. If it is a long day's shoot you should provide meals every six hours. It is not unusual to have shoot days last 12 hours or more. Hire a caterer if necessary. Your cast and crew will do anything for you and everyone will perform at a higher level if they are well fed, and this will be reflected in your results.

Also make arrangements for bathroom facilities if there are none at the location. Yes, this may mean springing for a port-a-potty. We've had our share of "watering the bushes" but you don't want to put your people in that situation.

PROP AND SUPPLIES LIST

As you write your script, you should be taking notes of the props and supplies you'll need. If you haven't, then it's time to go back through it and do this. Some of them you may need to order in advance. Go through your script and develop a props breakdown which is essentially mapping out when and where the props or supplies will be used throughout your video. If you have a script supervisor or production assistant, make it their job to keep track of these things and make sure they are where they need to be, when they need to be there.

Some scriptwriting software will do this for you. Final Draft, Adobe Story, and Movie Magic, for example, can compile a list of props automatically. If your needs are simple this may not be worth the expense.

If all you will be doing are screen-capture movies, this means getting all the website addresses, videos, and graphics you want to include organized together in one place on your computer so that you can efficiently visit the sites you need.

WARDROBE AND MAKEUP

You should have wardrobe details worked out in advance. Regardless of who is going to be on camera, give them a heads-up as to the type of clothing they should wear. If you're shooting over a few days, you should make sure that they have the same clothes on in every shot unless there is a specific reason not to. We often buy several of the same shirt so that in case one gets soiled, we can switch shirts and keep shooting.

If you are not providing wardrobe, at least communicate with your talent what they should and should not wear. Some busy patterns, fine stripes, and saturated colors, especially red, can wreak havoc with digital cameras. Stay away from that type of clothing.

Neutral colors work best for shirts and blouses. Pinstripe and herringbone patterns are bad. Solid black or solid white clothing should also be avoided. Also some types of material, such as nylon, may make loud sounds when touched, which could end up being a nightmare if you are using a lavalier microphone.

If money is no object then hire a makeup artist. If you are like the rest of us, however, learn to apply basic foundation makeup to a person. Lancome 'Pure Focus' T-Zone Powder Gel is an excellent all round shine control that gives a nice even skin tone. Put a tube of that in your gear bag.

Everyone looks better on camera with makeup. The older they are or more uneven their skin tone, the more they should be wearing makeup, men included. Some people get stressed out on camera and start to sweat. This has to be dealt with. Have tissues on hand to wipe off sweat and do it often if necessary. You'll kick yourself later if you don't. You can't take it off in post-production.

LOCATION SCOUTING

You're going to have to scout, line up, and coordinate your locations in advance. Time spent scouting locations will save time during the shoot and improve the end product. Don't let first impressions cloud your evaluation of a location. Look at the shot as the camera might see it, not for the great or terrible furnishings, paint job, or view from the room. You can do a lot with careful framing.

Here's a trick for seeing a location as the camera would, without having a camera on hand. Cut a 1-1/2" by 2" hole in a card. Trim it to about 2-1/4" by 3-1/2" to fit in your wallet or leave it larger to fit in your pocket. Or find an old 2×2 slide holder. With a black felt pen make a line around the inside of the frame. View the location through this frame, held a couple of inches in front of your face.

Audio conditions at the location will also need to be considered. If you have them, bring your camera, microphone, and headphones to test listen while scouting. Clap your hands and listen for echo problems.

When you look at a shooting location, consider what would be needed to shoot it. Will the lighting be right at that time of day? Will you need permission or have to pay for permits? Will noise be a problem? Are the people involved likely to be cooperative or have to be paid? (I have plenty of experience with state park rangers and museum docents interrupting a shoot.) Will there be enough parking for vehicles? Is there enough working room for camera and cast in the best location? How many hours will it realistically take to shoot the scenes? (It always takes longer than you think.) Is this the best location available? How about safety? Will the location say what you want it to say? Will people have to be fed? Where are the rest rooms? Will people need protection from the sun, heat or cold?

See, there are a lot of considerations when scouting a location.

When we shot our *The Properties of Soil* video, we had to find very specific locations that visually demonstrated what we were talking about. We had to find places where there was erosion, search the country around us for specific types of rocks and soil, where we could show the effect of wind, etc. Scouting was an important part of that production.

For Dave Sheahan's exercise video series, our challenge was finding a house that would not only look appropriate on camera, since one of the key benefits to his program is *home* workouts, but also gave us enough space for him to do the workout and for us to shoot it. We needed high ceilings for lighting and the ability to shut out daylight to give us complete control of the light. Plus we needed a house he could actually stay in with his family since he was traveling here from Ireland. We wanted to leave our lights set up overnight but allow his family room to live in at the end of the day's shoot. Fortunately, we live in an area where there are several vacation homes and found a perfect place that was reasonably priced.

When shooting on location, it is always good to have a backup location in mind and arranged if the weather or circumstances don't cooperate. This is especially important if your shoot is time-sensitive and you only have this one chance to shoot it. Lighting, audio, the environment—all of these add challenges when you're at a location where you have limited control. This is especially true if you're shooting outdoors and in a public place. You'll have to interact with the curious public who may get in your shot, whether on purpose or not. You'll have to pay attention to noises that on most occasions you probably tune out such as car engines airplane traffic, yard work, air conditioners, refrigerator compressors, neighbors hammering, garbage trucks, etc.

BE PREPARED

We've dealt with almost every imaginable circumstance when shooting on location. When we shot some of Dave's home workout series outdoors, we dealt with leaf blowers, ambulance and fire engine sirens, low flying helicopters—even an impromptu dance rehearsal happening in the parking lot beside where we were shooting. We had fog so thick some mornings when we planned to shoot outdoors that you couldn't see 25 feet. We shot in parks with inquisitive children and dogs, and had sprinklers come on in the middle of shots.

The message here is that you need to be prepared for the unexpected. Try to stick to the plan but be flexible enough to do whatever is needed to get your video finished.

Action Steps

- Decide on the type of "talent" you will need—on-camera narrator, voice-over narrator, or both. Decide on who that person will be and if he or she represents your video well.
- Decide if you will use professional or amateur talent.
- Set up auditions with on-camera narrators—especially if you haven't worked with them before.
- If you're going with a voice-over, listen to their voice demo reel or MP3 to decide if they are right for your project.
- Determine if you will need to hire production help and what skills and experience you need them to have.
- Review your shot list/storyboard and script to come up with a shooting schedule to give to your talent and crew.

- Look through your shot list/storyboard and script and note all of the supplies and props you will need and when and where you will need them.
- Purchase the props and supplies you need.
- Decide on what you want in a location and scout the place out. Have more than one location in mind in the event the first doesn't work out.

Chapter 12

Permissions—Releases and Permits

Chapter Objectives

- Learn about the different permits and releases you need.
- Understand why you need to have signed releases and permits.

When you are producing any kind of video for sale you need to make sure you have proper permissions. Using release forms to get permission in writing is a standard practice in video production. Releases help protect your rights and also help keep you out of legal difficulty in the future.

Since you need to be aware of this aspect of video production, we will cover some of the most common release forms and types of permits we've encountered. This is not intended to be legal advice; we aren't lawyers and do not profess to know all the ins and outs of this area. Laws covering permits and the use of images of individuals and property differ based on jurisdiction—from country to country and even from state to state. If you have any specific legal questions regarding permits and releases, you need to consult an attorney familiar with this area of law to ensure the release form you use will cover all the points related to your situation.

States, counties, and most large cities will have film commissions or film offices that can assist you in getting filming permits. Be aware that when you go through these organizations to get shooting permits you may be required to show proof of insurance as well. This can all get complicated so you want to evaluate if getting permits to shoot on public streets in a major city is really what your SIV needs.

Following are descriptions of three common release forms we have used. This is not an all inclusive list:

- Video Appearance Release Form (also called Talent Release Form)
- Materials Release Form (for photos, illustrations, documents, etc.)
- Location Release Form

VIDEO APPEARANCE RELEASE FORM

A signed video appearance release form gives you legal permission to use the video and audio recording of the person for commercial and non-commercial purposes. It is designed to protect you from litigation if the people you filmed were to come back later in a court of law and claim they didn't give you permission to record them or that your recording is an invasion of their privacy or unfair or slanderous use of their image. A signed release shows the court that the person did in fact give you such permission.

If you plan to use a person's image for commercial purposes, you need to get a *signed* video release form from that individual. This is especially true if your performers are portraying someone other than themselves as in reenactments or commercials.

I'm the publicity coordinator for a large annual Renaissance Festival. In order to be a participant we require every person to sign a form giving us permission to use any photos or video taken of them in future advertising. We have over 500 costumed participants and this makes it possible for me to shoot them all weekend and use the footage for future advertising. I also had to do this when I was shooting a series on Californian history where we hired reenactors. We had a whole cavalry of riders who had to sign the forms.

In the United States, if you are shooting for an educational video of a crowd scene in a public area and you use the footage in the context in which it was shot, you generally do not need a video release form from every person in that crowd. According to U.S. law, when we are in a public area, as opposed to a private area, i.e., our home, office, private party, etc., we give up our reasonable expectation of privacy. So if you are shooting on a street, at a public beach, at a park, etc., you wouldn't need a talent release form, unless there are local laws which control the recording of images, or the use that may be made of them without the subject's consent. Any local laws would take precedence.

Keep in mind the context in which you are shooting and how you are portraying the people in your shot. The key is identifiability. People in the background are not a problem. Focusing a tight shot on a person crying would probably be crossing the line.

I avoid lingering shots that focus on one person in a crowd. If you are shooting a woman in a bikini at the beach and use the image in a way that could be considered lurid or demeaning, you can bet you'd better get a signed release or just don't use it.

If you are making an educational video about fitness and are shooting individuals in a public park, showing them walking their dogs, playing Frisbee, jogging, etc., you probably wouldn't have to worry about a release since they are positive examples of your message. But if you decide to pinpoint specific individuals who are really heavy, eating, drinking, showing them in an embarrassing or negative light, then you may get in trouble without a release. In general, showing a person in a negative light would be a bad decision without a release. That's the kind of thing people would feel constitutes an invasion of privacy. It just makes sense.

Here are some other shooting situations in which you'll want to get a release form:

- *You're shooting a how-to video and you interview someone or shoot footage of an instructor.*

  You'll want them to sign this form.

- *You're shooting video at a workshop or event.*

  This is a private event and so you may need to get signed video release forms from each audience member who appears on the video—especially if you plan to use clips of identifiable audience members for promotional purposes. If you are conducting the event, it's a good idea to have the forms completed at the check-in table. Post a sign, make an announcement and make sure all participants know the event will be filmed.

- *You're shooting video at a private event, within a place of business, or a home.*

You will also need to get permission from the owner or organizer of the event before you start filming, in addition to video release forms from each person you get on camera. Being in a home or business falls under that reasonable expectation of privacy clause.

Getting a video release form signed by identifiable participants in your video is a good idea not only to protect you, but it also can make it easier to sell the rights to your video footage in the future. Some video distributors want a signed release from everyone shown in a video.

You should *always* have signed releases where minors' faces are identifiable. A good way to deal with this is to shoot them from an angle where you do not see their faces and cannot identify them.

Make sure you get the talent release signed before turning the cameras on! Imagine if you don't and then later the talent refuses to sign the release for whatever reason. You will have wasted all that time and money spent in shooting anything that person was seen in and may have to spend more time to reshoot with another person.

Talent releases are not necessarily required in an interview situation because you already have tacit approval by the fact that they are there, in front of the camera and microphone and aware of what's happening, but it's still a good idea to get one. This is called consent by conduct, meaning an ordinary person should realize that with a microphone and camera pointed at them and with their willing participation, they know they are being filmed.

If I don't have a talent release form I'll often ask a person as I'm recording them on camera if I have permission to shoot them. We've used this technique at times when we hadn't planned on shooting and had no release forms with us. We go even further and have them tell the camera that they give us permission to record them along with their address. However, we recommend doing this only in an emergency and then mail or fax them a release.

A good practice for obtaining permission for shooting a person at a special location is if a reasonable person would *assume* that permission must be obtained, you should get permission.

 Have an iPhone? You can download the mRelease app for appearance releases, property releases, location releases, and crew releases.

In most U.S. jurisdictions, minors must sign their own talent release forms if they are old enough to understand the nature of what you are producing and how they will be portrayed. However, you also have to get these signed by a parent or guardian as a safeguard. Legal age varies from state to state so you should check out your specific state's requirements before shooting. Always be particularly sensitive when shooting minors, especially young children.

Shooting in a School Setting

I always get permission in advance when shooting at a school and this can take a few days. What likely happens is that after I contact the school, they will send a notice home with the students and have the parents give explicit permission for their child to participate. This gives the school time to assess if there are any children who should not be included in the shot. The classroom teacher will be notified and you will know which students to avoid.

It really should go without saying that you need to make sure you have clearance from the school to shoot there—never just go onto school grounds and start shooting, even though it is a public place. Most likely you'll have to check in with the front office. We've had to sign in at some schools and be issued visitor badges. Even if they don't require you to check in, it's a good policy to do so. Schools are sensitive areas in which to shoot and for good reason. You don't want to come under suspicion of any sort. At least I don't!

There is an example of a simple video appearance release form included in Appendix G. We also have it available as a download at www.shoot-to-sell.com. To reiterate, if you have any questions, it is a good idea to consult an attorney to make sure that the release form you use covers all the points that are appropriate to your situation.

MATERIALS RELEASE FORM

This type of form is used for photographs, video, film, music, or other media that may be copyrighted or owned by others. You want to make sure you are not using any copyrighted material without permission. You also want to make sure if you are hiring someone to produce media for you, such as illustrations or photographs, that it is done as a work-for-hire and that there is no expectation of future money from the sales of your video. Your work-for-hire agreement should explicitly state this.

Unless you pay for the commercial usage rights or get written approval from the artist, videographer, photographer, or writer to use their work, *do not use it*. Just because you find it floating around the internet, don't assume it's OK to use it. Even if you use apps such as SoundHound (www.soundhound.com) and they don't show it being a commercial work, don't use it. If you bought the CD or downloaded it from iTunes, found it on Flickr (a photo sharing site) or Google Images, if you use it on YouTube or Facebook and they haven't said anything to you, even if you don't see a © or copyright notification on the work, *do not use it*!

Also do not plagiarize written works when you are writing your script and narration—unless you have big bucks for a lawyer. Because you are going to be selling this product in a public venue, you need to be more vigilant than if you were only producing it to show to friends. Technically and ethically that's not permitted either, but that's not the same situation as producing something with the intent to make money from it. This advice is important regarding any promotional videos you are planning to show on sharing sites like YouTube as well.

Do not succumb to the temptation to use popular music, either. Music has a fingerprint and there is software that can decipher and track that piece of music, especially if it is on the web. You don't want your buyer to discover that your work contains pirated material. Imagine that you have a video selling well and it suddenly gets pulled for copyright violations. Your sales, and your reputation, will be ruined.

While you can use common information you find in books, articles, and on the web in your research, you have to write what you've found in your own words. Most information is not new but you need to put your unique spin on it.

If you do want to use someone's exact words, you can get permission to quote them. Quotations of up to two sentences normally don't require permission. When in doubt you should always get permission and you should always cite your source in the credits.

You can purchase the usage rights of copyrighted material for a fee but also many writers or artists may give you permission without a charge in exchange for the exposure. *Always* give them credit, even if you don't pay them for the use of their work. And, of course, you want to send them a free copy of the program. We loved a few passages from Gwen Moore Kelaidis's beautiful book, *Hardy Succulents: Tough Plants for Every Climate* and wanted to use them in a voice-over narration at the start of our *Hooked on Succulents* video. We contacted her and received approval.

You can get legal music rights through a music library. Look up "royalty free music" and you'll find a lot of options. The same applies to stock video clips. Look for "royalty free stock video" and you'll find a lot of sources where you can purchase the right to a huge range of video clips at affordable rates and it's legal.

We have included samples of a typical materials release form in Appendix H. It is also available as a download at www.shoot-to-sell.com.

LOCATION RELEASES AND PERMITS

A location release should be completed when you are shooting on someone's private property. The property's owner should sign it. By signing the release, the owner of the property forgoes the right to sue for specific types of claims.

You may also need to get permission or even special permits for some public places, like libraries, gardens, state and national parks, etc. They may have a policy that supersedes the public space rights we discussed earlier. You may need to pay what is called a shooting fee. It is always a good idea to have permission beforehand, especially when that location is key to your video. For example, we shot our succulent and cacti videos at the Huntington Botanical Gardens in Pasadena, California, and had to call down weeks in advance to get permission. When we arrived, we checked in with the appropriate staff to make sure we still had permission to shoot on the grounds. I also received advance permission to shoot the landscaping director at the Getty Center. Only one problem though—he didn't realize he had to get permission from security. He had no authority over the Getty security force so we had to stop filming.

Any time you shoot a public event you have to think about privacy issues and shooting permits. It can be cumbersome and expensive to get shooting permits, and sometimes you simply cannot get them, but this should be part of your pre-production planning.

I know plenty of run and gun shooters who shoot clandestinely and take their chances. I do this myself and I will continue to do so but I've also been caught and had my shooting stopped a few times, too. Let me share a cautionary tale about a time this backfired and cost me a lot of time and money.

Around 2005 I was working with a partner on a documentary about a man with cancer who, near the end of his life, wanted to set a world speed record on the Bonneville Salt Flats during Speed Week. My partner and I drove out to the event in Utah and spent about five days shooting him with his pit crew. The event organizers welcomed us with open arms and couldn't have been nicer or more accommodating. I shot him and his crew as they wrestled with constant nagging problems with the car. They finally got a run near the last hour of the last day, which coincidentally was his birthday. We got some great footage although he didn't come close to getting that speed record. It was bittersweet and the story wasn't over.

Kim and I met him later that year at the veteran's hospital in Palo Alto and shot him as he was getting a chemo treatment. We had some really powerful footage.

Well, I wanted to follow-up the next year as he again tried for a record on the salt flats. I arranged a hotel in Wendover, Nevada, flew out to Salt Lake City with all my gear, rented a car and drove to the event. I even brought along a heavy and expensive gyroscope to stabilize my shots because I planned to get some aerial footage. I showed up at the check-in site with a big smile on my face, happy to see the woman who had been so welcoming the year before. "Where's your permit?" she asked. "You can't shoot without a permit." I explained that I didn't have one and that she had allowed us full access to the event the previous year. "Don't you remember?" I asked. "You have to have a permit," she insisted, telling me that it would be $5,000 for the week! She further told me that if they caught me shooting without a permit I would be thrown out and that lawyers would be after me and there would be all kinds of hell to pay. She was the exact opposite of the previous year.

I never did find out what her issue was, but of course I did not pay the fee. I hung around for a day and shot some intimate footage of the family members praying at their site, but kept my camera well out of sight. I managed to wrangle a ride in a Cessna 182 to get aerial footage of the event, but really didn't get much usable footage. The trip cost well over $1,000 for very little footage. What made it even worse for me personally, just a few days before the trip I had had cancer surgery on my nose, so I was out there in the heat, sun, and salt with stitches in my nose, constantly having to treat it with medication and change the bandages. It was a miserable time even without the indignity of being turned away.

I regret that I eventually abandoned that project. I gave the footage to the family after my friend died. I just felt so defeated by the turn of events and my inability to continue shooting him as he tried to achieve his goal.

The lesson I want you to take away from this is that shooting permits are becoming a bigger issue all the time. When the economy is bad you will find every venue looking to boost their income and one way is by charging for shooting permits. Sometimes just having a camera on a tripod is enough to trigger an official inquiry about your intentions. At least do your research before you spend a lot of money going to a place, only to be thrown out. I was on a movie set once with a large cast and crew, only to be thrown off the beach because the producer tried to avoid paying the shooting fee to the state park, which at that time wasn't that much. I felt it was short-sighted of him not to pay the fee when he already had spent the money on the cast, crew, film, food, fuel, etc.

With the current trend toward shooting high-end video with digital SLR cameras and small HD camcorders, you can often get away with more run and gun shooting. It's hard to tell if you are just a tourist taking pictures or a cinematographer shooting b-roll for a film. Just be prepared to be stopped. And keep in mind that even if you get your footage, you may need a signed release to legally use it in your video.

Can you imagine if you had a best-selling video that had footage from a Disney theme park and you were dealt a lawsuit and they won? You'd have to pull the video off the market or maybe pay out more money than it is worth. So I would definitely have your I's dotted and your T's crossed, especially if the location you are choosing is really well known.

You will find a sample of a location release form in Appendix I. This form is also available as a download at www.shoot-to-sell.com.

WHAT DO YOU NEED IN A RELEASE FORM?

A good release form should be in writing and include:

- What is being released (video, images, audio, photographs, location, etc.).
- Language outlining that you may sell or assign the right to use the images or other materials to third parties.
- A statement that the release is irrevocable. If that isn't in there, the release could be terminated by the person giving it at any time.

I want to reiterate that this isn't intended to be a comprehensive treatise on all the permutations of releases, permits, or copyright uses. We're not in a position to give you legal opinions on this but what I will say is: if you are in doubt about the legality of something you are using or doing, take the safe route and ask for permission. You'll be surprised how often the answer will be yes.

By now you see how much emphasis we place on planning and preparation in every area of video production. Better planning means a better video, and that's where we sow the seeds of success.

Action Steps

- Collect all necessary releases and permits *before* you start filming and check what is required in your jurisdiction. If necessary, consult an attorney.
- Make sure you have appropriate permission to film on location.
- Get clearance and permission if you are going to be shooting at a school.
- If in doubt, get a release.

Part III

Production and Post-Production

Chapter 13

Equipment

Chapter Objectives

- Learn the most important tool for making a great video.
- Learn what you need in a video camera.
- Get familiar with concepts such as depth of field, white balance, image stabilization, etc.
- Know what audio features you should have in a camera.
- Understand the need for a good tripod.
- Familiarize yourself with your options in lighting equipment.
- Discover some editing software available to you and what is required for your computer.

We are living in an amazing age of technological wizardry.

When my production department at the university started shooting videos around 1980, the field production cameras we used were large, heavy, expensive and, to be honest, not all that good.

We initially shot on 3/4″ (U-matic) tape. The recorder was a separate and delicate piece of equipment connected by umbilical cables to the camera, an awkward and unwieldy setup. Our tapes were the size of hardbound books and the recorder ate batteries for breakfast. In fact, the tapes alone were bigger than many of the camcorders we use today!

Video editing was a nightmare compared to the ease of non-linear editing that everyone does today, and the equipment limited our creative capabilities. You had to have separate pieces of hardware for everything. We had time code generators, black burst generators, audio limiters and compressors, graphics generators, a paintbox, a vectorscope, a waveform monitor ... it was a long list of mysterious and expensive boxes. I had no idea what most of those things were; it was so complicated that we had to have an engineer install and run the equipment for us. It was kept in a special air-conditioned room because it generated so much heat.

I am glad to say that is all in the past. What used to be reserved for the few in "the industry" is now affordable and available to the masses.

The ability to shoot and edit videos is now almost universally available. I never cease to be amazed at the quality of videos that are shot with cameras costing under $500 or even on cell phones. Many computers come bundled with basic video editing software that runs rings around what we did with all of that complicated equipment and it is so simple and easy to use that young children are making their own videos. What we have access to today would have sounded like science fiction to us back in 1980.

There should be no excuses about not having access to software and equipment as your reason for not getting started in special interest video publishing. It is affordable and easily accessible.

So, what do you need to get started shooting your own special interest video? Not that much, as it turns out. I've seen some awesome videos shot and edited on an iPhone. I don't recommend that you use a cell phone as your main video camera, but the astounding thing is you can do it.

YOUR MOST IMPORTANT TOOL

I feel that the most important piece of equipment you'll use lies between your ears: it is your mind. Having a scalpel does not make you a surgeon anymore than having a pencil makes you a writer and having all the latest video gear does not make you a video producer. It is your ability to tell a story, demonstrate a process, engage and educate the viewer that will make your videos successful. This book should help you with that.

Now I'll get off my soapbox and say that having professional gear will serve you well in the long run if you know how to use it. It's built to last, has an edge in quality over consumer gear and can do more. It's also more complex, capable, and far more expensive. Cameras evolve so quickly that this year's hot item is next year's discontinued relic, so there's a real danger of investing too much in a professional camera that will be replaced by a newer and even more capable camera in six months. If you are considering buying a professional camera, it's a good idea to rent one first to find out if it is a good fit.

Before I go any further I want to clarify something. If you are an experienced professional videographer you can probably skip this section. You already understand the advantage of XLR audio inputs; large image sensors; separate iris, focus and zoom rings; a wide range of frame rates; zebra stripes; histograms and all of the things that come with a pro camera. I'm writing this section for someone who is starting out without much experience, has a limited budget and wants to get equipment that will do the job but not overwhelm him. That's what we're going to cover.

EQUIPMENT YOU NEED

Now, let's get down to specifics. If you will be shooting with your own gear you will need at least some equipment in the following categories:

- Video Camera
- Audio Equipment
- Stabilization Gear
- Lighting
- Editing Software.

Video Cameras

People ask me all the time what camera they should get. I'm not going to make specific recommendations here because by the time this book gets into print things will already be changing. Three years from the time I write this any camera I recommend may be obsolete and discontinued, a footnote in the history of video cameras. The technology is changing that fast.

I've worked with cameras at all price points. I recently started working with some pro-sumer and consumer cameras and am very impressed with them. Prosumer is an official category that lies somewhere between consumer and professional gear. The difference in the quality of the image between those and a professional camera will not matter unless you are aiming for very high quality large screen projection, or where your lenses cost more than $10,000, or where you are spending a *lot* of time lighting your scene. Especially if you are just beginning, the difference in price is not worth it.

I used to think that showing up on a project with anything less than a professional camera was a poor reflection on me. I admit that I love big, important-looking cameras. However, a couple of years ago I hired a videographer whom I respect to help me on a pro-ject. This was a run and gun shoot requiring the camera operator to be nimble and incon-spicuous. He showed up with a tiny Canon HV10 and an HV20. These cameras fit easily in the palm of your hand. Quite frankly, I was embarrassed for my client to see us with these cheap-looking consumer cameras. They looked like toys to me. "What are these?" I asked him.

Later that day we went back to his studio and he showed me some footage from a documentary he was shooting in Vietnam with those cameras. He showed it on a 42 inch HD monitor. I was blown away at the quality! How could you get such beautiful shots on a camera that looked like he bought it at Toys R Us®? This was a revelation to me.

It took some time to get comfortable with the fact that these consumer cameras would work fine on many of my projects and especially for the budding videographer. I've done plenty of research and now know that you can get excellent camcorders for $500 and even less. I've seen some great videos on cameras in the sub-$200 range. Mike Dejure, one of our case studies, creates beautiful videos with a camera that only costs about $100. In the $1,000 to $2,000 range you can get a serious camera with better optics and more controls.

So, if you are just starting out and on a budget I'm going to recommend that you look at consumer or prosumer cameras.

I should mention a trend that you will see of people using digital SLR (single-lens reflex) cameras, referred to as DSLRs, to shoot videos. This is what most people think of as a still image camera, but the latest generation of these cameras in most brands are capable of making stunning, feature film quality images. Their advantage is they have a much larger imaging chip than most video cameras, which gives them better low light performance and the ability to display a more shallow depth of field (DOF), depending on the lens used.

DOF means the area of the shot that is in focus. A shallow DOF would allow you to do something like focus on a person's face, while everything in the foreground and back-ground is out of focus. The majority of scenes shot in bright light and medium wide angle with a camcorder will show most of the scene in focus, giving you little control over DOF. Neither is right or wrong, but shallow DOF is a creative tool that is useful to direct the eye to certain objects in a scene. It is also the way we are used to viewing movies.

Another advantage of DSLRs is the ability to change lenses, going from super wide angle to extreme telephoto. You can use very high quality lenses and have an amazing cre-ative range with these cameras.

The down side of shooting with DSLRs is that keeping a moving image in focus is very challenging and they are not, at least at this time, the best choice for recording audio.

None have XLR (professional) audio inputs and many of them do not offer volume control and audio level meters. Serious shooters resort to recording audio separately on a high quality digital audio recorder. This adds a lot of complexity because you have to synchronize the audio with the video in post-production. There are software tools to do this, such as Singular Software's PluralEyes.

While I love the look you can get with DSLRs, they may be a bit too challenging for the beginning SIV producer.

You can shoot your SIV with the simplest of camcorders or even a cell phone if you have excellent lighting and audio. However, I know you want some suggestions about a camera so here are some features I would look for:

- The camera must have an external microphone (mic) input.
- It must have a headphone input jack.
- It must have manual audio controls and level meters.
- It must have the ability to focus manually.
- It must have white balance control.
- Optical image stabilization is desirable, but not absolutely necessary.
- If you are going to do any zooming you want an optical zoom lens. Skip cameras with only digital zoom.

Take this list with you when you are shopping for a camera and don't be afraid to ask the sales person for these specifications. There are many inexpensive camcorders that meet these specs.

Audio Requirements

You want the external mic input because you should always use an external mic for just about anything. The built-in mics on these cameras are the weak link in a good image. You'll read more about audio in the following chapters and in the audio requirements section below, but take my advice and only choose a camera with an external microphone input. You also want the ability to manually control the audio level.

Consumer and most prosumer cameras (and DSLRs) have a 1/8″ stereo mini-pin microphone input. That is not a professional grade input. It will work fine most of the time but in some situations it can lead to a hum in your audio. If you use professional mics you will probably have to use an adapter to get the signal into your camera. This is called a *Mini Stereo Male* to 3-pin XLR and sometimes a pigtail XLR adapter. Alternately and for a lot more money you can buy a small mixer from a company like Beachtek or JuicedLink that takes XLR cable inputs and then outputs to the 1/8″ stereo mini-pin. This is one of the differences between consumer and professional cameras. Professional cameras will usually have a direct XLR cable input.

You also want to be able to control the audio levels. Otherwise the camera will be raising and lowering the audio automatically based on what it thinks is the norm, effectively raising and lowering the audio volume. Having the ability to manually adjust the audio level by referencing audio level meters allows you to adjust the volume to an optimum level and avoid this automatic volume adjustment effect.

Adjusting Your Camera's Focus and White Balance

If you are just starting out you want a camera that you can point, shoot, and get an excellent image. Most cameras today will deliver that. Automatic exposure is fine in some situations but it can be fooled or not realize what you want to focus on, so you want to be able to override that with manual focusing. In low light many cameras will "hunt" for focus, meaning they go in and out of focus, so you want to be able to set focus manually.

Most cameras will have a manual white balance control in addition to presets. Make sure yours does. White balance calibrates the camera so that colors are accurately recorded no matter what the light source. Your brain does tricks so that a white shirt looks the same to your eye under a streetlight at night, in broad daylight, and under fluorescent lights. Cameras can't do this and can give you some ghastly images until you help the camera understand the light source. This is white balancing and you must be able to do that manually.

Getting to know and use your manual settings and white balance control is not as difficult as you may feel they are at first. If all you've been shooting with up to now is your phone, of course it may seem daunting. Your camera manual will show you how to use and adjust all these settings.

More Camera Considerations

Image stabilization is a mechanical adjustment the camera does to stabilize a shaky shot. It is nearly impossible to hand-hold a shot and not get some jitters, but an image stabilized camera will really smooth things out. Unless the camera needs to be moving for an effect or you are on the run, shooting on a tripod or monopod is preferable. If you do shoot on a tripod, turn image stabilization off.

Some very compact cameras, like cell phones, do not have an optical zoom lens. When you "zoom" with these cameras, the processor is really just magnifying the image, which further degrades the more you zoom. In this case you are better off moving the camera toward your subject.

I tend to shoot on the wide angle end of a zoom lens and don't care so much about how strong the telephoto reach is. When you are shopping for a camera be aware of how wide or telephoto the lens will go. If you know you need a really wide angle lens, put that on your checklist.

> Good filmmaking doesn't use zoom shots much anyway. While zooms do have their place, a good practice is to make your zoom adjustment, frame the shot, and then press record. Don't incorporate too many zooming shots or it will look amateurish. You see zooms incorporated in television shows specifically to simulate amateur camera work.

Another thing to look for is the size of the image sensor (chip). Most consumer camcorders will have 1/4″ chips. The larger the sensor, the more ability you have to use DOF as a creative tool because you can create shallow DOF. A larger sensor will also give you some advantage in low light. A three chip camera is better than a single chip camera, but the price goes up considerably.

Finally, be aware that what you see in your flip-out monitor or viewfinder may not exactly match what the camera is recording. It may actually be recording 5 percent or more than you think, so learn how your camera performs so that when you frame a shot you are really getting the image you want.

Tape cameras are fast disappearing so you'll probably get one that records to some kind of flash memory. I have mixed feelings about this but that's just the way it is. I like tape as an archival storage media. The alternative is having more and more hard drives used strictly to store my digital footage. If I fire them up in 20 years, will they work or will the software even recognize them? All I can do is hope. Because most camcorders sold today are high definition, the file sizes can get quite large and require a lot of storage space.

As to file format, that's another area that will be changing. Today AVCHD (advanced video coding high definition) is taking the lead in most consumer and prosumer cameras. It uses a compression standard called MPEG-4 AVC/H.264. Don't worry about that, just make sure that your editing software and computer will handle it, as it puts a lot of demands on your computer processor. Compression formats are bound to evolve over time.

That's about it for my camera recommendations. Look for these features and you will be in great shape.

You should spend a good bit of time practicing with a new camera before shooting something serious. Under the stress of a real shoot is not the time to be figuring out a new camera. Learn the menu items, where certain controls are, and how to use them.

Using a checklist will help. It's easy when you are under pressure to forget a simple thing like setting white balance or checking your audio levels. You'll find a helpful checklist in Chapter 15.

Audio Equipment

Viewers will watch a video with mediocre or poor image quality but excellent sound (and content) much longer than they'll sit through a video with good imagery but unintelligible sound.

That's why I insisted that you get a camera with a microphone input and manual volume controls. You will want to use an external mic in every situation possible. It will yield far better results than the camera's built-in microphone.

Microphones

There are four major categories of mics you are likely to use: lavalier, shotgun, head worn, and hand-held. All four types can be either wired or wireless. Wireless mics, also called radio mics, use a transmitter on the microphone and a receiver at or near the camera.

Mics can get very expensive but you don't need to spend a bundle. I've seen lavalier mics with mini-pin connectors that cost $30 that sound good enough for a lot of applications. They are definitely an improvement over the built-in mic. I use an industry standard lavalier mic, the Sony ECM 44-b. You can find these new under $200 and it is the last lavalier mic you'll ever need. I bought a couple of them used on eBay for around $70.

A lavalier mic is meant to clip to a person's clothes. They give the person "presence," a much more natural sound. They can be clipped between the second and third button of a blouse or shirt, which may be just out of frame. They are also often clipped to a tie or the lapel of a jacket. If you don't want it to show it can be placed underneath clothing with tape but you have to be very careful about clothing rubbing against the mic it can sound like thunder. I get my friend the Hollywood sound man to help me with shots like that.

You can use a wired or wireless system. When possible it's usually better to go with a wired connection as it will be less likely to have electrical interference. Wireless is the way to go if the subject is moving a lot or is a long distance from the camera. Expect to spend

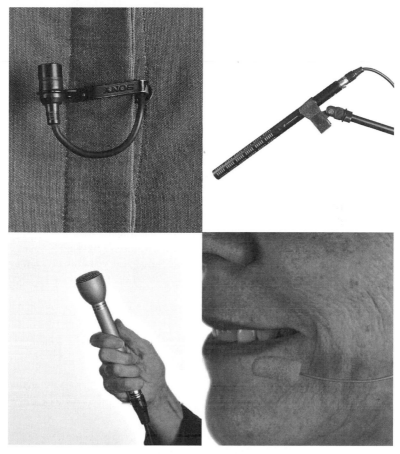

FIGURE 13.1   Lavalier Microphone (*top left*); Shotgun Microphone (*top right*); Hand-held Microphone (*bottom left*); Head Worn Microphone (*bottom right*).

upwards of $500 for a good wireless set with a transmitter and receiver. You can find inexpensive wireless mics for sale but I've found them to be too susceptible to radio interference and lacking in range. Don't waste your money on them.

If you are recording several people in the scene and they are moving around a lot your best choice might be a shotgun mic. Contrary to what most people think, a shotgun mic doesn't "reach out" and bring audio closer. The way it works is it is not as sensitive to sound from the sides and behind it, so that you hear more of what is in front of it. This works well unless the subject is standing in front of a noisy background, like an air-conditioning unit or crashing surf. It will magnify that as well.

Shotgun mics can be mounted on boom poles so that an operator can follow the actors with the mic held just out of the camera's frame; you see this all the time in behind the scenes photos of movie productions. Of course if you are going to use it like that you will need a mic boom and a boom operator.

A shotgun mic can be mounted on a mic stand if the person speaking is stationary. Shotguns sound best when kept as close as possible, yet out of the frame. Three to four feet is a good distance. You have to be aware of what is behind the person speaking as it can magnify that background sound.

A technique to get optimal sound quality when using a shotgun mic is to have something behind the person speaking that will absorb the "splash" or bounce of the sound if shooting indoors. Sound bounces off of hard surfaces like wood floors or bare walls, causing an echo or empty sound. You can muffle that splash with fabrics like drapes on the wall or a rug or carpet on the floor if the mic is pointing down.

Another mic that is useful in the right situation is the head worn mic, also known as headset or ear worn mic. You see exercise trainers, ministers, and music performers wearing these. They keep your hands free, can be so small as to be almost invisible, and keep the mic right at the speaker's mouth. I used a Countryman E6 headset mic on my exercise video series and it sounded great, even when Dave was doing strenuous exercises. With all of his movements there was no other choice.

A head worn mic would be a good choice if your SIV is about someone demonstrating a technique where he'll be moving around a lot and will need full range of motion with hands and arms. You can find models like the Countryman E6 that are very thin and that come in a range of colors so that they almost disappear on the person wearing them. This particular model is intended to be wireless.

Hand-held mics have their place, too. They are great for doing interviews in the field, like you frequently see news reporters doing. These can be wired or wireless. They are great for quick, impromptu interviews where you don't have time to put a lapel mic on a person. You can find models that are better suited to loud, noisy environments, like stage performances, or that pick up more of the environmental sounds. I make a hand-held mic a standard part of my audio kit.

If you do decide to go with a wireless mic system, choose one that is dual diversity. This means there are actually two active receivers that switch between themselves automatically if one is getting interference. You also want to have the option of many different radio channels (frequencies) so that you can avoid noisy channels. Most sets, even expensive ones, are limited to about 100 feet and work best when there is nothing between the transmitter and receiver. Walls, vehicles, buildings, and other solid obstructions can interrupt the transmission.

A good microphone should last for many years, so get the best you can afford.

Some manufacturers have recently introduced some excellent small digital audio recorders for film, video, and music producers. They are affordable and are a good alternative to putting a wireless mic on someone. You just slip one of these recorders in his pocket, connect a mic and record that way. This eliminates the possibility of radio interference that you get with wireless systems. The main concern with this type of system is that you have to sync the audio and video together in post-production when you are editing.

Stabilization

There are times when hand-held shots are appropriate, such as when you are representing the point of view of a person on the move. Hand-held shots give you the ability to move quickly in all directions and they take almost no setup time. However, too much hand-held work will look unprofessional.

Tripod shots add a professional look and give you the ability to study composition, contrast, lighting, and your actor's performance. Features to look for include a standard quick release plate (the plate the camera attaches to) that is interchangeable with other tripods or monopods you may own, a bubble level for ensuring that it is level, separate pan and tilt controls, and a fluid head. The fluid head is something video tripods offer so that you can get a smooth pan or tilt shot.

A medium weight tripod with good build quality will last for many years. Expect to spend $500 to $1,000 for a decent tripod (legs and head). You can get inexpensive video tripods under $150 which will work for light use. The good thing about investing in a good tripod is there is no way it can become obsolete.

Just make sure the tripod you choose is built to support the weight of your camera and attached accessories.

All camcorders will have a tripod socket on the bottom. Cell phones do not have them but you can find adapters for most models so you can use them with a tripod.

A monopod is a tripod with two legs missing. I love monopods and I have different sizes for different uses. They range from a short, 8-ounce travel monopod to big, heavy professional monopods with fluid heads and flip-out feet. A monopod will give you more stable shots than hand-held while allowing you the mobility to pick up and run to your next shot. Several years ago we had a contract to create a documentary about the college's marching band. The monopods were indispensable in allowing us to keep up with the band during a performance and still get smooth shots. I can quickly go from low to very high shots for some unusual angles that add production value.

At last count I owned five tripods and six monopods, so that tells you how important I think these items are.

Lighting

Cameras love light. I'm sure you've seen photos of movie sets out in broad daylight where they are throwing lots of additional light into the scene. This is necessary because cameras do not have the ability to render detail in very dark and very light areas at the same time to the degree that your eye can. This is called dynamic range. By throwing light into dark areas, even in bright sunlight, you can get a smoother, more pleasing image or you can create a more dramatic look.

If you are shooting in a dark environment you'll see a dramatic improvement in the quality of your video if you add some light. The camera has to work hard to get an image in a dark area. It will do this by increasing the gain. This means it is amplifying the image signal, which results in a grainy image. This is sometimes called mosquito noise because it looks a bit like a swarm of tiny mosquitos.

Light is a creative tool. You can create moods and emotions by manipulating light and shadows. Think of how Rembrandt used light to create a brooding or melancholy mood.

You can spend thousands of dollars on a lighting kit or you can do it yourself with work lights from the hardware store. Work lights are cheap and powerful and work well if you use a diffusion material like spun glass over the lights to diffuse them. They throw light in a broad area and you can't focus them, but they will work fine in many situations. They do generate heat so be careful not to get flammable items too close.

Remember that I said you want to pick a camera with manual white balance controls? This is why. Every light has a certain color temperature, measured on a scale called Kelvin. Color temperature varies on the Kelvin scale from cool blue at one end to red at the other end. Every light source produces light at some point on that range of colors. Tungsten lights like household bulbs and those work lights, are measured around 3,600 degrees Kelvin and are on the red end of the scale. Daylight falls toward the blue end of the spectrum and is around 5,600 degrees Kelvin. Your brain adjusts what it is seeing under all kinds of light to look normal, but a camera cannot do that. If you white balance for those tungsten work lights, any daylight will look bluish. If you white balance for daylight the tungsten lights will look reddish. So if you are mixing light sources you will have to white balance to adjust colors as close as possible to what your eye sees.

Tungsten light sources use bulbs or globes that generate a lot of heat. They are not energy efficient and the bulbs can be short lived and expensive. They are still commonly used in film and video production but we're seeing a shift to other light sources.

LED (light-emitting diode) lights are getting more powerful and affordable. They are lightweight, sturdy, and efficient. They can come in many different color temperatures and some are adjustable from tungsten to daylight.

Fluorescent video lights have also become popular. The typical fluorescent lights you find in an office won't work very well because they will appear to flicker and can have a sickly green cast even when you do white balance them. However, the professional video fluorescent lights are very nice. I have a set that consists of five large softboxes (diffusers) that each output the equivalent of 1,200 watts while only using 300 watts. This allows me to use a lot of lighting in my studio without generating much heat or blowing my fuse box. They are also daylight balanced so I can use them as outdoor fill lights. Fluorescent light is soft and efficient.

You can get fluorescent video quality bulbs now that screw into a standard light socket. You can get a few of these bulbs and a couple of those shiny, clip-on light fixtures (about $10) at hardware stores and you have the beginnings of a workable light kit for under $50.

I like to put these fluorescent fixtures into round paper "Chinese lanterns" for a very soft, wrap-around light. You can find these in import stores such as Pier 1. I wouldn't do this with tungsten bulbs but the fluorescent bulbs put off so little heat that I use them.

When shooting outside in daylight you have the best light source available—the sun. By using photo reflectors, white boards such as foam core, or architectural structures like reflective floors and walls, you can fill in shadows without needing electricity.

I carry reflectors with me all the time. These fold up into compact packages but pop out to about three feet across. They have removable gold, silver, and white surfaces so you can "color" a scene, and they also have a thin diffusion material that acts to diffuse strong overhead light. Get one of these multi-surface reflectors and you're set for many challenging lighting situations.

Editing Software

Once you've shot all of your beautiful footage you will need to edit it. This is another area where I hesitate to make specific suggestions because software comes and goes and what I recommend today might not exist in a few years.

I use two powerhouse non-linear editing programs for the Mac: Apple's Final Cut Pro and Adobe's Premiere Pro. I like both of them but the Adobe Creative Suite is quite expensive with a list price of $1,699. Final Cut Pro X is now just $299.99 and a real bargain.

These programs may be overkill for you. Even I don't use a lot of the functionality so I know a beginning editor can easily get by with less. Adobe makes a scaled-down version of Premiere Pro called Premiere Elements. This is far less expensive than Premiere Pro and will suit most needs. Apple includes iMovie free with every new Mac and it is an excellent editor for most people working on Macs.

I'm afraid I don't have much experience on the PC side of editing so I can't speak from experience about programs for that platform. There are certainly many more options for the PC than for Macs. Adobe makes all of its editing programs available for the PC. There is also CyberLink PowerDirector, Corel VideoStudio Pro, MAGIX Movie Edit Pro,

Roxio Creator, VideoPad, Windows Movie Maker, Pinnacle Studio HD by Avid®, Sony Vegas Movie Studio, Roxio Video Lab, and several others, all priced under $100.

Conceptually, most of these work the same way so if you learn on one it should not be too difficult to migrate to another, possibly more powerful, platform later.

The primary thing you have to look for when shopping is that the software supports the file format your camera produces. Some require more computer processing power than others or will perform better with certain hardware items, like the video card, so take your time to select the right package for your camera and computer.

RENTING AS AN OPTION

If all of this equipment talk makes you think you'll need to spend a lot of money, keep in mind that you can rent everything we've covered here. If your needs are limited and short term it might make more sense for you to rent than to purchase equipment. You might find that if you need a particular item for a long period of time then it is more economical to purchase it and sell it when you are finished. I do this a lot.

Here's a budget for a good consumer quality camera that will meet every requirement I listed, a small fluorescent light kit with stands, lavalier mic, decent quality headphones, and a tripod that will do the job for several years.

Camera, Batteries, Memory Cards	$450
Lights	$150
Lavalier Mic	$30
Headphones	$50
Mic Cable	$15
Fluid-effect Tripod	$150
Total	**$845**

You can spend less than this. You can find an inexpensive tripod without the fluid head for $25. You may already have headphones. You can buy work lights or those clip-on lights and fluorescent bulbs for about $50. You can also spend more than this but you don't have to in order to start making SIVs that you'll be proud of.

Action Steps

If you are going to be shooting your own production, you will need to invest in either renting or buying the following:

- Video camera—Look for:
  - an external microphone input
  - manual audio controls and level meters
  - the ability to use manual focus
  - manual white balance control
  - image stabilization
  - an optical zoom lens.

- Audio equipment—Assess your needs before you buy an external microphone. Decide if you need a wired or wireless system.
- Stabilization gear—Invest in a sturdy tripod and get a monopod if you are going to be doing a lot of fast shooting.
- Lighting—Look at your shooting situation and decide if you can get away with using simple work lights. For outdoors, invest in a reflector/diffuser.
- Editing software—Make sure the editing software you get is compatible with the file format your camera produces. It doesn't have to have all the bells and whistles, just the ability to do basic editing.

Chapter 14

Basic Camera Shots, Lighting, and Audio

Chapter Objectives

- Understand the basic shot types and when to use them.
- Learn to frame and apply the "rule of thirds" to compose shots.
- Know the basic types of lighting angles you'll use.
- Learn some microphone techniques and the importance of using headphones.
- Learn about basic camera movements.

BASIC SHOT TYPES

Here are three basic shots you will incorporate into your video: wide, medium, and close-up. Each one serves a different purpose so think about why you are choosing a particular shot before setting it up.

Wide Shot

Wide shots reveal a lot of information about a scene. You will often want to begin a scene with a wide shot. When I say "wide" I don't necessarily mean a wide angle but a shot that reveals the environment into which you are taking the viewer. More often than not it is shot from enough distance to indicate the setting and maybe include some action or audio clue that sets the stage for things to come.

For example if you were making a video about woodworking you might start with an establishing shot of the outside of the workshop, moving down from a sign to the open doorway. The viewer hears a saw buzzing. The next shot will take them inside the workshop.

In the example shown in Figure 14.1, taken from my exercise video series, the widest shot is of the interior room where we'll be demonstrating the exercises.

Establishing shots are often the first shot of a film, video, or scene. They are usually wide shots.

There is also an extreme wide shot that is as the word implies, extreme. This can involve a very wide angle lens, even a "fisheye" lens which gives a distorted perspective.

FIGURE 14.1 Wide Shot.

Medium Shot

After a wide shot you may move into a medium shot of the talent (one or a couple of people on camera) to establish their presence (Figure 14.2). This has the effect of the camera bringing the viewer into the scene. The talent could be speaking directly to the camera or to each other. This will probably be framed from the waist up. Also when you're framing the shot, watch the head space (head room) above their heads; don't have too much distance above their heads to the top of the frame but don't cut the head off either (save that for the close-up). This is also called a "two-shot" if it is a medium shot of two people.

Close-Up Shot

As the name implies, this is a close shot of your talent or an object (Figure 14.3). This shot functions to focus the viewer's attention tightly on this person or item. If it is a person's face then it is telling the viewer that this is an important shot, pay attention to what is being said!

If you are demonstrating something, like our woodworking analogy, it could be a close-up of the saw cutting wood.

As in the wide shot, there is also an extreme close-up shot that is used very effectively to show emotion, like a person's eyes or an expression.

Since we are often demonstrating a process in SIVs, the close-up is a handy shot. It is also one where careful attention to camera focus is critical. Once you are focused very closely, any lack of sharp focus will be very evident.

It is important that as you set up these different shots you keep the exposure and white balance consistent between them. Otherwise the different look of the shots will jolt the viewer and you'll lose the flow. If you are shooting a scene with multiple cameras be sure to white balance them off the exact same white object in the same light.

Once you've established your scene you'll mostly be cutting between medium and close shots until you either change the scene or come to the end. There is no set formula for this

FIGURE 14.2   Medium Shot.

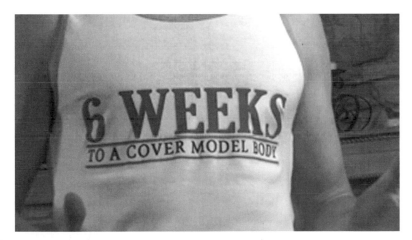

FIGURE 14.3   Close-Up Shot.

but that's a typical pattern. Always give the editor a wide variety of shots including the establishing wide shot, and plenty of medium and close-up shots. This will allow them to create more visual interest.

CAMERA FRAMING

Framing is the process of creating a composition rather than just pointing a camera at something and shooting. The rules of framing video images are essentially the same as those for still photography. Following just a few key rules will improve your composition.

Your horizontals should be level, and your verticals straight up and down unless you are intentionally going for a tilted effect.

FIGURE 14.4   Divide your frame into nine sections. Place the center of interest at one of the intersections.

Follow the "rule of thirds" by dividing the frame into nine sections, as in Figure 14.4. You'll have three vertical and three horizontal sections, evenly spaced. The point of interest should happen at one of the intersections. Avoid placing your center of interest dead center unless you are doing it for effect.

If a person is looking off-camera leave more space in front of them than behind them. This will avoid a crowded or claustrophobic look.

TITLE SAFE AND ACTION SAFE ZONES

Older televisions varied in how much of the entire image was shown. Some cut it off more than others. For that reason most cameras and all editing systems display guides that show safe zones (Figure 14.5). The Title Safe zone is an area inside the image where graphics and titles should display without being cut off on any television set or monitor. The Action Safe zone is further out but still does not include the entire image. This is an area that should show on most monitors. You may or may not be able to display these guides on your camera. Most modern flatscreen TVs can show the entire image being recorded.

CAMERA VIEWFINDERS AND MONITORS

Look carefully through your viewfinder or monitor. A common error is to accidentally include items in the shot that you didn't see. This happens because some viewfinders only show 90 to 95 percent of the frame, so there may be things being recorded on the edge of your shot, such as a shotgun mic, that you don't want included. That's why

FIGURE 14.5   Title Safe and Action Safe indications.

it's important to learn how accurate your viewfinder is so that you know to compensate for this.

BASIC CAMERA MOVES

Here are some of the main camera moves:

Pan

The camera moves over the scene from left and right. There is no moving up and down. A fluid head tripod makes this a smooth look.

Tilt

The camera moves up and down without changing the horizontal position.

Zoom

You can zoom in and out in a scene, making it appear as if the camera is moving closer or farther away from the subject.

Follow

This is a shot where the camera physically follows the action, be it a person, car, horse, whatever. It can be hand-held or mounted on any number of support systems. The simplest way to do a follow shot is hand-held. News crews often do this with shoulder mounted cameras.

Tracking or Dolly

This shot is similar to the follow but instead of hand-holding or mounting the camera on a shoulder mount, the camera is mounted on a camera dolly, which is a wheeled platform that is pushed on rails or tires while the camera is running. This type of shot can add a lot of production quality to your video. The shot doesn't have to last long: just a few seconds of subtle movement will be very effective.

A camera support item that has become very popular recently is the "slider." This is basically a small rail system, usually three feet long or less, upon which you mount a tripod head to hold your camera. You can get very smooth, slow dolly shots with these. It is a nice touch if not overdone. They still tend to be expensive, averaging over $300 for a well-built slider.

I have also used a cart, wheeled office chair, and child's wagon as a dolly.

Most camera moves are a combination of these basic moves. The best advice is to move the camera as little as possible, and only when it makes sense in the context of the shot.

CAMERA POSITIONS AND ANGLES

Think of the camera as the viewer's eye—every choice you make about the position and angle of the camera is where you are visually placing your viewer. You should be making them view the scene from a certain perspective for a reason, so be clear on why you pick certain positions.

Eye-Level (Point of View)

This view shows the subjects in your scene as they would be seen in real life by a human standing in that position. This common angle is the one with which we're most familiar. It is often used to portray the point of view (POV) of a person in the scene.

In some circumstances the POV will be at a low level. If we were trying to show the world as seen by a dog, the POV would be lower.

High Angle

In a high angle, the camera is angled down towards the subject, showing the person or scene from above. This reveals a lot of background information. It can make a person seem small or helpless (Figure 14.6). Bird's eye is an extreme type of high angle.

Low Angle

Opposite of the high angle, shooting the subject from below gives the viewer the impression of larger than life and the subject dominates the scene (Figure 14.7). If this is a POV shot it can imply that the viewer is vulnerable or hiding.

Slanted

This angle is also known as a dutch tilt and is when you purposely tilt your camera to one side so that the horizon is on an angle. It's an effect that you see in a lot of music videos. It implies off-balance or gives a unique look at something.

Use angles carefully. Unusual angles keep things interesting but don't just do it for the sake of doing it. There needs to be a good purpose for the shot. A high or low angle can be

FIGURE 14.6   High Angle Shot. © Dmitriy Shironosov | Dreamstime.com

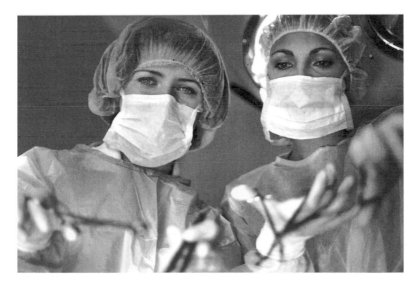

FIGURE 14.7   Low Angle Shot. © Lyudmila Bubentsova | Dreamstime.com

too extreme and not make sense within the context of the scene, so use discretion. More likely you will be switching between medium and close-up shots for variety.

LIGHTING

Have you ever seen the paintings of Rembrandt van Rijn? Faces glow out of rich, dark backgrounds.

Johannes Vermeer used window light to create magical paintings. Go to www.essentialvermeer.com and see his stunning use of a single light source. Brilliant!

These artists knew that light was just as essential a tool in the artist's toolbox as paint and brushes. It is just as important for filmmakers and videographers.

I'm not saying that you need to light your SIV as artfully as these paintings, but you do need to become aware of how light is used. Not only do you use it to direct the viewer's eye to certain objects, you use it technically to get the best image possible out of your camera.

Here are some lighting terms you should know:

Key Light

The dominant light on people or objects is called a key light. Outside it's the sun. Indoors, you have to pick one main light. It is often at 45 degrees off-center from the subject. The height depends on how you want the shot to look. With older people I lower it to reduce the appearance of wrinkles.

Fill Light

This is a light that fills in the shadows not lit by key light. Outdoors, natural fill light is often from the sky or clouds. It can be supplemented by artificial or reflected light.

Back Light

Back light comes from behind to light the edge of a person or object to separate them from the background. This is also known as hair or shoulder light and is usually placed behind and above the person.

Top Light

Light directly from above is a difficult situation. Shooting people at high noon is a challenge due to harsh facial shadows. This is an unflattering time of day to shoot faces. My recommendation is try to avoid shooting people outdoors at this time of day. Putting people into broken shade, such as under tree branches, can also work if the background is dark enough to balance with the foreground lighting.

Hard Light

Light from the sun or bare bulb is called hard. Hard light creates hard shadows and accentuated detail such as lines in the face.

Soft Light

Light that comes from many directions is soft. Light from the sun on a foggy or overcast day is natural soft light. A softbox is a lighting device that diffuses light, softening shadows.

Eye Light

A light reflecting in a person's eyes is eye light. It can add life and sparkle.

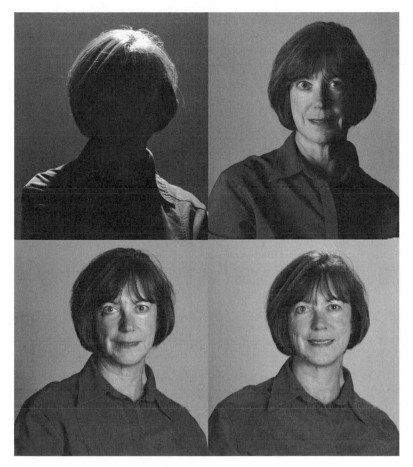

FIGURE 14.8   Back Light (*top left*); Fill Light (*top right*); Key Light (*bottom left*); Final Shot (*bottom right*).

 A trick to getting the lighting the way you want it is to turn all of the lights off and then turn them on one at a time and individually adjust each light to the way you want it. Then turn them all on and make final adjustments.

SHOOTING OUTDOORS

Learning to deal with the moving sun is important. The camera operator has to plan to shoot the master shot when the light is best or can be modified to look good. Then he must plan how and when during the day to get the necessary coverage (close-ups and inserts) so that the lighting will match the master shot. Clouds and the passage of time can make continuity in an outdoor shoot challenging. Watch movies and TV shows carefully and you'll notice the light changing even though the shots are supposed to be just seconds or minutes apart.

When you're shooting outdoors, don't have your subject looking in the direction of the sun or they'll squint. Shooting at high noon is generally to be avoided. Early morning and mid to late afternoon are better times. The "golden hour" is that hour just before sunset when the sun's color is warm and the light less intense.

An error we see frequently in outdoor shots is using too much fill light. If you use a reflector, use it with discretion. If there is a strong back or side light, don't completely fill in the shadows on a person's face. It looks unnatural.

Bright sunlight can be a problem, producing too much contrast on a face. In auto mode your camera may shift into a high shutter speed to compensate for the abundance of light, which can cause a stuttering look on playback. Your camera should have a neutral density (ND) filter or switch. This is the equivalent of sunglasses for your camera. If it doesn't automatically turn on then do so manually. Shooting on an overcast day or in the shade helps reduce contrast. You can also place a diffuser to soften the sunlight on a person. An umbrella, if out of the shot, can soften harsh sunlight.

Avoid getting too much sky in your shot if it is much brighter than your subject. When you have a very bright background behind your subject the camera will want to expose for the bright area, leaving your subject a silhouette.

When scouting a situation, look for existing possibilities that can solve your needs. Indoors, if a light source is too bright, switching to a lower wattage bulb will help the scene balance. A light can be turned on or a shade added to help the overall balance. A couple of white sheets (satin is best) can reflect light to fill shadows. Outdoors, moving a white vehicle near a shot can provide fill light.

Start observing your environment to learn where the light is coming from. Look to see if it's coming directly from the sun, the open sky, or reflected off a building. Also think about the things that can block light: trees, buildings, overhangs. Just changing positions a bit can turn a problem shot into a workable situation.

If you're shooting run and gun documentaries you only need adequate lighting, the best you can get under the circumstances before you miss your opportunity. Often wisely selecting a good position for the tripod will provide a good background and lighting. In these cases it's more important to get the shot while you can rather than fiddle with getting perfect lighting.

At some point you will most likely have to shoot in low light situations. Modern cameras will do a pretty good job of automatically adjusting for good exposure under most conditions, but low light can be a problem. First, be sure you have switched your neutral density (ND) filter off. As light levels decrease the gain is automatically increased with no indication in the viewfinder. This will cause noise or a grainy appearance in the picture as auto gain kicks in. By using manual control you can reduce the gain if needed. The best solution here is to add light to improve your picture quality. A little bit of added light can make a big difference in the image quality

If you are shooting at night and you want the scene intentionally to look dark you will have to switch to manual exposure mode or the camera will do its best to brighten the scene, spoiling the look you are going for.

> To simulate firelight or a candle, point a light source at a reflector with a crinkled golden surface and gently rock it back and forth. White balance the camera first with the light pointing at a white object in front of the subject before you bounce the light off the golden surface so that the end result is a warm glow.

Today's video cameras do an amazing job of capturing acceptable images, so a little effort to improve the lighting can go a long way. You just have to use your imagination sometimes. I was on a night movie shoot once and the electric generator ran out of gas. We were in an isolated location so running out to get more gas was out of the question. We couldn't get those actors together again to shoot it on another night so we had no choice but to find a solution. We ended up driving a truck up this very steep hill, pointing the headlights at the scene and it worked great.

AUDIO

"Sound is half the picture." It really is. If you have great audio, a good script, and decent lighting, you are head and shoulders above the crowd.

Think about home videos you've watched. Did it sound like it was shot in a giant tin can? Are the background sounds overwhelming the person talking? Does the person speaking sound like they are far away even though they aren't? Those are all the result of using the camera's built-in microphone. You don't want to do that.

When we talked about cameras, I stressed picking one with an external microphone input.

For many situations where the person on camera is stationary, your lavalier mic works great. In most situations we aren't concerned if a lavalier mic shows, as long as it is not dangling in front of a person's clothing. We try to snake it up inside a coat or shirt and just pop out at the point of attachment for a neat appearance. You can hide mics inside a person's clothing by using tape, just make sure the clothing isn't rubbing on the mic. Hollywood soundmen will often hide a mic in a person's hair or a hat.

Be careful when using lavalier mics. People who are not used to wearing them may pick at them unconsciously, rustle papers close to them, or even hug things to their chest, creating a lot of rumble and noise. For this reason I often use a shotgun mic on interviews.

Shotgun mics allow you to mic a person without having to place a mic on them because they emphasize the sound directly in front of them. A shotgun on a boom allows your actors to move around without being encumbered with a wire or having a lavalier on them that shows or may pick up clothing sounds. Watch your viewfinder carefully if using a boom mic to make sure it doesn't dip into the frame. Also know if your viewfinder is only showing you 90 to 95 percent of the scene or else you might have that mic in the shot and not know it.

Lavalier mics tend to be forgotten once a person is on camera, whereas a shotgun mic pointing at them may make them nervous, especially if dangling overhead from a boom. A shotgun mic is great if you have to cover multiple speakers close together.

> If you use a wireless lavalier or head worn mic on a person, make sure to take it off when finished. Since they are not tethered by a cable and it is small and lightweight it is easy to forget that they are wearing it. They might just leave and you won't have a mic!

Plant mics and boundary mics can be used discreetly on a table or in a plant or other object to place a mic closely but out of sight. A boundary mic is a plate-like, low profile mic that has a wide pickup area. A boundary mic placed on a table can pickup several people sitting there, as in a panel situation.

Watch Audio Levels

When I talked about equipment, I recommended that you get a camera with manual audio levels and audio level meters. You can display the meters on your viewfinder or monitor. There will be a mark labeled -12 dB. On colored meters this may be the point where the colors start to turn from green to orange. Use this as your target for most audio peaks. The loudest levels can go a little higher than this but never let your audio go all the way to the top end of the scale. Once digital audio peaks there is nothing you can do to improve it.

Headphones

Headphones are "our viewfinders to sound quality." Using headphones is imperative because it is the only way you know what sound you are recording. Without headphones you have no idea if you are getting unwanted noise or even if the microphone is working.

I prefer "closed ear" headphones, meaning they have a shell that fits over your ears that has no ventilation holes. This keeps more exterior sounds out so you know what the mic is hearing. Open ear headphones do have ventilation and are more comfortable but you'll have a harder time discerning what sound is coming from the mic and what is sound you are hearing through the headphone. I don't personally like ear buds because they let in too much sound from the environment but they can be used in a pinch and are better than nothing.

There are a lot of good headphones on the market. You can't go wrong with a set of Sony MDR-7506. Expect to spend $90 to $100.

Be sure to visit our companion website at www.shoot-to-sell.com for more tips and tutorials on camera framing, lighting, and audio recording.

Action Steps

- Know your basic shot types—wide, medium, close-up—and vary them to focus attention and maintain interest.
- Pay attention to composition. Use the "rule of thirds."
- Incorporate basic camera moves—pan, tilt, zoom, follow, or dolly.
- Vary your camera angles between eye-level, high, low, slanted (dutch angle).
- Look at light as a creative tool. Study the list of lighting styles and practice lighting individuals and sets.
- Mic your talent carefully and always monitor the sound through a good set of headphones.

Chapter 15

Shooting Your Special Interest Video

Chapter Objectives

- Get familiar with items you'll want to bring on your shoot.
- Learn what to do on the day of the shoot.
- Read the camera operating steps on the provided checklist.
- Understand what you can do to make the editing job easier.
- Learn why you should slate your shots.
- Know why and how to use teleprompters.
- Know what chromakey is and how to shoot for it.

I have watched many low budget projects that have failed mostly because one or more skills were missing or the projects were too ambitious for the people involved. So, I highly recommend learning to drive in the parking lot before getting on the freeway.

Ron Dexter[1]

That quote sums up the essence of what I want you to get out of this chapter. Don't try to make your video into an epic your first time out. Learn to walk before you run.

To do that you need to keep your production simple and to the point. If you are a perfectionist it is going to cost you. You are eventually going to have to stop fussing and shoot, then use your best take. You have to learn to compromise in the fine-tuning of set quality, level of shot complexity, fancy camera moves, lighting, etc., and just say, "It's good enough, we have to shoot." Producing a video that is good enough but not a big compromise in quality is your goal.

There are already a lot of resources available on the topic of video production so this book isn't going to dive too deeply into the specifics of the subject. Click on the Film & Video tab at www.focalpress.com or search on www.amazon.com and you'll find very helpful books. You can find a lot of hands-on production tips and instructional videos on our companion website, www.shoot-to-sell.com.

No, our key focus (pardon the pun) with this book is more on how to choose a topic and then successfully market your final product. What we will explore in this chapter is how you can make your production flow smoothly and avoid common mistakes.

THREE VERY IMPORTANT ELEMENTS IN YOUR VIDEO

It is important that you bring the following three elements to your video if you want it to look professional and be enjoyable to watch:

1. A good script.
2. Excellent audio quality.
3. Good lighting.

I listed them in that order for a reason. That is my suggested order of importance. Regardless of the subject or the equipment you are using, those three elements are the foundation of a good video.

If your production has a bad script, no matter how pretty the images or how tricky the camera work, people will lose interest. They won't be able to follow it. People buy your SIV primarily for information, so the most important goal is to present the information in the best way so that it is easily accessible. If you have a great script and then give them clean audio and good images, you're well on your way to success.

Assuming you have your script ready, let's ...

GET READY FOR THE SHOOT

You're all packed for the shoot. Sure you packed everything? The last thing you want to do is get there and discover that your batteries are dead or you forgot your microphone. Following is a list of what I take on a typical shoot when I'm driving there. Obviously, I can't take as much when flying.

Checklist of Items for Your Shoot

I bring a lot of stuff to a shoot in addition to my camera and tripod. If I'm flying I have to cut it back to the essentials, but if I'm driving to a job I bring everything but the kitchen sink and I've never regretted it. Nothing will stress you out more than being on a shoot and seeing the blinking "replace battery" notice in your viewfinder when you don't have another battery. Arrgh. Or running out of tape or seeing your flash card filling up, all without a backup.

Don't forget your human comforts, either. Always bring water, some snacks, sunscreen, a hat, maybe bug repellant, and aspirin or ibuprofen.

In addition to my basic camera gear I bring along equipment and supplies that will serve me well in a wide range of situations:

- Band-aids
- Bottled water
- Business cards
- Camera, plus a backup camera
- Camera batteries—more than one backup, preferably three or more
- Camera battery charger
- Cell phone
- Clips—metal clips and wooden clothes pins, useful for all kinds of things
- Color correcting gels

- Digital audio recorder
- Dulling spray—takes the shine off of objects, found at art supply stores
- Eyeglasses (if needed) and sunglasses
- Extension cords—industrial quality
- Flashlight
- Gaffer's tape—a special kind of tape that won't peel paint off walls but holds well. Not duct tape. Order from www.filmtools.com.
- Hat
- Hairspray
- Headphones—preferably a closed ear style, like the Sony MD-7506
- Ibuprofen, aspirin, etc.
- Lens cleaning materials—a camel hair brush and lens cleaning cloth
- Light stands—make sure they fit your lights
- Lights—bring spare globes (bulbs or tubes)
- Makeup—at least basic foundation makeup
- Microphone batteries—lots of them
- Microphone boom pole
- Microphone cables (XLR and mini-pin adapter cable)
- Microphone shock mount
- Microphone stand
- Microphone wind muff—fits over mic to prevent wind noise
- Microphones—a lavalier, shotgun, hand held, wireless or wired—depending on the situation
- Monopod   always handy
- Multi-tool—combines screwdrivers, knife, bottle opener, etc.
- Multiple power outlet—get one with a fuse so you don't melt it
- Notebook
- On-camera light (used for eye-light)
- Paper towels—you never know why
- Pen
- Rain gear for inclement weather
- Recording tape or flash memory cards (bring plenty)
- Reflector and diffuser
- Reflector holder boom arm and stand
- Safety pins
- Sand bags or weights of some kind
- Slate (clapboard)
- Snacks
- Still camera
- Sunscreen
- Tissues—for wiping off sweat
- Tripod—*make sure you have the camera plate*
- Zip lock bags

WOW! That's a lot of stuff. No wonder it takes me so long to pack.

> If you have multiple camera batteries it's easy to confuse the fresh one from the spent ones. Put a rubber band around all of your camera batteries. When they are fresh, place it lengthwise. When they are used up, turn it sideways. That way you know which one is dead and which one is fresh. Also, if you have several batteries, get stick-on labels and number them sequentially.

NOW WE'RE READY TO SHOOT

Finally, everyone is on the set. What do you do now? The director and camera operator (could be you) must decide on camera angles and moves. These things should already be spelled out on storyboards or a shot list. The more you can do in advance of the day of the shoot, the better. It's time now to run your talent and crew through the shots. This is called "blocking" and will involve placing your talent on the set and doing final lighting adjustments.

Lighting and audio needs to be arranged with the talent and props in place. That's the only way to know if you are creating distracting shadows, if your subject is lit well, and if all the props needed are where they should be.

Good lighting will make a huge improvement in the look of your video so give it the attention it deserves. A lighting setup can be quick and simple or it can take hours. Know in advance what you want to do so that you don't waste time on the set figuring it out while people wait for you.

If you are shooting indoors and are not going for a dramatic look you'll want to light your set as evenly as possible. This means lighting it so that your talent can move around without causing the camera to change exposure radically. Those inexpensive work lights can do this. We use big fluorescent softboxes, which throw a lot of soft, broad light across a set. Putting two lights in front of your set at about 45 degrees on either side from center, pointing toward the center, will provide even lighting. The further from the set you place them, the more even the light will be. A back or hair light will help to separate the subject from the background.

Be sure to get any audio issues worked out before you start to record. See the following checklist for more tips on that.

> Try to avoid having your audio cables crossing or laying alongside electrical cables. This can induce a hum. If you are hearing a hum in your headphones, try moving audio cables away from other electrical devices. Lights, especially fluorescent lights, can also cause a buzz so check that out too.

Here is a checklist of things that are easy to miss, so before you call ACTION, go down this list:

- The camera lens is clean and free of lint or dust.
- The camera is in sharp focus.
- You have plenty of battery power and have backup batteries at the ready.

- You have a tape or a memory card with plenty of storage in the camera and cued up.
- The shot is properly framed.
- The exposure is what you want.
- You have properly adjusted the white balance.
- Both video and audio gain is turned off unless specifically needed.
- If you are hand-holding the camera, turn image stabilization on.
- The microphone is positioned, turned on, and connected to the camera.
- The camera has the mic input selected as the audio source. Sometimes it does this automatically; on some cameras it is a menu item setting.
- The microphone has a fresh battery (not all mics need batteries).
- Audio is manually adjusted to the proper level.
- If you are using a shotgun mic, make sure it isn't sticking into the frame.
- There is someone monitoring the sound through headphones.
- There are no buzzes in the audio.
- All lights are turned on and correctly positioned.
- There are no distracting background elements.
- All unnecessary noises (air conditioning, refrigerator, etc.) are silenced.
- If you are doing a pan or tilt, the tripod head is not locked.
- Your talent's hair and clothing look good and their face is not shiny.
- Make sure the tripod is steady. Use sandbags if necessary to stabilize it. Wind can really shake your tripod so be aware of that.
- Be sure to press RECORD (don't leave it in standby).

Some of these things sound obvious but I don't know a professional videographer who hasn't made most if not all of these oversights.

Also, while not absolutely necessary, it's a good idea to have your cameras connected to larger monitors. This allows you to see what is going on in the frame better than on the camera's tiny flip-out monitor or worse, a viewfinder. It is particularly helpful when you want several people to watch a review of a take with a critical eye.

ROLL CAMERA!

Shoot for a few seconds on every shot before you call ACTION. This gives you a "handle" for creating transitions in editing. Double check to make sure the RECORD light is blinking or it says RECORDING on your monitor or viewfinder before you call ACTION. Don't be too quick to cut when shooting interviews. I've also learned that in interviews if you leave the camera rolling after the subject thinks you're done you'll often get some of the best materials from them. Interviews are such an important subject in SIVs that we dedicated the entire next chapter to it. Be sure to read that.

DIRECTING NON-ACTORS

Don't expect non-actors to act. This includes most aspiring actors. The key to directing real people is to let things happen that you prepare for. Allowing them to say things in their own voice will sound more genuine than if you force them to read words they didn't write. A script should sound like talking to the viewer, not reading.

You will most likely have to shoot multiple takes of a scene. This happens when an actor flubs lines but is also a good idea anyway because shooting a scene multiple times from different angles gives the editor various shots to work with. Be careful to keep the audio levels the same each time.

I find that it helps to keep my camera at a distance. If I'm operating the camera I "hide" behind it so that the talent cannot see my eyes and are not distracted by looking at me instead of into the lens. I rarely look at the talent while we're recording. Sometimes I'll pretend that we're just rehearsing but will actually be recording. Once people find out that you have been shooting and they survived, they usually relax.

Wait a few seconds after the shot is finished, then call "CUT." If you are using a tape-less camera and have the time, review your take. I don't like to do this with tape cameras because of the possibility of damaging the tape, the danger of taping over part of a good take, or not aligning the next shot up so that you break continuity in your time code.

If you are happy with the take, then mark it off on your shot list or script and move on. If you aren't happy, then do it again until you are. Keep track of how many takes you shoot of each scene and if there were problems worth noting. If you make notes about which take you liked best it will make life much easier during the editing process.

Work your way down the script, shot list, and storyboard. Make copious notes of anything that will be helpful to the editor. If in doubt about any scene, shoot a "safety shot." A safety shot is basically shooting the scene again. It is not a bad idea to do this with every take. Sometimes the safety shot will save your bacon. If you have time, do several, changing the camera angle or zoom in or out. This will give you more to work with in post-production and will add visual interest.

BE KIND TO YOUR EDITOR

Look for any b-roll opportunities. B-roll is the cutaway of something relevant that the viewer sees while a narrator is talking. Think of what you're seeing on the news when the camera cuts away from the reporter. If they are on the scene of a house fire they show the house, the fire truck, firemen at work, neighbors, fire hoses, smoking embers, anything to visually tell the story besides looking at the reporter. Be alert to opportunities to get b-roll on your location. In an interview situation you might want some shots of the person's hands holding an item while he talks or shots around the set or location. Look for things that support the story. These can even be shot on a different day.

Editors love b-roll because it can cover a myriad of problems when you would otherwise have a bad shot or a jump cut. A jump cut is when the camera position stays the same but because of an edit decision the actor or action suddenly changes, or "jumps" in the frame. If you're going to cut to a new shot it should be different enough that it doesn't appear like you just sliced out a bit of film. Be nice to your editor and shoot lots of b-roll.

Editors will also thank you for giving them lots of "coverage." While b-roll can be anything the narrator is talking about, coverage generally will be a variety of shots taken on the set: medium, wide, and close-ups of the talent. I simplify this process by shooting with multiple cameras. I like to have a medium to wide shot on one camera and a much closer shot on another. I can cut back and forth for visual interest. Like b-roll, it helps cover mistakes or retakes when you have to cut to another angle. Be sure to get a wide or establishing shot to set the stage.

Be aware of continuity breaks when shooting coverage. Props shouldn't suddenly move around, clothing and lighting shouldn't change if it is supposed to be the same time and place, liquid in glasses should be the same level, etc. Even if you are picking up the scene the next day, you want to ensure continuity.

LISTEN THROUGH HEADPHONES

You may have to shoot in a noisy location. It could be traffic sounds, electrical equipment, wind, running water, ocean surf, cows mooing, dogs barking, babies crying, a rooster crowing … I've had all of those. Sometimes it can't be avoided. In this case you should record a couple of minutes of just the background sound so that you can put that in during editing to create continuity in your audio track. You don't want the background sounds to suddenly cut in and out so this track will cover editing breaks.

Tell everyone on your set to be quiet while you record the ambient sound of your location. You want *no* voices, only the sound of where you are. When shooting interiors we call this getting "room tone" and your editor will love you for it. It is especially important if you are using a voice-over narrator. Putting that room tone or ambient sound behind the narrator will greatly improve your audio continuity.

As I shared earlier about shooting the car detailing video in Chicago, we were pretty much right under the flight path of O'Hare International Airport. We were shooting outdoors so there was no way to get shots without the constant sound of jets overhead. My way of dealing with this was to shoot several dramatic scenes of the jets overhead for the opening, to establish the fact that we were under the flight path. Then the viewers accepted the jet sounds because of the location.

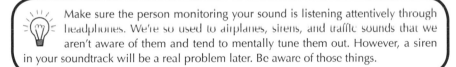

Make sure the person monitoring your sound is listening attentively through headphones. We're so used to airplanes, sirens, and traffic sounds that we aren't aware of them and tend to mentally tune them out. However, a siren in your soundtrack will be a real problem later. Be aware of those things.

TELEPROMPTERS

Once only found in professional studios, teleprompters continue to come down in price, making them affordable on even low budget productions. Shooting with a teleprompter can significantly increase your productivity if your talent is working from a script. It displays the script or notes on a reflecting glass in front of your camera's lens so that when someone is reading the script scrolling by, they are looking directly into the lens. The camera does not see the reflection. You can have the script scrolling at reading speed or it can just hold a still image such as bullet points. There are models now that work with cell phones and tablet devices. A teleprompter is ideal for when a narrator has to get through long stretches of narration.

WHEN TO STOP THE CAMERA

If someone on camera is having hair, makeup, or wardrobe problems, stop the camera and fix it. I used to be too timid to tell someone, especially someone like a CEO or a celebrity, that their hair looked bad or their face was shiny and needed makeup. Then I would beat myself up in post-production for not saying anything, but it's too late at that point. You're in charge, so just go ahead and fix what needs fixing. Everyone wants to look their best on-camera and it is your job to see that they do. They'll thank you for it later and you'll thank yourself. Just do it as soon as you notice. Once they get going it's a bigger interruption than doing it at the start so make that decision as early as possible.

SHOOTING FOR CHROMAKEY

The software has become widely available to do what your local weatherman does on TV when he's standing in front of the weather map: you can put yourself in into any environment you want. This is a post-production process known as chromakey compositing. You often hear this technique referred to as green screen or blue screen. The object is to shoot your subject in front of a solid color that is so different from anything else in the shot so that you can select that color in editing and make it transparent without affecting the talent or props. That way another background can replace it.

While the background you can shoot against can be virtually any color, a brilliant green or blue color is often used as the backdrop because they don't occur that often in clothing or skin tones. Blue can cause problems with blue eyes so a particularly brilliant shade of green has become more common. You have to be sure no clothing is similar to this color or it may disappear, too!

Most editing software today can do this, some much better than others. The trick to getting a good result is to light the background as evenly as possible at about the same intensity or a little brighter than the subject. Soft, broad light sources work well for this type of lighting, like those work lights we talked about, or softboxes. You would typically place a light to either side of the backdrop at approximately the same height and angle to get even lighting across the entire backdrop.

Keep your talent far enough in front of the backdrop that they don't throw a shadow on it. This also keeps the green screen or background color from "splashing" back on them. Be aware of wrinkles or spots on the backdrop. The smoother and more even it is, the better it will "key out."

 Don't happen to have a chromakey background on an outdoor shoot? If it is a cloudless sky, you can shoot up and use the blue sky as a background. Or if you have a solid color wall handy, use that.

You can replace the keyed out background with anything you want. It doesn't have to be a video clip background, either. I've used this to place solid white or black backgrounds behind people being interviewed. That's a nice effect.

Thanks to the rapid improvement in chromakeying software, what used to be an expensive and challenging technique is now easy and commonplace. It can look cheesy if you don't take into consideration things like the lighting on the subject and the light on the substituted background. For example, it won't look right if your background is a warm tropical sunset but your talent is in bright white light with the direction of the light all wrong.

WHY YOU WANT TO SLATE YOUR SHOTS

In feature film production they use a clapboard, also called a clapperboard or slate, to identify information about a shot at the beginning of a scene. You've probably seen this. This is to indicate to the editor where the shots go in the film and which take it is, i.e., Scene 4, Take 7, etc. Otherwise the editor would have no idea where in the film the clips should go. Other information such as the name of the film, date, director's name, and camera angle are often included. The clap sound is also used to sync the audio to the film. With camcorders the audio sync function isn't so necessary but in film production the sound is recorded separately from the camera and must by synced up later. The visual image and sound of the clap make this easy.

You don't need a clapboard for some SIV formats, such as seminar recordings, but it can be very helpful if you are shooting a lot of different scenes, angles, and takes. It is essential if you are handing your footage off to someone else to edit who knows nothing about the intended sequence of your video.

When we shot the 42 videos in our fitness series, a slate was a huge help in editing because the beginning of each video looked similar. The slates gave visual confirmation that we were working on the correct day in the sequence. It also made it easier to keep track of which take we preferred.

Wooden clapboards can be found for under $10 while electronic ones that display timecode cost over $1,000. Acrylic dry erase versions are popular and affordable. We often simply use a small whiteboard with a marker pen. That works fine. It doesn't have to be fancy, you can even use a pad of paper. You can get a fantastic clapboard app for the iPad or iPhone for $25. My sound guy keeps a palm-sized acrylic slate and marker pen in his camera bag and it has proven handy many times.

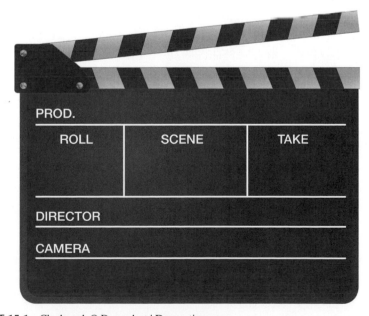

FIGURE 15.1 Clapboard. © Dogandcat I Dreamstime.com

REVIEW YOUR DAILIES

At the end of the day (or each scene) it is typical for the director and camera operator to review the shots, called dailies. If anything needs to be shot over, it's better to know about it now rather than later. If you are working from tape, I recommend that you go ahead and capture your tape to a hard drive while you are reviewing it if possible, just to eliminate unnecessary winding and rewinding of delicate tape. Never reuse tape. Tape is cheap so always record on fresh, unused tape.

If you are recording to tape be sure to push the little "write protect" switch on the cassette at the end of shooting, label the tape, and store it someplace safe. Always handle tape carefully. Keep it away from magnets, heat, and moisture.

If you are recording to a memory card you may need to move your files to a hard drive at the end of the day so that you can clear your card for the next day's shoot. Make sure you review the files before you reformat the card, just to make sure they transferred correctly. That's the weak point in shooting to flash memory—there's nothing to go back to if your files get erased or corrupted. I back up my backups. I'm fanatical about that.

One thing you can count on is that not everything will go according to plan. It may rain or be windy, you'll have a camera failure, you'll run out of tape or batteries, a light will blow a bulb in the middle of a shot, an actor will be late. It's always something. Be sure to allow some slack time for such events.

Before everyone leaves the set or location, make sure all cast and crew have call sheets and are informed about shooting times and locations the next day.

At the end of the day be sure to also charge up all of your rechargeable batteries and replace any non-rechargeable batteries with fresh ones.

Action Steps

- Review your script and shot lists to make sure you are keeping it simple and to the point, and making the shots appropriate for your audience.
- The three best ingredients for a professional production are:
  - A Good Script—Have a solid shooting script written before you turn on the camera. Make sure your cast and crew know what they will be shooting beforehand.
  - Good Audio—Ensure you have everything on hand so that you get the highest quality audio.
  - Good Lighting—Be aware of the available light and have additional lighting on hand if needed.
- Have the set ready for the cast and crew.
- Make sure everyone received a call list and knows their call time.
- Have plenty of nutritious food and beverages on hand.
- Follow the checklists provided to prepare for shooting.
- Mark off shots on your script or shot list as you go.
- Look for b-roll opportunities.
- Record ambient audio and room tone.
- Have wardrobe backups.
- Have makeup on hand and know how to apply it.
- Carefully store tapes at the end of each day.
- Check digital files before reformatting memory cards.
- Recharge batteries at the end of the day.
- Allow time for the unexpected.

Shooting an Interview

A common component of special interest videos is interviews. These can be shot in a home or hotel, in a studio or in the field. They usually have their share of challenges but with some experience and preparation you should be able to get a good interview.

For example, we had arranged to shoot a series of interviews in Venice Beach, California. I was concerned when I saw the tiny size of the room and the fact that the walls were bright orange. Cars kept driving up right outside the room, slamming doors or leaving their motors running.

However, we did have some nice sidelight coming in through the window and by carefully positioning and framing the interviewee we were able to throw the orange wall out of focus. It actually looked like a seamless backdrop and worked out great. We did have to stop several times during the shooting session to wait for the car noise to go away, but we managed to shoot a dozen short interviews within the space of an hour. You can't give up in situations like this, you just make the best of a situation and sometimes, you'll surprise yourself.

Following are some guidelines for shooting interviews. Thanks go to my friend Ron Dexter for sharing some of his personal tips with us.

MAKE THE INTERVIEWEE COMFORTABLE

Few people are comfortable with a boom microphone dangling over their head, lights in their eyes, a camera in their face, and an interviewer asking embarrassing or dumb questions. The trick is to turn an informal chat into an informative interview.

Your first order of business is to have your camera, sound, and lighting all ready before the interviewee arrives. Keep the situation appearing casual but as much under control as possible, even if you're having technical difficulties. Don't let it show if you are nervous.

GETTING ACQUAINTED

Perfect lighting, a great background, good sound and camera work is nothing if the interviewee is not at ease. An ideal situation is if an assistant can bring the interviewee into the interview room with makeup and wardrobe adjustments already done. Take any name tags off and be sure there is no noisy jewelry near the lavalier mic. Be particularly mindful of noisy necklaces or dangly earrings on women.

Be ready to explain how the video will be used. Being part of "the event" is much better than seeming to be making a documentary for some unknown and possibly negative purpose. Avoid making commitments about editorial control by the interviewee.

As the interviewee sits, keep the chatter going with non-interview "getting to know you" questions while you, the camera operator or coordinator attaches the lavalier mic to the person. If you are the interviewer and have someone else running the camera, it's best if that person does not get acquainted with the interviewee. It keeps the interviewee's attention on the interviewer. You want the camera operator to "disappear" behind the camera.

We have found the interviewer–interviewee distance of about seven feet ideal. It's intimate but not threatening.

INTERVIEW QUESTIONS

Write down the questions you want to ask in advance. You might want to give the interviewee an idea of what you'll be asking, but don't give him the exact questions. Some inexperienced guests will try to memorize their answers, which will then sound canned. Let them be spontaneous.

During the interview you'll want to keep this list of interview questions handy so that you can make sure you cover everything you need to cover. If they or you are nervous, it's easy to lose focus. They may be thinking ahead to what they want to say and miss a key point. The same can happen to you: you may miss asking them something important.

If you find they are stumbling, it's OK to have them start over unless this is a live interview. It's in their best interest to deliver their "lines" well and they'll thank you for it when they see how good you made them look on camera, even if they seem a bit impatient at the time.

The ideal question is one that requires the interviewee to repeat the question or at least give a complete answer not requiring the question to be included. Sometimes "how about XXX" is enough. The interviewee then will have to explain in their own words what you are talking about. "What did you think about the current national elections?" would elicit a better answer than "Did you think the recent election was a fraud?" You want to avoid questions that can be answered with a "yes" or "no."

Asking questions that start with what, how, who, when, where, and why are good conversation starters. These types of questions elicit detailed answers.

THE INTERVIEWEE'S CHAIR

Consider the interviewee's posture and what you want it to be. Is it comfortable and relaxed, authoritative, or in the "hot seat?" A deep comfortable chair may relax the interviewee too much and limit their body language. Couches often block much of the background and are usually too comfortable. People can sink into overly soft couches and chairs. An armless chair may tire people for a long interview. A swivel office chair allows them to swing around and has a greater chance of creaking and changing your lighting.

The chair should also "belong" in the situation it is in. Your audience shouldn't notice the chair unless it is an important prop. The best chair is one that is quiet, comfortable, dark colored, and appropriate to the location. What seat would be appropriate in the woods—a log, a stump, or a rock? If you never see the seat, it makes no difference. The interviewer, camera operator, and other crew present also need quiet chairs.

Our favorite is a lightweight, padded backless stool that folds flat. It makes people sit up and they don't spin around in it. We always take it with us on interviews. We've had a lot of famous behinds on that stool.

When people stand, they tend to preach. When they sit, they are more friendly. Of course, you need to make the decision of how this interview's look will fit into your final program. Remember, you are the director!

WARDROBE

Just as with your on-camera talent, what your interviewee wears is also important. If possible, give them advance information about what to wear and more specifically, what not to wear. Neutral colors are best. Light clothing on dark complexions should be avoided. A white shirt under a darker jacket is OK but a light blue shirt is preferable. Avoid anything with sparkles or sequins. As I shared previously, video cameras have problems with saturated reds, thin stripes, and small patterns, but we often have to live with such problems to avoid making a big issue of it if the person shows up wearing such a clothing item. I know videographers who keep a selection of neutral colored shirts in their studio in case people show up wearing taboo clothing colors.

SETTING UP THE SIDE-BY-SIDE INTERVIEW

In a two person side-by-side interview, attach the mics as far apart from each other as possible, but close to the mouth. This reduces echo if the two mics are mixed together. Later the audio tracks can be mixed separately. In an emergency, if you have only one lavalier, attach the mic high on the shoulder of the person with the softest voice, on the side toward the other person. If using a shotgun mic, put it on a mic stand and aim it between them if you don't have a boom operator.

Put the lighter complexion person farther from the light source. (Do this as they sit down.) If shooting a dark skinned person you may need to add light or adjust exposure for good skin tone and detail. If one person is taller and might block light on a shorter person, place the taller one farther from the light.

AUDIO CONSIDERATIONS

Before the shoot, make signs that say "QUIET PLEASE, SOUND RECORDING." Put these signs on doors to not open, toilets to not flush, etc. Have signs made for the interview room door that says "Recording in progress. Please do not enter." Unplug the refrigerator (put a large sign on it to turn it back on and don't open often while it is off). Bring tape and sign posts if necessary.

Be still and listen to the room. Is there an air-conditioner vent nearby? Is there traffic noise coming through a window?

A big empty sounding room can be a problem. Clap your hands to check for bad echoes. If the location is good for everything but echoes, putting the mic close helps, but consider adding things that help reduce the echo. In studios they use sound blankets. Moving blankets work almost as well. I buy them from my local moving company for $15.

If you are using a shotgun mic on a boom, be aware of what is behind the interviewee. It's usually better to aim it down at the subject rather than up at them. Aiming at the ceiling can create a hollow sound. If the interview room has bare wooden or concrete floors, putting rugs or blankets on the floor around the interviewee can improve the sound. It also reduces noise your interviewee may make if they shuffle their feet.

Sometimes air-conditioning controls are not convenient or can be locked up. Tungsten video lights make a room much hotter and can trigger the air conditioner to come on. A wet napkin over a locked and covered air-conditioning control will fool it. (Make sure you take it off when you leave!)

When people are nervous they can get a dry mouth. This will show up in audio, so have bottled water for both the interviewer and interviewee.

LIGHTING

Some meeting rooms already have adequate lighting levels but it is from mixed light sources. If possible, bring your own lighting to either supplement or replace existing light. Don't forget to white balance your camera to the key light source.

If you are using window light and the interview is long, the angle of the light will change. It may get too harsh or disappear altogether. If you are cutting the interview up and skipping or rearranging segments this will be particularly apparent. Anticipate such problems.

Large picture windows with bright backgrounds are tempting to use but can be very difficult to work with. If you don't add fill light your subject will be a silhouette against the bright background. If you expose for your subject the background will be overexposed or as we say in photography, "burned out." The only way to save a shot like this is to add a lot of fill light on your subject, but beware of reflections in the glass. A better idea would be to reverse the setup, putting the camera operator's back to the window and let the light fall on the face of the subject like I show you in Figure 16.1.

Trying to balance indoor lighting with daylight is challenging. In these situations you have to match the color temperature (white balance) of your artificial light source to daylight. The new daylight balanced fluorescent lights help a lot in these situations. If you are using tungsten lights then you'll want to place a blue gel, known as CTB (color temperature blue), in front of the light source to bring its color temperature close to that of the daylight. You can buy these gels in different sizes and grades of blue, depending on the amount of correction you need to do. It's a good idea to keep some of these gels with your lighting gear if you're using tungsten lights. You can buy them from many sources online. Do a search on "CTB color correction gel."

WATCH YOUR BACKGROUND

Here is where a lot of looking will pay off. When selecting backgrounds, consider where the camera will go and if the interviewee will have decent lighting *and* good sound. To be

FIGURE 16.1   Example of how changing your camera position improves lighting on your subject.

safe. I often bring along a portable photographer's backdrop. You can find a good selection at www.backdropoutlet.com, www.cowboystudio.com, www.dennymfg.com, or just search online for "photographer backdrops." Dark to medium gray is a good choice. If you order from a backdrop outlet they will also sell portable stands to hang them from. Don't forget things when you leave.

FRAMING

Staying on the same shot, like a medium shot, of even the most interesting person soon gets boring. If a person is using their hands to communicate, include them, they help tell the story. During more intense or intimate times, slowly zoom in for a dramatic effect.

We often use two cameras on the interviewee, one set to a medium tight head and shoulders frame. We have another right beside it that we can zoom in and out with to get varying tighter shots or a cutaway of hands. We set exposure and white balance carefully to match and this gives the editor much more variety to work with. A third camera off to the side gives your editor lots of choices to keep things interesting.

Frequently you see the shot framed so that the interviewee is looking not at the viewer but off axis, at the interviewer who is out of the frame. In this case there should be more space in the frame in front of the interviewee's face than behind their head, otherwise they will look cramped and claustrophobic. In other words, they should be looking out of the frame with more room in front. You can do this type of shot even if there is no interviewer. This happens when you are both interviewer and camera operator. Tell the interviewee to look at a spot on the wall and act as if there is a person there.

For close-ups, putting the person's nose in the center of the frame works. If you zoom out, change your frame so that you are placing some room (not too much though) above their head and keeping more room in front of the person's head than behind. I like to use about 1/8 to 1/10 of the frame for head room. Be sure you know if your viewfinder is revealing the whole shot.

If available, have a stand-in sit in the interview chair before you start so that everything (chair, background, lights, etc.) is set up and positioned as you want before the interviewee shows up.

 Tape over or turn off the "record" light on the camera. That red light can make people nervous. A little piece of gaffer's tape works great.

WHEN THE INTERVIEWER ISN'T ON-CAMERA

Here is a common scenario: you are the camera operator and the interviewer, so you can't be on camera during the shoot. If you want to show yourself conducting the interview, frame the interviewee fairly close, like head and shoulders. Here is where having a portable backdrop is ideal. Have them direct their answers just off camera, as if you were sitting there interviewing them.

Even though you are not on camera, record your audio so that you know exactly how you asked the questions. You'll want to know this later because you are going to set up a shot that looks like you are in the same room during the interview. It can be a different day and different place, but should look reasonably similar. Using that same portable backdrop will make this possible.

You will ask your questions on camera and edit them in with their responses. Try to shoot thoughtful expressions of the interviewee listening to your questions. When you shoot yourself, be sure to get reaction shots to use as you listen to their answers.

When you do similar lighting this should edit together to make a believable interview situation.

GET A RELEASE

Be sure to get a signed release before the interviewee leaves. Granting an interview is an implied consent, but one on paper is insurance.

WHEN THINGS GO WRONG

If during an interview the sound or lighting goes bad for some reason tell the interviewee that you (not the interviewee) have a problem and stop to correct it.

If the interview is interrupted, the camera operator should remember when the problem occurred so the interviewer can repeat the question. Writing down the words will help.

Action Steps

- Make the interviewee comfortable.
- Check the room for unwanted sounds and do your best to control them. If necessary, make and post signs stating "Recording in progress."
- Choose the interviewee's chair with consideration about how you want them to look.

- Let your subjects know in advance what colors are best and which should be avoided.
- Choose your background carefully. Set up a backdrop if you have one available and it's needed.
- Have the interviewer or another person chat with the interviewee in advance to relax them.
- Be prepared with your questions. Don't ask questions that can be answered with a "Yes" or "No."
- If things are going wrong, stop the camera and fix it.

Chapter 17

Shooting a Stage Presentation

Chapter Objectives

- Discover how easy it is to turn a presentation into a video for sale.
- Learn why you want to consider investing in a videographer.
- Understand what you need if you aren't going to be using a professional videographer.
- Learn how to deal with lighting and audio challenges unique to live presentations.
- Discover why you may want to look into live-streaming your event.

If you are a speaker or presenter, you have the perfect venue for a special interest video: shoot your presentation and then produce and sell the videos. The people in your audience have likely traveled quite some distance and spent a lot of money to attend. Why not let others get the same information for less cost and trouble by purchasing a video of your presentation? You'll also find that audience members will want to purchase a copy. Have an order form ready so they can purchase it the day of the presentation. You can send it to them later.

This is one of the simplest and most efficient types of SIV to produce but you still want to make it look and sound as good as possible. Because your video's viewers know that you are filming a live event they will excuse the audience rustling, coughing, etc. What they won't tolerate is if the audio is *really* bad and they can't hear you! Also if the lighting is poor, the camera movements are shaky, and the video quality marginal, your viewers will wonder if this is a reflection on the quality of the content you're delivering. The higher the price you are asking, the higher the expectations will be for a quality video.

That is why we stress aiming for the best quality possible. The great thing about these types of videos is that they don't require a lot of bells and whistles so your budget can be focused on basic production.

If you decide to hire a videographer, ideally, you want to hire a professional who has experience shooting live events. It's even better if you can get one who shoots with more than one camera and has at their disposal a video switcher. A switcher (or video mixer) is a device used to select between several different video cameras and then composite the footage together to create one video. While switchers can also be used to add transitions and special effects, using a switcher at an event with more than one camera basically gives you a finished product at the end of your presentation. You can even have the signal fed into a DVD recorder so that you are creating a DVD as you go. Although this type of set up is usually more expensive, you will save on the back end in reduced editing time and expenses. You will be able to deliver the finished video much sooner.

One caveat with using a switcher, though—since the footage will already be mixed onto one track, you can't change your mind later and choose a different camera angle during the editing process.

The other reason to hire a videographer is they will be able to deal with audio and will most likely bring in additional light sources if needed. You will not just want to use the microphone you will use during your presentation, you also should get a separate audio feed directly to a camera so that you will have cleaner sound. This will most likely be a wireless lavalier mic.

While having a single camera shoot is the least expensive, having additional cameras can give your video a higher production value. One camera can get another angle of you speaking, can capture any PowerPoint slides you may be showing, get audience reactions and cutaway shots, all of which is much more interesting and informative than watching you pace back and forth on stage.

If you aren't hiring a professional and want to do it on your own then I advise you to invest in a decent low light camera, a good wireless microphone, and a good external light or two.

Although turning off the lights helps your audience see your PowerPoint presentation better, unless you keep a light pointed on you, you are going to be disappointed in how you look.

A common challenging audio situation with seminar presentations is how to record questions from the audience. Since the mic will be on the presenter, it is difficult to hear an audience question. The best way to deal with this is to have the speaker repeat the question or comment. If you're not the one presenting, remind your presenter to repeat the audience member's question. You might even tape up a sign to remind him to "Repeat the Question."

If you are prepared you might have a hand-held wireless mic that can be passed around the audience. You just have to have someone to handle it for you and turn it off when not needed. Also remind the audience member to hold it close enough to their mouth.

If your presenter fails to repeat the question, try to remind them to do so. I shot a workshop presentation recently with this exact situation and the audience was constantly interrupting the speaker with questions. At the time I knew I should remind her to repeat the questions but to my chagrin I let it slide. Now I'm kicking myself for not speaking up and telling her to do so. This is one of those situations where it is better to interrupt and say something than regret it forever later.

Make sure you have permission to shoot your event. Some events and venues have restrictions against this and it's best to know that up front, especially if you plan on hiring a professional videographer. Also if you are using music, video, and images in your presentation make sure you have permission to use them in a video. If you are getting reaction shots, make sure the audience members have given their written approval. (Refer to Chapter 12.)

If the logistics at the event will preclude shooting it, consider setting up a staged presentation where you invite an audience and you are able to *totally* control your audio, the light on you and the audience, where you can stop and start over, get unique camera angles without being concerned that the camera operator will block a paid audience member.

LIVE-STREAM YOUR EVENT

Another option is to live-stream your event. By making your presentation available as a live-stream you can sell internet access to your event as it happens. The biggest concern is getting a good internet connection on your end. There are several software platforms that allow you to live-stream events. Search on "live-stream provider" and you'll find plenty.

Live-streaming could be another way to increase the income from your event.

Action Steps

- Strongly consider hiring a professional videographer to record the presentation. Make sure this person or company has live event videography experience. Call a few companies and get quotes before you commit.
- Use a good low light camera, wireless lavalier mic, and bring lighting if you're not hiring a videographer.
- If you or the presenter will be answering audience questions, remember to repeat the question before answering it. If you have one available and are able to do this, pass a hand-held mic to the questioner.
- Get the proper permissions to shoot at the event, from the audience, and for the usage of any music, video, or images you use in your presentation.
- Consider setting up a staged presentation where you can control the production.
- Consider offering this program as a live stream and look into the logistics of doing so.

Chapter 18

Producing Videos Without a Camera

Chapter Objectives

- Learn the software applications available to make videos without a camera.
- Understand how people are using them to make videos they then sell.

So what if you don't want to be the camera operator, editor, audio person or grip *and* you don't want to work with a videographer or partner? No problem—you can still be a video producer without even turning a camera on. With nothing more than a reliable internet connection, you can create all kinds of marketable educational and how-to videos using video screen capture software.

This software makes what are called video screencasts. I've also heard them called video screen captures. A screencast is simply a recorded movie of your computer monitor while you are doing various actions, such as you moving your mouse across the screen as you demonstrate something, showing a PowerPoint presentation, clicking on desktop icons, typing text, opening web pages, etc. You can also record a narration as you do this.

For example, if you wanted to demonstrate how to do a simple computer function you would start up this software, click the record button, then every keystroke and movement you make will be recorded. If your computer has a microphone, what you are saying is recorded as well. It basically turns your computer into a camera that is recording itself.

The more advanced programs allow you to add in supplemental video as well as slide presentations, highlight areas of the screen, draw on the screen, zoom in and zoom out, all recorded as you are doing it. After you stop recording you will have a file that you can further edit or upload to a server. Some of the most robust systems even have fairly advanced editing tools so you can do a lot of embellishments afterwards.

 One thing I have found very helpful in making effective screen capture videos is to get a program that highlights your cursor/pointer so that it is easy for the viewer to follow your actions. I use a program that puts a big red circle around my cursor.

One of the attractive benefits of creating screencasts is that you can create videos very fast this way. You can turn on the record function, run through the program or exercise that you are demonstrating, and you are done!

WHAT YOU CAN "SHOOT" TO SELL

Because they can help demonstrate and teach the use of software features, you see many software developers use screencasts to show off their work. But many others have found this software to be an incredible communication tool as well and have learned to expand on it to monetize these types of videos.

Because this technology involves the computer, how-to and educational videos are well suited for it. You can also turn PowerPoint slide presentations into salable products. Online courses are also perfect for this type of technology.

It's an additional tool to use, even if you are just planning on shooting your video mostly with a camera. When we shot our video on *Make Money Selling Your Own Videos*, I wanted to show the viewer how to use Google to do research. I used a program called Snapz Pro X and was able to walk the viewer through the keyboard steps as I did it. This was combined with footage of me on camera.

When new computer technology comes out many people are searching for tutorials on how to use it. While these aren't evergreen topics and go out of date quickly, they can be a way to turn what you know about this new technology into profits very fast. I've seen screen capture videos like these selling for just a few dollars up to $20 or more. You can do a screen movie and have it for sale within hours. Even though there are a lot of free screen-cast videos available we've found that there is still a market for solid, trustworthy information that will help people solve a problem.

Since these videos are created on a computer, they are easily put online. They are very popular within protected membership and coaching sites. This is what internet marketing coach, Gail Bottomley, (next page) is doing with great success.

PROGRAMS AVAILABLE

I won't be going into too much detail on the specifics of all the different software programs available since the technology is constantly being updated and changing. You may visit www.shoot-to-sell.com for the latest resources.

At this time the software leader in this field on the PC is Camtasia. My favorite on the Mac is ScreenFlow. These programs are not free but if you do an online search for free screen capture programs you will find a number of them.

We use ScreenFlow and really like it. It's easy to learn and there's a lot of great functionality. Camtasia is also highly regarded and if you were to do a poll among users, you would probably find them neck and neck. Less expensive Mac options are ScreenRecord Studio, Voila, and Snapz Pro X. For the PC, there's Debut Video Capture and Snagit. Before you buy, make sure they give you what you need. Some of them lack video editing capabilities.

Free Programs

At present there are a few free open source programs available that would allow you to experience just how this tool might work for you. Most of the paid versions also have a free trial period.

Gail Bottomley, Founder of www.gailbottomley.com and www.immacademy.com

We met Gail and her husband Gary a few years ago at the pool of a hotel in Fort Lauderdale, a few nights before we were headed to the Caribbean on a marketers cruise. Spying our conspicuous button designating that we were one of the 400 or so marketers on the cruise, Gail came up to us with a hearty, "G'day!" It was obvious they had traveled a long distance, from New Zealand as a matter of fact. It was also not long before we got to talking internet marketing and we discovered how successful she was. A big part of her business was teaching others how easy it was to set up websites and get into internet marketing and producing videos was a strong component of her business.

Gail started making web videos around 2004 or 2005, when YouTube came on the scene.

At that time I was actually part of a network marketing company and I tried to figure out how on earth I could tell people about, the different products that I was selling. And so I thought the best way would be to just do videos.

So she did all sorts of videos, but a few in particular did very well.

I did one for a product that a horse could eat. I got a friend who had a horse and had her feed the horse the product on a sandwich and that was really funny! It got so many views, which was excellent. I actually drove so much traffic to my main website from all the videos I was making and I was able to sell a lot of products and get a lot of interest from them. So I decided then that video is the way to go.

Although Gail has done a lot of videos in her home studio, she confessed,

To be honest, for me the screencast movie is the easiest to do because I don't have to set anything up. Right now my lights are sitting in a wardrobe. And so, it's just a whole lot easier for me. I think, "Oh, oh, that's a good idea." And I can sit down and do a screencast and have it up on YouTube, all done within 30 minutes or even less. And because my main niche is within internet marketing, it's also a lot easier for me to show people what I'm talking about rather than just talking about it.

Gail has a high level mentoring course on setting up membership sites where most of the videos she needs to show are of the "back office" of all the different memberships sites and they are all screencast movies.

I teach people how to put a video up on their website, how to add things to their website, all that sort of stuff, show them how to do a screencast video as well with just using the programs like Camtasia and Cam Studio and Movie Maker.

And so you really do need to be using screencast for those. I would say that 96 percent of my videos are screencast videos. I have about 260 on my YouTube channel but I also have hundreds that are all part of membership sites that we have. I use PowerPoint and a screencast movie program called Camtasia, which is such an easy program to use. I used to use Cam Studio, which is still around. It's nowhere near as sophisticated as what we have available now.

She also sells the screencast movies that she makes on DVD as well.

Camtasia is really good because you can set each video up as a chapter on a DVD. So if you've got a series of steps, like Step 1, Step 2, Step 3, Step 4, you can go from one thing to the next and to the next. Now, not everyone wants to send out a DVD but there are companies like Kunaki where you just load your video up there and they'll print it and send it out for you.

Gail also works with webinar software to create movies she sells.

What I've done many, many times is I've held a webinar that was an hour and a half long. Then I take that webinar and split it up to make 4 or 5 more videos out of it. Then the next week I'll present another webinar. And before you know it, I've got a series of videos done!

If you have a product that's online, then screencast is certainly the way to go and it's just so much easier and so much more informative than just talking about it. Much easier to show I believe and people like to be shown how to do something. I think we learn quicker that way. So that's one of the main reasons that I've been doing the screencasts. And of course, when I first started, I didn't use screencast because I didn't know that Camtasia was as good in those days as it is now.

But the other thing I do with videos is I get them transcribed. So not only do I have a video, but now I've got a book or a PDF that people can download as well with all the information in that. The other thing I do is strip off the audio as well. So then I actually have three products. That's what I love about video; you can create three products and it might have taken you 10 minutes!

Her advice to get started with video?

Use whatever you're comfortable with to create your videos. It's more important to get comfortable and get it up there. I have a friend who did 75 takes on a two-minute video because she's a perfectionist. That's crazy. Just get it out there!

You don't have to be perfect. As long as you've got a really good message and really good information. In fact, one of the biggest, most viewed videos I've seen is a white screen and the guy's typing on this flipping notepad as he's talking. It's not all about being perfect, it's about really giving good content.

It's an amazing way to get your information out because people love video. I mean let's face it. How many hours a day do people spend watching T.V.?

And this is just another form of T.V. really isn't it?

You can hear more of that interview at www.shoot-to-sell.com.

Two popular open source programs are CamStudio (www.camstudio.org) and Jing (www.jing.com). CamStudio is just for PCs. Jing can be used on Macs or PCs. There is a paid version of Jing called JingPro.

Because Jing and CamStudio are free, there are some huge limitations. Both only save the video as SWF files, which only play with Flash players. At this time, many smartphones and some computers (Apple products) aren't able to view Flash videos without plugins so the better method of saving them is as MPEG-4 videos, which you can do in JingPro and Camtasia.

The other really big problem with using Jing for making a video to sell is that you can only record five minutes of video at a time. What Jing is really good for is working with others at far-flung locations, such as partners and off-site editors. As a work around, you could make your videos into five minute or shorter segments, then use an editing system to string them together; but doing so adds more time and, of course, time equals money. There is also no email or telephone support for these free products and as open source programs, there may also be stability issues.

Due to these limitations, if you decide that screencast movies are something you want to make I suggest you invest in one of the paid screen capture programs such as Camtasia (PC and Mac) or Screenflow (Mac only). They are reasonably priced between $30 and $99.

Problems with Screen Capture Videos

Although it is getting better, a common problem with screen capture video is the action is jumpy and doesn't flow smoothly. This is due to low frame rate. Many PCs on which screen capture movies are made are not fast enough to play videos and capture them at the same time at the higher frame rate, such as 30 frames a second (the speed at which a video ordinarily runs). Now it may not be a problem or issue for you, but if you are going to mix it in with other footage you've shot, you may not like the quality.

Webinars

Webinars are another way you can make video information products without a camera. The term webinar is short for web-based seminar and like the name implies is a presentation, lecture, workshop, or seminar that is transmitted over the web to distant locations. Large groups of people can attend simultaneously as long as they have an internet connection and a password. The program may include screencast videos and PowerPoint presentations as well as other video. Webinar software also allows your viewers to interact with you (the moderator) either by telephone, typing in a text box (live chat), or both. The moderator can also share links in the live chat box.

GoToWebinar (www.gotowebinar.com) is a source we recommend although there are other services available at varying price points. The price depends on several factors, one being how many participants you have on the conference. While many people use these programs for live-streaming programs, you can also record your webinar to share it with others later, either free or for a fee. Free webinars have become one of the biggest and most profitable marketing strategies today but you can also offer them for sale as well.

> Gail shared one of her strategies with us during our interview. She will put on a 90–120-minute free webinar as a list-building strategy, record it, then cut it up into three or four sections, convert them into MPEG-4s, and then "drip" them weekly in her paid membership program. That way, she can create content for her members very quickly and efficiently.

The biggest challenge with webinars and screencasts is audio. GoToWebinar supports only one audio channel, so if you are doing screencast tutorials about audio topics, this format would be a challenge.

Other Video Web Applications

There are also web applications that produce trailer-type videos from photos, video clips, and music. While you may not have much success selling these styles of videos (I have heard of people doing this to varying degrees of success), using this type of software lends itself more to producing promotional and marketing videos.

The application we like and recommend is Animoto (www.animoto.com). They employ an easy to use system where they take your images and videos, lay them over a bed of music you provide or choose from their music selections, then run it through a process that creates a video out of all these pieces that is similar to a movie trailer. You can make an unlimited number of 30-second videos for free. The paid version allows you to make longer movies. If you do a web search you'll find many other similar applications available. Look for "slideshow software." Some of these sites let you make videos and then sell streaming versions through their site.

FINAL THOUGHTS ABOUT SCREENCASTS

Make sure that your audio recording capability, whether that is your computer's mic or an external mic, is of good quality. Even more than regular video, screencasts require good audio and a good voice-over for maximum impact. If you do not have a good speaking voice you may want to hire a voice actor to record your narration.

Because of the ease of making these types of programs, there is increasing competition in many obvious applications like software tutoring, so research your topic like we've previously covered before investing too much time in a project. Then find your market niche and promote aggressively.

Also with screen capture videos and webinars, you still need to make sure you have the appropriate permissions and are not violating anyone's copyright.

Even if you are doing a screen capture demonstration of a process you are familiar with, it helps to have a brief script or outline in front of you so you don't miss any key points.

Action Steps

- Download Jing or CamStudio and see how you might be able to use this software in creating your video information product.
- If you decide you want to produce screencast movies, sign up for the trial versions and see what software works best for you.
- Research the possibility of offering recorded webinars, live and for sale.
- Go to Animoto and see what types of videos you can create there.

Chapter 19

Post-Production

Chapter Objectives

- Learn which activities are covered under post-production.
- Understand the importance of organization and taking notes during production.
- Learn what to do—and not to do—to keep your program from looking amateurish.
- Learn how to stay out of legal trouble by respecting copyrights.
- Decide how you will deliver your final video and learn what formats you will export it to based on that decision.
- Learn what goes into DVD packaging and the types of duplicating options available to you.

Post-production is where you finally assemble all of the pieces that you so carefully planned and shot. It includes all of the functions that occur after shooting is finished, including video editing, special effects, sound effects, creating a musical soundtrack, graphics, color correction, creating a master, preparing it for online distribution or, in the case of DVDs, authoring the DVD.

Today's amazing editing software gives a person the power to do every step of post-production on a single computer—editing, graphics, titles, special effects, mixing the musical soundtrack, sweetening the audio with sound effects, color correcting, and more. Whereas post-production used to take a team of artists and could last longer than production, in today's budget-conscious post-production environment you may be the entire team.

Teaching in-depth film editing techniques is beyond the scope of this book although I will cover some basics. Many of the technical points of editing are covered in video tutorials which you can view online (these are SIVs!). If you are editing with Adobe Premiere Pro or using Adobe After Effects you can find many fine tutorials for free at tv.adobe.com. If you are editing on Apple's Final Cut Pro system or Adobe Premiere Pro you should visit www.larryjordan.biz or www.rippletraining.com. There are tutorials for both PC and Mac platforms at www.lynda.com. Just do a web search for the topic you wish to learn about.

While our SIVs have less lofty artistic goals than feature films, editing is still a crucial phase of production. Post-production can make or break a film or video. A cut at the right moment can startle, thrill, or distress the viewer. A cut at the wrong moment can drain the power from a scene. Good editing doesn't draw attention to itself. You, the viewer, just get so caught up in the program that you are "in it." Bad editing makes this experience difficult. Just keep in mind that as we've said many times already, time is money, so don't let editing be a barrier to finishing your video. If you aren't familiar with editing or you don't feel your skills are up to the job, this is the time to hire a good editor to help you finish your project. You don't want to blow it at this stage.

Places you might find video editors include www.freelanced.com, www.elance.com, www.odesk.com, www.angieslist.com, www.local.com, www.weva.com, www.iov.co.uk, or just do an internet search on "video editor needed YOUR TOWN." (Substitute your own city or town for YOUR TOWN.) You will typically pay $25 to $75, or more, per hour in the U.S. Overseas editors may be much less expensive. You can try www.odesk.com for overseas editors.

Organization is an important aspect of editing. That's why we told you that you should be making copious notes on your script or shot list during production. You or your editor will use these to determine which take you liked best, scenes that were added or deleted, changes in dialog, anything that can help the editor work more efficiently.

Here's a story from Kim about why you can't take enough notes during shooting …

One day when Rick was deep into editing the series of 42 exercise videos we shot for *Dave Sheahan's Home Workout System*, he turned to me with a look of panic in his eyes and announces, "We have to shoot the first video again!" He couldn't find the footage on his computer. I went looking for it and it looked like he was right—it didn't look like the shots were there. My stomach sank and Rick was sick about it.

Since we were dealing with such large, long files, Rick didn't have the time while getting them off the camera every evening to watch and log each one individually. It would have taken over two hours a night just to watch the main camera, and we shot with three Cameras.

He just assumed that all was going correctly during his transfers until … uh oh … he couldn't find Day 1, Camera 1.

Reshooting was going to be a *big* problem since we no longer had access to the house and set we shot it in. But that wasn't the biggest problem. Dave was back in Ireland! Reshooting that scene wouldn't have just been exorbitantly expensive, it would look like we messed up and oh, how we hate to admit that!

While on the shoot, I took the role of script supervisor while Rick was the main camera operator. I had a folder where I had put all the notes I took while we were shooting and there I saw where I wrote that we were having problems with the mic that first day and had to do some retakes. So I meticulously went to the place in the clips where I noted the problems and … voilà, there was the missing shot! Whew! Without my notes Rick wasn't finding it.

The files were numbered randomly and Rick, being the main shooter, hadn't really remembered that we had the mic problem on that particular day which caused several false starts. I hadn't remembered it either since it happened on Day 1 of an 11-day shoot, over three weeks ago. But my notes did!

He found the file and all was fine. Boy, was he relieved!

NON-LINEAR EDITING SYSTEMS—HOW THEY WORK

If you are new to editing and want to try it yourself, here are some of the key concepts you'll need to know and my suggestions for organizing your editing project. I'll also cover some basic editing techniques. Although I won't be discussing any particular system, most have the same general features and use similar terminology within the software.

Most likely you will be using a non-linear editing system (NLE). Names you'll frequently see include:

PC	Mac
Adobe Premiere Pro	Adobe Premiere Pro
Adobe Premiere Elements	Adobe Premiere Elements
Avid Media Composer	Avid Media Composer
Corel VideoStudio Pro X5	Final Cut Pro
Cyberlink PowerDirector	iMovie
Microsoft Windows Movie Maker	
Pinnacle Studio (HD & Ultimate)	
Sony Vegas Movie Studio HD	

Microsoft Windows Movie Maker (PC) and iMovie (Mac) are included free with the purchase of a new computer. They offer plenty of capability and are among the easiest to use, so you may not need more than that. You can get far more powerful, complex, and expensive programs if and when you decide you need them.

With non-linear editing, you have great freedom to quickly move all of your video assets around on the timeline to suit your needs. The timeline is a visual representation of your video, running left to right. This is a vast improvement over older linear editing where your scenes had to be edited in chronological order, from beginning to end. You could insert a clip but you had nowhere near the flexibility of a non-linear editor.

Think of it like the difference between typing on a typewriter and using a word processor. On a typewriter, if you decide to make a change after you typed most of your document and wanted to insert a new paragraph in the middle, you would have to retype it up until that point to add the paragraph, then retype the rest. In word processing you have the ability to copy and paste and move text around at random. You are doing the same sort of process with a NLE, except that you are moving scenes around. You can work on any section at any time and move entire segments up or down the timeline, which is a graphical representation of your program's flow. You can see how the life of the editor is made so much easier with a NLE system.

Most non-linear editing systems generally function the same way, conceptually.

In every system you will create a new project where all your editing will be done. In most editing programs you have an area where you import and store the media (video clips) you shot during production, plus additional graphics, music, sound effects, etc. We'll call this a bin. This is basically a library of every component you'll need to make your video. You will have a window where you can review this media, trim it, make color adjustments, etc.

You will arrange these assets on a timeline, from left to right, following your script. As we said, this is random access so you don't have to start at the beginning and work forward. You can start anywhere and continually revise and move things around. You can apply a wide range of filters on both the audio and video tracks as desired to make adjustments and for special effects.

Finally, you'll have a way of outputting your final project to any number of formats, such as DVD, tape, web delivery, etc.

ASSEMBLING YOUR ASSETS

In your bin you can organize clips into "folders" by whatever criteria makes sense to you, such as by scene, location, subject, day, etc. The important thing is to organize your assets in a way that makes it easy for you to find what you need quickly.

If your clips just have numeric names that make no sense, renaming them to something that makes sense for you or another editor may be helpful. You can view clips by name, by icon, and by scrubbing (playing) through them.

TIMELINE

Video clips are placed on the timeline on a separate track from the audio, although they generally come in synced to each other. You have one window or monitor where you preview an asset and can trim it to the length you want (this window is called various names in different NLEs), and another window (monitor) that shows you a preview of how things look on the timeline. Most NLEs will let you have as many tracks on your timeline as you need for audio and video. Try to arrange tracks logically to keep things neat: track 1 could be the narrator, track 2 for interviews, track 3 for b-roll or graphics, etc. The more you mix things around on tracks the more potentially confusing it will get.

You can create your video in "chunks," called sequences. For example, you might create an opening sequence, like a company logo, that you put at the beginning of all of your videos. Then you might have a beginning, middle, and end sequence. Once created, you can treat these sequences just like individual clips, dropping them onto a timeline and moving them around as needed.

When importing your video clips it's important that you have your project's sequence set to the correct aspect ratio of the clips. You're most likely to be working in either 4:3 (standard definition like a regular TV) or 16:9 (high definition, wide screen TV).

CUTS AND TRANSITIONS

As you assemble your clips on the timeline you can choose how to move from one clip to the next. You can simply use a cut, which is a change in perspective; a dissolve, which indicates a change in time or place; a wipe breaks the current story and takes the viewer someplace else. Those are simple transitions. Please resist the temptation to use most of the fancy special effects transitions, like spins and bouncing stars, that are available to you. Using a lot of fancy transitions is the sure sign of a beginning editor who's fascinated with all of the new toys in the toy box.

If you are going to use some of the transitions in your NLE, only use a few and use them consistently. Don't mix a lot of effects into one program; it just looks amateurish and distracting. When in doubt, just do a straight cut from one scene to the next. You can't go wrong with a cut. Look at feature films and you'll rarely see any transition effects, just straight cuts.

If you do feel you need a transition, choose one that fits the style of what you are editing. A dissolve is a good choice in many situations. It doesn't scream for attention but does offer a bit of effect. A soft cut is a very short dissolve. It is so subtle that most people don't notice, it's just a nice soft transition.

A dip-to-black (fade) is a nice effect for the right situation. The video briefly dips down to black and back up again. This can happen in the space of 20 to 30 frames and is good for a transition indicating passage of time. I call this a PBS-style transition.

LOWER THIRDS, GRAPHICS, AND TITLES

A "lower third" refers to the text that appears underneath a person, displaying their name. If they are an important person in your video you may want to identify them with a lower third. If you do use a lower third you don't also need them to say their name on camera (you should record it, but it's redundant to use that part).

Your NLE probably includes some templates for lower thirds and you can either add more or create your own. I recently bought some I like from www.darkroomdesign.net.

All NLEs have some capability to make titles, charts, and other graphics. You can also create titles and more complex graphics in photo editing software like Adobe Photoshop or drawing programs like Adobe Illustrator or Corel Draw. If you are working in these other programs be sure to export the file in RGB mode and save them as JPG or PNG.

PUTTING IT TOGETHER

With SIVs the formula will be fairly straightforward. You will arrange the best takes of your shoot in a linear fashion on the timeline, starting at the left and running to the right. You will most likely have some type of opening sequence or logo, then go right into the production, stacking things like b-roll, graphics, titles, etc., on higher and higher tracks, like a stack of pancakes. Just remember to try to keep same with same; host on track 1, b-roll on track 2, graphics on track 3, etc., Figure 19.1 is taken from one of my projects.

Remember when we were telling you to shoot b-roll and coverage while on a shoot? This is where it can make a huge improvement in your video. Nobody wants to watch a "talking head" for 10 minutes or more. Use your cutaway footage as much as possible to add variety to what the viewer is seeing. Try to illustrate for your viewers what the person on camera is talking about. The cutaways should make sense in the context, and should add relevant information to the scene.

As editor, you are now the eyes and ears of your viewer. See what you are doing through their eyes and make it as clear and understandable as possible by the clips you choose and the way you arrange them.

Keep your shots as succinct as possible. You may fall in love with your footage but your viewer has a short attention span, so be really objective about what needs to stay and what should go. If you can cut a 15-minute video down to 12 minutes and keep the message strong and clear, it will be more powerful.

There are exceptions, of course. If you can linger on a beautiful or meaningful shot and it fits the style of your video, that can be a nice effect. Some of the documentaries

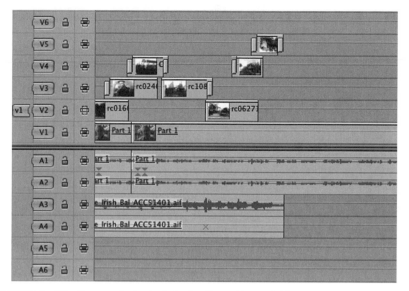

FIGURE 19.1   Timeline sample that includes b-roll, graphics, and titles.

you'll see on National PBS hold onto shots for a long time while a person is speaking. If it is a photo or illustration you may notice a slow pan or zoom within the image. This has been dubbed "the Ken Burns effect," a tip of the hat to documentary filmmaker Ken Burns, who brought this technique to high art in his *The Civil War* series. This works very well in the hands of a talented and sensitive editor with the right subject matter.

WORKING WITH POWERPOINT SLIDES

It is quite common to incorporate PowerPoint slides into a seminar or classroom presentation. This can give an editor fits because in a wide shot that includes the presenter and the screen, one or the other is going to be poorly exposed. Here's a good workaround if you are producing a video like this. Rather than shoot the PowerPoint during the event I'll focus on getting good shots of the presenters. I'll ask to get the PowerPoint slides from them in the correct order they were shown. Then it's just a matter of placing them in the editing timeline where the speaker refers to them. I can then cut back and forth between speaker and slides. That way the slides and speaker both look great.

Some new programs have recently come out to significantly streamline this process. Singular Software Presto™ (www.singularsoftware.com/presto.html) will automatically combine your slide images with a closely tracked inset of your presenter. It is available for Final Cut Pro, Adobe Premiere, and Sony Vegas Pro as of this writing.

COLOR CORRECTING

Despite your best efforts to white balance your shots in production, they can always be improved in editing by adjusting the color (color correcting) and matching that correction throughout all of your clips. Most NLEs offer similar tools for color correction via a color correction tool. You may have more than one.

Typically you will click an eyedropper tool on what should be a white color, which tells the software what your benchmark for white is. A white shirt, a wall, anything that should be white will do. From there it will make adjustments, which you can override. You can make some wild color variations by clicking other colors with the eyedropper tool.

You may hear the term color grading. This is not the same thing as color correcting. Color grading is a different process in which the editor or grader will adjust the overall "color" of a film. This can be used creatively to establish a mood or emotional tone. A film can be made to look warm or cool, old or nostalgic by the color palette the color grader applies. There are plugin effects you can apply to clips or entire videos to get these color effects easily. Use them sparingly.

We don't usually do color grading with our SIVs, but we do want visual continuity throughout the video and this will usually involve color correcting for white balance. You can also adjust brightness, contrast, and color saturation to bring out details or to focus the viewer's attention.

I've been amazed many times at how a clip that looks bad can be made to look totally acceptable with careful color correcting. It can be a bit like letting the genie out of the bottle. Once you correct one shot you'll see such an improvement that you'll want to correct all of your scenes. This will invariably improve the look of your video at the expense of editing time.

MUSIC—THE FINAL TOUCH

Adding music is putting icing on your video cake. Music can make such a big difference in the quality of your video but it has to be the *right* music to set the tone you want. Music should not call too much attention to itself. For example, a hard rock tune under a tender moment feels all wrong, and tender music under a fight scene would not match. Music is there to set the mood, lift the energy during a period of slower pacing, and indicate to the viewer how they should be feeling. Think of the triumphant music after a victorious fight scene or the tender music as lovers gaze into each other's eyes. In many SIVs you may only have music at the beginning and end, and maybe during key transitions or major subject matter changes.

It may surprise you but when I show one of my videos and ask people afterwards, "how'd you like the music," and they say they didn't notice it, I like that. This means that I picked music that matched the subject matter and didn't distract them or take them out of the story.

SWEETEN THE AUDIO

Once you have your narration, sound effects, and music tracks, you need to balance them and do any clean up needed. This is known as sweetening, the act of making your soundtrack as clean and beautiful as your video.

You may need to get extra sounds to replace missing or poor quality clips. Consider shooting them yourself or finding what you are looking for at a sound effects library. As with music, someone else's recorded sound effects are also copyrighted so you can't just pull them off the internet and use them without permission. I use Sounddogs (www.sounddogs.com) a lot. Their prices are very reasonable and they have a gigantic library of sounds and music. I shot a horror film a few years ago and we needed lots of scary, creepy sounds that we didn't record when shooting. Sounddogs saved the day for me. Look on www.shoot-to-sell.com for more sound effect and music resources.

You want to balance your audio so you can clearly hear the most important part—the voice. If your voice (whether voice-over or on-camera narrator) was recorded properly you shouldn't have to do much to it. However, if you picked up a steady background hum or buzz, which is not uncommon, you can usually remove those kinds of sounds without damaging the voice quality. I currently use Adobe Audition for this but there are many other programs available. You should start with an equalizer audio filter from your NLE and try to isolate and suppress the offending frequency.

Adjusting your soundtrack is part art and part science. It is too big a subject to cover in detail here. Let it suffice to say that you want your viewers to clearly hear the voice without straining. The music should be audible but it should not overwhelm the voice. When you are making these adjustments, wear a good set of headphones or listen through high quality speakers at a high enough volume to really hear everything. It never hurts to bring in a friend and get a second opinion.

KEEP IT LEGAL

As I shared in Chapter 12, you cannot put just any music into your video. There are clear rules on ownership of creative works and you can get in trouble fast by using someone's copyrighted music without getting permission from the songwriter *and* the recording company. Recorded music technically has two copyrights: (1) the song itself, and (2) the recording of the song.

If you get permission you may have to pay a fee. Popular music will likely be too expensive to even consider. There are many "royalty-free" music libraries available that sell varying rights to use their music, and they often have tunes that sound similar to popular music but you can use them legally once you pay the fee, which can vary depending on the use of the material and how many times you can use it.

Royalty-free does not mean the work is free; it means that although there is a fee to use it, it is free of royalties. What I mean by this is that after you pay for the right to use the music one time you will owe nothing more, regardless of how much money you make off the video. If it was not royalty-free, the musician or recording company might have a claim to some of the future earnings of the video.

Some music libraries sell "buy out" CDs where you can do anything you want with the music once you buy it. Others restrict you to one time use. Every music library has online samples and you can usually buy individual cuts online. Visit www.shoot-to-sell.com for our recommendations for royalty-free music.

There is another category of license called *Creative Commons Attribution 3.0*. You can read the full license wording at www.creativecommons.org/licenses/by/3.0/legalcode. If someone allows you to use their music for free under this license, the only restriction is that you must give the musician attribution.

Even if you get a verbal OK to use a musician's work, get it in writing. Things can change and you want to be protected from legal action. To find out who to ask for permission regarding music, check out the three licensing agencies that handle the vast majority of published American music:

- ASCAP (American Society of Composers, Authors and Publishers) (www.ascap.com)
- BMI (Broadcast Music, Inc.) (www.bmi.com)
- SESAC (www.sesac.com).

If you can't find the agencies through those sites, do a web search. Ask for the name of the artist/song with the term "licensing" or "licensing information."

The same thing applies to images. If you start incorporating footage you find online or maybe something you shot of private property without permission, you may be in trouble. We can't stress enough, if you're ever in doubt, ask for permission. If you have to pay something up front it is better than having to pay a lot more later to a lawyer and possibly having to scrap your project due to legal problems. Review Chapter 12 if you need to refresh yourself on this issue.

Like with music, there are many stock image agencies that will license the use of video clips, still photos, graphics, and animation. These can increase the production value of your video and may well be worth the investment. If your video is about politics for example, stock footage of the United States Capitol building or of a foreign capitol can make your video much more powerful.

Before I leave this topic let me say one more time—do not use any music or images that are not your own without seeking permission and paying any required fees. Then make sure you have your license or permission in writing. There is software that will sniff out illegal music in seconds on places like YouTube and other social and video sharing sites. We should respect the rights of intellectual property rights owners if we want our rights respected.

PREPARING FOR ONLINE DISTRIBUTION

If you are going to show or sell your videos online as "video-on-demand" or VOD, you will need to prepare them for the web, which means compressing and exporting them properly. You may just want to put a teaser sample on a user generated video sharing site like YouTube, Viddler, Vimeo, Blip.tv, or dozens of others. Each one of these sites has a slightly different audience and purpose and you can submit to multiple sites. If that's the case, it's pretty simple to upload videos. You may not have to do anything special to put your video on one of these sites. Look for video hosting sites on Wikipedia for an extensive list of current options.

What if you want to host your videos yourself? The question I hear often is what format to do it in: FLV, AVI, MOV, WMV, SWF, QT, MPEG, or other formats? There are services that will encode any one of these formats into all of the other formats, host your videos, and stream it out at the appropriate bandwidth for the connecting device. We use ClickStream (www.clickstreamtv.com) that does this and our videos look and play great whether watching them on a computer or on our iPhone. It's easy and convenient. I predict we'll see more of these services doing business at varying price points.

We also place a lot of our videos on Amazon S3. This service is inexpensive and reliable. If you are preparing your videos yourself for upload, here are some suggested output sizes

For standard definition (4:3 aspect ratio):

- Modem (56 k): 160 × 120
- DSL: 320 × 240
- Cable: 512 × 384
- Cable/corporate LAN: 640 × 480

Frame sizes for high definition (16:9 aspect ratio):

- Modem (56 k): 192 × 108
- DSL: 384 × 216
- Cable: 448 × 252
- Cable/corporate LAN: 704 × 396

If you place your video on Amazon S3 or similar service you will need a media player. The media player allows your user to view the video. We've been using EzS3. There is a modest monthly subscription fee but we feel it is good value. You can choose to build players for a range of different styles of FLV/MPEG-4. Flash has been a popular online video format for many years. However, Adobe, the developer, is dropping support for it in several browsers and Apple products have never played Flash without requiring the user to add plugins. Flash will still be around for a while but over time will be phased out. HTML5 is becoming a widely supported option.

DVD DISTRIBUTION

If you are delivering your videos in a physical format, most likely that format will be a DVD, whether standard definition or Blu-ray. Up until 10 years ago we sold a lot of programs on VHS tape but we haven't had a VHS order in years and we advise that you don't bother making VHS tapes.

I keep hearing that the days of DVDs are numbered also but I believe we will be seeing them for many more years. We are selling more videos via video-on-demand or subscriptions but the majority of our sales are still physical DVDs. There is something to be said for having a physical product that you can keep on a shelf and not have to worry about losing the link or the file. Therefore, you may want to make your videos available as DVDs, in addition to online access.

DVD AUTHORING

DVD authoring is the process of assembling all of the program's components and then programming the navigation of your DVD. These components are not only the video and audio files but graphics for the navigation menus as well. Common DVD authoring programs include but are not limited to the following:

PC	Mac
Adobe Encore	DVD Studio Pro
DVD Movie Factory Pro	iDVD
Roxio MyDVD	Roxio Toast 11 Pro
Sony DVD Architect Studio	
Sony Vegas Pro 11	
Womble EasyDVD	

Again, I won't be going into the specifics of authoring a DVD in this book. If you wish to do this yourself, there are resources and courses available. The editor you work with will probably know how to do this and deliver you a finished product. But if not, you'll need to know a few steps to get your project into a format your DVD authoring software will recognize.

One of those steps is exporting your video and audio files into a format that your DVD authoring software will work with. This is done in your NLE system. The most common format you will export will be an MPEG2 (not the same as the MP4 usually used with compressing video for the web.) Many authoring programs will also accept MOVs as well. Once your DVD project is done, you will run it through a build and burn process.

There are stand-alone DVD recorder units available that have basic authoring functions built-in, however you have little or no control over the layout of your DVD menus. If you are making a video to sell, you may want more creative control, such as the ability to have motion menus, music playing in the background, and attractive graphics. Some people creating videos of events will use these recorders because at the end of the event the DVD is already done.

The other thing you can do with DVDs is to add documents such as PDFs, Word Docs, JPGs, Spreadsheets, etc. If your customer loads the DVD into a computer, they'll be able to open these documents. The DVD will also play in the computer's DVD player. There is a way to have clickable links on your DVD, so if a person is watching your DVD on an internet connected computer, they would be able to click on a link and then be sent to a website.

One of the most convenient features of a DVD is that you can navigate the video by scenes or chapters. Unlike cumbersome VHS tapes, with DVDs you don't have to fast forward or rewind to find the section of the video you want to watch; they have random access. You can go to a particular scene or chapter easily on a DVD. That's why we recommend that you produce your video in topical sections and have a chapter menu, so that your customers can watch a particular part repeatedly. This is especially useful in school settings.

Modern DVD authoring programs have come a long way in becoming user-friendly. Still, DVD authoring is one area where you may wish to seek professional help, especially if you want to do more high-end stuff like having motion menus and custom buttons. You'll also want attractive graphics for your menus.

DVDs can deliver a lot of extras that increase value and can justify a higher price, such as adding guides, reports, resources, extra teaching material, etc. For example, in our *My Secrets of Producing Successful Special Interest Videos* DVD, we include a script guide and an exercise for picking a topic. These are also printed out and slipped into the case, an added feature of sending a physical product like a DVD in an Amaray (the plastic case which folds around and snaps closed) case.

Teachers *love* getting guides with classroom videos and this will definitely help your marketing efforts. Teaching guides can include vocabulary, exercises, tests, resources, and even a transcript of the script. Make sure your marketing material tells them they're getting these extras.

PACKAGING—GIVE IT SHELF APPEAL

Here is another area where you'll have to decide how you want to present yourself to your customer. There are many packaging options. You may choose paper cases, plastic or jewel cases, Amaray cases, notebooks with special DVD sleeves or custom-made packaging.

You should have attractive graphics for the box and DVD face. The Amaray case is considered the standard packaging for DVDs. You can insert color covers, just like the retail DVDs you see for sale in stores. Design your DVD cover with shelf appeal, meaning good photos that illustrate the content and appealing sales copy that would entice a person to purchase it (see Chapter 30 on copywriting).

This is an area where I recommend hiring a graphic designer, preferably one with experience working in an ad agency, since what you are designing isn't just a cover, it is a marketing tool. You want a cover that will catch your viewer's eye and sell the video.

If you don't have a graphic designer you can try 99 designs (www.99designs.com). You post your graphic design project specs on the site and graphic artists will compete to win the job. You select the winning design. This is a great way to see how a lot of different artists treat your design.

If you plan on selling your DVD in retail outlets, you'll need a UPC code graphic on the DVD packaging. You can buy UPC codes at www.barcodestalk.com/bar-code-numbers. Many services that offer DVD packaging and duplicating will include a UPC code free so check with them before you invest in a code.

MANUFACTURING YOUR DVD

Once you have your DVD master and your artwork, you need to decide if you will be manufacturing your DVDs yourself or sending them out. The cost of doing it yourself may be less than sending it out but it does take time and access to the right equipment, so you need to decide if that is the best route for you.

The two processes involved in manufacturing a DVD are called duplication or replication. The difference between the two methods is that duplication is the process of copying data onto a recordable DVD, like what you do at home when you burn to a blank DVD. Replication is the way commercial DVDs are manufactured where the information is physically "stamped" or "pressed" onto a DVD from a glass master that is created from your source DVD. For replication, you need to send your master to a company that does this service. It's normally used for higher quantities (1,000 or more). For smaller runs, duplication is the way to go. Theoretically the replicated discs will play more reliably on more DVD players, but I think that was more of an issue years ago, due to manufacturing variations in DVD players.

There are many on-demand duplicating services in the market, so do a web search for "on demand DVD duplication" then compare prices, benefits, and features. A search on the term "DVD replication" will unearth companies who will do larger orders.

For single DVDs, Kunaki (www.kunaki.com) is a very cost-effective option. You upload all your artwork along with your built file and they'll duplicate and package it for you on demand. You can have them mail you a batch of DVDs and you handle shipping. Or you can have them ship it to the customer for you. Because it is all done automatically, they can keep the price really low but that also comes with some negatives. There is no human customer support so if you encounter problems, you can send a support ticket but can't call up and talk to a human. If you have several DVDs in a set, you would have to send your customer each title in an individual case because they don't bundle them into other packaging or binders. I haven't used them so cannot personally vouch for them but I know a lot of people who have been happy with their service.

Another option is going through Amazon's CreateSpace (www.createspace.com/Products/DVD/). Going this route isn't the least expensive way we've found but there are some nice features, like they'll give you a free UPC code and you can buy the DVDs from them so you aren't restricted to just selling your videos on Amazon. They also have the ability to convert your video into a video-on-demand format and sell them through their site.

What if you have more than one DVD that you want to sell in a series? Many of the duplication companies now offer multi-disc package options that can hold more than one DVD. They are attractive and can give a professional look to your DVDs. They can also be expensive. Some companies that provide multi-pack packaging include Discmakers (www.discmakers.com), Molding Box (www.moldingbox.com), and Speaker Fulfillment Services (www.speakerfulfillmentservices.com).

DUPLICATING DVDs YOURSELF

At the time we started selling a wide range of DVD titles in small batches there weren't the low priced duplication services available like now, so we decided to do it ourselves. You may decide this is a good option for you too.

We use a nine-bay duplicating tower to duplicate our DVDs in small batches of 200 or fewer. Beyond that I usually send them out. We use a Primera Bravo Pro Printer to print them. We print the color covers on an HP printer, trim them on a paper cutter, and insert them into Amaray cases. Our cost per DVD is about 60¢ this way. This combination has been a great convenience for us. If we suddenly need a few DVDs of one title we can knock them out quickly and inexpensively.

There are many different types of DVD duplicators available. You can get models that both duplicate and print the DVD. We chose to use a tower duplicator with a separate printer. With a large tower duplicator you can burn (duplicate) quite a lot of DVDs in a short time and then just stack them in the printer and do something else while it prints them. You can get tower duplicators that only do two to three DVDs at a time, or bigger models that will burn 13 or more per batch. I like having a separate duplicator and printer because if I have a problem with one of them I can still be using the other.

We print the covers on Staples® brand glossy brochure paper. Photo paper is too expensive and regular ink jet paper doesn't look good. We then trim them on a paper cutter and insert into the case. Our printer is an ink jet machine but if you do a lot of printing you'll find a laser jet printer costs less in the long run. We use a small shrink wrap machine to finish them off. This costs about 7¢ each. If you need a lot of covers it will be less expensive to send the printing out to someplace like www.printplace.com.

That's the post-production process. It includes everything from after the shooting stops to getting your video ready to sell, whether online or as DVDs. And now, it's time to move on to pricing and fulfillment.

Action Steps

- Decide on if you are going to be outsourcing your editing or going to be doing it yourself.
- Import your video assets (clips, graphics, images, music, etc.) into your editing project. When they are imported, organize them into bins and folders.

- Use your final script, shot lists, and storyboards to guide your editing process.
- Decide on the look and style of your titles, lower thirds, and transitions. Avoid cheesy transitions!
- Add in b-roll, music, and graphics in an organized way and according to your script.
- Get copyright clearance for music, video, and images.
- Color correct your footage to adjust for white balance or a special look.
- Sweeten your audio.
- Export for the web if you are delivering online or export for your DVD.
- If you are going to be distributing DVDs, decide if you will be outsourcing the authoring or doing it yourself.
- Package your DVD with "shelf appeal." Purchase UPC bar codes if necessary.
- Decide if you will duplicate your DVDs yourself or send them out.

Part IV

Getting It Ready for Sale

Chapter 20

Pricing Your Video

Chapter Objectives

- Learn what goes into determining a price for your video.
- Calculate the break even point for your video.
- Learn how perception influences your sale price.
- Understand the advantages and disadvantages of selling wholesale.
- Know how to raise your price with Public Performance Rights.
- Learn how to test your prices.

You've probably been mentally toying with the price you'll charge for your video since you first started thinking about it, right? You can't help but wonder what you can get for it. It's fun to fantasize about all the money you're going to make from your brainchild. I do it too. It's important and you *should* do it. In fact, you should be thinking about pricing, your market, and your profitability from the very beginning. Among other things, your profitability will depend on how you set your price.

As we'll discuss further in Chapter 32, pricing is one of the key variables in your marketing mix. There are several factors, both internal and external, that will come into play when setting your price. Externally, your market and your competition will play a large role in determining what price you will be able to ask and what you will most likely receive. Looking at this will show you the ceiling. Internally, you have to look at your pricing objectives such as:

- Do you want to focus on maximizing your short-range or long-range profits;
- increase your sales volume;
- increase gross profit per sale;
- desensitize customers to price or match competitors' prices?

You want to know the ceiling and floor of the price for this type of product in your market so you can decide where you want your video to be in that range. You'll also want to learn the prices and quality of your competitors' products because you'll be using this information to set your prices too. It's also important to be aware of economic forecasts and conditions in your market.

You may be thinking to yourself, "my product is going to be so much better than anything else in the market, I'm going to break through that price ceiling." Optimism is good, but look at the reality of the economic climate. Are premium-priced products selling well in your market or are people in an economizing mindset. I'm not saying don't do it, just listen to what your market is saying at the time you're pricing your video.

It's time to put on your objective glasses and look at your costs. You have to look at the total investment you'll make in this video as well as what you have determined your market will pay in order to know if you'll actually be able to make any money. Look at your hard costs such as cast and crew, equipment, travel, and your own investment of time. All of this should be reflected in your production budget.

So what will be the total cost of producing your video, from inception to packaging? How much time will you put into it and what is that time worth? You have to recoup these costs before you are making a profit. Then you need to look at all the costs that go into producing your DVD. There are a lot of other factors you'll want to consider but we'll do a simple exercise to explain how you can start.

Let's say you've determined that your actual cost to produce and sell a physical DVD will be about $2. That includes all costs associated with printing, packaging, duplicating, shipping it to you in bulk, and processing a credit card sale. If you are selling on-demand videos it may be less. You also have costs like packaging materials and shipping to your customer but I'm assuming you will be charging for shipping and handling, so let's stick with $2 for the following example.

This is how I go about it. Say you calculate that it will cost you $5,000 to produce your video, including your time. If you sell your video for $20 and your profit after duplication is $18, it will take you 278 sales to break even.

How long do you think it would take to sell that many? A month? Maybe, but realistically if your product is new and you don't already have a list of targeted buyers to market to, you'll be lucky if you sell that much in a year. If that happens it will take you a year to get your initial investment back.

Let's continue … if you sell that same video for $50 it will only take 105 sales to get there. If it was a $75 price it would take only 69 sales to break even. Sell it for $120 like my friend does and you only have to sell 43 and you're in the clear. Quite a difference, eh?

You'd have to sell seven $20 videos to make the same profit as one sale at $120. If your market will bear it, obviously go for the higher price. If your potential market is small and you know you will only sell a limited number of copies ever, you have to raise the price to the point it needs to be to make the profit you need within a reasonable time.

This is why we encouraged you at the beginning to look first at markets where the price could be higher, like schools and institutions or specialty markets. If your market will bear a $75 or even a $95 price, don't sell it for less. If your competition is selling for $120, you sell yours for $120. Don't underprice it. You can always have a sale or cut the price later but it is very difficult to raise the price once people have seen the product at a lower price point.

A better approach would be to price it higher so that you can afford to offer incentives for people to purchase, like bonus items or discounts.

Pricing is often driven by the size and income of the market. I've been contemplating dusting off my private pilot license and getting current again. Looking at the price of videos to help me refresh my skills, prices for single title lessons on DVD or download mostly fall between $49 and $119. That's average; some titles are far more expensive, especially if they are dealing with the latest aviation equipment training.

These flight training videos are selling to a small niche market that clearly has disposable income, since flying is an inherently expensive proposition (that's why I quit flying).

Since they won't sell them in the millions or even thousands they have to make it up on price, not volume sales. If they sold them too cheaply they'd never make a profit. Because pilots want them and have the money, they'll pay that much.

There is definitely a perception of value based on price. If your product is the most expensive then people will naturally assume your video must be superior, else why the high price? If it is the cheapest video then people may suspect that it is inferior and therefore worth less.

To recap, you have to assess your market's ability and willingness to pay, be aware of what your competition is charging, and decide where you want to position your product between least and most expensive. If you feel your product is the best of its class, then go for the top of the range. You'll want to focus on its benefits, features, production values, even your packaging to position it as the obvious choice for those who demand the best. Use "exclusivity" to justify a higher price. Your particular market may be price sensitive or it may be the kind that will buy a video on your topic at any price. Ultimately, the only way to know for sure is to test.

Public Performance Rights (PPR)

One way to significantly increase the price and value of your video is to add Public Performance Rights (PPR). This is so that a person or organization can legally show your video to a general gathering, possibly even charging admission. By law, you can't buy a DVD in a retail store for $9.95 that only has home use rights and then show it in an auditorium and charge admission. You have to have PPR to do that.

Unless videos are sold or rented with public performance rights they should be considered "home use only" and should be restricted to private showings in the home to a "normal circle of family and social acquaintances." In other words, it's OK to show at a home party but not to a paying audience.

According to the U.S. copyright law (Title 17, United States Code, Section 110), a public performance is any screening of a videocassette, DVD, videodisc, or film which occurs outside of the home, or at any place where people are gathered who are not family members, such as in a school, library, auditorium, classroom, or meeting room. You can authorize the rights to show your video as a public performance.

The only exception to this rule is the face-to-face teaching exemption that allows instructors to show videos in a classroom as long as the activity is a teaching activity and not recreation or entertainment. This exemption is also covered in Section 110 (1) of the U.S. copyright law. If they are showing the video outside of their curriculum for entertainment, during a rainy day, or for a treat then it is not allowed and the PPR rights should be purchased.

It's impossible to enforce this, but we put FBI warnings on all of our videos and PPR versions say so on the packaging. On the home use videos we state that the video is for Home Use Only and not for viewing by a general audience.

On our videos with PPR we raise the price to $75 or $95. Libraries and schools respect this and order the correct version. Most organizations will understand this distinction when you explain it to them.

By granting the rights to show your video in a public venue you are increasing the value and justifying the price.

BUNDLE TO INCREASE VALUE

Another way to increase your sales price is to bundle multiple titles or add ancillary items. Maybe your market won't pay $95 for a single DVD but what if you have a set of three or four DVDs for $95? That sounds like a lot better deal. So if your video is two hours long, break it into four 30-minute parts, put it on multiple DVDs and you have a "kit" or a "complete package." Checklists, ebooks, and PDFs add value. The more you can add, the higher the perceived value of what the customer is getting and the more you can charge. It doesn't cost you much more to make but it is viewed as getting more for the money.

I'm not suggesting that you water down the content or be deceiving, just break it out into logical chunks so your prospect can see the value of what they are getting. When it comes down to it, people will pay what they think it is worth.

PHYSICAL PRODUCTS vs DIGITAL

Our experience is that people still want to own DVDs over on-demand videos. We have one line of videos that deals with pain relief and those sell far better as videos-on-demand because people want relief immediately. Aside from those, the majority of our sales are DVDs. A couple of the people we interviewed for our case studies found that to be the case also, while the others found online video worked better for their market.

There is a higher perceived value in a physical product. In my own shopping experience I know that files can get lost, links can get forgotten, and hard drives crash, so whether it's true or not I think I'll have access to my DVDs longer than if they were just digital files.

SPLIT TESTING

So how can you really tell what price will work? One of the best ways to determine this is to do split testing (also called A/B testing or bucket testing) which is a method of market testing where you test one marketing variable (in this case price) with a different aspect of the variable (different price) among segments of your prospects.

Split testing has been used in direct mail marketing for decades. When selling on the internet, the same testing tactics can be employed very successfully and many times less expensively than with direct mail.

In the example below we took a list of 3,000 names, split it into thirds and sent the same email to each list of 1,000 but with a different price only: $19.95, $29.95, and $49.95. Notice that the lowest price had the highest response rate, but the least profit. A higher price can be perceived as a superior product and result in a higher response rate at a higher price.

Testing 3,000 Names			
	Test A—$19.95	Test B—$29.95	Test C—$49.95
Printing	$210.00	$210.00	$210.00
Mailing	$190.00	$190.00	$190.00
List Rental	$110.00	$110.00	$110.00
	$510	$510	$510

(Continued)

Testing 3,000 Names (Continued)			
	Test A—$19.95	Test B—$29.95	Test C—$49.95
Response Rate	3.00%	2.00%	2.50%
# of Sales	30	20	25
Cost of Goods	$2.00	$2.00	$2.00
Net Profit	$538.50	$559.00	$1,198.75

SELLING WHOLESALE

If you are going to sell copies of your video wholesale then the dealer will probably want a 40 to 50 percent discount off your retail price, sometimes more. Although this may lead to a higher sales volume for you it will be at a highly reduced profit margin. We'll be talking more about working with distributors in Chapter 22. What I want to leave you with here is that you want to price your videos to take into account working with distributors. You want to make sure you are making a profit on each sale. If you only have a 40 percent profit margin yourself then you cannot sell it to a wholesaler at 50 percent off. Know what your profit margin is.

LISTEN TO YOUR MARKET

When all is said and done, your market will tell you what the correct price is. If your videos are flying off the shelf faster than you can duplicate them, your price may be too low. You won't truly know that unless you test your price points. That is one of the beauties of having your own website where you can raise and lower your prices to see what is working for you. If you're getting lots of interest and great feedback but nobody's buying, ask some questions. You may be charging more than your customers can afford, no matter how much they'd like to have your video. Or maybe they would rather have the video in a different format (online or physical product) so it may not be a pricing issue at all. Talk to your customers and listen to what they tell you.

AIM HIGH

I hope you weren't expecting me to tell you what price you should charge. I can't because I don't know your product, your market, or anything about your marketing plan. What I hope you got out of this chapter is that, with your product and customer in mind, you should make any changes you can to get your price as high as possible. I usually start out at the top of the ceiling knowing that it is much easier to decrease prices than increase them. Like I said, that also allows you to offer special discounts and incentives and still generate a profit.

It's likely that you won't sell thousands of your video. There are a lot of variables but the average independent video will typically sell under 1,000 copies in its lifetime; 2,000 if you're doing well. If you want to make $50,000 from your video and you expect to sell 1,000 copies, you need to charge over $50 each to do that. This brings us back to the task of knowing your target market. Do they have the money to purchase your video at the price you need to ask, and are they willing to part with their money?

Remember, our goal is to build *multiple* streams of income. So $50,000 isn't bad, and if you produce 10 titles that each earn you $50,000 that would be a very nice income. Maybe a more achievable goal would be to produce 20 videos that each earn you $25,000 to make the same amount.

That's a lot to consider. Coming up with the right price isn't so simple and you should spend serious time thinking about your price and testing it with your market. Then go out and do it.

Action Steps

- Consider how you will be distributing your videos—DVD or online or both.
- Research your market to determine what they will pay.
- Find out what your competition is charging.
- Calculate your production costs, your manufacturing costs, and your anticipated profit margins to come up with your floor price and your break even point.
- Determine how you want to be positioned in the market (high, low, middle).
- Split test your price (place ads, send emails or letters to your list, etc.).
- Use your product's features, benefits, and production value to differentiate it from the competition and get your price as high as possible. Add extras such as guides, reports, transcripts, etc., and sell them in sets.

Chapter 21

Fulfillment
Delivering Your Video
to Your Customer

Chapter Objectives

- Know the pros and cons of doing your own fulfillment.
- Choose the best shipping method for you.
- Understand what fulfillment services can do for you.
- Understand what Video-On-Demand (VOD) is and how you can use it.

Having the greatest video in the world won't earn you a cent until you exchange it with a customer for cash, which means you need a method of getting it to them. The industry term for the process of following through a transaction from ordering through delivery is fulfillment.

The activities involved in product fulfillment include warehousing, assembly, quality control, and delivery of your video directly to your customers. If you decide you are going to sell your videos as DVDs, then you'll have to make decisions on how you will handle all of these processes. Now that you are able to offer online delivery of video, you can bypass some of these and focus on delivery.

You have to decide if you want to do this yourself or job it out. If you decide to do it in-house, you'll be dealing with maintaining inventory, storage, buying packaging materials, investing in a postal scale, and getting the packages to the shipper. You may find that your time is better spent marketing and creating new videos than duplicating, packaging, and shipping.

If you have the time and capability to handle your own fulfillment, it will cost less than using a fulfillment service. They will charge a fee per package shipped that you won't have to pay if you do it yourself. You'll have to decide if this is a good use of your time and if you even have the space to do it.

SHIPPING IT YOURSELF

If you do decide to do your own shipping we recommend the United States Postal Service for its value. USPS Media Mail is a great bargain for shipping DVDs and books. This used to be called Book Rate but has been renamed Media Mail to include all types of media. You can ship books, films, DVDs, CDs, and sound recordings under Media Mail, but not magazines or any type of advertising. You can ship large boxes up to 70 pounds via Media Mail for much less than UPS or FedEx. Just don't include any advertising material such as catalogs and don't put any handwritten notes in there either. You can get optional delivery confirmation for a small charge. Delivery confirmation will show the date and time of delivery or if the delivery was attempted but not successful, plus the date and time of the attempt but it won't show you the tracking of the package like other shippers (UPS, FedEx) offer.

Media Mail packages are typically received within seven to nine days, but this can vary by location. The further away you are shipping, the longer it will take. Within your own state it may only be a day or two. In very busy times, like Christmas, it can take longer than nine days. Within my own state of California I have found that Media Mail packages are usually delivered within one or two days, sometimes the next day.

If you are only shipping one DVD then it can go via 1st Class Mail at about the same cost as Media Mail, and is usually delivered in one to two days. Today 1st Class postage for a single DVD is averaging $2.50.

Don't just put your DVD into a bubble envelope or worse, a plain shipping envelope. The Amaray cases break easily and you stand a good chance of getting a call from an unhappy customer. We get some great single DVD mailing boxes from Uline (www.uline. com). The box number is S-10395. They sell boxes of all sizes to fit any need. Invest in good shipping materials and pass the cost on to your customer.

The free USPS Flat Rate Priority mailing boxes and envelopes are a very good value for heavier items that need to be delivered fast. As the post office says, "If it fits, it ships." You can sign up with USPS.com and use their Click-N-Ship® option which will allow you to print out labels (you don't have to buy labels, you can print them out on your own paper) at a reduced shipping rate and get delivery confirmation for free. Since you pay online, you don't even have to go to the Post Office to mail, just put your label on the Priority Flat Rate mailers and take it out to your mail box for your carrier to pick up.

I've always looked at shipping as a profit center and set my shipping fees to cover the cost of the package, postage, and the time it takes to package and ship the item. You should not be underwriting the cost of shipping; that will eat into your profit. The challenge here is setting a price that covers all of your costs plus a little for your time without allowing the shipping cost to get so high that it starts hurting sales. Make sure you at least break even on your shipping fees.

FULFILLMENT SERVICES

If you don't want to bother with shipping you can find a fulfillment service to do it for you. These services range from simply warehousing and shipping your goods to taking the orders over the phone or internet, putting the component parts together to make your package, then shipping it. Some of them can even handle your ordering and DVD duplication needs. If you do an internet search on "fulfillment services" you will see scores of options. Some of these companies are geared to larger businesses and others will cater to businesses of any size. Amazon offers Fulfillment by Amazon with reasonable rates. Their website at www.amazonservices.com/content/fulfillment-by-amazon.htm is easy to understand and is a good introduction to the topic of fulfillment.

Once your sales justify it, getting a fulfillment service is a good move as it allows you to spend your time on more important activities than packaging and shipping items—like making more SIVs!

Choosing Fulfillment Vendors

Choosing a fulfillment option for your business is an important business decision. Besides the cost and quality of the services there are other things to consider like the type of goods to be delivered, the volumes of orders, warehouse locations, and the dependence of fulfillment activities on other business processes.

VIDEO-ON-DEMAND

We can now skip the DVD process, and all that is involved with it, entirely through online video delivery or VOD. The best part of VOD is that your customers get to view the video as soon as they purchase it and you get their payment sent into your bank account right away! There's no inventory, no packaging supplies, no shipping or handling to deal with, no worries from either party that the video will get lost in the mail. Other than for shippers like the USPS, Fed Ex, and UPS, it's good news, especially for the small producer. For us it is a very liberating way to do business.

Most VOD providers will handle everything, from hosting and streaming your videos to processing credit card sales for you.

Like any new technology, VOD does have its challenges. Bandwidth, or the user's connection to the internet, can still be an issue. If a user has a slow internet connection or underpowered computer, the viewing experience can be unsatisfactory. Even with a very fast internet connection and a powerful computer, sometimes when we watch videos online they buffer for a long time, stutter, or even stop while playing. It can be frustrating.

Companies offering VOD are popping up regularly as the technology gets better and more affordable. Some offer free services for a small number of videos (basically as a trial) and costs can go up to over $1,000 per month if you are hosting a really large number of videos that are getting played a lot. Pricing is usually based on both the size of files you are storing on their system and the bandwidth used to deliver videos to end users. There are scores of players in this area with more starting up all the time. One of the larger ones that I feel confident will be around for a while is Amazon's own brand, Amazon Video On Demand™, available through their CreateSpace company. Check www.shoot-to-sell.com as we'll be updating information on VOD providers there.

These VOD providers usually have excellent tutorial videos to guide you through the process of setting your video files up. Some of them bundle other services with VOD such as live-streaming, video email, custom video interfaces, and more. As always, do shop around to find the provider that best fits your needs and budget and don't be afraid to contact their support lines if you need help.

An alternative to paying a service to do this for you is to do it yourself. It can seem a bit daunting at first but if you take it one step at a time you can do it. As I shared in Chapter 19, we're doing this ourselves using Amazon S3 hosting service, which is very inexpensive. You will need PayPal or a credit card merchant account to take orders, and then you'll need some way of protecting your videos so that only legitimate users can view them.

You have to think about security. There are lots of people who would "share" your video with friends if they could, and then they would share it with their friends, and before you know it thousands of "friends" will have your videos without paying for it. There are ways to deal with this.

Many of the video-on-demand hosting sites serve your video in a secure fashion so it is difficult (it's never impossible) to steal. Some go so far as to restrict playing to one

IP address, meaning one specific computer. This can be a bother, as a person couldn't watch the video on a different computer without getting the VOD provider to switch IP addresses. That's too much hassle for my taste.

Membership sites are a good way to deal with security because a member must have a username and password to get inside to view the videos. Membership software packages deal with the issue of security in various ways. A good WordPress plugin to secure videos stored on Amazon S3 is S3 Media Vault (www.s3mediavault.com). It allows secure access to videos stored on Amazon S3 and provides a video player to play Flash, MP4 and MPEG videos.

This software also is always changing so I'll refer you to www.shoot-to-sell.com for the latest recommendations.

A WORD OF CAUTION ABOUT ONLINE VIDEOS

I like the idea of delivering video-on-demand and not having any inventory to deal with. We're definitely going to see more of that model in the future. I would be remiss, however, if I did't tell you the downside of that.

Many of the videos going online now are high definition and can be played full screen. They look great. Here's the catch: even though the end customer is watching a streaming video, meaning it never is downloaded to their computer, they can use screen capture software to record it while playing and—violà!—they have a copy. The quality of the copy depends on the quality of the online video. Since it is a digital copy it can be duplicated over and over and every copy will be identical. Unscrupulous or uninformed people could get a copy and share it with friends or put it on social sharing sites like YouTube, where millions more people could view and share it. From selling just one copy, hundreds, thousands, or even millions of people could view it.

Your customers may not know about screen capture software or they might not be the kind that would copy your video, but it just takes one. In Chapter 23, we'll discuss some ways you can deal with this issue.

Action Steps

- Decide if you want to do your own fulfillment.
- Will you be doing your own shipping? Consider USPS Media Mail as the least expensive option.
- Use good shipping materials to protect your DVDs.
- Charge enough for shipping to cover your costs and your time.
- If you don't want to ship, shop around for a fulfillment service.
- Consider distributing your videos as on-demand (VOD).

Chapter 22

Distributing Your SIV Through Others

Chapter Objectives

- Learn about some of the distribution options you have for DVDs and online delivery.
- Understand the pros and cons involved in selling your DVDs through distributors and to large retailing chains.
- Find out how you can find specialty niche distributors, retailers, and catalogs.

There are many ways to sell and distribute your videos. Later on we'll focus on setting up your business to sell retail but let's turn our attention to selling your videos through other distribution networks first. We'll be talking mostly about physical products such as DVDs but, more and more through the availability of online technology, you can sell your video through distributors who deliver it digitally.

When you sell through distributors, you will sell your video to them at a discount. The standard industry practice is from 40 to 50 percent off of your established retail price. It is common to have a sliding scale so the more they buy, the bigger the discount. It could be based on units ordered or total dollar amount. You will need to set this scale in a discount schedule and apply the same discounts equally to every distributor.

The distributor can be an online or retail store, a mail order business, or a middleman who in turn supplies the videos to retail stores.

There are pros and cons to selling through others. Since you'll need to sell your videos at a significant discount, you'll have to sell a lot more videos to recoup your initial costs. On the plus side, if your video sales take off, you can see large numbers of sales occurring through larger retail networks. Another plus is someone else is handling the process of distribution for you.

Also don't necessarily count on distributors to do a good marketing job for you. Most likely your product is just one among hundreds or thousands they sell. You still need to be involved in marketing to create desire for your videos. Supply your distributors with sales copy, images, banner ads, anything to help them do a better job of promoting your videos. Send out press releases and mention where people can get the videos. If you just sit back and wait for the money to roll in, you'll probably be disappointed.

WORKING WITH A NATIONAL CHAIN

Almost every partner I've worked with wondered if we could get our videos into a national chain. Getting your video picked up by a large retailer used to be one of the main ways you could get your video into the hands of your consumer without setting up a mail order business yourself. Maybe because of this, it seems to be the frequent goal for producers.

They start to talk Walmart or Barnes & Noble and they see dollar signs. I have had limited experience trying to get into large national chains and have learned a lot of reasons why it may not always be a good fit for the small SIV producer.

First, it's very difficult to get your video into a retail outlet buyer's hands. There are many layers between you and that person. In fact, many retail outlets only work with wholesale, independent, or sub-distributors and if your video is not available through those companies, they won't even deal with you. You need to find who they buy from and try to get listed with them. Some of the wholesale distributors that work with videos are Baker & Taylor (www.baker-taylor.com), Ingram Entertainment (www.ingramentertainment.com), and WaxWorks VideoWorks (www.waxworksvideoworks.com/). Barnes & Noble works exclusively with Alliance Entertainment (www.allianceentertainment.org). The only way they'll consider your DVD is if it is listed with Alliance. Walmart only buys DVDs through Anderson Merchandisers (www.amerch.com). For other retailers that sell DVDs, go to their websites and search for "Vendor" or "Supplier" information.

Getting picked up by these wholesalers is quite a process and requires that you actually have a DVD "shelf ready," complete with attractive packaging and UPC code. They'll want you to send copies for their review. (Here is where investing in a smaller DVD run would be smart. If there is interest shown in your video, then you can order larger quantities and get your expenses down.) Additionally, they may ask for your marketing plan, any reviews you have on your video, and financial information, among other things. This isn't meant to be discouraging, it's meant to show you some of the steps involved in getting onto their shelves.

Most of the big distributors don't want to deal with you if you only have one title. They want to work with producers who have at least a dozen titles. Brokers will sometimes handle getting your videos into the big chains but they will take a big cut, the chain wants a big discount and you end up getting very little from each sale.

That's why I wouldn't produce a DVD with the express intent of getting it into a big chain unless you have a prior arrangement with a distributor or broker.

There are other things to consider. When you sell to large companies, you have to agree to their terms of sale and most require you to guarantee your products are fully returnable if they overstock it (meaning if they don't sell them, they'll ship them back to you), make you pay to ship your videos to them, and most have 90-day payment terms. In essence, your inventory is on loan for 90 days and may all come back to you.

If you do go with a distributor or chain, don't enter into an exclusive contract with them. They have to allocate their marketing budget to the most profitable and best-selling products. Yours may be one of them but if they find it does not sell, they'll not spend any more time or resources to market it. Unless they let you out of the contract, you're stuck. You can attempt to drive people there to buy, but you can't sign on with any other distributor who may do a better job for you.

They also may wish to sell them at drastically reduced prices, which tarnishes the image of your product in the eyes of other possible distributors. They can also go out of business and you're back at square one. Think of Borders and Circuit City.

This is where the trend toward digital video-on-demand favors the small producer.

I'm not against finding distributors to handle your sales. On the contrary, I sell wholesale to special market distributors but I personally wouldn't enter into an exclusive contract and not also market them myself. We have videos now that are in distributor catalogs and sold through their websites. They may give them only two inches of space and a photo, if we're lucky. (You'd be surprised at how many distributors in the education market don't even put sample videos on their site!) Our videos are just one among hundreds of titles they offer, so how much marketing focus do you think ours get? Almost none.

When your DVD is new, it may be featured but if it doesn't perform as it moves into the later stages of the product life cycle, it will drop down in their marketing budget. It will get smaller and less desirable space in a catalog or website until they drop it.

I've known producers who will not sell to distributors for a period of time, like the first six months or year of a new product's life, so that they can recoup as much profit as possible, as quickly as possible, before discounting it to distributors. The more crossover there is in their customer lists, the less inclined they are to let a "competitor" buy their videos at a discount until they've skimmed the cream off the sales. As sales to their own market slow down they can afford to let more people buy it from them for resale, particularly if they will be selling to a different customer base.

The risk in doing that is that some large distributors don't want to touch your seasoned product—it's not new enough for them. They want to cash in on the new video sales.

I always build my own web page for new products. The advantage of this is I can provide a lot more information, testimonials, photos, and videos. I can have related products for added sales (see Chapter 24). I can provide valuable content and build a relationship with prospects by having a site they can visit. Better yet, I can offer giveaways and collect email addresses so that I can communicate with potential customers who may buy from me in the future. This step is crucial in building your mailing list and will be covered in depth a bit later. We also always put a sample of the video on YouTube and other sites with links back to our website. You have to do everything you possibly can to get your video found.

We talked with video producer Rich Ferguson about his experiences working with a large discount retailer.

Kim and I met Rich Ferguson about 13 years ago when I was teaching him Final Cut Pro and Kim was teaching him After Effects for a local vocational school. Rich had just walked away from a secure job at UPS to embark on a career involving his talents as a magician and his desire to get into producing media. Smart move as it turned out.

He was recently a guest on the Ellen DeGeneres Show, is an award-winning member of the Academy of Magical Arts in Hollywood, has a #1 book ranking on Amazon, was a finalist on NBC's reality show Phenomenon, opened for Jimmy Kimmel Live and Jay Leno casino shows, and has performed for corporate shows all over Las Vegas. Corporate jets fly in to pick him up to do shows. Suffice it to say, Rich has done well for himself and has some fascinating experiences in the video publishing world, which he has agreed to share with you.

Rich Ferguson, Magician, Mentalist, Author, Motivation Speaker and Creative Consultant (www.theicebreaker.com)

One of the very first DVDs I produced, I did on my own. It was on poker chip tricks, which is really a niche market within the poker community. I had an interest in poker and I had a very big interest in psychology, so those two worlds collided with the explosion of Texas Hold 'Em. I happened to be very into coin magic and so everything collided at once.

I noticed a trend and I thought, "Wow! I know how to do a lot of really cool things with chips and coins. I wonder if I can make a DVD on tons of fancy things to do at the poker table and sell it in the very niche market of poker?" And so I produced it quickly just to beat anyone else to the punch. It did very, very, well—very fast.

I immediately started making the next version which had about 75 poker chip tricks in it. I didn't know all those tricks, I only knew about a dozen. I had a tiny bit of knowledge in it and then I just attacked it.

That's some great advice about seeing an opportunity, taking advantage of it and not waiting until you are an expert to get started. I also wanted Rich to share his experience about working with a big (name withheld) box store:

If you're going to try to get your DVD picked up by something like Warner, let's say, they're not going to touch you unless you have maybe 10 titles. They just won't touch you. So you might have to find yourself a broker who can be the in-between. So I had to find a relationship with a broker who has thousands of titles and they represented me and they took a 50 percent royalty cut.

The problem was you have thousands of copies of different titles going into the different big box stores, and there's a lot of money that gets paid for marketing, then there's all the returns and all the damages and there are no guarantees at the end of the day. Although we made a lot of money, much of it was eaten up by expenses. It's just not an efficient system compared to the ease of a really good, optimized website and blogs pointing traffic to Amazon, for instance.

I'm doing much better with just online sales than the big box store ever did for me. I had four DVDs selling for $15 to $19.99 each and they wanted the entire four-disc set put into a package and sold for $19.99 for all four, and then of course they want 60 or 70 percent off the price, and then you have to pay your broker, and then you have to pay everyone that's involved, and it just doesn't equate to a ton at the end unless you're selling millions of copies, and that's just not going to happen for the little niche market I had.

I didn't walk away thrilled but I was glad it happened. It's great for the resume to say you've gotten into this particular store and it kind of shocked the magic world a bit. They're like, "Dang Rich! How'd you do that because that's not that common?" But it didn't really change my life.

What works really well, at least in my industry, is finding who the main distributor is within your industry. Every industry has their own version of that, a main distributor to all the stores and niche stores. I have found that to be such a great thing because although you don't make a ton of money you make a good amount consistently, forever. They just continually buy, continually stock the stores. And I get a nice check.

I asked Rich how he managed to do so much.

I find the time by scheduling, working hard, and it's all in the calendar. I set a lot of daily, weekly, monthly, and yearly goals and you have to. You can't just have a pipe dream, "I hope to have a book someday." You have to start writing or it's never going to get done.

That's how I want you to think about producing your special interest videos!

Our interview covered a lot of fascinating details that I don't have room for here, but you can read the entire interview at www.shoot-to-sell.com.

SMALLER NICHE DISTRIBUTORS AND RETAILERS

Does your video serve a niche market like Rich's? Smaller distributors and specialty retailers may be seriously interested in your title. We sell our DVD, *A Sense of Place* to several museum gift stores in Florida. They are much easier to contact, are open to negotiation, and offer better terms. These are the kind of distributors we look for.

Do a search through the periodicals you referenced when researching your titles. Look online for retailers and other distributors. Find out if your DVD is a good fit for their business and, if so, get their email, fax, and physical mailing information. I usually start with an email introduction before I send a sample DVD to them. I like to establish a relationship first to learn if they are interested in my DVD before I put a lot of expense into wooing them.

GETTING INTO CATALOGS

This is another option to consider and one we've employed. Print catalogs are still a viable business and the nice thing for the independent, small producer is that they are easier to reach, pay faster, order in large quantities, and usually pay you to ship your product to them. Catalogs also have a long shelf life, so as long as you are listed in the catalog they'll do business with you. It's also good advertising for you.

The downside is they may want to dictate your price, request a much deeper discount, and sell your videos for less than the retail price.

Where do you find catalogs? Do an internet search on your topic adding the word "catalog," go to your local bookstore and your library where you will find *The Directory of Mail Order Catalogs* and the *Directory of Business to Business Catalogs*. Also look for the *National Directory of Catalogs* and the desk reference, *Direct Marketing Market Place*. Online you can go to www.catalogs.com.

With the internet, many of these catalogs will have companion websites as well, which further increases your exposure to buyers.

ONLINE DISTRIBUTION CHANNELS

You may find some VOD business who would want to represent your title, or you can build your own catalog at places such as www.mindbites.com. If your video is a documentary, check out www.filmbinder.com. Again, look into Clickbank to see if that service would work for your title.

www.distribber.com is a service that will place your video in a number of high visibility outlets like Netflix, Hulu, Time Warner Cable, iTunes, and more, but they are expensive.

Action Steps

- Research the type of retail outlets and distribution companies that would be a good fit for selling your videos.
- Get your marketing plan, financials, and appealing packaging buttoned up. Make sure your DVD has a UPC code. Have your review copies made.
- Contact distributors to find out what they need from you and how you can apply to be listed with them.

- Do the same with national and specialty retailers.
- Research the types of catalogs available and what you need to do to get them to sell your DVD.
- Look into all the online distribution options and methods of protection and consider making your videos available through those avenues.

Chapter 23

Protecting Yourself from Piracy

Chapter Objectives

- Learn how you can protect yourself from piracy.
- Discover what is included in a copyright notice and how to craft one.
- Find out what you can do if you find someone who is infringing on your intellectual property rights.
- Learn who holds the copyright on your video.

You're starting to see steady sales of your videos then one day, you happen to trip across a listing on eBay or another site and see your video title ... being sold by someone else! How can this be?

When you start seeing some success in selling your videos, you may find that your website, marketing copy, articles, videos, and your other intellectual property have been copied without your permission. This is especially true in the online world, but it can happen in the offline world as well. Even if you use software to protect your DVDs, a determined person can crack and copy them.

When I was working for the university, we discovered an individual who was buying our videotapes, copying them, and then selling them under his own business name. He couldn't have been any more blatant about it. This was pre-internet and he was selling our titles via catalog mailings—and we were on the mailing list! Well, we noticed that although he kept sending out these catalogs, he never purchased any inventory from us.

We hired a private investigator and busted him. When confronted, he admitted it. That ended up costing him a lot in the end because we got a judgment against him and he had to pay us $120,000. We were lucky in that regard because he stupidly had us on his mailing list. If he hadn't, he might have gotten away with it for a long time.

There are some people who will take your profitable idea and create a similar product. Don't let that fear keep you from producing and creating though. Except for the above situation, I've never had anyone do that to me again—that I know of. And even though on the internet it is easier for unscrupulous (or lazy) people to steal your ideas or words and try to profit from them, the technology also makes them more transparent and easier to find as well.

First and foremost, the main purpose of the copyright is to tell people that this is not public domain material and that it is illegal to copy it. A work is considered public domain if: (1) it was created before copyright laws (before 1923 in the U.S.), (2) its copyright protection has expired, (3) it never had copyright protection or its protection was lost, (4) it was dedicated to the public domain.

You don't have to file with the U.S. Library of Congress to have copyright protection (this may not be the case in other countries so you need to research the copyright law where you live). Just putting it in print using the copyright symbol © does the job. Currently a copyright is good for the creator's life, plus 70 years. That doesn't stop anybody who is determined to steal it, but it does put people on notice. That is why we put a copyright on all of our product packaging. If you do want to take legal action in the form of a copyright infringement lawsuit, you do need to register your copyright.

 A copyright notice needs to include the word "copyright" or the symbol © followed by the year of the first publication and the name of the copyright owner. An example is © 2012, Panorama Studios.

For people who outright steal your intellectual property or use your website copy word-for-word, there are ways you can discover if you're being pirated, protect yourself, and fight it without spending tons of money on an office full of lawyers.

I suggest doing these things:

- *Sign up for Google Alerts at www.google.com/alerts.*

Set the frequency of your alerts to get daily updates from Google. Then add words unique to your site and/or product to your alert. You will see if your sites or products show up under other listings.

Using a longer word combination will get you more specific results. For example, we have a video program we sell at 10MinutesToPainFree.com so we choose as our Google Alert query, "10 minutes to a pain free neck," rather than the more generic "pain free." The first is actual copy on our site. That way, the search is much more specific than just "pain free" or "pain relief."

- *Periodically do a manual Google search on a specific phrase on your website or product copy.*

Copy the phrase exactly as you wrote it and surround it with quotation marks. So if your copy says, "fly fishing advice that is guaranteed to bring home the BIG one," enter it just like that. Although there is a chance that the offender changed your copy, many times they don't, due to laziness. They also may feel it was working well for you, it will also work for them, so why change it? They are also wanting to take advantage of your good reputation.

If you find someone is copying your site or selling your videos on their site and you don't want to deal with the guilty person, find out where the website is hosted. You can find who owns a website or domain name by searching the WHOIS database. Go to www.whois.com/whois/ to check their database. Once there, enter the offending website and you'll find the Internet Service Provider (ISP) who hosts the site. Then write to the host notifying them, using strong terms and an authoritative tone, about copyright infringement by one of their users.

Internet service providers by law are expected to remove material from their customer's websites that appears to violate copyrights. ISPs are usually very quick to pull the offending website down since they don't want to run into legal problems that would jeopardize their business. This should also work if the website they host is selling a video that infringed your copyright.

You can also often find the owner of the site and their contact information on whois. com. If you do, contact them directly. If they are uncooperative, you may have to seek legal advice. As a first step, you may want to look into the cost of having a lawyer write a strongly worded cease and desist letter. For an hour of their time, it may be worth it. If you've never received one of these, it's pretty ominous and scary enough for most people to stop. (I can attest to that since I've been on that side too when using the words *Tarzan and Jane* on an art print. Edward Rice Burroughs's estate sent us the letter and we quickly renamed it *Jungle Love* and they were satisfied.)

- *Search eBay, Craigslist, and other big auction sites for illegally copied DVDs and videos.*

Look for DVDs on the same topic as yours. If you find someone selling exact copies of yours on eBay—and they are selling them as brand new and not just selling their own copy for a little extra cash—you may request the removal of listings on eBay that offer products that infringe on your rights through eBay's Verified Rights Owner (VeRO) program. At Craigslist, you can report abuse at habuse@craigslist.org.

One word of caution: think twice about selling anything to China and other Asian countries where it is highly likely your product will be copied, mass duplicated, and resold. Because we can't police it that well, copying is rampant.

With all this said, don't let your fear of copyright infringement keep you from producing and selling your own work. It may not happen to you and you would have missed out on months or years of sales and good income.

WHO HOLDS THE COPYRIGHT ON A VIDEO I DID WITH A PARTNER?

So who holds the copyright on a special interest video you do for a client: you or the client? Do you split/share/assume the copyright from your clients? This is one of those things you need to hammer out at the beginning and have it written into a contract or letter of agreement.

If the client is paying you to create the video for them, they will be the one who owns the copyright if they contracted you as in a work for hire agreement. Don't construe this as legal advice because it isn't, but the person creating the source material, i.e., the video clips, audio, graphics, etc., often can claim that they own the right to that material, and possibly extend that to the final product that they created. It really comes down to how you negotiate it, so do clear this issue up with the client to avoid any problems later on.

We feel that if it is a joint project and the other party did not pay you for the production, (i.e., you funded it), then the actual footage, videotapes, editedmasters, the DVD authoring, graphics, packaging, etc. are your intellectual property. You may pay your partners a fee up front or incrementally as the DVD sells, like a royalty, but you may own the copyright.

We often work with technical advisors or subject matter experts and this is typically how we work with them.

For example, our cactus and succulent DVDs were done entirely by us with the help of advisors. We worked out a deal with those advisors to pay them a royalty of 10 percent. The DVDs are our intellectual property and the copyright belongs to us.

In another project we copyrighted the videos but we made it clear in a letter of understanding that our partner is free to develop other projects using the name, in this case it is 10MinutesToPainFree.

It is very important to get this type of relationship in writing. The expert needs to understand that they are also bound by that copyright so if they reproduce the DVDs without your knowledge or consent, they are in violation.

This issue is not black and white and so you have to take every case on its own. Again, let me emphasize that you should get the copyright issue cleared up with any partners right at the beginning to avoid future problems, and seek legal advice if needed.

Action Steps

- Add a copyright notice on all your intellectual property.
- Set up a Google Alert on keywords and key phrases related to your videos and your business.
- Do a Google search periodically on these keywords and key phrases to discover if someone is selling your video or using your copy, artwork, etc., without permission.
- Run a search on eBay and Craigslist periodically and use their abuse protection programs to report if you find someone is selling your video without permission.
- If you do find a business that is infringing on your copyright, contact them immediately. Look into having a lawyer compose a cease and desist letter to send them.
- Register your copyright if you intend to take the offender to court.
- If it is a website that is infringing on your copyright, you should also research their ISP provider and inform the provider to report copyright infringement from one of their users. You can usually find this information at www.whois.com/whois/.
- Get your copyright ownership issue in writing when working with a client and partner. Have people you subcontract with—crew, talent, etc.—sign work for hire agreements and talent releases so that they are clear they do not own the copyright.

Chapter 24

Expanding Your Product Line Fast

Chapter Objectives
- Understand the need to have more products available.
- Know what affiliate programs are and how to find them.
- See ways to expand existing videos into new formats.

Let's assume that you have finished your SIV, it's available for sale and someone buys it. Yay! Good for you. What's next?

Unless you have other products to sell to your new customer, your relationship is over. You'll spend a lot of effort converting them to a customer and getting them to trust you enough to fork over their money. This is the best time to offer them something else related to what they have just bought. If you don't have anything, that's an expensive mistake. If you don't yet have another video produced to sell, it's a good idea to begin thinking about offering other related products they would find beneficial, and the sooner the better.

The cost of converting a prospect into a customer is much higher than the cost of keeping one. You'll invest time and money to make the video, set up your eCommerce site, plan your marketing, take the steps to get them into your marketing funnel, send a string of emails, maybe spend money on advertising, offer enticing discounts and bonuses, only to end your relationship—unless you have more to sell them. The thing is, they will probably want to buy more stuff from you. So go get some stuff and add it to your product mix!

In Chapter 3 we stated that you would want to develop multiple titles on a topic. Not only can you bundle them together to get a higher price, it's also better to have six 20-minute videos for sale on a topic than one 120-minute video. Maybe a customer will buy them one at a time over a period of weeks or months. That goes back to our metaphor of having lots of little streams of income feeding into a mighty river. It's more profitable when you own your own products but there are many ways to add products to your offerings immediately without creating them yourself.

I'm going to say something that sounds like heresy coming from an SIV producer: sometimes I'd rather read a book or ebook than watch a video. I can skim through a book, look at the index, and find information faster than I can in a video. That's why I like to offer both formats together. Books have been some of our most successful products.

We recommend that you do add books to your product line. It adds depth and some people will prefer a book to a video, or in addition to it. Where can you find books on your subject to sell? While you can get a wholesale account with a large book distributor like Ingram Book Company, to get really favorable discounts, you'd have to agree to buy a large amount over the course of a year. Then you have to deal with inventory and getting them shipped to you and then you shipping them to your customer. But you don't have to buy and ship physical inventory to sell books online.

Amazon and Barnes & Noble have partner programs where you earn a small percentage of every sale that is generated from a link they provide you. It isn't a large amount, usually 4 to 6 percent, but if you do a lot of sales this can add up. With these partnership programs, you can offer such a broad selection of related books that it will make you look like a big publisher overnight. You can go from selling a single video to offering a catalog of related products. Your average order size will go up as people add multiple items to their orders.

Amazon sells a lot more than books and some items cost hundreds and even thousands of dollars, so your potential can be quite good. Sell a $3,000 camera through your link and you can earn $180 just for connecting the customer to Amazon.com. Mighty Google also offers a program similar to Amazon.com.

This is known as affiliate marketing and there is a whole industry built around it. Look on many web pages and you may see a small link, often at the bottom of the page or under the About Us tab that says either Affiliates or Partners. These are opportunities to become an affiliate and represent and recommend those products. Many people who want to get into internet marketing but who do not have any products of their own get started as affiliate marketers and are very successful at it.

Affiliate marketing is great for both the company and the affiliates. Affiliates essentially become commissioned sales agents for the product. The company gets the benefit of having a large sales force but they only pay when an affiliate facilitates a sale. Affiliates can build an online business without having any product of their own. They may never even see the product they are selling.

The way this happens is a web visitor clicks on a link or banner on the affiliate's site. That places a piece of computer code called a "cookie" on their computer. When this person finally transacts a sale, that cookie tells the company who the affiliate was that sent them there and they get credit for the sale. There is usually an expiration date for cookies. Affiliate commissions can range from a few percent to as much as 75 percent of the sale.

There are several other large sources of products. Clickbank (www.clickbank.com) is a major player in this area. At this time Clickbank products are all digital, so there is no actual inventory. You can find Clickbank ebooks and video tutorials on just about any topic, so the chances are good that you can find Clickbank products that will complement your video titles. Clickbank also pays higher commissions than Amazon.com, often as much as 50 percent or more.

Commission Junction (www.cj.com) is one of the largest sources of affiliate relationships. They represent thousands of affiliate programs in every area of business but primarily physical goods. They are also a good place to learn about affiliate marketing because they operate one of the most robust and current information and training resource centers in the industry.

Linkshare (www.linkshare.com) is another leading provider of affiliate marketing programs. ShareASale (www.shareasale.com) is another. None of these programs requires exclusivity and we promote products from all of them.

Amazon.com's affiliate program, Amazon Associates, also offers a feature called the aStore (astore.amazon.com). You can build an entire catalog of products which you can either hand select or just choose a broad category of products. You have a certain amount of creative freedom in matching the look of the catalog to your website and it is a simple matter to connect the aStore to your website. You can actually have hundreds or even thousands of products in your aStore. For example, on our website for the car detailing DVD we have an aStore offering all kinds of car washing and detailing products. It fits perfectly with the DVD.

One word of advice before I continue, stick with affiliate products you use or trust. You want to build an ongoing relationship with your customers and if you start recommending books and products that aren't really related or complementary to your videos, you're going to lose their interest and loyalty.

EXPAND YOUR EXISTING PRODUCTS

There are ways to turn a single video into additional products. For example:

- You can strip the audio out and sell it as an MP3 or an audio CD.
- You can transcribe the audio into text and create an ebook. This works especially well with instructional videos. With the booming popularity of ebook readers, this can be a nice source of additional income at almost no cost to you.
- Break your video into individual modules and sell them separately.

You want to keep the relationship alive with your customers. Producing additional videos along the same subject line is the best way to do this, but pursuing these other methods will give you additional products quickly and at little or no cost to you.

Action Steps

- Join affiliate programs and sell related items.
- Look at your own products. Can you create new products out of them?

Chapter 25

Selling Online Without a Website

Chapter Objective

- Discover ways you can sell over the internet without setting up a website.

eCommerce is the business of selling online and it is changing everything. Whether you want to sell your videos through the internet or not, you really have no choice. People shop online and if people can't find your product online you are missing in action.

DO YOU REALLY NEED TO HAVE A WEBSITE?

We strongly recommend that you do build a website to establish your brand and have an internet presence but you don't absolutely have to have your own website in order to be found online. There are alternative ways to get an internet "store" without spending any money up front. For example, you can build a business page on Facebook, complete with payment processing applications like Payvment. Cost? Just a little for order processing, which you have to pay for any payment collection system. The downside of this is that Facebook could change its policies or cancel your account for some transgression and your store goes POOF. I do this but only in addition to building my own websites.

You can also use CD Baby, eBay, or Amazon.com to sell your DVDs. This way your videos are available for sale on the internet and you don't need a website or a merchant account.

AMAZON.COM

Amazon is the 800-pound gorilla in the room when it comes to book and DVD sales. Anyone can sell through the Amazon Advantage and/or the Marketplace program, both of which require you to have a UPC code to sell DVDs.

Amazon Advantage is a consignment program: they'll stock your DVDs and pay you when they sell. They handle shipping to the end customer. The downside is they take 55 percent off the top and don't pay you to ship your goods to them. This doesn't work too well if your price is low. For example, if your retail price is $12, you're only going to get $5.40 from them and then you have to pay to ship to them, so there goes a couple dollars more for packaging and postage. If they only order one or two DVDs at a time, most of your profit will go to getting your products to them. They also charge an annual program membership fee of $29.95. Since they are the ones dealing directly with the customer, you also lose the opportunity to communicate with that person which can be valuable in future marketing efforts.

Amazon's Marketplace program takes less of your sale but you have a fixed monthly fee and Amazon does not stock your item. It is a program similar to eBay. When your DVD is sold, it will be up to you to send an email to the customer to let him know when you are shipping the DVD, and then ship it. What I like about that is you get the customer's contact information and so can communicate with them about additional products. You can also request that they review and rate your DVD and make a recommendation on Amazon.

We use the Amazon Advantage program for our better-selling and higher-priced DVDs.

If you list with Amazon.com, make sure you write up an enticing, keyword-filled description and include images when you list your videos.

Neither of these programs actively promotes your items, so it's still to your advantage to create awareness of your videos and drive traffic to where customers can make a purchase.

eBAY

While it is free to sign up with eBay, sellers are charged an insertion fee to list items and a final value fee when it is sold. Once you set up an account on eBay, listing is fairly straightforward. They have very good seller support and pages of helpful guides, tools, and tutorials.

Here are some basics for listing your DVD:

- They have a category for educational videos but also consider listing in other categories as well. They don't have to be DVD categories either.
- Add the word DVD in your title.
- Under your description, what you say matters. Refer to Chapter 30 on copywriting. Bullet your benefits and features and try to include a sample of the video.
- You should include a real picture of your DVD, and pay the small extra fee for the gallery shot.
- Choose the Buy It Now option for your DVDs.

One thing I like about eBay is that you can test your prices easily. You can also choose to sell one copy at a time or more. Although listing more than one is less expensive, selling them one at a time may show scarcity and encourage buying. If you have it set to Buy It Now, once one is sold, you can relist again. In fact, you can set it up to automatically be relisted within your eBay seller settings.

eBay has an online catalog option that helps you create listings faster and automatically increase the possibility that your listing will appear in searches. Although you do not need UPC codes to sell on eBay, you will need a UPC code in order to take advantage of this feature. Learn more about the eBay catalog at www.pages.ebay.com/sellerinformation/ebaycatalog/home.html.

Be aware though, that eBay doesn't actively promote your items. Sure, people can do a search and find your product based on your listing (that's why you want to create a keyword-filled listing), but to get optimum sales you'll need to do some marketing yourself to build awareness of and demand for your product and drive traffic to these sites.

Guest postings on blogs, forum participation, and article marketing are promotional avenues that don't cost anything and don't require you to have your own website. We cover those in Chapters 37 and 38.

> Even if you do build your own website *you should still list your items on Amazon and eBay*. Both have partner relationships with Google so that when someone searches on Google, if there is a matching item on Amazon or eBay, it has a good chance of being displayed at the top of the Google search results page. Just think of that; one listing in Amazon and eBay gives you exposure on Google too. It's quite a deal; you get twice the exposure for a small price.

For videos-on-demand there is also Video On Demand™ a service of Amazon. Another company that sells digital products is Payloadz. You can sell from your own site, their store, and eBay, among others.

Those are just some of the ways to sell online without building your own website. You'll probably discover more. For now, let's assume that you are going to build a website. The first thing you'll need to do is choose a domain name.

Action Steps

- Look into Amazon's programs (Advantage, Marketplace, and Createspace) and decide which works best for your video product.
- List your DVD with eBay.
- Research online services such as Payloadz to see if those channels would be a good option and fit for your video programs.

Chapter 26

Choosing a Domain Name

Chapter Objectives

- Gain an understanding of why you'd want Universal Resource Locaters (URLs) for your name, company, and product name.
- Know how search engine optimization relates to your domain name.
- Understand why keyword-rich URLs are effective.
- Know how to easily find options for your URL.
- Choose a URL suffix the works best for you.

PICKING YOUR DOMAIN NAME

If you've been around the internet for a while, you've probably heard or seen the word "domain name." It is another word for Universal Resource Locater (URL)—otherwise known as your web address.

If you don't have a domain name yet, this is where you need to start. The good news is that you can usually pick them up at a great price. They can be found starting at $7.99/ year. Some web hosting services will throw them in free when you sign up for hosting, and some URL merchants will throw in free hosting when you buy your URL from them. It's worth shopping around.

Your domain name is essentially your online business name and can do many things for you, from branding you and your products to helping your search engine optimization (SEO). Choosing your URL is an important step and deserves serious consideration. That's why we're going to spend some time talking about it.

There are different types of domain names to consider using. You can use *your* name, your *business* name, or your *product* name, or all three. You can choose something that is short and catchy or long and keyword-filled. A keyword-filled name would be something like AutomobileTransmissionRepair.com. Every word would be a highly descriptive search term that someone looking for that type of product or service would likely use.

Which type of domain name you use depends on what type of website you're building, i.e., to promote yourself, to promote your business, or a specific product.

My position is that your business's name should communicate something as to what the business is about. There are many stunning exceptions to this of course, with creative nonsense names like Google and Zazzle for example, but we're not Google. I take the safe route.

YOUR NAME AND SEARCH ENGINE OPTIMIZATION

Before we go further, we should talk a little about search engine optimization (SEO) as it relates to a domain name. SEO is all about improving the ranking or visibility of your website in search engines in "natural," or unpaid search results. You'll also hear this called "organic" or "algorithmic" searches. Search engine ranking refers to where your site appears in the unpaid results of a search engine query. That page of result is called a search engine results page or SERP for short.

You want to increase your chances of appearing high in the search results when people search for your type of business so that you can be easily found and get a lot of traffic to your site, which you hope will convert to buyers. If your site appears anywhere except the first page, your web traffic will suffer—a lot. The top half of the first page that shows without scrolling is known as "above the fold," in reference to how newspapers fold, and that's where you want to be found on your key search terms. The more effort people have to put into finding you the less likely they'll do so.

I just did a search on Google on the term "food." I see that it found 3,490,000,000 matching results. If your website was about food you would want to be found among the top 4 or so results above the fold on the first page, out of those over *three billion* results. You can imagine if you fell somewhere around the 500th page of search results; you'd never be seen! This is why learning to optimize your website for the best possible search engine results is so important.

The principles of SEO should also be applied to the choice of a name for your video as well as your web content and other marketing endeavors, which we'll discuss in more detail when we get into copywriting in Chapter 30.

Earlier I mentioned the word keyword-filled domain name as something to consider when choosing your URL. Now why is keyword-filled so important? (You will also see it described as keyword-rich.) And how can that help you?

Keywords are descriptive terms that search engines use to index you. Indexing is the process where a search engine scans through your website, looks at all your pages and stores a list of keywords it found on your site into their database. These keywords are then used to select pages to display in the search results when a user performs a search on a keyword. *So to be found, the first imperative is to get accurately indexed.* The more accurately the search engine thinks you match the search terms and the better the rank you have earned over time, the further up you'll be on the SERP.

Let's say you own a fly fishing tour company called Backwoods Fly Fishing Tours and you live in Alaska. You'd probably want to buy BackwoodsFlyFishingTours.com. This is great for branding your business. But in terms of SEO it would only be good if a person enters in the word Backwoods in their search. Now if it's my business and at less than $10 a year, I would choose that name. My video production business is called Panorama Studios so I have PanoramaStudios.com as a domain name. Also consider this …

Your name is Jane Doe and along with running the fly fishing tour business, you're well known in your niche and are looking to establish your business and brand under your name too. In that case, you would try to get JaneDoe.com. (Unless you have a very unique name, you may find them much harder to get. I couldn't get the name PatrickSmith.com when I went to set up my dad's website, think how many Patrick Smith's there are. My workaround? PatrickSmithOnline.com.) Adding "online" to an already owned name is a good workaround.

But you also want to buy a keyword-rich domain name as well. In this case, more people are probably searching for "fly fishing tours in Alaska" than for your specific business name Backwoods Fly Fishing Tours since they may not know your name or even that you exist. Unless you are the only fly fishing tour company in Alaska (not likely in Alaska!), one of the best ways to capture this traffic is to also pick up the keyword-driven name which in this case would be FlyFishingToursAlaska.com or AlaskaFlyFishingTours.com. And that's exactly what Alaska Fly Fishing Tours of Homer, Alaska, did.

While these are examples of how to approach this for your business and personal name URLs, I use them to illustrate the thought process that should go into this. You'll do the same with the title of your videos.

Since you want to use the power of SEO, the key is also to find out exactly what people are searching for in Google and other search engines, and pick up the "exact match" keyword domain name. (We'll show you how to do that later.) So, if people are typing in *Alaska fly fishing tours*, you want AlaskaFlyFishingTours as the first part of your domain name.

If you decide to turn your fly fishing expertise into video information products, your video publishing business may benefit from a domain name that explains what your business is. For example, if your business is fly fishing videos, why not make it clear by choosing a URL like FlyFishingVideos.com? A person is more likely to search for "fly fishing videos" rather than for your name or business name and you have all three words in your URL.

Going the opposite direction, you may also think about using something short and catchy. You want a name that rolls off the tongue that may not be really descriptive but will be memorable. If doing this, the shorter the better. Google likes short. Try to use 12 characters or less. But keep in mind this makes your SEO more challenging when you're starting out because nobody is searching for that term, so I tend to steer clear of catchy, kitschy words.

One reason it's a good idea to use a shorter name is if and when you use it in pay-per-click advertising (PPC), the number of characters you can use in the URL address line are limited. Good examples of successful and catchy URLs that don't describe the product line at all are: Zappos.com, GoDaddy.com, Yahoo.com, and once again, Google.com. (To be honest, if you're going that route, I would stick with a word that sort of relates to your business and your product if you can.)

If you did decide to go with a short, nonsense name you would want to fill your website with highly descriptive and popular keywords so that you would be indexed properly.

However, if you're going to build sites that get most of their traffic from Google searches, a keyword-filled domain name is preferable. This is how your video title name can help your SEO and corresponds with your business and product. Good examples of this come from the book publishing world, like a recent book I purchased from Marc Ostrofsky, *Get Rich Click*. He also scored the domain name GetRichClick.com. So if you can title your video with the most likely keywords people will search on, great!

KEYWORDS ARE THE KEY

We're going to be using the term "keyword" a lot from here on. There's a whole science to choosing the right keywords, and we'll cover some of that, but you really want to spend time choosing words that are being actively searched on, not words you think sound good.

Let's revisit that topic of niching it down that we first talked about in Chapter 3. The more you can choose words that are specific to the way people will search for your niche, the better.

How do you find the keywords your target market is looking for? You can do this by conducting keyword searches. The best free tool I found to do this is the Google keyword search tool, KeywordToolExternal. This tool is part of Google Adwords and you don't need an Adwords account to access it. However, when you do a search without an account they limit the number of results to no more than 100. To expand that search, I recommend setting up an Adwords account. It's also free to set up and you aren't required to run any ads to use these tools.

How does it work? Go to https://adwords.google.com/o/KeywordTool and type in a word or phrase describing your topic, you can see how much search volume there is for that keyword. For example, say you typed in "fly fishing," you'd find 1,220,000 monthly global searches for that word. Obviously, there is a lot of interest in fly fishing. Niche it further and search for "fly fishing videos" and that number drops to 8,100 monthly searches. Narrow it further to "Alaska fly fishing videos" and you come up with 28—big difference in search volume.

This is just a simple search. A good search also factors in how much competition there is for that word with pay-per-click advertisers and what they are paying to get clicks on that word. The higher the amount people are bidding on a keyword, the better that keyword is performing. The best combination is to find a keyword with high value and low competition. We have a short tutorial on using Keyword Tool External that shows you how to look at those factors at www.shoot-to-sell.com.

IS YOUR DOMAIN NAME AVAILABLE?

Now you've decided on the perfect URL and you want to know if it is available. You can use a service like www.godaddy.com to check that out. I also like to go to www.nameboy. com to see which URLs are available based on the keywords I enter. Nameboy is fun to play with because it suggests lots of permutations on a name. It will suggest dozens of variations on a domain name and tell you which ones are available. This may help you find a name that never occurred to you. There are similar services, like www.domainsbot.com and www.instantdomainsearch.com.

You can buy many variations on a name and have them redirect to your main site. At $10 or less per year for a URL, that's cheap marketing.

If you plan to mostly attract people to your site by word of mouth, or through social media sources, consider choosing domains for your name, business, product title, and product line.

A couple of the reasons to do this are:

- It's a smart move for your branding strategy.
- You can protect and manage your own name, business, and product's trademark or copyright and online reputation. You don't want someone else to own it, do you?
- You want to future protect your title if it becomes a best seller.

I've also found that I don't want to limit myself to buying one domain name for just one video program for these reasons:

- I want to see which domain names will be found the most in searches. You can put different tracking mechanisms behind the scenes, done through a shopping cart and other ad tracking programs, so that you can see where people are finding you.

- I don't want my competitors to "scoop me" on a good name! If you have the .com name you don't want someone else to get the .info, .biz or .org name. People might get confused and go to the wrong site.
- I may want to make variations on my product's name and price, for different markets.

For example, I own CaptivatingCacti.com and SuccessWithSucculents.com where I sell these two videos to the consumer market. I repackaged and renamed the DVDs, added teaching guides, and also sell them to schools at HookedOnSucculents.com and CrazyAboutCacti.com. At a cost of $40 a year for those four URLs I only have to sell a couple of DVDs in one year to pay for the extra URLs. I'm always experimenting to see what works best.

Don't worry, you don't have to set up sites for all of them right away, you can redirect URLs to point to your main site initially or just "park" them. When I find a really good URL I'll buy it even if I don't need it, just so nobody can snatch it out from under me. I have a lot of URLs waiting to be developed into profitable websites when I get the time. In the meantime, nobody else can buy them.

THE SUFFIX OF YOUR URL MATTERS

When choosing your domain names, choose those with the .com extensions first if they are available. They are still preferable to any other domain extension, especially for commercial purposes. It is the most well-known and widely used extension and people are likely to type .com first on any URL. Other options to use are .net, .org, .biz, .info, .co, .me, .tv, and a whole host of others. However, I would stay away from .org unless you just want to set up a blog on it and you're not selling anything, because .org is, in many people's minds, still associated with its original purpose of serving non-profit organizations.

If your domain name with the .com is taken, and you feel strongly about using it, you can choose one of the other suffixes. Keep in mind if you don't have the .com and someone else does, that other site will pick up some traffic that would otherwise go to your site. Also remember what I said about simply adding "online" to the name and then usually you can get the .com suffix.

If the .com is available for registration, grab it before someone else does. You may find that the .com you want is taken but is for sale by a second party for a few hundred dollars or more. You'll have to decide if the asking price is worth it. You can also find out who owns a URL by going to www.whois.com/whois/ and doing a WHOIS lookup. You might be able to contact the URL's owner and buy the URL from them. A lot of people buy URLs with the sole intention of selling them at a profit. URLs are virtual real estate and there is a robust business in buying and selling them.

For example, there's a premium domain name that I want to buy but the owner is asking $1,188, so I'm not biting just yet. For names I'm really itching for, I like to put a domain buy order in so my domain service will purchase it automatically in case the current owner fails to renew it. I have used www.snapnames.com to do this and have purchased several important URLs for my business that way.

Several times this year I've been contacted by people who own URLs very similar to ones I own. They wanted to know if I wanted to buy them. I said no but watched as their expiration date got closer (I found this again at www.whois.com/whois/). On the day they expired I grabbed them for about $8 instead of the hundreds they were hoping I'd pay. If someone owns a URL you want you can try to grab it on the day it is due for renewal.

Want to see what URLs have recently become available because the owner forgot or failed to renew them? Go to www.justdropped.com. You can enter keywords and see what URLs with those words have recently become available.

 A lesson here is for you not to let *your* URL expire even for a second, lest someone pounces on it!

If you scored your .com, congratulations. Now you may decide you would also like to use other suffixes in addition so that you can not only do market testing and redirects, you can also keep them from your competitors' clutches. I know that when I buy a .com from Godaddy.com they offer the .info (if available) for an additional 49¢, so I always take it.

Also think about buying any common misspellings that might attract traffic. Buy www.yourdomain.com, too. Dropping the first period is a common typing mistake that may make that URL valuable too. Then you just redirect that to your main site.

WHERE TO BUY IT

Finally you're ready to buy your name(s). You can purchase them from many companies. www. godaddy.com, www.namecheap.com, www.networksolutions.com, www.cheapnames.com, the list goes on and on. Do an internet search on the term "best domain registrars" and you'll see lots of current articles and resources.

 Before you buy, do a Google search and you may find coupon codes that will allow you to buy the name cheaper. I always find good coupon deals at www.fatwallet.com. Also, if you do a search on the term "cheap domain names" you may find highly discounted offers from even the biggest registrars.

The place you buy your hosting account, covered in the next chapter, may either include a domain name in your purchase or sell it at a discounted price, so check that out first.

Be careful about renewals. When you buy a URL you can set it up to auto-renew. These auto-renewals are often at much higher prices than the original cost. Make sure you know the renewal terms and have a good notification system in place so that you'll know in advance that it is coming up for renewal. I turn automatic renewal off on my URLs but make sure I am getting renewal notifications in advance. Then I look for those discount codes and save a lot on my renewals.

Choosing your URL is a business decision that should not be taken lightly. It affects your search engine results, your image in your customer's minds, your ability to branch out with additional products in the future; it can be limiting or expansive. Have fun using tools like www.nameboy.com when looking for a name but take your final choice seriously. Finally, if you do find the name you want, don't hesitate! Buy it immediately before someone else does. I've had that happen to me in the span of minutes.

Action Steps

- Decide if your URL should be about your name, your service, or a specific product, or all of them.
- Write down a list of all of the search terms a user might try to find your product or service.
- Conduct a search on those words using Adwords.Google.com/Select/KeywordToolExternal.
- If you don't have a clear idea of what URL you want, go to www.nameboy.com to see some variations on your keywords. Also visit www.justdropped.com to see what URLs have very recently become available.
- Go to a service like www.namecheap.com, www.godaddy.com, www.networksolutions.com, www.domain.com, www.cheapnames.com, or any of dozens of similar places to purchase your URL. Consider buying the .info, .net, and other suffixes for your name to prevent your competition from buying them.
- If your chosen URL is not available, see if you can get it with a different yet appropriate suffix. If you don't want to go that route, look at that list of search terms again to see if something else will work. Consider adding the word "online" at the end of the words you want.
- If you really want the name that is not available, put a domain buy order on it. You can do this through www.snapnames.com or many of the registrars. You can also find out who owns the name and contact them directly.

Chapter 27

Your Own Hosting Account

Chapter Objectives

- Learn what web hosting is.
- Understand what to look for in a web host.
- Learn how to connect your domain name to it.

Once you have your domain name, you'll need a place to host your new site. Hosting refers to the place where your website, store, or blog will reside. Many domain registrars include free basic hosting as part of their domain name registration package but if you are running a website critical to your business, you'll want to evaluate these "deals" carefully. If you accept their free hosting you may also have to accept their own branding or advertising on your site. I prefer to host my sites at a place where hosting is the main business, not a sideline.

As you are shopping for web hosting look to see if they include a URL for free with it. If you haven't already bought your URL this will save you some money.

The most important thing you want with your web host is reliability. If your viewers can't visit you they may never return, so you want your website to be up 100 percent of the time. You also want it to be fast and to give you all of the storage space and bandwidth you need. Bandwidth refers to the monthly volume allocated to your website.

The second most important thing is responsive technical support. Support is so important I'm tempted to say it is the #1 thing to look for. I dropped a host a few years ago because every time I asked tech support a question I received an answer that seemed to not have anything to do with my question. Either they didn't understand English, they were giving me the runaround, or there was a robot attempting to answer questions with pre-written answers that made no sense. If you get a service like that drop them and move on.

There are lots of companies competing in the web hosting market; choosing the right one can be a confusing ordeal. If you look at the ads, most of them promise basically the same things: unlimited disk space, unlimited bandwidth, unlimited mailboxes, unlimited databases, site building software—they all sound similar, including their pricing. Most of these things don't really matter because your site won't be that big, you won't need unlimited mailboxes, and you won't need unlimited databases. They know that, but promising it sounds like a big deal. It isn't.

You should not pay more than $10 per month for all the features you need and you can probably get it for several dollars less. Do some online research at the time you are shopping to see who is getting the best reviews. The hosting service I've used for the last five years is www.hostgator.com and I have been happy with them.

Here are some things that you need in your hosting account:

- Email accounts
- Email forwarding
- Autoresponders
- AWStats (statistics software)
- Toll-free telephone technical support
- 24-hour online support
- Data backups
- Addon and sub-domains (allows you to add additional websites to the one hosting account)
- WordPress hosting (a popular blog platform that we recommend you use)
- MySQL databases (a common database that WordPress uses)
- PHP 5 (don't worry about understanding it but some software requires it)
- Shopping cart software (usually includes osCommerce, ZenCart, or Cube Cart)
- cPanel
- Fantastico De Luxe.

They are all important even if you don't yet know what they mean. The last two are deal breakers in my opinion: cPanel and Fantastico (or Fantastico De Luxe).

Most web hosting accounts come with cPanel, which is an area that contains controls for the many functions available to manage the account. It is referred to as the dashboard. I go into my cPanel every day to check my visitor statistics through a program called AWstats. It tells me how many visits I've had, what pages were viewed, and how long people stayed on the site. You can set up email accounts, build databases, install software, manage files, and much more in your cPanel. There are currently 46 programs available in my cPanel, so it can look a bit overwhelming. Don't worry about that; I don't know what most of them do and I simply ignore them. You'll probably only ever use a few, like checking your visitor statistics or setting up email and using the utility called Fantastico De Luxe to install other programs on your site.

Fantastico De Luxe is a handy utility that contains a library of scripts that automate installation of dozens of additional programs and functions including blog platforms, shopping carts, image galleries, discussion boards, forums, website builders, mail list management, project management programs, and many more. You should get all of this included with your hosting account, so I recommend that you make sure you get a hosting account that has Fantastico De Luxe. You do not need these things at first but as you grow you may want to add some things like a forum or an image gallery.

POINTING YOUR URL TO YOUR DOMAIN NAMESERVERS

If you purchased your domain name through your hosting account, you can ignore this section because it will already be set up. If you purchased your domain name elsewhere you need to tell that company where the hosting account is. This is known as pointing the URL to the nameservers of your hosting account. This is not as scary as it sounds. Let's walk through the process.

When you purchase your hosting account you'll get an automated "Welcome" email that has account information in it. It will include such things as your Username and an automated Password. You can change this later. It will also give you something called your "Nameservers." There will be two things listed: NS1 and NS2. This is what is used to tell the URL where the website exists.

To do that you go to the account that was set up when you purchased your URL. They all look a little different depending on where you bought the URL, but it will be similar to what we're telling you. You may have to drill down a level or two but you are looking for an area that will be called **Domain Name Server Setup** or just **Nameservers** or something similar. Look for a link that says something like **Set Nameservers**. Click that link. Another panel will show you the default nameservers. You want to substitute the NS1 and NS2 information that you received in your welcome email from your hosting account. These are the **specific nameservers** you want to use. The link where you'll paste them will say something like Specify Custom DNS Servers (your own DNS Servers). If you cannot figure this out then contact customer support where you bought the URL and they can help you. They may even have an online tutorial to show you how it is done.

Once you do this and save changes it can take from 20 minutes to 24 hours for this to take effect. This is called resolving the domain name. My experience is it takes a couple of hours. Until the domain resolves, if you enter your URL in a web browser it will take you to a page that says it is "parked." After it resolves it will take you to your hosting account but until you build a website there all you will see is an empty Index page.

So now it's time to put a website on there!

Action Steps

- Find a hosting service that meets your needs. Research online reviews. Look for the features listed.
- Point your URL's nameservers to your hosting account if you didn't buy them through your hosting company.

Chapter 28

Building Your Own Website

Chapter Objectives

- Understand your options between building an HTML site and a WordPress site.
- Know what makes a website attractive. Build trust with your website visitors.

I previously stated that you don't absolutely have to have your own website to sell online. While that is true, I also highly recommend that you do build your own site because you will have more control over every aspect of it. It is also a place where you can establish your brand.

One of the benefits of having your own site is that a talented web designer can make your site look like a million dollars and suddenly you are an international company and people all over the planet can find your "store." How is a web visitor to know if you are operating your eCommerce site out of a brass and glass corporate building or your bedroom? They can't, and that is an incredibly empowering thing.

If you're breaking out in a sweat and your heart is starting to race at the mere thought of making a website, relax. If you aren't the technical type then you certainly will be better off hiring someone to do it for you, and there are plenty of people who will be happy to help you. Expectations are high these days and a poorly designed website is almost as bad as no website at all, so even if you can build your own site, you still might be better off hiring a designer to build an attractive site and do the "under the hood" work needed to get your site found quickly. Then you can learn to take over and do occasional updates if you wish.

No matter where you live there are probably web designers who can help you out. Look in your phone book, on www.craigslist.com, www.angieslist.com, www.elance.com, www. odesk.com, or others. Do a web search on "web designer YOUR TOWN" (substitute your town or city for YOUR TOWN) and you'll probably find some locally. There are also lots of web designers advertising online. Competition is fierce and many of them will build your website at reasonable rates.

There are also all-in-one eCommerce solutions which include website builders, shopping cart software, eCommerce hosting, and payment processing. Some providers of these solutions include Amazon Webstore (webstore.amazon.com), Yahoo (smallbusiness.yahoo. com/ecommerce), Instant eStore (instantestore.com), Volusion (www.volusion.com), Intuit (intuit.com/ecommerce/create-your-online-store), and more. Do an online search on "eCommerce store" and you'll find plenty of options.

If you are the do-it-yourself type your choice will probably be between building an HTML site and a WordPress site. HTML sites require knowledge of the HTML programming language. Templates simplify this but you'll still need to know some basic HTML coding. An HTML site may be fine if all you want is a landing (home) page; there are a lot of done-for-you templates readily available for simple applications like that. For almost anything else we recommend that you build your site in WordPress.

WordPress is a highly popular blog platform that has taken the internet by storm due to its ease of use. It is also free and easily installed via the Fantastico De Luxe utility you get on most hosting accounts or you can download it from www.wordpress.org and install it manually. (Not wordpress.com, which is also a free blogging service by the same people who offer wordpress.org. Because you don't install it on your site, you only have to sign up, but it comes with restrictions such as a limited selection of themes (designs) and the ability to customize and add plugins (features). That's why we recommend going with a WordPress.org site instead.) Even though the platform was designed for bloggers, you don't need to use it as a blog. It lends itself well as a general website.

We highly recommend using WordPress because of its ease of updating and adding content. There isn't a big learning curve and once you understand how it works you can quickly make changes and additions to your website yourself. You customize the look of WordPress with "themes" which are simple to upload. Themes are how you control the look, also known as the graphical interface, of the site. There are thousands of them available for free or you can find premium themes for a fee. There are so many available that you will almost certainly find one to fit your particular needs. They are also easy to customize.

There are thousands of plugins which expand the utility of WordPress. Plugins are pieces of software that are written to give WordPress more functionality. There's a plugin for almost anything you can think of. You can find hundreds of free plugins and themes at www.wordpress.org. Specialized plugins, like for operating eCommerce sites and membership sites, are available for a fee.

> A common mistake is loading WordPress up with unnecessary plugins, which can slow down loading of a site. At a certain point your web hosting service may shut your site off if it is causing too much of a load on the server because of this. I have had this happen a couple of times with my WordPress sites, mainly due to plugins that were going out and actively searching in the background for videos or other information to automatically post. I avoid any plugins that do this now and recommend you do the same. Put only the plugins you need on your site and keep it as light as possible.

The beauty of using WordPress is that you can easily integrate articles, news releases, photos, and valuable content along with your sales items. This makes it more of a resource and less in-your-face sales. This fits in with relationship building, which we'll cover in Part V on marketing. You can do so much with WordPress, such as integrate advertising and create paid and unpaid membership sites. WordPress sites can be set up to alert blog directories, known as pinging, every time you make a change or enter a new item. This keeps the search engines indexing your site more frequently which helps you maintain a higher position in the search results.

Even if you do hire designers I recommend that at some point you learn enough about WordPress so that you can enter your own blog articles, upload photos, illustrations, and videos, and do quick updates to the site when the muses strike. Fast action is important in internet marketing so the more you can respond promptly to new ideas or problems with your site, the better. You might find as I did that you enjoy doing the work yourself. Just make sure that is the best use of your time.

We're not going to delve into the specifics of building websites here. That is much too big a topic for this book. There are many books on this subject, just check at Amazon. com where you can find *WordPress For Dummies*, *Web Design For Dummies*, and many other simplified, helpful publications. Wordpress.org itself has a very active and informative group of forums.

However, I do want to point out some of the key elements that your website needs.

MAKE IT GOOD LOOKING

Whether you design it yourself or get help, your website needs be attractive and intuitive to navigate. It should have the right look for your products or topic area. Don't use flashy animations or multimedia unless it makes sense. Search engines don't like them and they annoy your visitors.

Your homepage should look like, well ... home. It should quickly communicate what the site is about and show all of the navigation options of the site. The most important elements should be visible "above the fold." A user shouldn't have to scroll down to see them. You only have a few seconds to convince impatient web surfers to stay on your page so make your message clear. There should be a return link to the homepage from every other page on the site.

Strive for excellent quality photographs and graphics. If you don't have your own photos you can find free ones at www.morguefile.com or purchase them from any number of stock photo agencies. We use www.dreamstime.com a lot. We also use www.istockphotos. com. Make sure they are royalty-free and able to be displayed on websites.

Color is one of the tools you'll use to make a statement about your website. The colors of your site should work together. Even edgy, grunge-style websites conform to a color theme (the good ones do).

One trick to get a good color palette is to design your colors around a dominant photo. A helpful tool to do this is www.degraeve.com. You can give it the URL of a photo and it will suggest a complementary color palette. A similar tool is www.colorhunter.com.

MAKE IT LOAD FAST

Speedy loading is right up there with quality content in earning a high page rank. It'll also keep your web host happy. Photos should be compressed to make them as small (file size) as possible so they load fast. Compression is a process of reducing the amount of bytes it takes to create the image. It's a balancing act between keeping the photo looking good and reducing the file size. Reducing the actual dimensions of the photo helps too, but compression software will be your key tool.

Photos should be in the JPEG or PNG format. Don't simply resize photos in your HTML editor or WordPress; that doesn't reduce the size or load time. There are lots of photo editing programs and utilities that will reduce a file's size while keeping the image looking good.

Photoshop is the king of photo editing software but is expensive and probably overkill for you. Photoshop Elements is under $100 and will do everything you want at less cost. If you do a search on "photo editing software" you'll find a range of products that are affordable. Search for "free photo editing software" and you'll be rewarded with free programs that probably do all you need. Pixlr.com offers a free online editing tool. Don't go overboard with photos—even a bunch of small ones will slow page loading down.

> When you name your images, don't use names like img463.jpg. Use keywords that not only describe the image but are part of your search engine optimization. Search engines can't index images but they can index the image name. For example, if "fly fishing DVD" are your keywords, name your image "flyfishingDVDcover.jpg."

These same principles apply to putting videos on your site. They need to be compressed to the smallest size possible without reducing the quality below acceptable limits. We covered this topic in Chapter 19 on Post-Production. All video editing programs are going to have an "export for web" option. Make sure to apply what you've learned about SEO and give the video a keyword-rich name.

MAKE IT EASY TO NAVIGATE

Navigation is how users find their way around your site. Good clear navigation is so important. You want your visitors to feel at ease in your site, not confused by too many navigation choices. It's much better to have drop-down menus than dozens of choices running across your page. Keep it as simple as possible.

You should have a link to your site map (a list of all of your web pages) and display a "bread crumb trail" or some way of telling the user where they are in your site. A bread crumb trail will look like this: Home > Store > DVDs > Fly Fishing 101. (WordPress does this automatically.) Make menu items and tabs that are descriptive and logical. Don't allow your users to wander into a dead end on your site. Users shouldn't feel like they have to work to find their way around your site.

SEARCH ENGINE OPTIMIZATION CONSIDERATIONS

From their perspective, search engines have one purpose—to provide the searcher with a satisfying response to their search in order to keep them coming back for more searches. Then they make their money off of advertising.

As I stressed before when we were talking about domain names, your goal is to get your site found easily in the organic (non-paid) search results and for it to be just what the searcher was looking for. If you do proper search engine optimization of your entire site, everyone will be happy.

Search engine optimization is a moving target and there are hundreds of constantly evolving guidelines to follow. Just keep in mind that, above all else, content is king on your site. The more original, quality content you add, the better. Content duplicated from another source will do nothing for your rankings and may even hurt them if you have too much duplication.

Everything you post should have the best search keywords in both the title and in the body, but don't repeat them more than five times or you might be viewed as "keyword stuffing" (using keywords unnaturally over and over again in an effort to get found and ranked) which will actually count against you in the eyes of Google. Here are some tips on using keywords:

- Try to keep your web page titles under a 70-character limit.
- Make sure your keyword is in there once, ideally lead off with your keyword first.
- Have a minimum of 450 words on your front page and have your keywords appear at least three to four times within those words. Just make sure your writing sounds natural.
- Have your keywords in bold at least once and in italics at least once.

The way this all works is search engines send out software called bots, crawlers, or spiders, that are continually scanning the web. They index your site based on the content these spiders find. They also look at the quality of the external links (websites linking back to you) to your site and quality sites, like a .edu or .gov site, help your SEO more than links from poorly rated sites. Their algorithms (formulas for ranking) are inscrutable, but if you follow the basic rules of good SEO your chances are good of showing up high on the search engine results page (SERP).

Since this is such a broad and changing topic we recommend that you go to Google and search on "search engine optimization" and "search engine marketing" to get the latest updates on this topic. You'll see us talk a lot about SEO in this book, especially where it relates to marketing.

BUILD TRUST

Customers are becoming increasingly comfortable purchasing online but they still want to feel that their personal information and their credit card numbers are secure. They will be much more likely to buy from you if you can convince them that your business is a legitimate, secure online store. One way to do this is by displaying a trust seal or symbol. (Having a clean, professional looking website also helps.)

Trust seals are issued by third parties and verify that the site has been inspected and verified as trustworthy. You can purchase trust seals such as Hacker Safe, Comodo, or eTrust. These services examine your site for vulnerabilities and allow you to display their badges, which state that your site is secure. I don't believe it is absolutely necessary to purchase trust seals, but it will likely improve your conversion rates, i.e., the ratio of your visitors who convert to buyers. Paid shopping carts offer trust seals. We'll be talking more about security when we get into the chapter on payment options and choosing a shopping cart.

One of the most important things you can place on your site to build trust costs you nothing. It is a guarantee symbol which I'll cover in more detail in Chapter 30.

ADD AN OPT-IN BOX

Although we'll be explaining exactly what this feature is in more depth when we talk about sales funnels in Chapter 33, keep in mind that you will want a process by which you can collect visitor's information so that you can contact them in the future. This is a sign up box, commonly called an opt-in form. This should display prominently on each page and offer something of perceived value in exchange for their email address and their permission to further contact them.

PAGES YOU SHOULD INCLUDE

Search engines look for certain pages and reward you with better ranking when you have them. They include:

- **About Us**—Who are you? Visitors like to know that there are real people behind a business, not just a nameless, faceless corporation. Add some personality to it.
- **Contact Us**—Make it easy for users to contact you. Add a phone number if possible. If you don't want to list a mailing address, at least tell them what state or province you are in. Your potential customer wants to know that you are a real company and that they can reach you in case there is a problem. If you want to add your email address, do so in a contact form which helps protect you from being spammed.
- **FAQs**—Provide a useful set of answers to the most commonly asked questions.
- **Privacy Policy**—State the terms of how you will handle private information that you may receive. Search engines look for a privacy policy and the lack of one can hurt your standing in the search results. WordPress plugins are available to automatically generate a privacy policy.

Action Steps

- Decide on the type of website you will build.
- Hire someone or do it yourself.
- Design your website to be clean, fast, and easy to navigate.
- Perform search engine optimization on your site.
- Display trust seals.
- Include the pages listed above.

Chapter 29

Membership Programs

Chapter Objectives

- Understand what membership sites are and how you can use them.
- Learn about evergreen and drip sites.
- Learn common ways to encourage people to subscribe.
- Become aware of things to look for in membership site software.

How would you like to make $19 per month for creating and sending an online video out to a subscriber? That doesn't sound all that lucrative, does it? Now what if you had 1,000 people paying you $19 per month for that same video? That's more like it!

This is the world of online membership programs also known as continuity programs. It's an exciting business model and a growing trend. Since several of the people we did case studies on do it with their video products, I felt that an entire chapter should be dedicated to this topic.

Continuity programs have been around for a long time. In the pre-internet world you would have known them by names like the Book of the Month Club and the Capitol Record Club. I think my family belonged to both. Even a magazine subscription is a type of continuity program.

Membership sites are an excellent way to sell your videos. Your subscribers are people who want your content on a regular, continuing basis and are willing to pay for it. You protect your intellectual property because it's locked behind the vault of the username and password-protected membership area.

This "pay-for-content" concept is especially well suited to video publishers who want to turn their hobby or specialized knowledge into a monthly income. Imagine that you have a group of people who share your interest in a topic and who look forward anxiously to receiving a new video, some news, articles, or other information on a regular basis. It's no more work for you to send it out to 5,000 people than to five, so you are really leveraging your time and talent to the maximum.

I've belonged to several membership sites. Bill Myers Online is one of my favorites. For the small fee of $9.95 per month, I get weekly screencasts, articles, and access to a vast library of resources and a vibrant discussion forum. It's all about developing videos and information products and how to market them. He occasionally sends his members free software that is worth more than the price of membership. When I'm busy I'll sometimes go for a month or two without visiting the membership site but all it takes is one or two great tips to make it all worthwhile. I wouldn't consider dropping it for the insignificant fee of $9.95 per month or $97 per year. I have no idea what the size of his membership is but I imagine there are a lot of people who feel like me and wouldn't think of dropping out.

Membership sites are growing in popularity because people are busy and this type of business allows them to get the information they need on a regular basis without much effort on their part. I know that if I have a video-related question I can pop over to the Bill Myer's forum (www.bmyers.com) and share my question with hundreds of like-minded entrepreneurs. It's like I have a bunch of consultants just waiting for my next question.

Some membership sites operate like a library. They are already stocked up with the information you need. You go to the site at any time and get what you need. In this type of site the owner has to first develop all of the content but once it's done, it's done forever. This is referred to as an "evergreen" site. Evergreen is basically information that is not likely to change, now or in the future. They will occasionally add new materials but it isn't a constant need, like a "drip" site.

A "drip" membership site sends content to members on a regular basis. This works well for tutorial programs where you want the member to go through the material one step at a time, starting from the date they sign up. Sometimes if you dump too much information on them at once it overwhelms them and they never get started. With the drip method you don't have to have all of the content finished before opening the program up; you just have to stay a few steps ahead of the drip.

Subscription programs are essentially the same as membership programs. Software programs that you have to pay a monthly fee to use are membership sites. If you stop your membership subscription, the software stops working. We've belonged to website template of the month subscriptions, SocialOomph for managing social media, coaching programs, and others.

Dave Sheahan designed his *Dave Sheahan Home Workout System* as a drip membership for the first 6 weeks. He wants his subscribers to go through it in a certain order to maximize their chances of success. Then they can access the entire program indefinitely. He requires them to watch the preparatory videos before they start the exercises, and then they have to go through the exercises day by day; no skipping ahead. The software he is using, Digital Access Pass, controls dripping the videos in a specific order.

An unusual membership site example comes from a friend of ours who is an artist. He runs a "Painting of the Month" club. People pay $75 per month to belong. He grids out a very large sheet of paper and paints variations on a theme in each of the grids. It might be a piece of fruit one month, a simple landscape the next, and so on. He does it like a production line and can produce dozens of original 6 × 9 inch paintings in a couple of hours. Then he cuts them up and sends them to his subscribers. Wow! This brilliant artist also teaches art marketing and yes, he also sells DVDs at $50 a pop. In a similar vein, I have a subscription to a service that sends me a digital package of website graphics every month. I get buttons, arrows, website headers, guarantee symbols, and lots of useful tools to embellish my websites. Think of how you can take your knowledge and expertise and apply this model. Sending a video a month is a logical application.

MEMBERSHIP SITE FEES

Membership sites charge fees from just a couple of dollars to hundreds of dollars per month. The expensive ones are usually high-end training that lasts from a few months up to a year. The smaller ones are sometimes called "micro continuity sites." One of the attractive features of micro continuity sites is that with such small monthly fees, as low as $4.99, people don't tend to unsubscribe. They barely notice that they are paying for it and if they get any value at all they feel it is worthwhile. A couple hundred people paying $4.99 per month isn't insignificant and once you have them on that list you have the opportunity to up-sell them with other promotions.

Some membership sites are free. I know people whose business model is to give their memberships away in exchange for the subscriber's contact information for subsequent marketing. People are happy to sign up for a "free" membership but in so doing they are handing over their email address and giving permission to the site owner to market to them. Then the marketer makes their money on up-sells and affiliate products.

MEMBERSHIP SOFTWARE PRICES

You don't necessarily need special software to build a membership site. You just need a way to collect fees, which could be one-time or on a recurring basis (monthly, annually, or other period). If you send the membership materials to the subscriber then you don't need membership software to protect it.

If you have a collection of content that the member gains access to when subscribing then it is worth looking into membership software. You could accomplish this by simply password protecting the site and giving members a password, but there is a lot more functionality you can gain from membership software.

The cost of membership software ranges from free to hundreds of dollars per month. Some only require a one-time payment and others charge monthly. There are several plugins that make WordPress a good membership platform. This is how we are currently doing it on our site www.specialinterestvideo.org. Popular plugins at this time include WishlistMember, wp-Member, MemberWing, Digital Access Pass, wp-eMember and s2Member (free), and more. Because there are so many choices in membership software and it is changing all the time we are not going to make specific recommendations. Do a search, read reviews, and check www.shoot-to-sell.com for updates.

You can get further security plugins, like S3 Media Vault, to protect your videos and podcasts stored on Amazon S3.

FEATURES OF MEMBERSHIP SITE SOFTWARE

Some features to look for in membership site software include:

- The ability to sign up both paid and free memberships
- The ability to sell products, both physical and digital
- Free and member-only access to certain content
- Free limited duration access and free trials
- Online payment processing for major credit cards and Paypal
- The ability to drip content
- The ability to offer multiple levels of membership
- Email autoresponders and broadcast applications
- The ability to sell recurring subscriptions (subscriptions that automatically renew on a periodic basis).

HOW TO ATTRACT MEMBERSHIP

You'll need to develop a strong identity for your membership site. This is called a Unique Selling Proposition or USP. The more you can help the prospective member understand why *your* membership program is the right one for them, the greater your chance of getting them to join your herd.

There are many ways to encourage people to join your membership site, including:

- Discounts, particularly time-sensitive offers (i.e., "For the Next Two Days Only").
- No Obligation—Let people sign up and pay later.
- Free Gifts—Have a bonus for signing up that has a high perceived value. Some people will sign up just for the gift.
- Free Trial—Let them try it out first to see if it is right for them.
- Installment Payments—"Just three small payments of …"
- Guarantees—Absolutely offer a money-back guarantee. Make it strong but protect yourself. A "double your money-back" guarantee may be too tempting for some people who will want to take advantage of you.

You'll revisit many of these ideas later when we get deeper into the subject of marketing.

You'll notice that when we talk about ways to encourage people to subscribe to a membership site or make a purchase, most of our tactics do not actually cost us anything. We rely on building relationships first, then moving the prospect toward a sale. Someone who is an expert at marketing on a shoestring budget and has a successful membership site is Jessica Swanson.

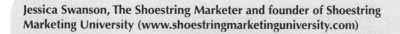

Jessica Swanson, The Shoestring Marketer and founder of Shoestring Marketing University (www.shoestringmarketinguniversity.com)

No matter what business you're in, here's the fact: the most successful small business owners are also the best marketers. Unfortunately, there are way too many small business owners today that don't take the time to learn the simple ABC's of marketing. They don't have a proven marketing plan that produces a substantial flow of traffic, leads, and sales. And if you don't have a marketing plan, then you don't have sales. It's as simple as that.

That solid bit of wisdom is from one of our mentors, Jessica Swanson. Following Jessica's advice is what landed us this book deal, so when she says something, you better believe we listen. The follow-up sentence to that thought is "The good news is that anyone can learn to be a good marketer."

Jessica has built a successful business helping small business owners learn to become great marketers on a shoestring budget. In fact, her business is aptly named the Shoestring Marketing University (SMU). She knows how to get high-impact marketing results at low-cost because that's how she launched her business.

The SMU is based on a membership model. Students join the SMU and get 52 online video lessons, delivered to them one per week for a year. Jessica creates the video lessons herself, mostly using PowerPoint, and records them with Camtasia. "I record my voice as I'm demonstrating something and it usually just takes one take." Jessica says that although Camtasia is a powerful and capable program she doesn't use all of the functions. "I don't do a lot of zooming and those kinds of things," she says. "I don't want the students to be overwhelmed or distracted."

Jessica says that she does all of her video production and marketing herself. "I feel that even if a site owner jobs out part of the business, they should 'get their hands dirty' and know enough about their site to do things for themselves." We agree.

Jessica used to be an English teacher so she has a lot of experience teaching people. "People learn in different ways," she says. "Some are visual learners, others need to hear the information and some learn best by reading. Video is the perfect way to teach for all of these learning modalities." To make sure her students get the information in the form that they respond to best she includes an audio of the lesson and a downloadable e-booklet so the visual learners can read through the entire lesson.

Unlike many membership sites, Jessica allows students to download all of her material to their computer for future study. We wondered how that was working for her: "I don't worry about people stealing them," she says. "I haven't had a problem with that." All of her content is kept behind the wall of her membership site, she uses Memberlist and WordPress, but once a person becomes a member they can download and keep the material forever.

How does she get people to sign up for the university? "You have to be creative and you have to develop a lot of trust because people are hesitant to have you bill their credit cards monthly," she says. She gives a free, 30-day trial to SMU to let people get to know her and decide if her membership program is right for them. "I haven't seen many membership sites do well that didn't give some kind of trial membership." She says 80 percent of the people who sign up won't leave the program. She also offers a 100 percent money-back guarantee if people are not happy with the courses.

Jessica attracts new students in several ways. One way is by giving away a free ebook called "121 FREE Shoestring Marketing Tools." People have to give their first name and email address to get this publication, after which she has them in her marketing funnel and can start sending them promotional emails.

Another effective tool is a five-part step-by-step marketing course called "The Shoestring Marketing Success Blueprint." This course is priced at $97 but you can't buy it. The only way you can get it is to accept a trial membership in the SMU. She says bonuses and giveaways are an important marketing tool.

"The membership business model has grown in popularity in the last few years and there's more competition today," Jessica says. "You have to offer a lot of value to be successful." In addition to the weekly video lessons, audios, e-booklets, workbooks, and action plans, students get access to a vast library of articles and marketing resources like marketing plans, press release templates, email marketing checklists, "asking for referrals" templates, pricing checklists, and more. They have full access to the library even during the free trial period.

Like we said at the beginning, we've personally benefitted by following Jessica Swanson's advice. Her methods of shoestring marketing certainly fit our budget and will benefit you, too.

IS A MEMBERSHIP SITE RIGHT FOR YOU?

If you are developing a series of video products and other content on a tightly integrated topic area, a membership site might be the perfect way for you to build your business.

If you decide that a membership site is right for you, think about the people who will be your members. Just like when we talked about deciding on a product and a target market, picture your ideal members. Do they have the money for a recurring membership and at what price? What is their problem that you can solve with your program? Knowing your ideal customer is the first step toward success.

Action Steps

- Decide if a membership site is right for you.
- Know what kind of membership site you need for your market.
- Shop for software.
- Put content into your membership site.
- Decide on tactics to attract membership.

Chapter 30

Copywriting

Chapter Objectives

- Learn about AIDA and how to implement it.
- Discover what a call to action is and why you must have one.
- Learn how to find and communicate your Unique Selling Position.
- Understand how to break copy into useful blocks.
- Learn about power words in selling.
- Learn how to build trust with your potential customer.
- Design ways to create a sense of urgency and an offer too attractive to refuse.

Before we go forward and jump into marketing, I need to introduce the subject of copywriting. Copywriting in this case means sales copy, the type of copy that will promote the sale of your video and other products on your site. The purpose of this promotional text is to persuade your reader, listener, or viewer to act: for example, subscribe to your list or buy your video. Sales copy will be used in your sales letters if you do direct mail, on your landing pages (those pages, homepage or other page in your site, where your visitors arrive after clicking on a link), even the types of posts you make on Facebook and what you say in your marketing videos. Copywriting concepts need to be followed in all marketing strategies.

Good copy will execute the following AIDA rules of good copywriting. That is:

A is for attention. You have to grab your visitor's attention. In the short attention span of the internet you only have a few seconds to do that. It's going to take a powerful headline, an interesting video, and/or an eye-grabbing graphic to get them to stick to the page long enough to move to the next step.

I is for interest. OK, you've grabbed your visitor's attention for a few seconds with a snappy headline or image, now you have to quickly instill interest in your product. If your headline stopped them from clicking off then you need something that will sink the hook a little deeper. Maybe the headline poses a problem and the subhead is promising a solution. Don't hold back—fire your best shot right up front or you'll lose them in the competitive tumult of the internet.

D is for desire. Now you have to move your visitor from simple interest in your product to desiring to have it. Compelling body copy that promises benefits, solutions, or pleasures will get the job done. This is like when you look at a delicious treat and in your mind you know how wonderful it would taste, your mouth starts watering and you just have to have it, right now!

A is for action. This is not the time to be subtle. You have to ask your visitor to take action, be it to sign up for your list, share the link with their friends, or buy your video. That is what marketers mean by a "call to action." Once you have their full attention, don't blow it by expecting them to figure out how to take the next step—tell them! If you want them to buy from you (and of course you do!), make it very clear that you want them to buy your thing with a big, obvious Buy Now button, then show them how to do it. Make the process as simple and straightforward as possible. A mistake some online marketers make is to give so many choices (size, color, weight, combinations of products) that the potential customer becomes overwhelmed or confused and either leaves or intends to come back later, which may not happen.

Good copywriting is a skill. It can be learned but if you are not inclined to write then this is a task best left to a professional. Good sales copy is crucial to the sales process. You can have a great product and an attractive website, brochure, or catalog, but the words in your sales copy are the key communication between you and your potential customer. Good copy will lead them to the cash register and transact the sale.

USE SUBHEADS AND BULLET POINTS

We already established that internet visitors have the attention span of a gnat; you have just seconds to grab them. They'll typically read your headline first, then quickly scan for sub-heads or bullet points that give them further information. If that is sufficiently interesting (the I of AIDA) they'll begin to read the body copy. You need to make sure that every step in this process is driving them toward desire.

This principle of scanning applies equally to printed material. You have a little more time with direct mail, but if your envelope copy is weak your package may go straight into the trash can.

There has been a decades-long running debate about whether or not to use long copy. I favor it, but it has to constantly add new information to the sales letter or landing page, not just repeat the same points over and over.

Because of the way people scan web pages and articles, you should use subheads and bullet points to break the flow of copy up into smaller, more manageable blocks. Each sub-head should make it very clear what the topic of the following block of copy is about and make the visitor want to read it. Each copy block essentially becomes its own mini-story. Bullet points are a good way to illustrate benefits of owning an item.

Break your copy up with appropriate, supportive photos or illustrations. They should be high quality and must be accompanied by a caption that tells a story that further creates interest in and desire for your product. A great photo tells a story in an instant. Add an equally powerful caption and you just threw a knockout punch.

Don't overlook video on your website either. We'll be talking more about using video in your marketing.

CHOOSE YOUR WORDS CAREFULLY

You have to pay attention to every word that you use. This is supremely important in head-lines and subheads, but also in body copy. Seriously, you should consider and weigh *every word you use*. Does it need to be there? Can you find a stronger way to say it without appearing clever, deceptive, or heavy-handed?

Here's an SEO tip that will come in handy, not just in the copy on your website, but also in blogging and social media marketing. Place your keywords at the beginning of your headline, subheads, subject lines in emails, sentences and paragraphs. You have to make it sound natural, but this is important not only to promote a sale but it will help your page rank. For example: "5 Easy Steps You Can Do TODAY to Stop Dog Barking" has the best keywords at the end and places the emphasis on "5 Easy Steps You Can Do TODAY." A much better arrangement would be "Stop Dog Barking—5 Easy Steps You Can Do TODAY." This places the solution first and improves your site's indexing.

There are widely accepted power words that always get attention. FREE leads the list and probably always will. Also NEW and YOU. More power words include COMPARE, DISCOVER, ANNOUNCING, YES, EXCITING, SECRETS, SHOCKING, AMAZING, MIRACLE, and IMPORTANT. These words get people excited and curious.

I personally dislike hyperbole and outright exaggeration. I see it overused, which dilutes the power of it. Don't say your thing was "Voted #1" or "World's Best" unless you have proof. You'll often get the opposite result of what you want. People will think you're full of it if you sound like you're bragging without proof or simply making it up. If you do have proof, tell them what it is. Then you really have something.

Also avoid pomposity. Don't throw in snooty foreign words or phrases as if everyone knows what they mean. You'll alienate your reader. Don't try to impress with your collection of big words. Don't write academically. Use short words that pack a punch. Just as we suggested in Chapter 10 when we talked about scriptwriting, you should be writing for a 5th grade level.

SELL THE SIZZLE

You'll need to develop a strong identity for your product. We talked about the concept of your Unique Selling Proposition (USP) earlier. The more you can help the prospect understand why *your* video is the right one for them, the greater your chance of getting them to buy.

Your customers don't want to own another video. A DVD is just plastic. They want the benefit they'll derive from the information on that video, whether that's entertainment or education. Don't make the mistake of talking about the fancy broadcast camera you shot this video with or the fact that this took six months to produce. People want to know "what's in it for me and why should I buy it from you?"—so tell them.

Be aware of overusing I or we in your copy. Don't write from your standpoint; turn it around and use "You" or "Your" as much as possible. "You will … " is much more powerful than "My … " Your copy should always be about the reader and the benefits they will receive, not about you or what a cool thing you did. (If you've been noticing, we've been doing that with you throughout this book!)

Spend some time writing down all of the benefits your customer will get from watching your video. Start by writing down the things your prospects have asked you to help them with that are being addressed in the video. Put yourself in their shoes and ask yourself if those things would encourage you to buy this video. Keep refining the benefits and put them into a bullet point list early in your sales copy.

If your video is going to solve a problem for them, state the problem and then tell how your video will solve it. "Stop Dog Barking" is the problem, "5 Easy Steps You Can Do TODAY" is the solution.

LET YOUR PROSPECT GET TO KNOW YOU

Build trust with your prospective customer. Don't ask them to take your word for it, offer a free trial or sample video. You should have a trailer or sample video excerpt to show highlights from your video. I highly recommend making a promotional video where you talk about the video you have for sale, explaining the content and benefits and showing samples from it. That video needs to be filled with good copy and a clear call to action too.

Customer testimonials are some of the most persuasive things you can use to get potential customers to trust you. People want to know that other people have been satisfied with your product, and the more they think those people are just like them, the better. A customer testimonial from J.C. in Kansas is OK. Much better is a testimonial from Joyce Cross in Wichita, Kansas. Even better is to show a photo of Joyce Cross in Wichita, Kansas, holding your product. Best of all is a video of Joyce Cross on camera, telling how much she loves your product and how she benefited from it.

Speak in their language. When writing copy it should sound like you know the product inside and out. If there is vocabulary unique to this group of people, use it. Don't use cute industry buzz words that might date it in a year or two, but use the language of your audience if such a thing exists. The more your potential customer can relate to you and your sales pitch, the more believable you are and the better your chance of making a sale.

THIS ALSO APPLIES TO YOUR PACKAGING

Everything we've said about writing sales copy applies equally to your DVD package. If it is going to end up on a retail shelf you have to give it sales appeal. The copy on your DVD box should follow the AIDA principles. Never stop selling.

Also apply these principles when deciding on a title for your video. Build in keywords and write it so that prospects know that this video is the perfect answer to their need or problem.

OFFER A GUARANTEE

Always, I repeat, *always* offer a guarantee. The stronger you make it, the better. The ultimate is a Lifetime 100% Money-Back Guarantee of Satisfaction. If your video or product is good you won't get many returns or have customers abuse these policies. This will get some reluctant shoppers off the fence. The fact that they know they can return it if they don't love it will relieve any angst about purchasing and will help to assuage buyer's remorse after a purchase.

Adding a printed 100% Guarantee Certificate with physical products will help assure that you'll get few if any returns. After a few days most customers will forget about returning things.

The longer the guarantee the better. Ninety days is better than 30 days. A lifetime guarantee is the ultimate risk reliever. It's a good idea to display your guarantee on the checkout page so if the customer is waffling on pushing the Buy Now button, they'll see the guarantee at the moment of indecision and that'll make the difference.

When I ran my media program at the university we went so far as to offer a lifetime free replacement policy on our VHS tapes (this was before DVDs) if they ever broke. I think we may have had to replace one, mostly due to customer mishandling, but that was it. Think how happy that made that customer and what a strong guarantee that was.

Admittedly, a guarantee is more complicated with digital products. Once they have the product there is nothing to return. My advice here is just to test it and see if it works for you. If you feel customers are abusing the guarantee, then make changes.

CREATE A SENSE OF URGENCY

It's annoying but things like "Limited Time Offer" or "For the Next Two Days Only" do create a sense of urgency. "This offer may be withdrawn at any time" may be all that's needed to get a customer off the fence.

"For the First 50 Customers Only" says that the item is scarce, so act fast. When I look at Amazon.com and it says they only have one in stock that makes me want to order fast before it's gone. Don't you?

Or say it's a digital product where there really is an unlimited supply. You can offer a lower price for the first 50 customers—you can set up both of these parameters in your shopping cart software. Don't go crazy scaring people with these phrases but a gentle push will often result in a sale.

Like we shared in Chapter 29, here are ways to encourage people to buy your video:

- **Pay Later**—Let people buy with a business purchase order. Schools buy with P.O.s so if you sell to teachers, they'll appreciate this.
- **Free Gifts**—Have a bonus for buying that has a high perceived value.
- **Free Trial**—Let them view a portion of the video to see if it is right for them.
- **Installment Payments**—"Just three small payments of … " Let them spread out payments, especially if this is a high-end course or video series. Offer a discount if they pay it in full.

THE "SWIPE FILE"

What do you do when you simply have no inspiration to write? You do what most copywriters do, you turn to your swipe file.

Come on, you didn't think every word and phrase those highly paid copywriters typed into their computers is original, did you? Of course not. They, and I, keep samples of things that inspire them. I do it on my computer as a collection of bookmarks. I have paper files stuffed with sales letters and ads that I turn to when I run out of inspiration. I have books of sales letters to use as a starting point.

Start doing this yourself, online and offline. A program like Evernote is nicely suited to organize your online swipe file. Recently I've been intrigued how I can use the new site, Pinterest, for this purpose. I also save my favorite email solicitations and Tweets that inspired me.

Pull out those file folders I told you to get. Clip out ads that you think you could emulate from the newspapers, magazines, and mail you get. Look critically at headlines and keep copies of the ones that inspire you. Keep bookmarks on your computer of web pages that you like. You don't have to start with a clean slate every time you need sales copy. Turn to your swipe file.

HAVE YOUR COPY REVIEWED

This isn't meant to be a course in sales copywriting. There are plenty of books and websites where you can learn more, but this should get you thinking about how to approach it. Even if you hire a copywriter you will now be more prepared to judge the quality of what they are presenting to you.

If you write your own sales copy, have some trusted friends read it and give you feedback before you launch it. It's hard to be objective when you've been slaving over every word, but you really need an outsider's opinion.

If you've hired a copywriter, try to put yourself in your customer's place as you read what they write. Does it speak to them naturally in a language they will relate to? If you do have some trusted customers, share it with them and get their feedback.

Finally, test it! As we get deeper into marketing, we'll be showing you how you can test your marketing formulas to see what works for you, because the bottom line is your customer is the one you need to attract and please, not you.

READ UP

There are library shelves bulging with books on copywriting. This is a deep subject, part art and part psychology. If you want to learn more you can find excellent books on the subject. A quick read with lots of good information is *Direct Mail Copy that Sells,* by Herschell Gordon Lewis. Also recommended is *The Copywriter's Handbook, Third Edition: A Step-by-Step Guide to Writing Copy that Sells* by Robert W. Bly. A good book about direct marketing in general is *Successful Direct Marketing Methods* by Bob Stone and Ron Jacobs. You can find these and many more books on the subject on Amazon.com.

If you are getting a lot of qualified visitors to your website but they just don't buy, don't blame them for being too dense to appreciate your fantastic video. You can only point at a couple of possible excuses: either your price is too high or you are failing to create desire to purchase, and that duty falls largely to the copywriter.

Action Steps

- Start writing copy to follow the four steps of AIDA.
- Decide on your calls to action. (We'll address this topic in greater detail when we get into the sales funnel and marketing strategies.)
- Write with strong headlines, subheads, and bullet points.
- Decide what your Unique Selling Position is.
- Lead off with keywords and use power words.
- Focus on benefits to the customer.
- Offer a strong guarantee.
- Create a sense of urgency and offer other attractive hooks.

Chapter 31

Shopping Carts and Payment Solutions

Chapter Objectives

- Learn what shopping cart software is.
- Know what you should look for in shopping carts.
- Know your payment solution options.

A good opening question for this chapter is, "How are you going to get paid?" In other words, how are you going to transact a sale with your online customers? As I shared in Chapter 28, you can choose an all-in-one solution that will do everything for you, but if you are setting up and hosting your own website, you'll need to look into how you'll collect payment.

If your needs are very simple, i.e., you're selling only one video or a single video course, you can set up a PayPal account, put a PayPal Buy Button on your site, and you're done. However, if you are offering multiple products from the same website, this is not the best solution. You'll need software so that customers can place multiple items in their virtual cart.

SHOPPING CART SOFTWARE

Shopping cart software allows customers to stroll down the virtual aisles of your digital store, select items, and place them in their "shopping cart." If the sole purpose of your site is to sell items, as opposed to being a blog, a shopping cart may be all you need because you can create an online catalog of products.

There are free and paid shopping carts. Free carts do not offer official customer support, they can be challenging to customize, and if your cart gets hacked it's your problem, not theirs.

Every hosting account I've ever seen includes some free shopping cart programs, so you likely already have a choice. Common free carts include osCommerce and Cube Cart. I used osCommerce for a few years until a couple of my stores were hacked, then I dropped them in favor of 1ShoppingCart (www.1shoppingcart.com). 1ShoppingCart is a paid service but they provide an SSL Certificate and are responsible for security and backups. I like the fact that all of my sensitive customer data resides on their highly secure server, not on mine, and they rigorously back up the data. The peace of mind of having them maintain and back up my data is one reason I switched from a free shopping cart; the other is all the marketing tools that are included.

I see a lot of people successfully using osCommerce; I just had a bad experience with hackers. If you'd like to see some shops using it, hop on over to www.shops.oscommerce. com. There is a bit of a learning curve but if you are on a tight budget, this is a good way to start. Because it is free they offer no official support but there are thousands of users and a very active user forum where you can get most questions answered.

Our friend Rich Ferguson, who you met in Chapter 22, built his store using the open source program Zen Cart. You can see it at www.richferguson.com/store. He built an entire catalog of items on this shopping cart. He did an excellent job and he designed and built the entire site himself.

Paid carts offer tight security, they maintain and back up your data on their site, they have helpful tutorials, are fairly easy to use, and include a lot of valuable marketing tools. Things you should look for in a paid shopping cart system include:

- The ability to create and use coupons. These work very well for special promotions. We use them all the time.
- Product up-sell and cross-sell, which is the ability to automatically market other items at lower or higher prices.
- Mailing list management.
- Autoresponder applications.
- Email broadcast capabilities.
- Affiliate program so that you can sign up affiliates to sell your products. This may be an added fee.
- Ad Trackers that allow you to test your marketing campaigns.
- Custom form features, which give you the ability to add opt-in forms.
- Popups—those windows that appear on top of (over and under) the browser window (don't dismiss using popups because you personally find them annoying. If used well in a giveaway offer they are very effective for building your list.)

Paid shopping carts do not reside on your server so are not taxing your website's resources. The downside is the cost. 1ShoppingCart, for example, starts with a scaled-back version at $34 per month and goes up to $99 per month for the full professional version that includes an affiliate module. The most sophisticated systems, such as Infusionsoft (www.infusionsoft.com) can cost up to $999 per month and are complex to use. Some provide some level of official support with your purchase and others offer premium support for a fee.

Setting items up in your cart is totally dependent on the particular system you choose and is too broad of a topic to address here. You'll usually have plenty of support material to guide you through the process.

You can find shopping cart review sites by searching online at places like www. shopping-cart-reviews.com. Names you will see a lot include 1ShoppingCart, InfusionSoft, SecureCart, Shopify, E-Junkie, MivaMerchant, ShopFactory, Cydec, and even Godaddy.com.

You can choose all-in-one options like Google Checkout, Bizhosting, Hostway, Volusion, and many others that will provide shopping cart software and handle your credit card processing for you.

CREDIT CARDS AND ONLINE PURCHASING

If you accept orders online it only makes sense to accept payment online, too. There are several ways to do this. Having your own merchant account is ideal, but there are fixed monthly costs and they are not always easy to get for the small startup company. Let's explore some options:

PayPal

PayPal is continually growing in popularity and acceptance. It allows you to set up "Buy Buttons" for your products and then PayPal conducts the transaction. They charge a small percentage and a per transaction fee. These fees are in line with what you'd pay with your own merchant account. PayPal is very popular. In fact, almost all of our international orders come through PayPal. PayPal is also a convenient way to send and receive money without purchasing anything.

PayPal offers a credit card services solution called Website Payments Standard that accepts all major credit cards and works with most major shopping carts. They also offer their own free, simple shopping cart and a virtual terminal. A virtual terminal allows you to manually enter credit card orders.

PayPal is a good and affordable solution for many people but it is not without some negatives. For one, you must manually move your funds out of PayPal into your bank. Some of the more sophisticated applications are complicated and require advanced programming. We have known people who have had their account frozen with tens of thousands of dollars in them due to having a sudden, large amount of sales during a product launch. This could be catastrophic if you need that cash.

Merchant Accounts

Depending on your situation, a PayPal account may be all you need. A "merchant account" is a traditional credit card account which allows you to accept PayPal payments along with major credit cards like Visa, MasterCard, Discover Card, and American Express. Having a merchant account in addition to PayPal will give you the most flexibility in receiving payments.

If you do an internet search on "merchant account services" you'll find a host of companies ready to take your business. Most charge a higher fee for online charges than retail. Banks are sometimes a difficult place to get a merchant account for a startup online business. Here are a few places I found that will work with eCommerce businesses: www.powerpay.com, www.merchantwarehouse.com, and www.charge.com.

Be aware of the extra charges when you apply for a merchant account and compare charges among service providers. Added fees to look for include:

- Application fees
- Monthly minimums
- Transaction fees (called the discount fee)
- Statement fees—sometimes you can get these waived if you agree to accept online statements only, so ask about this
- Higher rates for online sales

- Non-qualifying surcharge (meaning you don't have the actual credit card in front of you)
- Batch fees
- Annual fees
- Cancellation fees.

… you get the picture. Make sure they aren't loading you up on added charges.

You'll need a "payment gateway" which some merchant account providers will include but most don't. We use Authorize.net (www.authorize.net) as our gateway. The payment gateway serves like the point of sale terminal in a retail store. It provides you with a virtual terminal, which is how you can take phone or mail orders and process them manually through your computer. You want this. We use ours often. Expect to pay about $20 per month for your gateway account plus about 10¢ per transaction.

SELLING VIDEOS-ON-DEMAND

Are your products going to be video-on-demand? If this is your case you might want to offer your video as a www.clickbank.com product like Mike Deiure does. You can have a website and sell your videos through the Clickbank store and also get affiliate sales income if other affiliates drive customers to your website and they purchase. Clickbank is a good solution if you are only selling digital products since it handles everything for you; the delivery of your video, the credit card processing—if you sell through Clickbank you don't have to pay those expenses. Because Clickbank processes the credit cards you are not responsible for security. There is only a small one-time activation fee to get started and they have extensive support information to help you get set up. An added bonus? Sales of your videos made through productive Clickbank affiliate sales could even exceed your own direct sales. Paydotcom.com is another similar service.

GET A SQUARE

Are you going to be doing personal sales such as at a trade show, seminar, or kiosk? If so you might consider getting the "Square." This is a small device about the size of a postage stamp that plugs into a smartphone or tablet device. You swipe a credit card through it and it will process the sale for a small transaction fee. There are no startup or fixed monthly fees and the device itself is free. I think everyone should carry one of these around anyway. See www.squareup.com for more information.

BUILDING TRUST

As I shared before, although people are becoming more comfortable purchasing online, they will be much more likely to buy from you if you show them that your business is a legitimate, secure online store. How do you do that? For one thing, by displaying trust symbols such as Verisign, McAfee, Thawt, and GeoTrust.

If you are using a paid shopping cart it will include an SSL certificate. That stands for Secure Sockets Layer. An SSL certificate's main purpose is to authenticate the identity of the website you're connecting to. It also encrypts the data that is flowing between your customer's browser and the server where the transaction is occurring. When shopping in a secure site you should see "https" at the beginning of the address bar, along with a padlock.

You can purchase SSL certificates if you don't have one included with your shopping cart. Your web host or domain name provider can help you with this, or do a search on "SSL Certificate." Prices range radically, from as low as $25 to well over $500 annually. Names like Verisign, Geotrust, and Thawte are mainstays of the industry.

Authorize.net provides a "Verified Merchant" symbol which we like to display throughout our websites. When a user clicks on it they see a popup that states that we are a verified Authorize.net merchant, another way of building trust. Once a customer gets to our checkout page he will see both Verisign and McAfee symbols, courtesy of 1ShoppingCart.com.

Now that you're set up for business, you're ready to roll up your sleeves and do the fun work—marketing!

Action Steps

- Decide if you want a free or paid shopping cart. Assess the pros and cons.
- Choose a method of payment—merchant account, PayPal, Clickbank, etc.
- If you choose to go with a merchant account, research to find one that will meet your needs. Make sure you understand what type of fees they charge.
- Apply for a Square.
- Ensure that you have SSL and trust symbols. If your shopping cart doesn't have them, get them from a third-party provider.

Part V

Marketing

Chapter 32

Introduction to Marketing
The Five "P"s of Marketing

Chapter Objectives
- Understand what marketing is and how it guides the product development process.
- Understand why you need to be thinking about marketing throughout the video production process.
- Learn about the types of marketing activities you can use.
- Discover the key marketing variables you will be deciding on in your marketing mix.

IMPORTANCE OF MARKETING

Here we are at the transition from producing and distributing your video to sales for the rest of this book, which is all about marketing. Marketing is what stops a lot of people from producing their own SIVs. They have the ideas, they know how to produce them, they just can't figure out marketing. These next few chapters will take the mystery out of marketing.

Simply stated, marketing is a matter of perception in the mind of the prospect. It is how we persuade them that our product is the answer to their needs. We accomplish this through our public relations efforts, advertising, social media, public appearances, direct mail, and other ways we get our products in front of our prospect. Good marketing will position your product in a positive, memorable way in the mind of your prospect.

Now let's get down to the business of marketing your video. We told you at the beginning of this book that you should have marketing on your mind throughout the research and production process. Why? Because your success depends on producing something you can sell, not attempting to sell what you have already produced.

At the heart of this process is developing your marketing mix or plan. That should be centered around these five important variables, known as the five "P"s of marketing:

- **Products**—Primarily we are talking about your video information products but you may also include other things like books, CDs, eBooks, and services such as coaching.
- **Pricing**—You have to figure out what price your market is willing to pay and where within that spectrum you want your product to fall.

- **Place** (distribution)—These are channels your product will go through to reach the customer. As you saw, these can be online and offline, directly from you, through distributors, physical or video-on-demand.
- **Promotion**—This is how you raise awareness of your video with your target market and where we'll be turning your focus next. This component is what most people think of when the word marketing is mentioned. It can include activities such as advertising, public relations, and social media.
- **Positioning** (sometimes called People)—Here is where you will place your product in the mind of the consumer (not where you will physically place it). Positioning is largely a result of what you do in promotion to establish your product at the premium quality, middle, or the lower end of the quality/price scale for your product and market. It is also how you make it memorable.

Your videos will have a life cycle that goes from introduction through growth, maturity, and decline. This cycle falls nicely on an inverse bell curve. Where your video product is in this cycle will affect the marketing mix and your marketing strategies.

So how do you use this information? For example, you'll spend more effort and money promoting (launching) your product initially than when it is established and has its own momentum. You have to initially create market awareness and demand, then you'll hit a point where most of the people who are likely to buy your product are aware of it and you don't need to work so hard to convert them to customers. Then as your product has saturated the market and is in its declining phase, you should cut back further or you'll hit a point of diminishing returns on your promotional dollars and efforts.

It is important for you to be aware of where your product is in its life cycle and make adjustments to your marketing strategies on a regular basis.

TEST, TRACK, TWEAK, AND REPEAT

Marketing isn't science in the same sense that botany or astronomy are and although there are proven methods that have worked for most businesses, you are still dealing with people and their individual needs, tastes, and preferences. You can't base your marketing plan on what you like; you have to base it on your ideal customer.

What one direct mail catalog is to someone who disgustedly tosses it aside as soon as he opens the mail is an eagerly awaited delight to another. While Kim doesn't mind daily emails from Kohl's, to me they are spam. You'll go onto your Facebook page one day and see a rant against some company's R-rated YouTube videos and then you'll hear how their fourth quarter sales increased due to that ad campaign's popularity. Different strokes for different folks.

The only way to know for sure if your sales and marketing efforts are effective is by using the same process we talked about when setting your prices: by testing, tracking the results, then tweaking your process, focusing on what worked, and stop doing what didn't work. Then keep repeating this process.

Alright, it's time to get started on your marketing education. Let's start at the beginning, with the marketing plan and funnel.

Action Steps

- Get familiar with the marketing activities you will need to understand and the essential Ps of marketing. Each of these areas will factor in on the decisions you make regarding your video:
  - Products
  - Pricing
  - Place
  - Promotion
  - Positioning

Marketing Plans and Sales Funnels

Here's a story of what not to do …

I started out this book telling you about one of my partners, Holly Ziegler, the woman who had a large following in the field of Feng Shui and real estate and how we videotaped a presentation she did at the California Association of Realtors® conference. Producing that first video took us a lot of time. We spent many hours editing, overlaying her PowerPoint presentations, and adding additional b-roll and graphics to illustrate her concepts. I sweetened it with a beautiful music track and Kim spent a lot of time designing and authoring a nice-looking DVD set.

Once the DVD was done, we turned our efforts to designing the graphics and writing sales copy. In our zeal we ordered thousands of covers and advertising material for the videos. Additionally, Holly had made an audio book from her two best-selling books and asked us to handle the graphics, duplication, and sales of those as well. Her books were flying off the shelves and Holly and we thought the audio books would likely do the same, especially for busy real estate agents who spend a lot of time in their cars. So we ordered special cases that would hold all the CDs, had those covers printed, and duplicated hundreds of CDs.

At the time, we decided to put all of the DVDs and CDs together ourselves since Holly needed a large quantity quickly for an upcoming conference. I remember spending hours putting these together as I panicked that we weren't going to be able to keep up with demand once I built her website. I was happily calculating all the money we were both going to make.

Then the site went live. I knew it wouldn't have traffic right away so I spent a lot of money on pay-per-click advertising knowing, just knowing that once a struggling real estate agent landed on her site and saw what was available he'd buy! We also signed up with an email service and sent out emails to her list of thousands of names.

The people at the conference bought, we had a flurry of sales from her list as well, but not much activity after that.

So what happened? We knew that she was highly respected in her field and that we had a good product in a unique niche that would command higher prices. The site was getting decent traffic and I felt the sales copy was good. Where did we go wrong?

We didn't have a well thought-out marketing plan that included a strong sales funnel before we were counting our money. We were really just taking a stab at marketing. Once we put a plan into place, sales picked up.

YOUR MARKETING PLAN

You needn't make that same mistake when you have an overall plan for your marketing activities. That could be anything from placing ads in trade journals to email marketing. Timing is important for most products so you need to look at potential buying cycles for your product and plan to be promoting your videos through whatever means you choose with plenty of advance planning.

For our Christmas sales, for example, we start planning in summer and start implementing our activities in September, increasing the frequency as we get closer to Christmas. Our car detailing video sales slow down considerably in winter months and start up again in early spring as people get their cars cleaned up from winter sludge.

You could do this on an online calendar but getting a large dry erase calendar you can put on your wall is a good tactic because it is always in your sight, reminding you that you have to stay on track. Be sure to get the dry erase kind because you want to be able to make changes. A marketing plan should be fluid, not set in stone. You have to make adjustments as the market changes and as new opportunities arise.

Be planning at least six months in advance. Once you have some experience you'll be able to look a year out and plan based on previous experience.

You will want to forecast your expenses and for this the best tool is a spreadsheet like Microsoft Excel or OpenOffice. Most of the marketing tactics we advocate don't have much cost except for our time. We use email and social marketing, blogging, search engine marketing, and article marketing extensively, which don't have a cost associated with them. We do some direct mail marketing before Christmas and occasionally use pay-per-click and print advertising.

THE MARKETING BUDGET

As you are making your marketing plan you want to create your marketing budget based on the best cost projections you can get. You'll want to do this to project cash needs and to track actual expenses. Below is a very simplified marketing budget covering three months. You would want to expand this for an entire year. Build it so that it is summing up and placing totals for both projected and actual expenses.

Marketing Budget	Jan. 20XX	Jan. 20XX	Feb. 20XX	Feb. 20XX	Mar. 20XX	Mar. 20XX
	Projected	Actual	Projected	Actual	Projected	Actual
Renting Mailing List	$0.00	$0.00	$0.00	$0.00	$0.00	$0.00
Printing Brochures	$0.00	$0.00	$0.00	$0.00	$0.00	$0.00
Postage, Mailing Brochures	$0.00	$0.00	$0.00	$0.00	$0.00	$0.00
Monthly Trade Journal Ad	$0.00	$0.00	$0.00	$0.00	$0.00	$0.00
Email Service Fees	$0.00	$0.00	$0.00	$0.00	$0.00	$0.00
Trade Show Exhibit	$0.00	$0.00	$0.00	$0.00	$0.00	$0.00
Mailing Press Releases	$0.00	$0.00	$0.00	$0.00	$0.00	$0.00
Subtotal	**$0.00**	**$0.00**	**$0.00**	**$0.00**	**$0.00**	**$0.00**

Putting budget figures into a spreadsheet like this will help you prioritize your marketing activities and know where the money is allocated and where it actually went.

You want to put systems in place to track where your sales come from so you know which of these activities are profitable.

WHAT IS A SALES FUNNEL?

At some point in the marketing process, selling needs to happen. A good selling process usually consists of steps or stages you guide your prospect through in order to become a customer. Ideally you want a customer for life, who is so happy with your products that they will buy from you over and over again.

This sales process is often compared to a "*marketing or sales funnel*" which acts as a sieve to direct *qualified* purchasers through the sales process while filtering out less-qualified people along the way.

Picture a funnel (Figure 33.1). At the wide top of a sales funnel is a mix of qualified and unqualified prospective customers. Less-qualified purchasers drop away at each step as they move down the funnel towards the purchase process. The bottom of the funnel, the smallest part of the funnel, contains the most qualified prospects who will not only buy, but buy time and again, becoming loyal fans and advocates. In other words, they'll be the ones spreading the word among all of their contacts about how great your videos are.

Prospecting

Your Product's Story

Overcome Objections

Close The Sale

Follow-Up

FIGURE 33.1   Sales Funnel.

Prospecting

The first step in a funnel involves getting people into the funnel, which means prospecting for potential customers. You are looking for *qualified prospects* and the purpose of your funnel is to screen out the unqualified folks. You only want people who:

- Have a problem or have an interest that your video will solve or speak to;
- Are in the market for something that your video offers;
- Have the means to buy your product.

You can find potential prospects from a variety of sources including trade shows, commercially available databases or mailing lists, your sales records and in-house databases, websites, referrals, and other sources. You can get people into your funnel through search engine marketing, pay-per-click advertising, press releases, direct marketing, article marketing, email marketing, social media, video marketing, forum participation, and other means we'll be discussing in upcoming chapters. We'll also refer to this as "building your list."

You want to get a lot of qualified potential buyers into your funnel initially. You never know which ones can be converted into customers until you try, so at this first stage you want volume. Then you want to move them to the next stage in the marketing funnel. All through this process you'll use a range of marketing tactics that will bring them closer to a purchase decision.

One of the ways you've already started this sales funnel is through doing all that market research we encouraged back in the beginning of this book. I hope you kept those notes and lists you should have made because you'll be referring to them. Pull out your notes on your ideal customer, your competitors, and your target markets. Make sure your research was thorough. In the coming chapters you'll see where all that work will pay off.

Your Product's Story

Try to understand your prospect's needs and create sales presentations (web copy, videos, emails, etc.) that address the identified and likely concerns of your customer. You'll be refining this strategy as you learn more and more about your prospective customers and target market as you get into this process. Another way of saying this is that you're learning where their hot buttons are and how to push them.

During this portion of the sales funnel, you'll share your product's "story" in a way that speaks directly to the identified needs and wants of the prospect.

You want to show that you truly understand and care about their needs. You're offering your video as an answer to their need, not for your own financial gain. It's all about them.

Overcoming Objections

Don't think of objections as necessarily bad. They exist and you want to know them in order to address and overcome them. If you don't know what they are, you cannot begin to eliminate them.

An effective tactic is to have an "If/Then"conversation and deal with their objections before they even raise them. In this strategy we bring up the possible objection and shoot it down with our solution.

If your video was about weight loss, that might go something like this:

"If you think this will be too difficult … then you're going to be amazed at how fast the pounds come off."
"Don't worry about dieting … you can eat all you want and still lose weight."

A friend once told me, "the way to deal with a monster is to kill it while it's small." Get those objections out of the way early and move the prospect along in the funnel.

With online sales you may have to work a little harder to discover their objections. That's where social media shines.

Closing the Sale

This is the final decision point in which you may have to help the sale along by "asking" for the order and adequately address any final objections or obstacles. Closing does not always mean that you literally ask for the order, it could be more indirect, like asking the prospect if they prefer it on DVD or via an online download, do they want it with public performance rights, etc. In retail stores a similar tactic is to ask "would you like that gift wrapped?" It assumes that the sale is a done deal.

Follow-Up

Follow-up is an often overlooked but important part of the selling process. After an order is received, it's a good idea to follow-up with your customer to make sure the video was received in good condition and on time, and that the entire process worked well for the customer. This is a big step in creating customer satisfaction and building long term relationships with your customers. If they had problems you can intervene and ensure 100 percent satisfaction. In addition, follow-up helps you uncover new needs and video topic ideas and can lead to the customer making additional purchases. You also may get referrals and testimonials which can be used as sales tools.

By the way, if you get the opportunity to ask for testimonials, by all means, do so.

AN EXAMPLE OF AN ONLINE SALES FUNNEL

You may be thinking about now: Man, that's a *lot* of work and effort and it won't be worth it in the long run.

The fact is that you can do this online *very* well, very cost–effectively, and with little effort. Once we implemented this process on many of our sites we saw our sales increase substantially, so we know this works. Now we set this funnel process up with every video we sell.

If you are tempted to skip this section because you feel you don't need something like a sales funnel because you'll be selling your videos on Amazon or through eBay, don't! Even if you are not going to be dealing with any of the ordering or shipping processes, you want a way to build a list to increase awareness of and desire for your products and to send those people to locations where they can buy your videos.

The following is our basic sales funnel framework.

Capture Page

Also called a landing page or squeeze page, this is the start of the funnel where you will attract prospects and "capture" their information. This serves a couple of purposes: you not only build a list of people who are interested to hear more from you, this list is pre-qualified since they gave you their valuable information and approval to market to them.

It would be great if the majority of the people who visit your site would buy your video on the first visit. Unfortunately it doesn't usually happen like that. People like to shop around and yours may be just one site they stumble across. To get enough sales to sustain you on that type of hit-and-miss marketing involves generating *a lot* of consistent traffic to your website. And I mean *A LOT*, as in thousands a day. That's why you want to attract targeted traffic to your site, people who are predisposed to want your videos, and then have the sales copy on your site speak directly to their needs. Ten targeted prospects are far better than hundreds of random visitors.

Also once a visitor leaves your site you don't know if he'll return, and there's a good chance he won't unless you give him a good reason to do so. With all the websites available, he may have the intention of coming back but may lose your web address, misspell it, forget about it, etc. Happens all the time.

So what can you do to get a visitor to return and get to know and trust you as a source? Enter the concept of *permission marketing* through offering a giveaway. The first step in this is to have a way for them to opt-in to receive information from you.

What Do We Mean by Opt-In?

Opt-in boxes are special forms placed on your website where visitors can enter their name and email or other information in an online form in exchange for something. You could call it a sign up form. With that, they are giving you approval to contact them. Once they hit the submit button, their information is captured for you and you can start sending emails to move them along in the funnel.

Gone are the days when you could simply state, "For more information, enter your name and email address below." It also used to be effective to offer them a subscription to your newsletter in exchange for their information. That doesn't work well now because people already have information overload.

Today you need to crank it up a notch and offer a better giveaway. What can you give away? You want to give them something they will value. Free video courses, special "insider" reports, eBooks, audio podcasts, checklists, and guides are all good. For example, Mike Deiure gives a free video guitar lesson on learning to play a certain rock song. Dave Sheahan gives away a free workout video. We give a special downloadable report on avoiding pests on your plants on our Success With Succulents (www.successwithsucculents.com) site. Think about what you can give that your customers would value enough to trade their name and email for.

You can get opt-in software for your website if you don't have it as part of your hosting account or shopping cart software. Do an online search and you'll see dozens of options. There are many opt-in plugins available for WordPress and they are easy to use. You'll also need some kind of mailing list software to manage the names, and you'll want an autoresponder system such as AWeber or Constant Contact. Most mailing list management programs such as AWeber will provide you with opt-in code for your website or blog.

The autoresponder system is what will enable you to send emails that you set up in advance and are triggered by an opt-in or sale. These emails will go out sequentially and automatically in the order and timing you specify. Our shopping cart software, 1ShoppingCart, offers all of this, plus ad tracking software which allows us to test to see how different offers are performing.

Thank You Page (or Welcome Page)

The thank you page is where you want to send the person after they have opted in. You want to thank them for their trust in you and reiterate how valuable the giveaway they are getting is and to remind them how to access it. Reassure them they will get some good stuff from you, that you won't spam them, and you won't give or sell their contact information to others. You may want to make an offer to them for your product at this time or you may want to "warm them up" a bit first by giving them useful information without pushing the sale.

A smart idea is to design two thank you pages and run a split test to see which approach works best. You can use ad tracking software to create a switch, sending the first prospect to the thank you page without an offer and the second one to the page with an offer. The third goes back to the thank you page, the fourth goes to the offer page, and it keeps going until you collect enough data to see what page works better. Figure 33.2 shows you an image of one of our ad campaigns and what this process looks like. As you can see, sending them to the page with the offer performed better than the other page.

Campaign ID	519723
Campaign Name	Patrick Smith Birthday Sale
URL	http://www.on2url.com/app/adtrack.asp?MerchantID=101564&ID=519723

Campaign Info

Active	Destination URL	Clicks	Leads	Sales	Amount	Value
✔	http://patricksmithonline.com/birthday2.html	69 (80)	3 (4%)	4 (6%)	$159.65	$2.31 per click
✔	http://patricksmithonline.com/birthday.html	70 (80)	4 (6%)	4 (6%)	$99.85	$1.43 per click

FIGURE 33.2   Our ad tracking report from our shopping cart software.

Autoresponder

Once the person is on your list you now have permission to send them email messages. The neat thing is that you can write these messages all in advance and have them loaded into your autoresponder software and programmed to go out to your prospect on a predetermined schedule. You only have to set this up once for all of your prospects.

For example, you'll want to have an email they get immediately after they opt-in and you'll want to send one the next day, too. Then maybe you will send them another one every other day for a certain length of time.

Here is a sample of what you can do with an autoresponder:

Day 0—Thank you email that is sent right after they opt-in.
Day 1—Follow-up email to make sure they received the giveaway and re-send the information to access it again if they didn't already do so. Encourage them to keep this information.
Day 3—An email with a good tip they can use.
Day 5—Another email with a great resource you've found that can help them.
Day 7—An email with a 15 percent coupon off your video.
Day 9—Another email with another tip.

And so on …

You can have this sequence continue for as long as you like and you can also move people back into the beginning of the sequence and start over.

So how many messages should you send? I wouldn't send more than one autoresponder message per day. People may feel too uncomfortable with that and will unsubscribe from your list or worse, report you as spam. Too many spam reports and your account could get shut down. Besides, that's just annoying.

However, keep in mind that if you are clear with people as to what they are opting in for they will expect to hear from you on a regular basis. If they get emails from you too infrequently they may forget they signed up with you and report you as spam and unsubscribe. Think about the last time you signed up for a list: didn't you want to get all the information you were promised? I know that I eagerly open my the emails that come from B&H Photo & Video, and my favorite online guitar store. Your goal is to send emails they look forward to.

The frequency with which you mail is another aspect to test to find out your list's tolerance. We have found that for some of our lists, every other day is fine but for others we spread our emails out every four to five days.

Another thing to note—did you see how I didn't even talk about my video until the seventh day when I offered a coupon? That's because you want to offer 80 to 90 percent valuable information and 10 to 20 percent soft sales. You want them to get to know, like, and trust you first, then let them know how your product can help them. Make sure you have friendly follow-up messages packed with good information that supports the content your prospect signed up for.

What if they buy? Well, give yourself a little pat on the back! That's great. At this point you take them out of this autoresponder sequence and move them into another autoresponder sequence for another video or product. Once you set this up in your software, it will do it for you automatically.

What if they unsubscribe? I used to be bummed out when people unsubscribed. Now I take it in stride that this is a part of the qualifying process and that if I set up a good sales funnel sequence that is converting well for me, that prospect probably wouldn't have bought my video no matter what I did. Not everybody who walks into a store is going to buy something, nor is everyone on your list going to become a customer.

> Some email services will let you provide a survey that a person can complete on the unsubscribe page. These are helpful in knowing why they unsubscribed. Was the product wrong for them, was there too much email, or did their decision have nothing at all to do with either? (While I was focused writing this book, I had to unsubscribe from some lists just because I would get too distracted by the cool stuff they sent. Once I was done I opted back into many of these lists.)

The beauty of a system like this is that once you find a method that works well for you, most of your marketing effort goes into driving traffic to your capture pages. The rest of the process is automatic. Once you have a steady flow of traffic, you'll get a steady flow of income with little additional time invested.

WANT TO LEARN MORE? SPY ON YOUR COMPETITION

The information above is just to give you an idea of the steps in creating a simple sales funnel for your videos. There is a lot more to it than we can cover here so you'll want to do some research and study what others do. A good way to learn is to go to your competitor's website or another business you'd like to emulate, enter their sales funnel by signing up in their opt-in, and watch how they handle you. You'll get good ideas you can use.

HOW DO YOU GET PROSPECTS INTO YOUR FUNNEL?

So we've established that you need to get prospects into your funnel. Where do you find them? There are so many places you can go to find prospects. Avenues are cropping up every day. We'll be covering some of the top strategies we use in later chapters when we get into specific types of marketing. They encompass both online and offline methods.

A few examples of online prospecting involve posting your promotional videos on sites such as YouTube, producing podcasts for iTunes and your own TV channel website, doing joint ventures with other people's lists, asking your customers to refer others, and networking via social media.

Offline strategies include advertising in publications and on radio and television, sending out press releases, networking in person, blogging, direct mail marketing (fliers, catalogs, postcards, etc.), and speaking or displaying at a conference, show, or convention.

One of our partners, Butch Harrison, who produced *Florida Cracker Storyteller*, is just that, a storyteller who performs all over Florida. While he relies on me to handle his online marketing, he's out there cold calling, speaking at meetings and events, networking with almost anyone he strikes up a conversation with. He has gone so far as to put magnetic signage on his car and we have had orders because of that! He is the most determined person I've ever met. There is nothing he will not do to get a sale. He's out there building awareness of his video, displaying our URL on his car, and sending prospects to our website. That's a good partner!

Your greatest success will be to use all of the strategies available to you in combination to support one another. For example, if you are speaking at an event you could build and promote a Facebook Page about your product, Tweet about it, send press releases to all applicable media, take an ad in the convention's program, and place ads in publications related to that industry. Have someone take photos of you speaking and follow-up after the event by posting these photos and a brief recap in Facebook and on your blog. Be sure to capture all of the names, addresses, and emails you get. Don't be shy about self-promotion.

A key to attracting your prospects into your funnel and moving them through it to a sale is good sales copy. You will need to produce compelling sales copy every step of the way, from the post you make in Facebook to your order page, you're going to be educating them, overcoming their objections, convincing and coaxing them along to a sale.

Small businesses like us can't afford to do image advertising like soap commercials or automobile ads. We don't just want awareness of our product, we want a sale, and that's why the next chapter is dedicated to direct response marketing.

Action Steps

- Come up with your marketing plan and budget.
- Plan your sales funnel.
- Create a giveaway.
- Research and pick a mailing list management system.
- Install an opt-in on your site.
- Develop a sequence of autoresponder emails.
- Make a list of all the avenues where you can find your prospects and how you'll reach them.

Chapter 34

Direct Response Marketing

Chapter Objectives

- Learn how direct response marketing differs from image advertising.
- Learn some of the common forms of direct response marketing.
- Understand two common metrics of direct marketing.
- Learn some ways you can use direct marketing in your business.
- Understand the importance of testing.
- Instill the importance of the compelling offer.

Do you remember the Montgomery Ward catalog or the 4-pound Sears & Roebuck catalog that used to get delivered to every household? If you do, that dates you. I used to love them. I always lived in small towns with few shopping options but you could buy *anything* through those catalogs and have it delivered to your door. Sears even sold kit houses and automobiles. When I was a kid I'd gaze at guitars in the Sears catalog and dream, sure that if I could only get my hands on one I'd undoubtedly be a famous rock star. I eventually ended up getting one of their Silvertone amps, but the rock star thing … well, that never happened.

Those catalogs were the start of what today we call direct response marketing, direct marketing, or simply DM. These catalogs went straight into the hands of the consumer and made it possible for them to make a *response* (place an order) *directly* with the business, hence direct marketing.

Direct response marketing is a form of advertising, but it's done in a specialized, more measurable form. Most general advertising is meant to create awareness of a product or service, like an automobile ad in a magazine or laundry soap ads on television. They don't solicit a direct response, they're just making you aware of the product and brand. Direct response marketing, in contrast, is designed to present an offer and get a response or a sale right away. The desired response may not be an immediate sale but rather to get the person to ask for more information so that you can move them into the sales process. We covered that process in Chapter 33 where we introduced you to the sales funnel.

COMMON TYPES OF DIRECT MARKETING

Direct response marketing works well both online and offline and you may find that a combination of the two is the best formula for your business.

The main form of DM that we've found very effective in our small business is email marketing. That's such an important topic that we're devoting the next chapter to it in this book. Email marketing is the foundation of our online marketing funnel.

You've probably entered many similar marketing funnels when you traded your name and email for a free gift, free report, special video, or whatever. That action entered you in someone's marketing funnel and you soon, if not immediately, began receiving email from them. You became a prospect.

A common and annoying form of direct marketing is telemarketing. Those dinnertime calls asking, "How are you doing this evening?" are another way of asking for a direct response. I dislike them but they obviously work or people wouldn't be spending the money to do them.

Other DM tools include broadcast faxing (which is illegal and thankfully, disappearing), coupons, infomercials, inserts in your newspaper, stickers on newspapers and magazines, postcard packets like ValPak, voicemail marketing, pay-per-click advertising, and the granddaddy of them all—direct mail marketing. All of them are effective in the right markets when used well.

THE IMPORTANCE OF TRACKING

At its core, DM is all about targeting the right prospects with the right offer at the right time and right price, providing a strong and clear "call to action," and providing an easy way to respond. Finally, it's very focused on tracking and measuring results in order to continually refine the targeting component.

Direct mail marketing uses codes on each mailing piece to track response. Online marketing can track sales from specific landing pages and by using embedded code, called cookies for some mysterious reason, to track a sale.

In my catalog marketing days we would add a code before the order number of every product in the catalog. This code would change with every catalog. The Winter 2005 code might be W05 and would be added before the real order number for every product in the catalog. Most customers didn't know that wasn't part of the order number so they would include it on the order form. Then the person entering the order would know that the order came from the Winter 2005 catalog and would make note of it.

Since we did promotions throughout the year with many different mailing pieces that cost a substantial amount of money, it was important to know how each one was working. If we did a full-color flyer we wanted to know how well it generated sales compared to the catalog. This helped us refine our marketing techniques and economize on our printed pieces.

We also tracked our mailing lists with codes. Whether using our own customer list or a list purchased from a list broker, we added a code so that we knew where the list came from and which segment of the list that person belonged to. So, for example, high school horticulture teachers might be coded HSH on the mailing label. High school botany teachers might be HSB. We asked them to enter the code from their mailing label on the order form. (Teachers are very good about following directions.) We kept track of all of this so we knew how each segment of our mailing list was responding. Based on this information we might add more names from a segment that performed well and drop a non-performing segment.

Some of the more expensive mailing pieces have the person's name and code preprinted on the order form so they don't have to do anything special; you get the code automatically when they submit the form. If they order by phone the operator is instructed to ask for the code.

Those methods work well in direct mail but online ordering makes it far easier to know precisely where an order came from. Because of the incredible tracking and targeting that marketers can do with computers, the internet is a dream come true for direct marketers.

METRICS OF DIRECT MARKETING

One of the main metrics at the heart of DM is *"response rate."* Another word you see used for this in the online world is "conversion rate." This tells the marketer how many people out of an ad campaign responded to the offer and converted to a buyer. Those numbers are often low, usually in the single digits. Knowing them and striving to improve them is necessary in order to improve profitability.

If you do a promotion to 10,000 people and get a 2 percent order conversion rate, you'll get 200 orders. If you earn $20 per order with a profit margin of $16 per order, you've made $3,200 gross profit. If your marketing costs were less than that then you have made a net profit. If you didn't, then you lost money. Your future goal would be to improve the conversion rate, increase your average order size and/or your gross profit per order, or reduce your marketing cost.

In email marketing the terminology is a little different. You might send 10,000 emails and get a 20 percent open rate, meaning 2,000 people at least clicked on the email to open it. Then if you have a clickthrough rate of 35 percent of those 2,000, which is how many people clicked through a link you provided in the email you'd get 700 clickthroughs. If you then have a 2 percent conversion rate, you'll sell 14 items.

Testing is a word frequently heard in DM circles. To be effective, marketers must constantly be testing variables such as price, copy, offer, headlines, body copy, photos, colors, paper stock, timing, etc. Success or failure can hinge on the correct use of any one of these. Because the response to these tests is so trackable, marketers can continually refine their marketing campaigns.

I've seen studies where marketers go to extremes, such as not just testing a headline but testing the ink or paper color or even the font used in the headline. Any one of these variations can have a surprising impact on the results.

While we realistically can't test everything to that degree, it is very important to test major variables like price, headlines, and the offer. This is much easier and less expensive for internet marketers than for businesses working in the world of printed materials. For example, as I shared in setting up your online sales funnel, you can have multiple landing pages that test these variables and by using an ad tracker you can send equal numbers of random visitors to each landing page. The page that converts the most prospects to customers is the winner.

DIRECT MAIL MARKETING IS ALIVE AND WELL

Don't believe any rumors about the demise of direct mail marketing. It is still a very effective direct marketing tool; in fact, I think it is becoming more effective as the volume of direct mail is decreasing due to the growth of internet marketing. Now your mailing piece stands out more because there's less competition in your mailbox.

Direct mail marketing can take many forms: catalogs, flyers, brochures, postcards, sales letters, CDs, and DVDs. Even the envelope that direct mail is delivered in is a critical link in the creative chain. Heck, the copy on the envelope can make the decision between opening it and tossing it. There are writers who specialize in writing envelope copy, it's that important. Every single piece of a direct mail package should be thoughtfully considered to make sure the message is clear and consistent, and that all components are leading the recipient to the point of making a purchase decision.

Direct mail marketing is more expensive than email marketing because you have printing and postage costs. Color printing has become much more affordable in the last several years but postage is a fixed cost and is always going up. The cost is based on the weight and class of your mailing. Planning a direct mail campaign has to be done with a sharp pencil, but it can be very effective.

We're relying almost exclusively on email marketing these days due to the economy and efficiency, but we do include a direct mail campaign at least a couple of times a year. Postcards are cheap to print and still have among the lowest postage rates available. If you do venture into direct mail, speak with your post master or someone who knows the direct mail industry so you can take advantage of any bulk mailing savings available to you. Often a slight change in the mailing piece can result in postage savings.

HOW YOU CAN USE DIRECT MARKETING

How can you use DM to promote your videos? How about announcing a sale or introducing a new video to your existing customers? Sometimes direct mail is the best method despite the added cost. I find that retail businesses respond better to mail. They are not at their computer reading email all day and some don't even have business-related email accounts. No matter what form your DM takes, you need a mailing list.

As you've read throughout this book, I like marketing to schools. Schools and libraries respond better to mailing pieces than to email due to the internet firewalls that most school systems have. One of my longtime friends and associates, Joe Clokey, was willing to share his thoughts about direct mail marketing, knowing your customer, and marketing to schools.

Joe Clokey, Owner of San Luis Video Publishing (www.horticulturevideos.com)

Joe Clokey is one of the few people I know who's been in the special interest video business almost as long as I have. In fact, I helped him get his start in the business.

Joe was a horticulture student at Cal Poly in the 1980s, where I ran that video publishing department. As a child, he had some film background (his father was Art Clokey, who developed the Gumby and Pokey animation series), and he decided to do a horticulture video for his senior project.

Somebody recommended that I get a hold of you, and then you turned me on to one of the people that you had trained [Jim Harrigan, another horticulture student turned video producer] and he mentored me in video production. I made a video for my senior project and then I approached you about selling my video in your catalog, which you did.

That video sold so well that Joe continued to produce more horticulture videos with Jim Harrigan. We added them to our catalog, where they sold quite well. I encouraged Joe to start his own mail order company to sell both his and our videos. He did and has produced a catalog a year since then.

Joe's company, San Luis Video Publishing, has about 60 titles now, but he learned early on that even if you dominate a niche, it has to be a big enough niche to survive on. "Horticultural education is a small market," Joe says. "It wasn't big enough to support us so we added soil science, which is related. Then we expanded into botany and entomology."

Joe and I learned that if you are producing videos specifically for education you have to understand how they will be used. Joe says,

For instance, a Nova program on PBS will spend an hour on bees. A teacher doesn't have time to do an hour on just bees, they have to cover all of entomology in an hour or two, so I developed a four-part series that in an hour and a half covers all of entomology.

Pricing for schools is different than for consumers, too. If there's a limited number of teachers (or consumers) in a niche, you have to make your profit back over a smaller number of sales. Joe recollects,

When I started my catalog in 1988 I sold my videos for $39.95 but you put them in your catalog and marked them up to $75. The next year we raised the price to $75 dollars in our catalog it sold even better because the teachers realized that it was for them. When they saw a video for $29.95 or less, they would say, "Well this is for the mass consumers, it's not aimed at teachers."

One of the things Joe and I share is that we both spent over 20 years in direct mail marketing. Today I mostly do internet marketing but Joe still publishes a catalog. It's harder to get through school internet firewalls to directly contact teachers through email, so for now direct mail is still the most effective way to reach them. It is expensive, so you have to target your mail pieces very carefully. Joe explains,

Timing of promotions to schools is critical. When teachers come back after summer there's a heavy buying spurt because they're buying for their upcoming year. I have a two-week window to hit them with my catalog. Starting in January, they start buying again. There's another peak at the end of the school year when they spend money that they haven't spent.

School marketing is a subject that I have a lot of experience in, and Joe and I had a great visit talking about it. We share a lot more information about marketing to schools in our full-length interview, available at www.shoot-to-sell.com.

THE MONEY IS IN THE LIST

Unless you are doing direct response ads or newspaper inserts, the first thing you need is a list. Whether it's to an email list or a mailing list, you are going to be directing your message to a group of customers or prospects.

The best list you'll ever have is your own customer list. Those people have already trusted you enough to buy your video; hopefully they like it and you have established a relationship with them. They are far more likely to buy from you again than a cold prospect is. Always give your customer list top priority and treat them like VIPs.

You can mail to your customer list as often as several times a month. Until they start to complain loudly, keep contacting them with offers or a newsletter. This is one of the reasons why we told you in Chapter 24 that you want to be expanding your offerings and have more than one item to sell.

What if you don't have your own prospect or customer list? You can rent them from list brokers (see next section) or do a joint venture (JV) with someone who has a list that should respond to your video. Your JV partner will promote your products to their list in exchange for a percentage of the profits. You can also do pay-per-click advertising which we'll discuss further in Chapter 38.

You should always be building your list. Keep every contact you make, whether that is through an opt-in box on your website, a sign up sheet at an event, or a collection of business cards. Your mailing list is one of your most valuable assets. You should also have an opt-in form above the fold on your website and have something with perceived value to give away.

RENTING MAILING LISTS

Your customer list is always going to be your best performing list but there are times when you may want to rent prospect lists in order to gain new customers quickly.

There's a large industry built around providing mailing lists to marketers in every imaginable industry. There are list rental companies that specialize in a certain industry, dentists for example, and general ones that have lists of everything. From my experience, the more specialized the mailing list company is, the more accurate their list. You can deal directly with a mailing list company or a mailing list broker. A good company will help you choose lists that most accurately match your needs.

Mailing lists are either compiled, meaning someone gathered them from something like directories or public records, or response, meaning these people are proven buyers in that category. Response lists tend to be more focused and to respond better to the right offer. They are also more expensive. Expect to spend about $100 per thousand names with a minimum order size of at least 5,000 names.

It is important that you have clearly defined your ideal customer and know as much about them as possible before you buy a mailing list. Knowing your target market is crucial in order to choose a mailing list that matches it.

With few exceptions, mailing list companies rent lists, they don't sell them. That means you don't own the list you purchase, you generally just get to use it one time. Some companies allow you to use a list more than once for a limited period of time. If you are doing direct mail they'll either send you a file of the list or for an additional fee they'll print and send you the labels. Many mailing houses will also have the ability to print your mailing piece and do the mailing for you. Once someone from a rented lists buys from you they become your customer and then you can continue to mail to them.

An email list broker, to protect their list, will usually want to do the mailing for you. You send them your electronic DM piece and they handle it.

How do these companies keep you from stealing their lists? They seed them with decoy names. You have no idea which names these are but the decoy knows that they should receive only one communication from you. If they start receiving additional mailings from you then they know you've stolen the list and you are in deep trouble.

When you design your mailer, it's a good idea to give a good reason for the prospect to not just purchase from you but to also visit your website. That way, even if they don't become a customer from this mailing, they have the chance to visit your site and opt-in for your offer and you then have a way to keep the conversation going. The direct response you want might even be for the recipient to visit your website rather than to elicit a sale directly from the mailing piece.

COPY IS KING

Be sure to read Chapter 30 on copywriting because the way you construct your message is vitally important. Your potential customers are impatient so you have to very quickly convince them that your message is important enough for them to spend time reading it. This is one area where I feel direct mail still has an advantage over email marketing. Mail is tangible. People can set mail aside to read later but email promotions quickly disappear in the steady stream of email messages that most people get.

If your mailing piece is attractive people may keep it because it has a perceived value. Catalogs that look like magazines are kept longer. Beautiful postcards are hard to toss. Who doesn't like to leaf through a catalog of their favorite items? Do you keep some favorite catalogs on your nightstand?

If you use direct mail it will be to your advantage to get a graphic designer who is familiar with effective direct mail design. They can save you money at the printer through press-ready designs. Same for your copywriter.

TEST, TEST, AND TEST

Please don't go out and print 10,000 sales letters or postcards. Until you have a feel for your market you should be printing shorter runs and testing the variables. Do this in batches until you feel confident you know the right creative elements and price point. Only then do you roll out a larger, more expensive mailing. The same principle applies to mass email marketing.

Remember back in Chapter 20 where we went through an example of sending out a mailer to a list of 3,000 people to test prices? You can do the same with your marketing pieces.

Remember only test one variable at a time. In other words, don't change both the headline *and* the price on a split test. You won't know which variable caused the result. Be methodical and keep good records of your results. If you are doing this with different landing pages on your website, your ad tracker software will tell you which one worked best. If doing it on direct mail, place codes or different order numbers on items so you can tell which variation produced the most sales.

DON'T FORGET THE OFFER

Direct mail is about presenting an offer and asking for a response. It's that basic. Make sure that you present your product in its best light and include a clear, compelling offer and an equally clear call to action. Your goal is to make such an irresistible offer that there can be no other answer than YES. In fact, putting YES in a pre-checked box is an often-used ploy to move the prospect into action. The theory is that they have subliminally already agreed to YES. You should have your prospect thinking "this deal is too good to pass up."

An example of an offer would be: "This money-making four DVD set sells every day for $199, but this week only you can get it for HALF-PRICE! If you order today we'll also include (fill in the blank)."

Or "The first 100 people to sign up on my website by Midnight on April 1, 20XX will receive a free (fill in the blank)."

Always create a sense of urgency to place an order or respond NOW. People get busy and if you don't get the order or response when they're looking at the email or direct mail piece, you'll probably never get it.

I'm not saying that your copy should sound frantic or desperate, but you must present a compelling offer with a sense of urgency.

Finally, have people you trust read over your direct mail piece and give you feedback.

ADD A PRODUCT REGISTRATION

It sounds silly at first to register a DVD, but here's why you want to do it. If you're selling your DVD through distributors or some place like Amazon.com, you'll never get your customer's contact information. You can't follow-up with subsequent offers. However, if you include a product registration card in the DVD case, a good portion of customers will return it and you'll get their information for future promotions.

Call the card a "Lifetime Warranty Registration Card" or something like that. Say the DVD is guaranteed against defects in manufacturing for life but it has to be registered. Like I said, the money's in the list and your customer list is gold, so do what you can to bring all of your customers into the fold.

KEEP LEARNING

Direct marketing is a diverse and dynamic industry. I've worked in direct marketing for 30 years and am constantly learning new things. This book cannot begin to give in-depth instruction in DM. There are many resources available to help you. You can find lots of books on direct marketing on Amazon.com.

The Direct Marketing Association (www.the-dma.org) is the leading global trade association for DM. It is the single largest source of information on the topic. It is well worth your time to pay them a visit.

Action Steps

- Think about ways you can apply direct response marketing in your business.
- Build your customer and prospect lists.
- Pay close attention to your ad copy (review Chapter 30).
- Split test your campaigns to fine tune them.
- Analyze the results.
- Refine your campaign

Chapter 35

Email Marketing Basics

Chapter Objectives

- Become familiar with the CAN-SPAM regulations that cover emailing.
- Learn why you need to sign up with an email service provider and what it can do for you.
- Learn how you should build and communicate with your email list.
- Examine the different types of emails you can send: promotional, transactional, informational, etc.
- Learn the difference between autoresponder emails, broadcast emails and email newsletters, and when you want to use them.

Email marketing has been, and continues to be, a very effective marketing activity for us. We use it in conjunction with other forms of marketing: social media, video marketing, article publishing, blogging, and more. With any activity, it works best within a coordinated strategy where it supports other pieces of your marketing plan.

Email marketing stems from direct mail but instead of printed material, with email marketing you're communicating your marketing message in electronic form. All of the direct marketing basics are the same, you're just using another tool to reach your customers. It has many advantages over direct mail for doing business on the internet besides the economical cost. Not only is it a highly efficient way to immediately connect with your market, you can electronically track your conversion rates and sales from the links in the emails back to your shopping cart. Although email deliverability (or non-delivery) can be an issue, when done properly it is highly effective.

Before we go any further, you have to know that this is not something you should do on your personal email account. You will need to invest in an email service provider. Using these services not only makes your email marketing tasks much easier, they help ensure you will not be violating spam laws and your internet service provider's (ISP) acceptable use policies. The last thing you want to do is send thousands of unsolicited emails through your personal server and email account. I guarantee that you would get shut down.

REMAIN COMPLIANT AND LEGAL

The CAN-SPAM (Controlling the Assault of Non-Solicited Pornography and Marketing) Act, a law enacted in 2003, set the rules for commercial email, establishing requirements for commercial messages and giving recipients the right to have merchants stop emailing them. It also spelled out tough penalties for violations. What does that mean for you? Basically it means that all commercial emails you send must include an opt-out (unsubscribe) mechanism and your physical mailing address. You have to honor those opt-out requests within 10 days. (Another reason to use an email service provider: it handles the unsubscribing process for you.)

You also have to follow best practices with how you gather your lists. If you're collecting your prospect's email information in an unacceptable way, you'll be hit by complaints and spam reports and will get noticed by the large ISPs. When that happens not only will your email deliverability suffer, your account may be terminated and with that goes your list. I've even heard horror stories of your entire website being cut off from service due to spamming. You don't want that to happen!

Besides worrying about losing your ability to email, your list, or even your website, it only makes good business sense to send relevant, timely, targeted, and *valuable* emails to subscribers who have asked for them. None of us likes to be spammed.

To learn more about compliance, check out "The CAN-SPAM Act: A Compliance Guide for Business" available at the Bureau of Consumer Protection Services (www.business.ftc.gov/documents/bus61-can-spam-act-compliance-guide-business).

EMAIL SERVICE PROVIDERS

There are several email service providers you can choose from. They all have the basic features of providing code for opt-in forms that you embed on your website and into emails that capture your subscriber's information into a database; a send engine, which allows you to distribute your message to your subscribers; and an unsubscribe function that will automatically update the subscriber list to suppress those who wish to be unsubscribed.

If you will be using a paid shopping cart, most likely it will include a bulk email service. Shopping cart software such as 1ShoppingCart and Infusionsoft gives you the ability to send out newsletters and broadcast emails as well as autoresponder emails. This is a very handy benefit to have, so when you are looking for shopping cart software this is a feature you want to look for and it is usually included with the standard cost. They also feature the ability to automatically move your prospect into different lists and do sales tracking on your campaigns.

There are stand-alone email service providers that will allow you to send autoresponders, broadcasts, and newsletters. When you are just starting out and have a small list, it isn't necessary to spend a lot of money on this service. A highly regarded service that offers a complementary plan is MailChimp (www.mailchimp.com). You can have up to 2,000 subscribers and can send out up to 12,000 emails a month for free. The downside to their free version is that you don't have access to the autoresponder application. Some other services to compare are ConstantContact (www.constantcontact.com), VerticalResponse (www.verticalresponse.com), and Aweber (www.aweber.com). All of these have been around for several years and come highly rated. Many of them offer free trials. My recommendation would be to pick one, sign up for the trial period, then send some emails to see how that particular service works for you. When that period ends, decide if you want to continue with them. Whichever provider you choose, sign up for the lowest monthly rate that allows you to use all the features. Your costs increase only as your list grows.

It isn't impossible but sometimes unwieldy to move your lists from one service to another so this is a decision you want to make for the long term. We use 1Shopping Cart to send out our broadcast and autoresponder emails and ConstantContact to send out our nicely formatted weekly newsletters. One reason we like ConstantContact is that we can add names to our list that we get from other sources. Some mailing programs won't let you do that or they'll do it by sending out a blanket email to your list. They require the information to come in through their opt-in form, with a confirmation email sent requiring the person to click through a link to be on your list. This process is known as double opt-in and while it is not a legal requirement, it is good for getting legitimate sign ups, i.e., those with valid email addresses. The downside is that it is one more step you have to put the person through. If they don't click on that confirmation email link they won't be signed up on your list any longer.

BUILDING YOUR SUBSCRIBER LISTS

When we talked about prospecting and the sales funnel, we talked about how you can get people into your funnel. With email, that means getting them to opt-in to your email list which is also called a subscriber list.

What Is and is Not Acceptable Practice

It's easy to get seduced by the siren call of offers promoting questionable ways to get a big list *fast* and you may be tempted to do these black hat activities (unethical list building methods) to build your list, but in email marketing it's all about slow and steady. Your goal should be list quality over quantity because it's much more valuable for you to get a list of qualified people who are interested in what you are offering rather than randomly adding people for the sake of having a huge list. This can backfire with increased opt-outs, spam reports, and small open and clickthrough rates. These types of practices also affect your email delivery rates.

Here are good practices to follow

1. Build your list organically instead of buying lists of random names. You want to get true opt-ins. You can rent lists and contact a lot of people quickly but legitimate lists are expensive and may not be targeted enough to be worth the cost. Plus, when you rent a list you do not own it; you rent it for a one-time use only.

2. Ask for opt-ins wherever your target market can be found—on your website, at conferences, in your store, via direct mail, and on social media sites. Ask for them over the phone. I do this a lot when I get phone orders. I will let them know they can get their receipt emailed to them and that they will also be on our mailing list where they will receive other news and promotions.

3. Have your opt-in form on every page of your website along with copy explaining the benefits if they subscribe.

4. Be honest about how often they'll hear from you and the content they'll receive, and reassure them that their privacy is secured. We make a practice to always state that we will not spam or sell their information to anyone—and we stick to our word!

5. Send an immediate welcome email thanking your new subscriber for their interest and if they opted-in to receive a gift or bonus from you, let them know how they can access the gift you gave them.

6. Be sure to ask for opt-ins if you meet a prospect in person and they give you their card. Just because someone hands you their business card at a conference or makes a

purchase on your site does not mean they want to be opted-in to receive your emails. Doing so without permission can cause hard feelings, complaints, and spam reports.

Unsolicited Emailing

You may now be wondering if you are allowed to even send an unsolicited email! The answer to that, in the U.S. at least, is yes. According to CAN-SPAM, unsolicited emails are not illegal. What is a legal requirement is that if your email is a solicitation you must be very clear who you are, that it is a solicitation, and what you are soliciting.

You're required to include a physical address and contact information for your business. Hiding, altering, or using fake aliases or giving misleading information in your To, From, or Subject fields is a big no-no. You have to provide opt out information (unsubscribe option) within the email.

So although the good news is that you can legally collect addresses manually and rent lists, there are a few points to remember if you are going to send unsolicited emails:

- Never contact anyone more than once. If they go to your website and opt in, then that's different. They've agreed to get continued emails from you.
- Make this email the start of a conversation. Introduce yourself to your prospect and ask how you can help them. Put a lot of thought into your first email to them; put yourself in the mind of your prospects and think about what they might want to read about and what they won't find spammy.
- If you decide to rent an email list, only work with reputable companies. Also, make sure the email they send out for you contains your web address and a way for the prospect to opt-in to your email list.

WHAT SHOULD YOU EMAIL TO YOUR LIST?

You can use emails to send promotions, information, thank yous, tips, resources, announcements, etc. They can also be transactional, with embedded Buy Buttons that link to your order page so the recipient can buy directly from the email without having to be redirected to your website.

Emails are a way you communicate with your market so anything your market will value is a potential email subject. Your emails do not all have to be promotional in nature. In fact, I adhere to the 80/20 rule—give them 80 percent good information, tips, resources, and content, and only 20 percent promotion. Think about it from the perspective of signing up and attending an event where you hope to learn more about the presenter and their area of expertise. Upon entering the room the presenter walks up to you and launches into his sales spiel, urging you to "buy my stuff, buy my stuff!" If that were to happen to me, I'd probably turn around and walk out of the room. If, on the other hand, he came up to me, struck up a conversation and throughout the course of the presentation gave me a lot of great advice and helpful information, and then left me with an invitation to check out how he could help me further, I would be more compelled to buy and definitely to give him my business card to communicate with me in the future.

So before you decide on the types of emails you will send, take some time to list all of the tips and resources, promotional ideas, and valuable information you can think of about your topic. Start by asking yourself how you can provide value to your email subscribers. Then once you start getting opt-ins, ask your subscribers what they would like to receive.

TYPES OF EMAILS

The type of email you send out is determined by what you are wanting to do with that email communication. Is your goal to move your prospect through your sales funnel, trigger them to take immediate action (such as "like" a Facebook page, enter a contest, buy your video, etc.), or build trust and loyalty over the long run?

Autoresponders

As I defined in Chapter 33 on setting up a sales funnel, autoresponders are automatically generated emails you have set up in a sequence that is triggered when your subscriber opts-in. In addition to the marketing sequence to move your prospect through the funnel with the end result being a sale, some sophisticated email providers can generate autoresponders based on events, such as sales, birthdays, etc., and also targeted to sub-groups within your list. Refer again to the sample autoresponder sequence I shared in Chapter 33.

Broadcasts

When you have important information, special promotions, or anything you feel would benefit your entire list, you can send a broadcast message that will go out at the same time to all existing subscribers.

Newsletters

These are also called ezines and are set up to broadcast on a regular basis, usually on a weekly, monthly, quarterly, or yearly basis. Along with tips and industry news, a newsletter can contain product updates, new products, and new features.

Unlike common email promotions that focus on action, email newsletters focus on retention.

Promotional emails are generally short term, and if the recipient doesn't respond more or less immediately to the offer then chances are that the value of the email is lost. It has little long term impact or influence on the recipient.

Newsletters, on the other hand, are about building long term relationships. Of course you can include promotions and calls to action in the newsletter but the main purpose should be to strengthen your relationship with your customers and prospects. It is a valuable tool to get them to know, like, and trust you, which increases the likelihood that they will buy from you repeatedly.

You'll have to decide what you want to accomplish in your email communication to determine what you want to send. If you're planning regular mailings to customers or prospects, make sure you understand the distinction between promotional emails and newsletters, and design your email campaigns accordingly. One form of email marketing is not better or more effective than the other, it boils down to giving your subscribers what they expect.

If you sign up for a list where you know you are going to get offers and promotions, like what I expect from B&H Photo & Video, your tolerance for receiving sales notifications will be higher. However if you were promised a newsletter full of tips and resources but instead only received coupons and offers, you're likely to opt-out.

HOW OFTEN WILL YOU SEND YOUR EMAILS?

Determining how often you will send emails will again depend on your list and what they expect. It will also take some testing and tweaking. The key to successful email marketing is commitment and consistency, just as it is in any direct response strategy. While this marketing method may seem like a daunting and time-consuming task, as you get more comfortable and better at it and see how well your customers respond, it will get a lot easier. That's one of the reasons I like and recommend autoresponder applications. I can set my sequence up and except for occasionally checking to make sure my information is still valid and up to date, I don't have to worry about it going out regularly. Then when I want to communicate special offers and other cool information, I can send a broadcast.

My recommendation is to start emailing your list at least once a week to start. As you feel comfortable, experiment with adding more. Take a sample of your list and test increasing your frequency with them. If they respond well, i.e., more sales, no spam reports, less unsubscribes, then expand it to the rest of your list. You can actually ask them how often they'd like contact from you.

If you do decide that you want to go the route of a newsletter, start with sending it out once a month or at the very least quarterly. Newsletters tend to take a lot more time to put together and you want to make sure you will be able to meet your own deadlines. Keep in mind, they don't have to be lengthy. People are very busy these days and actually appreciate information delivered in small doses. (Another reason why newsletters are so popular.)

One formula we have found that works well is to put out a weekly newsletter that starts with a bit of news about ourselves, our businesses and current challenges, with the intent of sharing one or two products that have helped us that week. The second section is a longer piece where we share a business tip, strategy, or advice (since we've been blogging for a couple of years, we repurpose a lot of our posts for that section). Following that is a short section with links and summarizations of the past week's blog posts. We've had a lot of positive feedback on that newsletter. If you want to receive it, you can subscribe at www.howtosellyourvideos.com.

DESIGN FOR THE INBOX

Try to design your emails so that they are not more than 40 or 50 characters wide to be mobile friendly. Make sure that the top showcases you and includes your main call to action. You want this information "above the fold" area. Using images has been shown to increase conversion rates but many email clients (programs) block images or they may not show up on smartphones or take up too much prime real estate. Because of this, your call-to-action links should not be reliant on your images.

Getting Your Email Opened

We all get flooded with emails and a lot of them are obviously promotions. The tendency more and more is to just trash them, unopened. Your subject line is what will make the difference between getting your email deleted or opened so put some thought into this. Spend time coming up with noticeable and actionable subject lines, then test to see which works best for your subscribers. Try to keep them under 35 characters.

Gimmicky subject lines look like junk mail. Because of the increasing competition to get emails opened people are coming up with trickier and more dubious ways of getting their email opened. Subject lines like "Urgent!" or "Last Chance" scream junk mail.

You might not even get that kind of email delivered because spam filters will catch emails with subject lines that contain phrases like Click Here or anything with the word Mortgage, Make Money, Money Back Guarantee or Free. Don't TYPE IN ALL CAPS (it's the digital equivalent of yelling) and don't load it up with exclamation points!!!!! Essentially, the more pushy you make it sound, the greater the chance of it getting snared in a spam filter.

Spam filters also look at the content of an email so you want to follow these same guidelines regarding the body of your email.

If your email is a newsletter, say that it's a newsletter. "Here is your (insert name) Newsletter" will have a far better open rate than something that sounds like a sales pitch. If your subscriber knows that they signed up for special promotions then it's OK to have a subject line that says "10% Discount Coupon Inside," but that will turn off people who are expecting a newsletter. In fact, deceptive subject lines that don't accurately describe your email's purpose are what the CAN-SPAM Act forbids.

It far better to have a subject line that doesn't try to sell anything. Rather, just tell what is inside. It's that simple. An email I get from eBay gets me to open it every time. It says, "Check out the latest items from your favorite sellers on eBay." Of course I open it.

As we recommended in Chapter 30, keep an email swipe file too. Write down all of the subject lines that grabbed your interest and made you read further. Note the ones that annoyed you too. Sign up on your competitors lists and see what they are sending out. Don't copy what they are saying word for word; use it as a guide to learn how they manage their campaign, the language they use, the bonuses and information they are giving, and the subject lines they are using.

TESTING WHAT WORKS

How will you know email marketing is working for you? The only way to know this is to start emailing and test it. Email service programs make it very easy to split your lists and send out different email messages, calls to action, landing pages, etc., to see what works best for your audience. Run A/B tests on your subject line just as you did when you were testing your pricing and direct mail pieces. Don't be afraid to test the waters.

When we first started emailing our Patrick Smith (books and DVD) list, I worried about sending emails more than twice a month. A few years ago, we decided to try a more assertive campaign for the holiday shopping season and for six weeks we sent out weekly emails. What happened astounded me. Not only did our sales quadruple over the same time as the previous year, but when we looked at our reports we discovered that the percentage of unsubscribes did not increase and in fact the number of spam reports drastically went down. So we started sending out our emails weekly, and then went to twice a week. What works for one company may not work for you and vice versa. You'll never know until you try!

When you use an email service you will get reports on such statistics as clickthrough, opens, and bounces. Add an ad tracker and you will also see just how effective, in dollars, that email campaign was in generating sales or sign ups.

Figure 35.1 is an example from our shopping cart showing the results we received from a holiday email campaign and how the link was tracked and reported.

Campaign ID	521181
Campaign Name	Sense Of Place Christmas Email Sale
URL	http://www.on2url.com/app/adtrack.asp?MerchantID=101564&ID=521181

Campaign Info

Active	Destination URL	Clicks	Leads	Sales	Amount	Value
✔	http://www.marketerschoice.com/SecureCart/ SecureCart.aspx?mid=)C4673A-5074-43CF- 8414-02F1C8574&pid=a4563c5&bn=1	56 (64)	12 (21%)	32 (57%)	$909.50	$16.24 per click

FIGURE 35.1   *Sense of Place* Christmas Email Campaign.

You can also do this in a spreadsheet program also.

The most successful campaigns have a plan in place and of course you will make adjustments along the way as necessary. Having stated goals will help you measure how successful you are.

Action Steps

- Compile a list of all the content you feel your subscribers would read and group them under promotions and information.
- Research the email service providers we listed, comparing prices and features. Sign up for the trial period of your top choice when you are ready to start building your list.
- Place your opt-in form on your website and start driving traffic to it.
- Look into email list brokers to determine if that would be a good option for you.
- Compose some emails and send!
- Keep an email swipe file for your reference and use the techniques and strategies you respond to best.
- As your list builds, divide them for testing purposes then experiment with sending each sublist different messages, subject lines, offers, etc., and record and study the results. Do more of what is working.
- Learn how to interpret your email service provider's reports.
- Send emails to your subscribers asking for email ideas, survey them on what they like and don't like, if your mailing schedule is too much or not enough.
- Use email to build a sense of community and relationship—let your readers know who you are.

Chapter 36

Video Marketing Basics

Chapter Objectives

- Learn the types of videos you can use to help market your videos.
- Understand why web videos are so powerful.
- Get to know the advantages of self-hosted video sites over free sites and how to use each one.
- Learn what elements you need to include in these types of videos.
- Learn a few tips for using web video to drive traffic.

Video marketing is a fairly new form of promotion that can be very effective when used properly. As a video publisher, it just makes sense to use this visual medium when selling your products. Though visual marketing has been used for some time in the form of TV commercials, video marketing differs in some important ways.

While televised commercials tend to focus more on brand awareness with little or no way to measure results, video marketing, as we suggest you do it, is like direct response advertising. Video marketing uses short, attractive, and educational videos in order to convert viewers into fans and buyers, rather than just creating brand awareness.

WHAT MAKES VIDEO MARKETING SO EFFECTIVE?

Video engages more senses than any other media. Because it includes sight and sound, video has the power to affect people on a strong emotional level.

Whether you use video to assist, tutor, or entertain, your most important objective as a marketer is to build relationships that will result in trust, loyalty and, consequently, sales. Videos help create emotional connections between you and the viewer. Since people love seeing who they are dealing with, showing yourself via video makes your prospect more comfortable doing business with you.

Additionally, video can give your customer a lot of information in a short time. "Show it, don't say it" is a SIV mantra.

There are myriad ways you can deliver promotional videos to a large and receptive audience quickly. Thanks to the internet you're no longer stuck with the traditional avenue of producing commercials for broadcast. But before we turn to web video marketing, let's talk about offline video marketing methods.

OFFLINE VIDEO MARKETING

While the internet will be undoubtedly where you'll primarily target your prospects, you should be aware of some offline opportunities.

Commercials

Broadcast commercials used to be one of the only ways to get a promotional video to a wide audience. Commercials are still very effective for some video products. I frequently see commercials for Jillian Michaels, Tracy Anderson, P90X, and Insanity exercise DVD series when I'm watching late night TV.

You can purchase broadcast time to target cities around the country or you can buy time on cable channels locally or nationally. There are now a plethora of channels that have very defined niches such as home improvement, food, exercise, health, golf, fishing, and travel, to name just a few. This allows your message to be highly targeted.

Infomercials

If your video would lend itself to sales "as seen on TV," consider producing an infomercial. Typically this is a broadcast-length presentation about your product with a strong sales push. Not too long ago television stations turned up their noses at paid programming but now those same TV stations are searching for new revenue streams.

Infomercials are the most effective when they are done in an educational manner, hence the term "infomercial." This is an expensive route so you'll want to make sure that it's the right investment for you.

Don't overlook local public access stations either. Many of them are looking for programming that will benefit their viewers. Although their audience is not as large or targeted, air time is either free or purchased for a minimal amount.

Promotional DVDs

Maybe your target market would respond more to a promotional DVD. The DVD software enables you to loop your videos which is a perfect way to show your promotional DVDs at trade shows. Pass them out at conferences like you would a business card.

Remember our partner Butch, the Florida Cracker Storyteller? We send him batches of sampler DVDs that he takes with him and leaves when he meets with potential buyers at libraries, organizations, and gift shops.

Preview DVDs

Sending your entire DVD for your customer to review is also effective. This is common when working with teachers who often request preview copies to make sure the subject matter fits their curriculum. It's standard practice to let them have a preview copy for a certain period of time. Include a postage paid, self-addressed return DVD mailer to make it easy for them to return it.

We also give review copies to distributors and retailers as well as to some press outlets. You shouldn't expect those to be returned to you.

ONLINE VIDEO MARKETING

Online or web video marketing is an effective and economical way to reach and connect with a receptive audience. Why? As more and more people turn to the internet in search of information, watching videos has become one of the top activities people do online.

According to a Pew Center Survey, more than 70 percent of adults who went online in 2011 watched video.[1] Additionally, YouTube has become a close second to Google as the place where people search for information. I've even read some claims that say YouTube has *surpassed* Google in the number of searches people do every day. And it's not music videos and cute animal videos they're searching for. They are going to YouTube to find information about everything!

The Pew survey also found that shopping is one of the top five reasons people go online. Couple that with the growth of online video consumption and you can see why putting promotional videos online is a smart move.

WEB VIDEO IS GREAT FOR SEO

Search engine spiders don't really "read" and index video like other content, at least not at the time of this writing, but videos are important to your SEO for the following reasons.

Visit Length

Visitors are more likely to watch a quick two-minute video than they are to read a long page of sales copy. How does that help SEO? The longer their eyeballs stay on your site, the more the search engines feel your site is giving value and will rank it higher.

YouTube is an Authority Site

Second, the top video sharing site most of us use to put videos on is YouTube, which is considered an authority site by Google. Embedding the video you host on YouTube with a link back to your website will give you a high value backlink. Having a backlink from an authority site enhances your SEO. YouTube is currently enjoying a Google page rank of 9 out of 10! Now that's a powerful backlink!

Powerful Traffic within YouTube

YouTube is also currently ranked on the web usage information site Alexa as the third most visited site on the Internet. The traffic generated by YouTube alone is enough to accelerate the initial growth period of a new website. You can literally have a brand new website getting enormous amounts of traffic just minutes after you upload a video with a link back to your site.

Social Media Sharing

Don't stop at YouTube. Sharing your video on other authority sites such as Facebook, Delicious, Twitter, Reddit, and Stumbleupon also give your video SEO juice and are a good source of traffic.

New Google Algorithms Reward Content

With recent algorithmic changes on Google, consistently updated and valuable content like video has become king. Video is indexed right away by search engines, as opposed to web pages that can take months. It's a bonus if your website has a video and an article about the same keyword.

My assumption is that Google sees videos as high value because people love watching them. Web video has shown over and over again that it gives searchers value—exactly what search engines reward sites for providing by giving them a higher page ranking.

WEB VIDEO IS YOUR VIRTUAL SALES STAFF

Web video has other marketing benefits besides boosting your page rank and getting traffic to your website. It appeals to all learning modalities. You may learn better by seeing something demonstrated, your child by hearing the steps outlined, and your spouse by reading. If you are only offering your web visitors written content you're missing an effective strategy to reach and connect with your audience. Video is the next best thing to being there, informing and helping your customer.

Because it's online 24/7, you have a virtual sales staff that never sleeps, gets tired, or cranky. Every visitor gets the same experience, so make it a good one.

WEB VIDEO IMPROVES YOUR CONVERSION RATES

Statistics increasingly show that video and a more personable appearance on your website can dramatically increase conversion rates, i.e., the percentage of visitors who make a purchase, fill out a form, or make a donation.

Since video encourages visitors to stay on your site longer, they will have more exposure to your message, and the longer they stay, the greater the potential they are going to make a purchase.

Internet Retailer states, "visitors who view product videos are 85 percent more likely to buy than visitors who do not."[2]

PROMOTIONAL VIDEO FUNDAMENTALS

The major element you will need in every promotional video is a call to action. Ask yourself: What do you want viewers to do after watching your promotional video? Email it to a friend? Order a DVD? Click for more information? Just as in direct mail or email marketing, the goal in this strategy is to convert viewers into buyers. Tell them what you want them to do.

Make your videos informative, interesting, *and* short. Under three minutes is best. Just think of what you like to watch. A lot of the videos that go viral are humorous, awe-inspiring, educational, entertaining, unique, evocative and, yes, controversial. Incorporating one or more of these elements into your video will increase your chances of someone enjoying it, connecting with it, and sharing it with other like-minded people. When you are creating it for a specific target group, keep their interests in mind.

EXAMPLES OF WHAT YOU CAN DO WITH WEB VIDEO

There are so many ways you can use web video marketing. The following are a few ways we've successfully done it:

Sample Videos

Show samples from your videos so that your prospect can get a taste of what they'll get upon purchasing. While it's natural to show a sample of the video you're selling, you should also add some content to make it more of a promotional vehicle. Point out the benefits and add a call to action.

Promotion Videos

Made specifically to promote your video, it's essentially your sales message. Different from the sample, it's its own video production. I mentioned planning for this while you're shooting your SIV so that you can use the same set and environment, possibly the same narrator.

Trailers

A variation on the promotional video, this form is taken from the movie industry. These types of videos are meant to create excitement and anticipation and are usually produced in advance of your video launch. You can also make trailers to drive people to certain sites or places within your site. Trailers are a nice way to show samples of the video as you also promote it.

Trailers tend to be dramatic. You can buy trailer templates and music online. We use www.videohive.net because they offer a large and growing library of inexpensive After Effects templates. Their sister company, www.audiojungle.net (www.audiojungle.net) has music for trailers. Or you can use an online service such as www.animoto.com where you can upload still photos and videos and choose from a limited music selection. Animoto will then build a very dynamic trailer for you, although you don't have much creative control over what it does.

 If you don't have After Effects (it's a also a challenging program to learn), see if you can find someone on www.fiverr.com who'll produce a trailer from your template for around $5.

Welcome Videos

Welcome people to your site as you would welcome them to a brick and mortar business. In these videos, people can personally meet you and you can encourage them to explore your site, sign up for your free giveaway, offer them a special coupon code, or ask them to share your site on their social media sites.

Interviews

Interview your expert or partner. Interview your customers.

Tips or Tutorials

These types of videos are excellent for positioning your site as the "go-to place" for information. Doing so sets you up as an authority and builds trust with your viewers. They will see the quality of information they will most likely receive if they bought your video.

When Mike Deiure (www.rockguitarpower.com) started selling his guitar videos on the internet, he posted a couple of how-to videos on guitar maintenance on YouTube. They turned out to be very popular and sent a lot of traffic to his site. They are still highly watched and YouTube has become one of the main ways he gets customers.

Frequently Asked Questions (FAQs)

Offering videos that address specific questions is an excellent customer service tool and an effective time-saver. You can share more in a video in a shorter period of time than it would take the person to read your answer. The more you can address and answer a prospect's concerns, the more likely they are to buy from you.

Testimonials

Customer testimonials are highly valuable and on-camera testimonials are the best. Make sure they are the real deal though. The person giving the testimonial shouldn't be a paid actor (some countries, like the U.S., require you to disclose that) and they don't have to be polished. Make sure your customer gives their real name and, ideally, say where they live.

HOSTING YOUR WEB VIDEOS

Where should you host your web videos? Most likely you will want to use a video sharing site such as YouTube or Vimeo, as well as paid services.

While we advocate using these free sites, there are strong reasons for going through a paid service as well. We host our videos on Amazon S3, which is *very* cheap. We also use www.eZs3.com, a service that makes it easy to upload, download, and embed our S3 videos on our website. It also allows us to create different video player skins and make them "vidgets"—videos with widgets. A widget is a mini-web application that enables you to perform a function or access a service, such as share a post, "like" on Facebook, Tweet, etc. Their premium features allow you much more interactivity within your video.

Hosting on Your Site

Like having your own website, hosting your videos on your site ensures you have control over them. Remember when we warned you about having an eStore on a Facebook page and what would happen to it if Facebook went away? Nicholas Carr back in 2006 talked about that same risk when he coined the word "digital sharecropping." He used the term to refer to the concept of building your business on someone else's site much like tenant farmers grow crops on land that doesn't belong to them. When you post on a site you don't own and control, the content on that site is no longer yours, it belongs to the site owner, like YouTube or Facebook. They are in control. If they go out of business, you go out of business. If their server goes down, your business is offline. If they are hacked, your business could be hacked. If they don't like what you're doing, you are kicked out. Then there is always the possibility that they can "raise your rent" so to speak, by charging fees.

Before you post on one of these sharing sites, you have to make sure you're meeting its guidelines for usage. Some of these sites, YouTube being one of them, are very clear they don't want advertisements. That is the reason making the video more educational with a soft sell message has proven very effective. The video sharing site could pull your video if it feels you are not following its rules. That's happened to us and people we know.

Viewers can also double click on the video and leave your site and they may never return. That feature favors your competition. When a YouTube video ends, it presents a series of thumbnails linking to videos on similar topics or keywords you used. These videos may be from competing companies or may be promoting products similar to yours (sometimes they are embarrassing videos!). Then the person can click on that video and watch it—all from your site. You've just sent them to your competition!

The video players you get on the free sites are branded and yours looks like everyone else's. When you go through a service such as eZs3 you get an array of interesting players and skins to choose from. You also can add those vidgets I mentioned which allow you to add features like a comments box, email to a friend, ratings, to name a few. You can add powerful interactivity such as automatically redirect viewers, add a Buy Now button or show an opt-in form.

Posting to YouTube and other sites is a valuable marketing tool and a good source of backlinks—we've had great success with it—just don't rely on them exclusively to be your primary host. I advise hosting the videos that you want to have total control over, i.e., those that you want to make sure aren't pulled from your site by the video sharing site, on your own server, then let your YouTube videos lead viewers to your site and increase your SEO.

Build Your Own TV Channel

A growing trend is to create your own TV channel. You can do this on YouTube or www.blip.tv, but you can also buy a .tv URL and build your own channel, independent of the terms and conditions imposed by sites like YouTube. I know people who have had their YouTube channel shut down due to some transgression but if you build your own channel you don't have to worry about that. You don't *have* to build your channel on a .tv extension but it sounds glamorous and users will come to your site expecting to see syndicated video content and have an exciting experience. It's like warming up the crowd before the show.

By building your own channel you're really making yourself a web personality. Since you are in the video business, what better way to showcase your products? You can do this on—you guessed it—our friend WordPress. There are lots of great WordPress templates designed to showcase videos, from refined designs to outrageous and outright tacky.

What should you put on your TV channel? Samples of your videos, of course, plus testimonial videos, screencasts, product tours, video blog posts, live-streaming events, and anything else that helps build your own personality and showcase your videos. Treat these videos as your very own TV series by posting on a regular weekly basis. Web TV channels can be uploaded, syndicated, and featured on iTunes.

Even major Hollywood studios are building web TV channels and creating programs just for the web. Want to see some samples and learn more? Visit www.watch.tv.

Free Video Hosting Pointers

When you post your videos on the free sites, be sure to include that call to action to send viewers to your website. Also encourage them to share it with other people and to embed it on their websites. When editing the video, make sure you watermark it with your website's URL and add any pertinent information so that there is always a way for the viewer to find you! Don't rely just on the annotations functions where you can add this information to your video after you load it at YouTube or other sites.

When brainstorming topics and content for your videos, think again of the keywords that your target market is searching for. Add these to the description areas, titles, and tag sections when posting your videos to the sharing site. These sites not only have search functions within the sites, they are also being indexed by outside search engines like Google.

> Always put your URL at the beginning of the description box and be sure you include the http:// to make the link clickable. Not only does Google look for the link there, it also shows "above the fold" in the box. Then include it again at the end and encourage people to contact you.

Truthfully describe what's in your video and what they will get from watching it. Check out the DVD cover copy of some best-selling movies and books to get good ideas for copy that will get your viewer eager to watch your short movie.

Upload your video with the express purpose to be seen and shared. You want people to take it and "plaster" it everywhere so make it public by having your privacy settings set so that everyone can see your video. (This is usually the default option but check to make sure.)

To get your video on many sharing sites quickly you can use TubeMogul (www.tubemogul.com) which has a free service that will upload it to many sites at once, although you have to first sign up and register with those sites. Double check their usage guidelines to make sure of the type of videos you are allowed to post. Some discourage clearly promotional videos and will refuse to post them. That's another strong reason to produce educational and content-rich videos with a call to action for them to visit your site to get more information.

Traffic Geyser (www.trafficgeyser.com) is a paid service that will not only submit your video to scores of video sites, social bookmarking sites, blogs, and podcast directories with one click, but offers a built-in video maker, a built-in lead page generator, and audio file creator as well. This system is used by many top online marketers. They have a trial period for just $1.

BE CONSISTENT

Video marketing *will* work for you if you focus on the same tenets we covered in direct mail and email marketing: connect often and consistently. Shoot *a lot* of videos and post them on a regular basis. A large body of videos each drawing a healthy number of views adds up to *a lot* of views. Little streams flow together to make a river. (There's that analogy again!) That way you aren't reliant on any one video to do it for you. Just keep pumping them out and watch what happens.

Action Steps

- Review all the types of videos you can produce to market your videos and decide on the top ones you feel would work well for you.

- Produce several marketing videos following the guidelines we covered earlier for the videos you will sell. Pay special attention to writing your copy with sales promotion in mind. Make sure you include a "call to action."
- Look into automating services such as TubeMogul and Traffic Geyser.
- Sign up with YouTube and other video sharing sites appropriate for your niche.
- Sign up for an Amazon S3 account and look into the video players we mentioned above. Consider subscribing to a service like eZs3.
- Once you have your videos on your site and on video sharing sites, start sharing them with your list and your networks.

Social Media Marketing

Chapter Objectives

- Learn what social media marketing is, how it works, and why you should use it.
- Get to know a few of the top social media sites we use and recommend, and how they differ.
- Learn how to use these sites effectively in your marketing activities.
- Discover what is available to help you manage and automate some of your social media marketing functions.

Web 2.0 changed the way we do business when it ushered in this new phenomenon called social media. Now anyone with an internet connection or a smartphone has at their fingertips the ability to engage not just among a personal network of people but also with businesses worldwide. They can now share information and opinions and build and maintain business connections in a very public arena. Not surprisingly, although social media applications weren't designed specifically for business use, savvy entrepreneurs quickly discovered how to turn them into new marketing avenues. They also brought with them a sea change in marketing communication.

Through this blending of technology and social interaction, user- or consumer-generated content was born, giving the customer a whole new level of freedom and control. Marketing is no longer a one-way conversation, with marketers informing customers about products. Now customers have taken an active and powerful role in sharing with not just the marketer but the world at large what they think and feel about a product. Your customers have become participants rather than viewers. And each participating customer joins your "marketing department," influencing other customers with what they have to say about you—good or bad. With that shift, it's imperative that you get a handle on what's happening in social media and become active in managing and capitalizing on this whole process.

It may seem like a daunting task because this new world of social media is changing at lightning speeds. By the time this book is published another unknown social media site will be taking the world by storm and most likely the interfaces you just got familiar with on current ones will have changed. This is a great time to head over to our site at www.shoot-to-sell.com for the latest updates. We can't possibly know every little nuance of each social media site and tool but we'll have resources there for you to connect with people who make this their main business.

What I want to do in this chapter is to give you a basic understanding of how social media marketing works and why you want to get on board. I'll introduce you to some of the methods we utilize and show you how you can use this exciting new platform to your advantage.

DEFINING SOCIAL MEDIA AND SOCIAL MEDIA MARKETING

Social media basically refers to online communities where users can create and share comments, information, ideas, messages, videos, photos, and other communication (thus the term user-generated). This is done through participating in social networking sites like Facebook and LinkedIn, content communities such as YouTube, or micro blogs like Twitter. It is also done through internet forums, blogs, wiki collaborative projects (e.g., Wikipedia), virtual game worlds (e.g., World of Warcraft), and social bookmarking (e.g., Digg and Reddit), to name a few.

Social media marketing (SMM) then, at its essence, is using these formats to reach your markets and to get their attention, to build relationships with them and to share your content with their social networks. In so doing, this will attract new prospects and drive traffic to your product.

WHY DO IT?

Not only has this become an important avenue to reach and engage your customers, but actively posting on social media sites, blogging, video sharing, podcasting, etc., can generate significant traffic to your site. It has also become a perfect place to discover what is happening in the world and in your niche and industry. You can find useful information such as news stories, reviews, blog posts, etc., that will not only help you in your business but can be shared with your prospects.

We would be remiss to gloss over the fact that social media can also become addictive and can waste a lot of time, where checking online updates and comments can take the place of productive work. It is a powerful tool that must be used with discretion.

Social media can also help build backlinks that in turn support your SEO efforts because these networking sites are seen as authority sites. Allowing comments on your blog or participation on your forums also leads to incoming links from other potentially powerful sites.

Since this form of marketing acts as word-of-mouth marketing, it's a great referral marketing tool. By repeating your message through their feed, every user's connections are able to see the message, spreading it to many more people. As your message, post, offer, or giveaway spreads from user to user, it encounters less resistance because it appears to come from a trusted source (their friend) as opposed to your company.

Another key benefit is found in building "social authority," also known as "social proof." That's the concept I talked about when I recommended freely sharing lots of informational video tips and tutorials with your viewers, thus becoming the go-to place for information and help within your niche. As a result of social media and social media marketing, consumers today are highly likely to make buying decisions based on what they read and see in social platforms but only if this is from someone they have come to trust.

As if all that wasn't enough, social media also offer the benefit of providing another channel for customer support, a means to gain customer and competitive insight, the ability to recruit and retain new customers and business partners, and a method of managing your reputation online. It's amazing that we have all of this power and potential in something that is free or at least relatively inexpensive.

When you plan your SMM strategy, you should do more than set up your profile and Facebook page and post, tweet, blog, or publish videos to YouTube. Because it's the *relationships you create* by using these platforms that are important, you need to find the sites where your target market is hanging out, know what your objectives are in engaging with your market and what prospects are likely to respond to. Remember, it's not about technologies, it's all about building relationships.

WHAT SHOULD YOU BE DOING?

How you decide the best method for you will depend on where you find your target market and what type of engagement you wish to have with that market. Although these technologies are designed to get people to interact with one another and build relationships, they do have differences in how they go about it.

Some of the methods we have successfully used and will be discussing are:

- Social networking sites—Facebook, LinkedIn, and Twitter
- Content communities—YouTube
- Forums
- Blogs.

I recommend you get familiar with each of these, give them a reasonable try—test and tweak, test and tweak—then decide which ones you like and work best for you. A good strategy is to take them one by one and spend enough time learning about each one until you get a good handle on it, then go on to the next. I'll also be sharing with you some things that you can do to make this process more manageable.

I want to stress that the sites and technologies we'll cover are just examples. You may find a site we've not really worked with and won't cover here, like the new upstarts Google+ and Pinterest, that is perfect for you. Also, if you're reading this book five years from today then none of these may exist or massively successful new players may hold the field. So my approach is to give you the principles in how social media work, not specifics to each. I trust that the principles will still apply.

SOCIAL NETWORKING SITES

Although technically Facebook and LinkedIn are classified as social networking sites and Twitter is a micro blog site, for our discussion I'm going to lump them together since they all work similarly.

If you're hesitant to join in on these sites or feel your market may not be there, here are some statistics that may change your mind. Of the world's online population, 82 percent, in *all* age groups, is active (spending nearly one in every five minutes online) on social media sites.[1] That's 1.2 billion users, young and old! And Facebook leads the pack as of this writing.[2]

The key thing to keep in mind when you join these sites as a business is that it is all about relationship building and attraction marketing. I like to approach it like a huge ongoing networking event except it is online and global. Just like at events you attend in person, you can promote, help, chat, ask for feedback, learn some great stuff, and share resources, but it's best to keep your blatant promotions to a minimum and focus on building your authority and loyalty. Find out first what your prospects are talking about, what interests them, what problems they are having, and then tell them about you, how you can help them, and what you are selling.

Starting Out

You may already have accounts in all three of these sites but if you don't, here are the first steps to joining as a business.

In every social media site, there's an area where you set up your account and put in your profile information. Before you start posting, you need to fully complete this area. What you'll need is:

- Your name
- Bio (Twitter), About Me (Facebook), or Profile (LinkedIn)—Make this short, descriptive and powerful. I always include a call to action, i.e., an encouragement to go to my website.
- Photo—This should be a good quality, professional photo of *you*, not your car, your dog, a sunset, *you* (this is for your home account, you can use different images with your videos in your business page in Facebook and business accounts in Twitter.)
- URL—Where you want them to go for more information about you.

Because of the nature of these sites, your main account needs to be linked to a real human with a legitimate email address. They—and you—don't want the sites run over by bots so respect these restrictions. On all of the sites you can keep your personal information private through setting options. However, if you are going to use these accounts for your business, you want to make your posts and pages public.

Even if you don't decide to post or engage in these sites under your name, you do want to set them up under your name to protect and control your online reputation.

Find Friends, Connections, and Followers

One of the first items of business is to get people into your network. But how do you find them? The various sites will give you ideas on who to friend and follow so that is one place to start. You can also connect with your contacts through some email accounts.

All of these sites have a search feature where you can find people, groups, pages, lists, and what people are talking about. Search for people you know you would like to connect with. I like to follow and friend influential people in my industry. Also search for groups, lists, and pages within your niche. For example, when I first started on Facebook, I joined the Wedding and Event Videographers Association (WEVA) group. We don't shoot weddings but we sure want to connect with a lot of videographers and this is a great place to do that. We've since made a lot of friends there and gained many subscribers to our list from that group.

You can also use these search tools to find people who are talking about your niche. On Twitter, I looked for posts about certain cameras and filmmaking topics and found people there to follow. Of course you can look at who is following and friending the people in your network and that will give you another great place to find new connections.

If you have your target market clear in your mind, you will be able to find where such people are hanging out. And don't forget—this is a good way to gain intelligence on your competitors. So friend follow, and like their pages too.

With Twitter, you don't have to request a follow, you can just follow. However, in other sites most likely you'll have to get approved. When you ask to connect with someone, do so with a message introducing yourself and stating why you want to connect. I like to include a statement that also let's them know my area of expertise and include a link to my website. I also send a thank you message with basically the same information when I've accepted a connection or friend request. Once you start the process of friending, following, and connecting, you will find you'll soon be getting invitations and followers back.

While you have to set up a personal account to sign up with Facebook, it is Facebook Pages that allows businesses and brands to showcase their work and interact with "fans." They are designed with custom functionality appropriate to each category. You appoint an administrator, could be yourself and/or others, to manage that page. Also third-party developers have built an array of applications for pages. Instead of "friends," you'll want "fans" who sign on to interact with your page by clicking on the "like" button and "liking" it.

To build a following by way of "likes" on your Facebook page, start with your friend network within Facebook. You can only have up to 5,000 friends so you will want to set up a business page as well as your personal page. Pages can have an unlimited number of "likes." You can also add a share button on your website requesting "likes"; send your list an email to encourage them to "like" your page, tweet it, have a contest—use whatever you can think of to get people to "like" your page. The beauty of a page is that whenever you post, that post will show up on your "likers'" feeds—those people will get to see, respond, and share what you are posting on your page.

One of my tactics is to ask to be friends with big names within my industry. It only took a few to get started, then as more of these notables friended me I was able to parlay that into getting friended by still more notable names in the business. As people see my growing list of influential friends it becomes easier and easier to add more important names to my friend list. I now have exposure to not just them, but also to the people who follow them. Because of my "connections," I'm building "social proof" in their eyes as well and they may choose to friend me and/or "like" my page.

What Should You Post?

Determine what your marketing objectives will be first. For example, it could be researching what your market is needing and sharing, creating buzz by enthusiastic customers, spreading your message, helping your customers, or integrating customers into your business. Most likely it will be all of those.

The way these sites work is through joining and adding to the conversation. Don't be a lurker—the term for just reading what people are saying and not participating. The main way you join the conversation is through the status update feature in Facebook and LinkedIn, and tweeting in Twitter. Another word commonly used for that is posting.

Attraction marketing works very well in social media when you use your conversation with your prospects to connect, share, and help them. You should spend less time—*way less time*— promoting to them.

People don't care for marketing in general and they resent direct or overt marketing through social media platforms. As we've shared throughout this book, you can't expect people to be receptive to your marketing message in and of itself. On networking sites it is not only annoying, many people feel it is spamming, even though they may be interested in what you have to offer.

So how do you get the conversation started? Here is a list of ideas:

- Offer helpful tips.
- Answer questions.
- Ask questions.
- Provide links to great resources, blogs, videos, products.
- Report on industry news.
- Share photos with interesting captions to start conversations.
- Brag about your customers (get their permission first).
- Share testimonials (ones you give for others and ones people have given to you).
- Offer contests.
- Make announcements.
- Invite people to your events, webinars, etc.
- Share their videos, photos, posts, and information with a nod to them. For many sites, the @ followed by the user name is the way to do that. That way, they'll know you personally were talking to or about them.
- Share interesting facts.
- Share motivational quotes.
- Provide links to your resources, blog posts, videos, products.
- Inform them of special offers and sales.
- Provide links to affiliate products you recommend.

These are just some ideas. Once you get going, you'll come up with many more I'm sure. Watch what others are posting to understand how the conversation flows, then ease in.

Did you notice how a few of these ideas were related to promotion but the majority were about offering value? The crux of good attraction marketing is to become an influencer in a specific field or area but you must do it with a light touch. You want to be seen as an advisor, not a pushy marketer.

 On many of these sites, when you post a link, you need to put in the http:// to enable the link to be clicked through. Don't expect the person to copy and paste it.

How Often Should You Post?

Again, that depends. I've heard some people recommend no more than five a day, while some top social media marketers are posting constantly. Your market may respond differently so again this is a matter of doing it and then evaluating what works. If you are giving great information and value, mixing a bit of promotion in there, you'll get a sense of how often you should post. You don't want to be the obnoxious one that hogs the conversation, which always seems to revolve around him.

To be the most effective is to be active and consistent so my advice is to try to spend at least 15 minutes a day actively managing your sites, posting, approving friend requests, replying to people and adding comments.

Facebook, LinkedIn, and Twitter for Marketing Purposes

One of the best features in Facebook for you as a business is Facebook Pages because you can showcase your business and products and spread your reach further. You can also create groups and events. Groups are made up of people with a common interest and can be highly effective in gaining loyalty. If the members so choose, they can be informed via email every time someone posts on the group. You can also share events on Facebook and invite everyone on your list to attend. These events don't have to be in person, they can be virtual.

Facebook Insights give you information on the performance of your page: how many fans you lose, how many you gain, how much activity is happening on your site, etc. It's a good way to get an overview of how popular your Facebook Page is and what readers are responding to. Other sites offer these sorts of analytical tools as well. They give you good information on how you're doing with your audience so make sure you look at them.

Whereas Facebook was designed to connect people, LinkedIn was designed as a professional, business-oriented social networking site. Your profile on LinkedIn is more like a résumé. We've found LinkedIn to be a good source of finding business connections and partners. A couple of powerful features that I've found helpful are groups and LinkedIn Answers.

LinkedIn groups work similarly to Facebook groups. LinkedIn Answers allows you to view questions and answers posted by others. It also allows you to ask a question and get answers from users and experts outside of your network. You can then rate these answers. You not only can get great information, participating in your area of interest and expertise will set you up as an authority. There's that "social proof" concept again.

Twitter is like Facebook without all the apps and image sharing. You're limited to a maximum of 140 characters per tweet so it's a bit like texting with the use of abbreviations, numbers, and symbols in place of complete words. You can share links within your tweets. There's also a whole "lingo" connected with it that is a bit odd if you are new to it, not unlike the shortcuts that are used in texting.

In Twitter you don't "friend" as in Facebook, or invite connections as in LinkedIn, you follow and are followed. What I like about Twitter is the ease of initiating conversations and its culture of hopping into ongoing conversations without seeming to butt in.

Remember what I said earlier—these sites are *highly* addictive and can be a major time waster. Your goal with any type of marketing is to turn your efforts into tangible business results so have an objective, a plan, and set *strong limits* on the amount of time you can spend on these sites. A new industry of social media professionals and services has cropped up that will set up and manage your social media activities for you and they are worth looking into if you don't have the time or desire to do this.

On the other hand, you won't get anywhere if you set up your account and do nothing. In that case you're better off not to bother because if you do get traffic to your page or someone wants to follow you but they see no activity and your profile or page looks closed, they may think your business is too.

YOUTUBE

YouTube is not just a content community and video sharing site. It also has a large social media component: you can go to channels and see users' feeds that include videos they've posted, comments they've received and made, and channels they've subscribed to; people can comment on your video; you can subscribe to others' channels; you can share, embed, and "like" videos; you can showcase others' videos on your channel and offer information in the video description areas. Instead of a page, you build a channel. You're not restricted to just one channel either.

BLOGGING

Blogging is a social media function in that it allows the ability for readers to comment and share. It has actually been one of our most effective marketing vehicles. We're already recommending that you build your website on WordPress, which is primarily a blog platform, so if you've followed our recommendation you're ready to start blogging. WordPress lends itself well to providing a blend of useful content through the blog function and promotion of your products and affiliate products.

Assuming you are on WordPress, it is very easy to add articles, news items, videos, photos, and other information that has value to your reader. The more content you regularly post on a blog the better it will rank with search engines. Also because you can update a blog frequently, this gives your readers, prospects, and customers an incentive to return to read what is new.

The articles don't have to be long or academic—in fact because people are busy shorter items are better. Consistency counts more than the length of the article. It's better to have 50 short articles added consistently over time than to have two long articles but no recent updating. Videos make excellent content, so start posting short video blog entries. Be sure to use potent keywords and exciting copy when naming your articles and videos.

Invite guests to comment. When they do and if they added their URL, you have a new incoming link which is a boost to your search ranking and also enables you to build a relationship with that person. This "user-generated content" also adds depth to your blog for you, adding more unique content which the search engines like. You want to monitor this so that people don't post obscene or abusive things, but it is yet another way to attract more visitors and, in turn, sell more of your videos.

Also you don't have to come up with all the content yourself. Ask your readers to write articles for you. This is called guest blogging. If there is another blog that you follow, ask them if you can post one of their articles as a guest post.

Blogging consistently on your topic and sharing it on directories such as Technorati, social media, social bookmarking sites (Delicious, and Reddit), and through pinging, positions you as an authority figure. (Pinging is the way your blog lets your server and other ping servers know that its content has been updated.) You will be surprised at how quickly you become the authority figure people turn to when they think of your topic. You'll start to get backlinks from other blogs and websites, which also boosts your page rank.

FORUM MARKETING

Participating in online forums and chat rooms is another social media activity to build awareness of you and your videos at no cost except your time. If you can find active forums of people who would have an interest in your video topic then, by all means, join them. The key is to participate, not just lurk.

There are unwritten (and sometimes written) rules of etiquette about marketing on forums that are similar to marketing on social networking sites. Again your intent is to build authority and get people interested in what you have to offer, so don't burst onto the forum and start marketing your products right away.

When you see topics you can add to, jump in. Add advice, opinions, and value to the conversation. Only when the conversation turns to a topic where your videos are absolutely perfect should you make a pitch, and then keep it subtle. Forum marketing works, but you have to take it slowly.

It's usually OK to have a signature line with your web address listed. If so, do that but don't push your products in that area. Trust that over time people on the forum will become curious and will visit your site and probably sign up to be on your list. They really will, it happens to me all the time when I post in Bill Myers Online (www.bmyers.com) forums.

Some forums will have a special section where members can buy and sell goods. By all means, promote your products there.

MANAGING SOCIAL MEDIA

Don't let social media overload keep you from using social media marketing. You can hire others to help you but there is also a whole range of tools such as seesmic ping (www.seesmic.com) and SocialOomph (www.socialoomph.com) that have cropped up to help you manage your social media activities. Each of the networking sites I mentioned have their own internal organizing components you can use to segregate your friends, followers, and connections into lists as well. They also have notification settings within them.

There have also cropped up social network aggregation platforms (also called "dashboards") like Hootsuite (www.hootsuite.com), Tweetdeck (www.tweetdeck.com), and SocialOomph (www.socialoomph.com) that let you put all your social network activities under one control panel, which eliminates the need to jump from one social media network to another, trying to keep up with what's happening and what your customers are saying.

Action Steps

- If you don't already have one, open a Facebook and Twitter account.
- Make "friends" in Facebook who are influential in your topic area. Post a few times a day.
- Set up a Facebook Page for your business and your videos.
- Consider opening a LinkedIn account.
- Start your own blog. Add content on a regular basis. It doesn't have to be long but be consistent.
- Post videos on YouTube and engage with your viewers.
- Look for forums related to your video topic. Join them and participate. Don't push sales.
- When using social media marketing, make your participation 80 percent giving and helping, and 20 percent or less promoting your products.

Chapter 38

Other Forms of Marketing

Chapter Objectives

- Understand the broad range of additional marketing opportunities available to you.
- Research to determine the best marketing channels for your business.

We're coming to the end of the chapters on marketing but we've barely scratched the surface of the topic. There are so many ways to market your videos in addition to what we've covered. Briefly, here are a few more to consider.

SEARCH ENGINE MARKETING (SEM)

This is a broad category that includes striving to have your website found on search engine results pages through several means, both free and paid.

Search Engine Optimization

As I stated before, search engine optimization is enhancing your website so that it can be ranked high on the search engine results page (SERP) under the organic (non-paid) search results section by doing things like using accurately chosen keywords in headlines and body copy, filling your site with high quality original content, getting high value backlinks from authority sites and others with high page ranks, naming your images with keyword-rich descriptions, and doing a lot of the things that make Google happy. This is an area for further, continuing education and as soon as you think you've figured it out, Google changes the rules. However I do feel it is safe to say that if you focus on providing a content-rich website with a lot of value, that loads quickly and has high value backlinks, you'll continue to be rewarded with a good page rank. If you try to game the system, you may find your rank drops significantly.

Of course Google isn't the only search engine, but at this point in time it is by far the biggest. Other major players include Bing, Yahoo Search, Ask, and AOL Search. Although they work on different algorithms to rank pages, if you follow SEO practices that appeal to Google, you should rank well in all of them.

Pay-Per-Click Advertising

Throughout the book you've seen me use the words pay-per-click. Pay-per-click (PPC) is online advertising through many different channels, the largest one being Google AdWords but it's also available through Yahoo, Microsoft Ad Center, Facebook, and others. It is exactly what it sounds like: you pay per each click on the link you provide in your ad.

Do a search on Google. See all those ads running down the right column of your search results? Those are ads that businesses have created and targeted to the keywords you searched on. If you click one of those ads, the advertiser has to pay a certain amount that they have bid on for that keyword or search term, whether you buy anything or not. Now be nice, don't go clicking just to cost somebody money.

In order for Google ads to appear on a website, the site's owner has to sign up with another Google program, called Google AdSense. Then, if someone clicks on one of those ads they are displaying the owner gets a small commission, usually 25¢ or less but it can be much more, and the advertiser pays Google up to the amount they bid for that keyword for the click. Other online ad networks, like Chitika, work similarly.

You may wish to place ads on your site as a way to make extra money. However, keep in mind that if a person clicks through an ad, they'll be leaving your site and may not return. Is that small commission worth it in lost sales potential if that prospect never comes back? That said, there are many websites whose sole purpose is making money from people clicking on the ads they display so that is a business model to consider as an additional stream of income for you.

PPC is a good way to get a fast start on promoting a new website and building a list but you have to learn how to use it first or it can get expensive or be ineffective. The advantage to the advertiser is that, unlike traditional advertising, you only pay for performance. If no one clicks on your ad, you don't pay anything. Because you can set a daily spending limit you control your advertising budget strictly, but be careful. I accidentally bid $12.00 on a keyword once when I meant to bid 12¢. You can imagine my alarm when I started seeing clicks on my ads. You don't want to make that kind of mistake.

Google provides very detailed statistics on your ads which you can use to make adjustments at will. You can target your ads by country and language which can be useful if your videos have a regional appeal. There are a lot of targeting tools available, making PPC advertising very powerful when used correctly. Start off with a modest budget until you know what you are doing.

Google has some very strict rules about both their AdWords and AdSense programs. If you cross the line you can have your account banned without an explanation, so it pays to learn and abide by their rules. The other PPC channels are less strict and also offer good value, so look into them as well. Yahoo's PPC program is not as big as Google's but their rules are more relaxed and the results can be very good. Some advertisers say they get more bang for their buck with Yahoo and they don't have the complex rules of Google to cope with.

Facebook Ads is another PPC program to consider. In Facebook you can only choose keywords that are in their database and while this may seem restrictive, because these words are based on the interests, activities, books, etc., the millions of Facebook users have listed in their profiles, you'll be getting seen by a highly interested audience for those keywords. They are also less expensive than Google AdWords and you can add images in the ads.

Like other marketing tools, PPC is part art and part science. There is a lot of information available online and in books about PPC advertising if you want to learn more. Definitely visit the major providers and read their instructions and learn more before starting.

THE POWER OF THE PRESS RELEASE

Newspaper, magazine, and even online publication editors have pages to fill, they are busy people and they need news. They don't dig up all the news they print: people send it to them in the form of a press release. A press release is a good way to get the word out about your new video, and the price is right—it's free.

To maximize your chances of having your press release printed, you have to write it as though the magazine or newspaper wrote it; it needs to sound informational like news. Forget about using adjectives such as great, best, fantastic, breakthrough, etc. That sounds like puffery and the editor will see right through it. They're not going to run something that sounds like an advertisement. You must write the press release from a third-party point of view, without sounding like you're promoting a product, which means you must write from a journalist's perspective. Only use "I" or "we" in a quote.

When writing your press release, you need to find an angle to position your product as newsworthy. This means:

- Separate real news about your product from promotional hyperbole.
- Deliver a unique story angle that will be of real interest to the news reading public.
- If your product solves a problem, tell the reader about the problem and then explain how your product is the solution.

Reporters are hassled all day by PR people and really don't care about helping you or promoting your website, your video, your products, or your life story, unless you are providing something that helps make their job easier—that is, a well-written story.

How to format a press release:

- **Headline**—State your most exciting news, finding, or announcement in as few words as possible. Let the headlines you see in newspapers inspire you.
- **The Subhead**—Subheads are remarkably useful tools, yet usually overlooked by press release writers. Basically, the press release subhead gives you the opportunity to flesh out your story and further hook the reporter. They make it easy to scan for information.
- **The Lead**—The lead paragraph includes the "who, what, when, where and how" of the story. If the reporter were only to read the lead of a good press release, they'd have everything they needed to get started. There's no room for BS, hype, or sell. Just the facts!
- **The Body**—The balance of the press release serves to back up whatever claims were made in the lead and headline. Keep it as brief as possible.
- Be sure to include your **contact information**!

In Appendix J, we've included a press release template and a copy of one we sent right after we started selling the DVD we made about my dad.

Since your video will probably be in a narrowly defined niche, you may choose to send your press release to individually selected publications in that niche. If you can find the name of the editor and address it to them by name, great. Otherwise just "News Editor" will do. You can send your release through email if you have the editor's email address. A few years ago I would have said it's better to mail a physical release but now email has become standard practice. If you do submit your release by email make sure you have a strong subject line and it should state NEWS RELEASE. You can also attach images.

If your video has a general appeal you may want to make your press release available to the masses. There are many services, both free and paid, to help you distribute your release to hundreds or thousands of individuals and publications. PRWeb (www.prweb.com) is one of the largest but there are many more. Do an online search on "press release service" to find many such services.

A press release of a new product works best when it is brand new. You aren't limited to sending out a release just on your video, you can also send releases when you'll be speaking at a conference, if you won an award or received a commendation within your niche, or if you are sponsoring an event.

> Wouldn't it be great if reporters were looking for you and asking for your expert opinion? They are, it's called Help A Reporter Out, also known as HARO (www.helpareporter.com). When you join HARO as a source they will send you publicity alerts from reporters looking for information. If you happen to qualify, you can connect with the reporter and possibly get great media exposure. Prices for participation range from free up to $149 per month. The more you pay, the more alerts you'll get and you'll be able to build online profiles that reporters can see.

WEBINARS AND TELESEMINARS

Webinars are a great way to introduce people to the information found in your video, show samples, and take questions from the audience. They frequently incorporate PowerPoint-type presentations. The webinar organizer controls who can "speak" and manages the flow of information.

Webinars are used extensively in the internet marketing world as a tool to build an email list and to launch a new product. These types of webinars have a structure not unlike what you see from marketers on a stage. It is set up something like this: pick one of the key areas within your topic and offer an hour webinar about that specific area touching on the highlights, then 80 percent of the way through the webinar, you go into promotion mode, talking about how your video can help your listeners further, answering questions, then wrapping it up with a call to action. As incentive, it is standard practice to offer a bonus, drastic discount, or both. If this webinar is used to build a list, usually in preparation of a launch, then the wrap up would be to get people excited about what is happening—like a movie trailer excites your interest in seeing the movie.

Here's an example from Dave Sheahan:

At the beginning of the year he offered a webinar entitled Discover the 4 Steps to Transforming Your Body and Mindset for Success. *In that webinar, while he gave you the four steps, he was also explaining how these were the four key elements of his* Dave Sheahan Home Workout System. *Then at the end he encouraged listeners to sign up for the system by offering them a large discount for being on the call.*

Even if your prospect doesn't buy at that time, they are now on your list and you can continue to market to them. One of our other case studies, Jessica Swanson, also uses this marketing technique very effectively to build her list of prospects. That is how I came to be on her mailing list and eventually invested in her Shoestring Marketing Bootcamp video course and Shoestring Marketing University membership program. The other thing you see a lot in the internet marketing world is people with complementary products partnering up to deliver a joint webinar. You split the sales and also build your list at the same time.

Most webinars are live events but we're seeing more pre-recorded webinars that either play on-demand or at specified times. This is a very powerful way to allow people to attend the webinar at their convenience (minus the live interaction). It truly is a 24/7 marketing tool.

Webinar software ranges in cost from free for small meetings to $500 per month for meetings of up to 1,000 attendees. The actual connection of the attendees to the webinar is managed by the software. The service we see being used extensively is GoToWebinar (www.gotowebinar.com) but if you search for "webinar software" online you will find other service providers.

Teleseminars can be used in much the same way and are less technologically challenging. All you and your listeners need is a phone. You can find free teleseminar services but keep in mind that there may be transmission and support problems.

As with your video products, you also need to actively promote your webinar and telesminar, and social media is a great avenue for this.

TRADE SHOWS AND SPEAKING ENGAGEMENTS

This isn't for everyone, but if you can get up in front of a crowd and give a good presentation you can make a lot of money really fast by speaking and selling your products at trade shows, seminars, expos, and conventions. It is also an effective way to brand yourself and position yourself as the expert in your field. If people see you on a stage they will assume you are an expert.

"Back of the room sales" are your immediate goal at such events. You give a talk about your subject, give plenty of good useful information, but as you finish you promote your product and give a strong call to action to buy it right after your talk. Obviously, this works better with physical products that people can take with them but you could promote a special price on your online videos or a subscription to your membership program.

You have to make the push to buy right then because that's your only opportunity with this crowd. It helps to have a compelling incentive, like a huge price discount, big bonuses, etc. A common tactic would go like this: "This product is normally $297, but you're not going to pay that today. In fact, you're not even going to pay $197. For the next 20 minutes only, you can get this fantastic video for only $97.00, and as a bonus for buying today I'll throw in (fill in the blank). Now meet me at the back of the room to get yours. Remember you can only get it at this price today, for the next 20 minutes."

I also recommend announcing a drawing at the beginning of your presentation that will be awarded to only those in attendance at the end of your talk. That is a good way to keep them in their seats and also to collect their cards. (Of course, if you're doing that to add them to your email list, let them know that upfront.) Tell the event promoter that you want to do this and get their approval first.

If you are speaking on the stage of someone else's event you need to carefully read the terms you agreed to abide by. The promoter may be making their money by collecting a percentage of your sales, maybe as much as 50 percent, so they don't want you giving the audience your website information on your slides or business cards to order from later. They'll want to transact the sale through their ordering process and will later pay you your percentage. Professional speaker Alan Berg has found speaking to be a profitable way to sell his books and DVDs.

Alan Berg, Speaker, Author, and Marketing Consultant (www.alanberg.com and www.alanberg.tv)

I've been speaking professionally for over 10 years, but most of that time I was working for a major media company. When I left and became an independent speaker, author, and consultant I started ensuring that I got video of as many of my presentations as possible. I knew that they all wouldn't be high enough quality to sell, but I wanted as much "in the can" as possible. I started having my own presentations professionally taped in April of 2011 and produced my first DVDs in September 2011.

That's how professional speaker, author, and marketing expert Alan Berg got started in video production. I met Alan when we both were panelists for the Building the Ultimate Website: It Can Make or Break Your Business session at the Wedding and Event Videographers Association (WEVA) Expo in 2007. As VP at The Knot, the most-trafficked one-stop wedding planning solution on the web, he oversaw the sales, education, and training of local sales and wedding pros around the country.

Alan wasn't a videographer, he was at WEVA in his capacity as VP at The Knot, sharing his vast knowledge about building a strong website presence and how to use it to market a small business. But he really didn't need to know how to operate a camera to become a video producer.

Because of working with WEVA and other wedding videographers, I have a lot of contacts in the video industry, and I often trade my consulting services for their video production. Also most of my DVDs are my live presentations so there is no studio needed.

Therefore he can easily come up with video programs and get them on the market quickly. He looks to his audiences to determine which program most likely would do well.

The presentations that resonate the best with my audiences are the natural choices for distribution. Without question my best selling program is my video called Close More Sales, Today! I've already had to press [replicate] more copies of that DVD.

So how does he reach his target market?

Although I do have my DVD on my website www.alanberg.com, I've mainly been selling my DVDs "back of room" at my live presentations. I also just recently launched my online video site www.alanberg.tv so they can be watched anytime, anywhere and I've just started an email campaign to promote those online videos.

His DVDs sell for $49.95. At live presentations, he offers two for $80, three for $100 and all five for $150. "As my DVDs are mostly of live presentations I wanted the price to reflect the value and encourage them to buy more than one," he explains. He offers his online videos for three-, six-, and twelve-month subscriptions for $39.95, $59.95, and $99.95 respectively. "I also offer $10 off to members of certain trade associations."

Alan has found that selling physical DVDs at the back of room works the best for him.

There seems to be a lower value placed on the online video content. Consumers have become accustomed to getting so much free content that they seem reluctant to pay a lot for online video. They value the DVD more because they own it.

Content is still king, but you have to know how to connect it with your audience. My videos are between 35 and 75 minutes long. I'm rethinking that strategy and looking to try shorter content that can be offered at a lower price point. It's the podcast and iTunes mentality. If it's an impulse buy, at the right price, then you may have a better chance to get wider acceptance.

He also not only sells videos, he's an author as well and sells his books on his website.

His advice for you?

The internet has reduced the geographic barriers that existed before so anyone, anywhere can find you. That said, there are countless other sites vying for their attention at the same time, so identifying your target audience and getting in front of them is still the rule, only the medium as changed.

I have also had success at selling my DVDs when I spoke to non-profit groups and organizations such as libraries and book clubs. With many of these, I actually showed my video and then sold copies to the audience. In these situations I don't do a really hard sale at the end of my presentation but I will have a table at the back of the room or outside and invite them to talk with me further, ask me questions and let them know they can pick up a copy for themselves. Libraries have community programs and need speakers and presentations so don't overlook these opportunities.

Long term results from speaking consistently at events are that you will make money from immediate sales of your items, you'll build your reputation as an expert, you may actually be paid to keynote events and possibly offered discounted or free exhibit floor space, and you'll build traffic to your website where you can sell your videos on a continuing basis. Once you have a following, then building a membership site could be a logical extension.

ARTICLE MARKETING

Article marketing is publishing articles that deliver valuable content but which ultimately lead readers back to your website or sales location. The goal is to get the articles published on other blogs and online publications with your attribution and website link intact so that you get a backlink and a lead if the reader of the article clicks through. You want to see your article propagate through the internet so that you get many backlinks, which should boost your page rank and result in more web traffic. If your articles are on topic this should lead to targeted traffic.

Short articles are best. Keep it to 800 words or less. They should be informative and related to your video's topic but not sound promotional. You should select the title of your article with SEO in mind. Pick several keywords that people are likely to search on and make them the first part of your title. Write it so that it will solve a problem or promise a benefit. Make sure your keywords appear in the body of the article but do so with discretion. The article should flow naturally and not sound like you intentionally packed it with keywords. If it smacks of keyword stuffing and empty promotional hype then people will click off and may not read anything else you write.

You will have a "resource box" or "bio box" at the end of the article with your name, title, website hyperlink, and a thoughtfully written call to action. For example, add something like this in your bio box: "And you can discover even more about fly fishing and catching the BIG one in our FREE video course: Fly Fishing Made Easy!—Surefire Tips, Strategies, Techniques [and more!] when you visit flyfishingmadeeasy.com."

The fastest way to get your articles published is to submit them to article directories, where they become available for free to other publications and websites. Some locations you can submit articles to include:

- www.articlesfactory.com
- www.articledashboard.com
- www.ezinearticles.com
- www.ideamarketers.com
- www.goarticles.com

Once you submit your articles you can announce their availability at locations like:

- www.tech.groups.yahoo.com/group/aabusiness
- www.groups.yahoo.com/group/free-reprint-articles

Some directories want your article to be exclusively submitted to them. Read their terms of service to learn this. You'll be able to submit a summary of your article for the directory listing. Again, this should contain keywords in the title and have them in the body of the summary. This is how the directory will list your article, so put some thought into it and make it enticing and make the reader want to click through to read more.

You don't get paid by people using your article. What you do get is free publicity and a backlink to your website. The article directories have terms of service that state that users are free to use the articles as long as they keep all of your attribution information at the end of the article. If you are going to use more than one directory, you shouldn't submit the same article to each one. Google has cracked down on many of these directories for delivering regurgitated content, damaging their ratings and reputation, so they have become more diligent in not accepting spammy or duplicate content.

This is a no cost way to build your brand and establish yourself as an expert if done correctly.

GUEST BLOGGING

Writing blog posts for other bloggers is another way to gain authority and traffic to your site. It works in much the same way as article marketing. Start to follow blogs in your industry and check them out on Alexa (www.alexa.com) to find the best-ranking ones. Then look to see if they accept guest bloggers.

You can also find sites such as www.myblogguest.com, a site where you can offer your blogging services and also find guest bloggers for your site. Some of these blogs will pay you for your posts.

MOBILE MARKETING

Mobile marketing is about reaching the growing millions of consumers whom you can contact through their cellular phones or tablet devices. A common tool of mobile marketing is broadcasting simple marketing messages via text message. This is known as SMS (short message service). Text messages have a much higher open rate than email messages so your text marketing message has a better chance of being read this way than in an email.

Add to the high open rate the fact that most users have their phones with them and turned on most of their waking hours, it's no wonder mobile marketing is considered a hot new marketing channel. Users can respond to a message immediately on their mobile phone.

Mobile phone users can visit your website. Since phone screens are small, navigating a website can be a challenge. Scrolling and looking for information on a cell phone screen can get frustrating fast, which is a good reason to keep your website design clean, simple, easy to use and navigate on the reduced screen size of a smartphone. Ways to do this include having a fast-loading site, making navigation simple, designing it so that it isn't cluttered on a small screen, and using large navigation links like the all-important Buy Button that can easily be controlled with thumbs.

There are plugins for WordPress that make your website more mobile friendly, but many cell phone connections are still much slower than a broadband connection on a computer, so keeping a simple, elegant website design is a goal.

With the fast proliferation of smartphones we will undoubtedly see fast evolution of web standards for mobile users. To learn more about mobile marketing visit the Mobile Marketing Association (www.mmaglobal.com).

RADIO AND TV APPEARANCES

If you are asked to appear on a radio or TV show related to your video, it's most likely because you are already considered an expert. Any exposure like that is good. Just be sure to mention how viewers/listeners can learn more, i.e., send them to your website.

Local radio shows needs guests, especially talk radio, so be on the lookout for guest appearance opportunities. Start in your local area and get used to being on camera or in front of a mic. If you are in a city for a speaking appearance, contact local radio stations and inquire if there they would like to have you as a guest.

How about hosting your own radio show? Blog Talk Radio (www.blogtalkradio.com) is a place where you can create your own radio show and make it available to millions of potential listeners. You don't need fancy equipment to do it and it is very inexpensive. The cost ranges from free, with a limit of five simultaneous listeners, up to $39 per month with much larger audience capability and up to two shows per day.

PRINT ADVERTISING

Targeted print advertising is an effective way to get your product in front of the people you want to attract. The key to success is to pick the right venues, whether that's newspapers, trade journals, magazines, conference programs, classified advertising—that's all fair game and may work well for you.

With print advertising you want to know if it is going to the right audience, what the circulation is, and the cost. If you figure you might get a 1 or 2 percent sales conversion, will that cover the cost of advertising and yield a profit? Start small and test first.

Trade journals are highly targeted so check out any specialty publications in your niche. There also might be organizations that publish newsletters and magazines that accept advertising. Go back to the notes you gathered in Chapter 4 and look up the advertising rates in the publications you found. Also www.newspapers.com is a directory of thousands of newspapers all over the world.

The humble classified ad, when well written and placed in a highly targeted publication, can be very effective and economical.

PREMIUMS AND INCENTIVES

Premiums and incentives are very effective sales tools. People love to get those bonus items. It's human nature to want something for free.

Can you think of ways you could use a premium with your videos? It can be a bonus video, ebook, PDF, CD, MP3, or if you send DVDs, maybe you can give them something physical. For Christmas one year, we bought a batch of very inexpensive microfiber cloths and gave them away for free as an incentive if you bought more than one of our car detailing DVDs.

Here's a story about DVDs and offering a premium to schools ...

There's always an overlap of technology when transitioning from one format to another. Until the mid-1990s, my university media department was making all of our products available on VHS tape. When DVD machines started appearing in the consumer market, we wanted to get out of making VHS tapes and transition to DVDs, which are superior in every way. However, schools are very strict about how budgets can be spent. If they have money allocated for instructional materials, that's all they can spend it on. They can't use that money for equipment; that's a different budget item. So theoretically they could buy DVDs but not the DVD players to show them with. This made it very hard for schools to quickly migrate to the new technology.

Since our video series were already expensive, in the $250–$395 range, we decided we'd *give* the schools a free DVD player with every order for one of the big sets. We could buy the DVD players wholesale for $25, which amounted to about a 10 percent discount. This completely destroyed any excuse about not buying our DVDs because the customer didn't have a DVD player. Our school customers loved this and it was a very successful tool for selling high ticket items to schools. Joe Clokey still gives DVD players with every large order as an incentive and it is still an effective tactic.

Search online for "promotional items" and you'll find a bewildering array of offers. If you do use premiums pick something related to your topic that has real value.

WRAPPING IT UP

Trying to cover all of the marketing opportunities for selling your videos is like looking for the end of the internet. It's impossible! Hopefully, you'll find this an exciting range of possibilities and not be overwhelmed. You only have to do one thing first: pick something and get started. Spend some time testing it to decide if it is a good fit for you and your market before you turn to another strategy.

You don't need to do it all—when you find a few things that work really well, focus your efforts on those strategies and you'll see good results.

Action Steps

- Review this list of other marketing possibilities. Make a list of the ones that are appropriate for your videos.
- Many of these are free, some charge fees. Look at your budget and decide what you can afford.
- Take action! Pick at least one and get started.

Chapter 39

It's a Wrap

Chapter Objective

- To inspire you to get started!

Shooting permits, storyboards, camera moves, audio level meters, keyword research, shopping carts, URLs, web hosting, WordPress, security seals, email marketing, pay-per-click, Google AdSense, interview techniques, blogs, social media marketing … whew! We've covered a lot of topics in this book. Is your head spinning?

At first it may seem like a big mountain to climb but as they say, the way to eat an elephant is one bite at a time. If you've read this far then you've learned enough to get started and here is the most important step of all—just start. Don't fall victim to analysis paralysis. You are now far more prepared than I or anyone else I know in this business was when we started out.

Mistakes are bound to happen along the way. That's part of the learning process. As we've emphasized several times, this isn't a "get rich quick" business so be patient and stay the course. If you have a good product at the right price and know how to reach your market, you will be successful. You're going to always be learning, testing, making adjustments, and moving forward.

We meet people all the time with ideas that would make profitable special interest videos but so often they fail to take action. We've seen over and over that for many people it's the marketing phase that stops them in their tracks. That's why we've put so much emphasis on marketing in this book. If you take it one step at a time it takes the mystery out of it and it becomes achievable.

To summarize, here are the general steps you should follow. Keep your ideal customers in mind throughout the process and think how you can serve them best. Always be thinking of how you can reach them, how you can speak to their desires and you'll be well on your way to producing a video with a high chance of success:

1. Choose a topic. What problem or need will it satisfy?
2. Research your topic, market, competition, etc.
3. Identify your ideal customers. Can you reach them? How?
4. Niche it down. Have your topic be as specific and find your own unique selling proposition.
5. Outline your topic based on your research.

6. Choose the production style that best fits the topic; i.e., taped seminar, on-camera narrator, voice-over narrator, screen capture, etc.

7. Put a team together. Are you the expert or do you need a partner? Can you shoot and edit the video or do you need to find a production company or partner to help you? Have you signed agreements with your equity partners?

8. Create a production and marketing budget. Calculate your break even point. Is this realistic?

9. Create a storyboard, script, and shot list. Take your time. These are critical components.

10. Shoot your video. Don't over reach. Keep your first few videos short and simple.

11. Edit the video. Keep it as concise as possible.

12. Choose a fulfillment method. Starting out that could be duplicating and shipping DVDs yourself. Will you sell on-demand videos? Choose a service provider that fits your budget.

13. Try to expand your product offerings by breaking your video into smaller components, adding books from someplace like Amazon.com, find related affiliate products, etc.

14. Develop a marketing plan and design your sales funnel.

15. If you are going to sell from your own website: select a URL, get hosting, build a website with shopping cart. Or sell on Amazon.com, eBay, or an all-in-one online store like Volusion.

16. Write your sales copy.

17. Consider all of the marketing methods we mention: email, direct marketing, video marketing, social media, search engine marketing, pay-per-click, print advertising, article marketing, press releases. Pick a couple that you feel would work for you, learn more about them and start using them to build your list.

18. Launch!

19. Test, measure, test again. Keep refining your marketing.

20. Repeat.

When you break it down into steps it looks much more manageable, don't you agree?

You are not going it alone. We have your back and we really want you to succeed. Throughout this book we've mentioned www.shoot-to-sell.com. That's the website we've built to be the companion to this book and where we will keep revising our information and adding articles, resources, and equipment reviews to help you stay current. The one thing you can count on in this business is change. The website is free, so please visit us there often.

When we finish a day's video shoot we say, "It's a wrap." Time to power down the lights and camera, coil up the cables, put everything back in its place, and go home. That's where we are now. Thanks for reading our book.

It's a wrap.

Sample Work for Hire Agreement
(Consult with an attorney before using)

This Agreement is made this _____ day of _____, _____ between _____ (Company) and _____ (Recipient).

This document confirms the understanding between (Company) and (Recipient) regarding work to be done by (Recipient) as more fully described below:

1. You agree to provide video production services in a manner and form satisfactory to us related to _____ project.
2. We agree to pay Recipient $_____ You receive no further payment from us.
3. Recipient expressly acknowledges that your services hereunder, are being specially ordered and commissioned by us for use in connection with _____ (video). The Work contributed by you hereunder shall be considered a "work made for hire" as defined by the copyright laws of the United States. We shall be the sole and exclusive owner and copyright proprietor of all rights and title in and to the results and proceeds of your services hereunder in whatever stage of completion. If for any reason the results and proceeds of your services hereunder are determined at any time not to be a "work made for hire," you hereby irrevocably transfer and assign to us all right, title and interest therein, including all copyrights, as well as all renewals and extensions thereto.
4. Recipient agrees that we may make any changes or additions to the Work, at our sole discretion, with or without attribution to you. You further agree to waive any "droit moral" or so-called moral rights in the Work.
5. Recipient agrees that he/she shall at all times during this assignment be considered an independent contractor of Company

If Recipient agrees to the above, please sign below to reflect your agreement to the above terms and your intention to be bound hereby.

AGREED AND ACCEPTED:

_____ Date: _____

(signature of Recipient)

_____ Date: _____

(signature of Company)

Sample Letter of Agreement
(Consult with an attorney before using)

May 5, 2008

This LETTER OF AGREEMENT between Panorama Studios and (insert name) details the nature of our business relationship regarding horticulture videos produced by Panorama Studios with the assistance of (insert name).

In exchange for his valuable assistance in video project identification, outline and script development, assistance in arranging with people and locations to shoot, and overall project approval, the following applies:

1. Royalties of 10% of gross sales (wholesale and retail) will be paid to (insert name) from the sale of the DVDs made by Panorama Studios through its various marketing activities. Panorama Studios assumes the full cost of production, duplication, packaging, marketing and shipping. Royalties will be paid quarterly, based on a calendar year. Sales reports will be provided.

2. Current projects covered by this agreement include Hooked On Succulents and Crazy About Cacti, both scheduled for release by the end of 2008. Future projects under similar working arrangements will be included in this same agreement by way of an addendum.

Agreed: _____ Date: _____

Rick Smith, Panorama Studios

_____ Date: _____

Kim Miller, Panorama Studios

_____ Date: _____

(insert name)

Simple Production Budget Sample

Simple Project Budget Format

Pre-Production	Hours	TOTAL
Hourly Rate	$80.00	
Project Planning/Review Sessions	2	$160.00
Production Meetings/Storyboard/Reviews	2	$160.00
Script Writer		$2,000.00
	SUB-TOTAL	$2,320.00

Production		
Location Field Production		$2,000.00
Lodging & Meals		$500.00
Van Rental & Gas		$250.00
Purchase Royalty Free Music		$150.00
Cost of On-Camera Talent (one day)		$500.00
Equipment Rental		$500.00
	SUB-TOTAL	$3,900.00

Post Production	Hours	
Hourly Rate	$80.00	
1st Edit (includes music mix)	30	$2,400.00
Review/Consult	2	$160.00
Final Edit w/Corrections	5	$400.00
Package Design/Additional Graphics	8	$640.00
	SUB-TOTAL	$3,600.00

GRAND TOTAL		$9,820.00

A/V Script Template

TITLE: Your Video Name (Working title—this may change)

CLIENT: (If applicable)

DATE: (use date of each draft)

REVISION NUMBER:

PRODUCER/DIRECTOR:

ADVISORS:

WRITER/EDITOR:

LOCATION COORDINATOR:

NOTES/LEGEND: Section titles are <u>**underlined + bold text,**</u>
                                 Subtitles are **BOLD TEXT + ALL CAPS**
                                 Interviews appear as "quotations + italics
                                 Terms: CU = Close-Up Shot
                                        WS = Wide Shot
                                        MS = Medium Shot
                                        VO = Voice-Over
                                        OC = On-Camera Narrator

TREATMENT: This is what you want to get across with this video, the general outline and what the viewer will learn from this program.

Title of Project		
Date:		
SHOT # LIST	VIDEO—IMAGE	NARRATION—TEXT
Shot 1		
Shot 2		
Shot 3		
Shot 4		
Shot 5		
Shot 6		
Shot 7		
Shot 8		
Shot 9		
Shot 10		
Shot 11		
Shot 12		
Shot 13		
Shot 14		
Shot 15		

Storyboard Templates

STORYBOARD TEMPLATE 1

Project: _____ Page: _____

Location: _____ Date: _____

Shot # _____

Notes:

Shot # _____

Notes:

Shot # _____

Notes:

STORYBOARD TEMPLATE 2

Project: _____ Page: _____

Location: _____ Date: _____

Shot # _____

Notes:

Shot # _____

Notes:

Shot # _____

Notes:

Shot # _____

Notes:

Shot # _____

Notes:

Shot # _____

Notes:

Shot # _____

Notes:

Shot # _____

Notes:

Shot # _____

Notes:

Shot List Template

Title of Project: _____   Date: _____

Location: _____   Page: _____

Shot #	Video Image/Camera Movement	Notes
	Camera A	
	Camera B	

Sample Video Appearance Release Form

(Consult with an attorney before using)

I hereby assign the rights to the video recording(s), audio recording(s), motion picture filming, photograph(s), made of me this date, _____, by _____ (company name).

And I hereby authorize the editing, re-recording, duplication, reproduction, copyright, sale, exhibition, broadcast and/or distribution of said recording(s), film(s), photograph(s) for the purpose of _____ (video).

I hereby waive any right to inspect or approve the finished video recording(s), audio recording(s), film(s), soundtrack(s), photograph(s), or printed matter that may be used in conjunction therewith or to the eventual use that it might be applied.

It is understood that all of the Materials; audio media, videotapes and media, reproductions, photocopies, and electronic and digital copies of the Materials, are the sole property of (company name). I agree not to contest the rights or authority granted to (company name) hereunder. I hereby forever release and discharge Company, its employees, licensees, agents, successors, and assigns from any claims, actions, damages, liabilities, costs, or demands whatsoever arising by reason of defamation, invasion of privacy, right of publicity, copyright infringement, or any other personal or property rights from or related to any use of the Materials. I understand that (company name) is under no obligation to use the Materials.

This document contains the entire agreement between the (company name) and the undersigned concerning the subject matter hereof.

Signature of Participant: _____ Date: _____

Name of Participant: _____

Signature of Producer: _____ Date: _____

Name of Producer: _____

If the Releaser is less than 18 years of age, the following should be filled out.

I _____ hereby warrant that I am the _____ (Parent or Legal Guardian) of _____ (Name of minor subject to this Agreement), a minor, and have full authority to authorize the above Release, which I have read and approved. I hereby release and agree to indemnify the licensed parties and their respective successors and assigns, from and against any and all liability arising out of the exercise of the rights granted by the above Video Appearance Release.

Releaser's Parent or Legal Guardian: _____ Date: _____

Minor's Signature: _____ Date: _____

Sample Materials Release Form
(Consult with an attorney before using)

(INSERT YOUR COMPANY NAME), respectfully requests permission to use

_____ which will become part of the video program
entitled, _____ produced by (YOUR COMPANY NAME).

The rights I am seeking are world rights in all languages for reproduction in all forms and media, including electronic media, in this and any future revisions and editions of the work published by (YOUR COMPANY NAME).

Unless you indicate otherwise, credit will be given to _____ in the program's credit roll.

Fees for this use are: _____ Date: _____

(NAME OF FIRM OR ORGANIZATION) _____

Authorized By: _____

Position: _____

Address: _____

City, State, Zip: _____

Phone Number: (area code) _____

Sample Location Release Form
(Consult with an attorney before using)

This agreement is made this _____ day of _____, _____, between _____ (Name of Location Owner), hereinafter referred to as "Owner," and _____ (Your Company Name), hereinafter referred to as "Company," establishing the conditions under which Company may photograph and/or record Owner's location for _____ (name of video).

Owner's location will be visible in certain shots Company needs for the production. As such, Owner and Company agree to the following provisions:

Permission is granted for the purpose of photographing and recording scenes (interior and/or exterior) for video with the right to exhibit, as well as license others to exhibit all or any part of said scenes in video productions throughout the world; said permission shall include the right to bring personnel and equipment (including props and temporary sets) onto said property, and to remove the same therefrom after completion of work.

The above permission is granted for a period of _____ from _____ to_____

The permission herein granted shall include the right, but not the obligation, to photograph the actual name connected with the premises and to use such name in the program(s).

The undersigned hereby gives to the Company, its assigns, agents, licensees, affiliates, clients, principals, and representatives the absolute right and permission to copyright, use, exhibit, display, print, reproduce, televise, broadcast and distribute, for any lawful purpose, in whole or in part, through any means without limitation, any scenes containing the above described premises, all without inspection or further consent or approval by the undersigned of the finished product or of the use to which it may be applied.

The Company hereby agrees to hold the undersigned harmless of and from any and all liability and loss which the undersigned may suffer, or incur by reason of any accidents, on or about the above-mentioned premises, ordinary wear and tear of the premises in accordance with this agreement excepted.

The undersigned does hereby warrant and represent that the undersigned has full right and authority to enter into this agreement concerning the above-described premises, and that the consent or permission of no other person, firm, or corporation is necessary in order to enable the Company to enjoy full rights to the use of said premises, hereinabove mentioned, and that the undersigned does hereby indemnify and agree to hold the Company free and harmless from and against any and all loss, costs, liability, damages or claims of any nature, including but not limited to attorney's fees, arising from growing out of, or concerning a breach of the above warranty.

By:_____ Date: _____

    Signature of Authorized Property Representative

_____ Date: _____

    Signature of Producer

Press Release Template

Contact: Joe Owner   FOR IMMEDIATE RELEASE

Telephone: 888/555-1111   April 1, 20XX

Cell Phone: 888/555-1111

Email: Joeowner@JoeBusiness.com

Website: www.JoeBusiness.com

MAIN TITLE OF PRESS RELEASE GOES HERE IN ALL UPPER CASE

Subtitle Goes Here in Title Case (Upper and Lower)

Body of Press Release Body of Press Release Body of Press Release Body of Press Release Body of Press Release Body of Press Release Body of Press Release Body of Press Release Body of Press Release Body of Press Release

Body of Press Release Body of Press Release Body of Press Release Body of Press Release Body of Press Release Body of Press Release

Body of Press Release Body of Press Release Body of Press Release

Boilerplate Boilerplate Boilerplate Boilerplate Boilerplate Boilerplate Boilerplate Boilerplate Boilerplate Boilerplate Boilerplate Boilerplate Boilerplate Boilerplate

# # # # #

If you would like more information, or to schedule an interview with Joe Owner, please call George at 888/555/111 or email PR@JoeBusiness.com.

COPY OF ACTUAL PRESS RELEASE WE SENT

Contact: Rick Smith   FOR IMMEDIATE RELEASE

Telephone: 888/744-9381   March 31, 2005

Fax: 888-744-9381

Email: rick@panoramastudios.com

Website: PanoramaStudios.com

FLORIDA ARTISTS HALL OF FAME INDUCTEE PATRICK SMITH NARRATES FILM ABOUT FLORIDA'S PAST

Panorama Studios Releases Award Winning DVD About Patrick D. Smith, Celebrated Author of *A Land Remembered*

A newly released DVD, "Patrick Smith's Florida, A Sense of Place," provides an intimate visit with Patrick D. Smith, one of Florida's most popular writers, a resident of Merritt Island, Florida.

Produced by Panorama Studios, a studio owned by Patrick Smith's son, and narrated by Smith, the film takes viewers off the tourist path and into areas where Smith did unique research for several of his novels, including *Forever Island, Allapattah, Angel City,* and *A Land Remembered.* The film won a 2005 Telly Award and was honored with the Ron Tibbett Founder's award at the 2005 Tupelo Film Festival.

The film also includes historical illustrations and photos of Florida dating back to the 19th century and into the 20th century. One segment of the film follows the route of a summer vacation trip the Smith family took from Mississippi throughout Florida in 1933. It reveals a Florida strikingly different from today, and will be a nostalgic trip for older Florida natives.

"This film was born out of my desire to preserve the message that my father has given in hundreds of speeches across Florida and to personally introduce my father's southern charm and entertaining delivery to a broader public," says Patrick (Rick) Smith, Jr., "It is a tribute to my father who is now unable to make public appearances."

The author of seven novels and two non-fiction books, Smith is a 1999 inductee into the Florida Artists Hall of Fame. He has received more than a dozen literary awards, including the Florida Historical Society's "Greatest Living Floridian" award. He has also been a popular speaker all across Florida, speaking in venues from small town libraries to the Governor's mansion.

The producer of several films, Rick Smith resides in California. He also has won several film awards for his productions that have been broadcast on PBS and the Learning Channel.

For more information on Patrick Smith and the DVD visit http://PatrickSmithOnline.com. The DVD will be available in bookstores and can be ordered immediately by mail from Panorama Studios, P.O. Box 343, Cambria, CA 93428 or from PatrickSmithOnline.com.

Panorama Studios is a multi-media production studio specializing in documentary and special interest video projects. It is located on the southern tip of the beautiful Big Sur coastline in Cambria, California.

#

For further information, or to schedule an interview, contact Rick Smith at 888-744-9381 or email rick@panoramastudios.com

Throughout the book we referenced a lot resources we use and recommend. For your convenience here is a list of blogs, websites, video and photo equipment vendors, specialty supplies, and assorted tools we covered in the book plus some additional sources. This list is just a start. Do an internet search and you'll find many more great tools and services.

AFFILIATE MARKETING RESOURCES

These are some of the best sources of affiliate products, both physical and digital, that you can add to your product offerings.

    www.affiliate-program.amazon.com
    www.astore.amazon.com
    www.cj.com
    www.clickbank.com
    www.ejunkie.com
    www.linkshare.com
    www.shareasale.com

APPS

There are new apps coming on the market constantly. Just do a search for apps for videography.

    8mm Vintage Camera
    iMovie by Apple
    MovieSlate (Clapperboard & Shot Log) by Pureblend Software
    mRelease app
    Splice—Video Editor (free)
    StopMotion Recorder by graf

ARTICLE WRITING SITES

These are the places where you can find articles for your blog, hire article writers and also publish your own articles.

    www.articledashboard.com
    www.articlesfactory.com
    www.ezinearticles.com
    www.goarticles.com
    www.groups.yahoo.com/group/Free-Reprint-Articles
    www.ideamarketers.com
    tech.groups.yahoo.com/group/aabusiness
    www.textbroker.com

BACKDROPS AND STUDIO LIGHTING

www.backdropoutlet.com
www.cowboystudio.com
www.dennymfg.com

BLOGGING

Great links for bloggers. Do a guest blog on other people's blogs or find a guest for your blog. Also start your own internet radio show.

www.blogtalkradio.com
www.mybloguest.com
www.problogger.net

CLOSED CAPTIONING/SUBTITLING

Aberdeen Captioning—www.abercap.com
CPC—www.cpcweb.com

COMPLETE MERCHANT ACCOUNT SOLUTIONS

These are good options if you want an all-in-one solution for your online store, shopping cart, and credit card processing.

Amazon Webstore—webstore.amazon.com
www.instantestore.com
Intuit—www.intuit.com/ecommerce/create-your-online-store
www.premiumwebcart.com
www.volusion.com
Yahoo—www.smallbusiness.yahoo.com/ecommerce

COPYRIGHTS

www.copylaw.com
www.copyright.gov
www.creativecommons.org/licenses/by/3.0/legalcode

CROWDFUNDING

www.indiegogo.com
www.kickstarter.com

DIRECT MARKETING

www.catalogs.com
Direct Marketing Market Place www.dirmktgplace.com

Directory of Mail Order Catalogs www.greyhouse.com
National Directory of Catalogs www.oxbridge.com/ndccluster/thendc.asp
The Direct Marketing Association—www.the-dma.org

DOMAIN NAME

Shop for domain names or use tools like Nameboy to find permutations of a domain name.

www.cheapnames.com
www.domainsbot.com
www.godaddy.com
www.instantdomainsearch.com
www.justdropped.com
www.nameboy.com
www.networksolutions.com
www.snapnames.com

DVD DUPLICATION AND FULFILLMENT SERVICES

From inexpensive to beautiful multi-disc packaging and fulfillment, these are top names to turn to.

Amazon's Createspace—www.createspace.com/products/dvd
www.amazonservices.com/content/fulfillment-by-amazon.htm
www.discmakers.com
www.kunaki.com
www.moldingbox.com
www.speakerfulfillmentservices.com

EMAIL SERVICE PROVIDERS

Top names in email services. MailChimp has a free program.

www.aweber.com
www.constantcontact.com
www.mailchimp.com
www.verticalresponse.com

EQUIPMENT VENDORS

Our favorite online film and video equipment suppliers.

Adorama—www.adorama.com
B&H Photo & Video—www.bhphotovideo.com
Film Tools—www.filmtools.com
Full Compass—www.fullcompass.com
Markertek—www.markertek.com
Sound Professionals—www.soundprofessionals.com

FILM DISTRIBUTORS

Sources to get your film distributed.

> www.distribber.com
> www.filmbinder.com—Documentaries
> www.mindbites.com

GRAPHIC DESIGN

> www.99designs.com
> www.fiverr.com

INFORMATION PRODUCTS PUBLISHING

I'm a long time subscriber to Bill Myers's membership site and recommend it.

> Bill Myers Online—www.bmyers.com

INTERNET LAW

The CAN-SPAM Act (www.business.ftc.gov/documents/bus61-can-spam-act-compliance-guide-business).

KEYWORD RESEARCH

> Google Alerts—www.google.com/alerts
> https://adwords.google.com/o/KeywordTool
> www.dummies.com
> www.google.com/trends
> YouTube.com Keyword Tool—https://ads.youtube.com/keyword_tool

LINK SHORTENERS

> bit.ly
> tiny.ccurl.com

MERCHANT ACCOUNT SOLUTIONS FOR INTERNET BUSINESSES

> www.charge.com
> www.chargetoday.com
> www.ipowerpay.com
> www.merchantwarehouse.com
> www.paypal.com

MOBILE MARKETING

This is a great place to learn more about mobile marketing.

> Mobile Marketing Association—www.mmaglobal.com

MUSIC LIBRARIES

We often use these royalty-free music and sound effects libraries.

    www.audiojungle.net
    www.music2hues.com
    www.sounddogs.com

MUSIC LICENSING

    ASCAP (American Society of Composers, Authors and Publishers)—www.ascap.com
    BMI (Broadcast Music, Inc.)—www.bmi.com
    SESAC—www.sesac.com

OUTSOURCING SERVICES

These are good places to turn when looking for video, scriptwriting, marketing, administrative, and web design services.

    www.angieslist.com
    www.elance.com
    www.fiverr.com
    www.freelanced.com
    www.odesk.com
    www.scripted.com
    www.weva.com

PACKAGING AND SHIPPING

Uline has the best customer service of any business we have ever worked with.

    www.barcodestalk.com/bar-code-numbers
    www.uline.com—Box number for DVD mailer—S-10395

PAYMENT GATEWAY

    www.authorize.net

PHOTO EDITING SOFTWARE

    Photoshop & Photoshop Elements www.adobe.com
    www.pixlr.com
    www.portraitprofessional.com

PRINT ADVERTISING OUTLETS

    www.newspapers.com

PRINTING

www.printplace.com
www.vistaprint.com

PROJECT MANAGEMENT/BUSINESS MANAGEMENT TOOLS

www.37signals.com (Basecamp)
www.bizpad.com
www.box.net
www.docs.google.com
www.dropbox.com
www.evernote.com
get.wunderkit.com
www.market7.com
Open Office Productivity Suite—www.openoffice.org
www.pbworks.com
www.teamlab.com
www.workflowy.com

PUBLIC DOMAIN IMAGES

www.archive.org
www.morguefile.com

SCREEN CAPTURE SOFTWARE

Camtasia www.techsmith.com
CamStudio—www.camstudio.org
Jing—www.techsmith.com
Screenflow www.telestream.net

SCRIPTWRITING SOFTWARE

Adobe Story www.adobe.com
Scripped Writer—www.scripped.com
www.finaldraft.com

SHOPPING CARTS

www.1shoppingcart.com
www.infusionsoft.com
www.oscommerce.com
www.paypal.com
www.shopping-cart-reviews.com
www.volusion.com
www.zen-cart.com

SOCIAL BOOKMARKING SITES

www.delicious.com
www.reddit.com
www.stumbleupon.com

SOCIAL MEDIA MANAGEMENT TOOLS

www.bufferapp.com
www.hootsuite.com
seesmic.com
www.socialoomph.com
timely.is
www.tweetdeck.com

SOCIAL MEDIA SITES

www.facebook.com
www.linkedin.com
www.twitter.com

SPECIAL INTEREST VIDEOS

www.shoot-to-sell.com
www.sivacademy.com
www.specialinterestvideo.org
www.howtosellyourvideos.com

STOCK PHOTO AND VIDEO LIBRARIES

www.dreamstime.com
www.footagefirm.com
www.loc.gov/library/libarch-digital.html
www.pond5.com

VIDEO EDITING/DVD AUTHORING SOFTWARE

Adobe Premiere www.adobe.com
Adobe Premiere Elements www.adobe.com
Avid Media Composer www.avid.com
Corel VideoStudio Pro X5 www.corel.com
Cybelink PowerDirector www.cyberlink.com
DVD Studio Pro – www.apple.com
Encore www.adobe.com
Final Cut Pro www.apple.com
iMovie www.apple.com
Microsoft Windows Movie Maker www.windows.microsoft.com

Pinnacle Studio (HD & Ultimate) www.pinnaclesys.com
PluralEyes – http://www.singularsoftware.com/pluraleyes.html
www.singularsoftware.com/presto.html
Sony Vegas Movie Studio HD www.sonycreativesoftware.com
Womble EasyDVD www.womble.com

VIDEO EDITING/PRODUCTION TRAINING

Focal Press www.focalpress.com
Larry Jordan www.larryjordan.biz
www.lynda.com
www.rippletraining.com
tv.adobe.com

VIDEO EFFECTS

Animoto—www.animoto.com
www.darkroomdesign.net
www.videohive.net

VIDEO SHARING

Amazon S3 – Amazon.com/s3
Blip.tv
Hulu.com
ITunes http://www.apple.com/itunes/
Viddler.com
Vimeo.com
www.ezs3.com
www.trafficgeyser.com
www.tubemogul.com
YouTube www.youtube.com

VOICE-OVER TALENT

www.voice123.com
www.voices.com
www.voicetalentnow.com

WEB HOSTING

www.bluehost.com
www.hostgator.com

WEB VIDEO RESOURCES

www.reelseo.com
www.webvideouniversity.com

WEBINAR SOFTWARE

www.gotomeeting.com/fec/webinar
www.meetcheap.com

WEBSITE OWNERSHIP LOOKUP

www.whois.com/whois

WHOLESALE DVD DISTRIBUTORS

Alliance Entertainment www.allianceentertainment.org
Baker & Taylor www.baker-taylor.com
www.waxworks.com

WORDPRESS TUTORIALS

Christina Hills Website Creation—www.websitecreationworkshop.com/blog
www.wp101.com

A/B Testing Comparing two different versions of a sales element, i.e., copy, price, etc., with live traffic for a length of time, then measuring which version had better conversion rates.

Above the Fold Refers to the top portion of a web page that is visible once the page has loaded without scrolling.

Ad Tracking Software Software designed to manage and track your online marketing campaigns.

AIDA A common acronym used to clarify the four basic rules of good copywriting: attention, interest, desire, and action. It is a reminder to include all of these elements in your copy.

Alexa The leading internet statistics engine which computes the traffic rankings of all websites through analysis of web usage of not only its millions of Alexa Toolbar users but also data obtained from other traffic data sources.

Algorithm A set of rules or logic written into software so that a program will produce the intended results from given input.

Amaray The plastic DVD case that opens like a book.

Article Directories (Article Sites) Websites that collect and share an extensive assortment of articles written about many subjects.

Article Marketing A type of marketing strategy where individuals or businesses write articles and submit to publications and/or online article directories to increase exposure to their business and drive traffic to their website.

Aspect Ratio The dimensions of a TV or movie screen image described in terms of width by height.

Attraction Marketing A marketing technique using advertising and content marketing to build trust and loyalty among prospects through sharing valuable information about the topic and product.

Authority Site A website recognized by search engine algorithms as a leading online source of information. These sites have high page ranks and therefore inbound links coming from them to your site improves your page rank and traffic.

Autoresponder A program that sends an automatic email that you set up in advance and is triggered by an action such as signing up on an email list or buying a product.

B-roll Extra footage captured and added to your production when editing. It is used to add greater flexibility in post-production and also to enrich the video's story.

Backlinks (Inbound Links) Links from other websites that are directed to your website and are important in SEO.

Bandwidth As it relates to web hosting, is the amount of data that your hosting company allows to pass between your website and the rest of the internet within a time period.

Bid—Pay-Per-Click (PPC Bid) The dollar amount an advertiser offers to pay to secure certain keywords in his Pay-Per-Click advertising.

Black Hat SEO The techniques used to try to trick the search engines and get higher search rankings unethically.

Blocking Determining where on the set or on location the talent will move and be so that audio, lighting, and camera placement can be set.

Blog (Web Log, Weblog) A frequently updated, chronological personal online journal or publication filled with text, images, videos, or web links.

Blogger The author of a blog. It is also the name of Google's free blogging platform.

Boom Microphone A microphone attached to a pole or arm which is extended toward the talent.

Boom Operator The person who holds and operates the boom microphone.

Bounce Rate The percentage of your web visitors who leave after viewing only a single page.

Broken Link/Dead Link A link on your website that sends people to a bad (error) page or the wrong place.

Call Sheet An instruction sheet for the talent and crew denoting who will be needed for which scenes, when they will be required, and where they should be.

Call to Action The copy you use in your marketing message to urge the reader, listener, or viewer to take an immediate and desired action, such as Click Here or Buy Now.

Camera Operator (Cameraman) The person who operates the camera.

Campaign In this context, an advertising or marketing campaign. A series of promotions that follow a theme.

Capture Page *See* Landing Page

Chromakey A technique done in editing where a specific color background (chroma) is rendered transparent so that another background can show.

Clapboard (Clapper) A small board that holds information identifying the date, shot, and take number. Used in filmmaking where audio is recorded separately: the sharp "clap" noise is used in synchronizing picture and sound in the editing process.

Clickthrough Rate (CTR) The average number of clicks an ad or banner receives divided by the number of impressions.

Close Captioned (CC) A process that displays text of the program's audio portion on screen as it occurs.

Close-up (CU) A shot that reveals your subject in more detail because the subject is shown larger in the frame.

Content Marketing The marketing technique of creating and offering relevant and valuable content to a targeted audience with the objective of encouraging them to take action.

Continuity The seamlessness of the details of the physical elements, actions of the talent, placement of props, the lighting, clothing, etc., from one shot to another within a scene.

Conversion Rate The percentage of people who click through a link to your site and take the desired action, i.e., click through an emailed link, click through an ad and buy, opt-in to your email list, etc.

Cookie (In affiliate marketing) An ID tag the affiliate software places on a prospect's computer to keep track of which affiliate link referred each prospect so that if a sale is made, the referring affiliate will get credit and a commission.

Copy (Marketing Copy) Text that is written for promotional and marketing purposes to persuade the reader, listener, or viewer to act.

Copywriting The act of writing marketing and promotional copy.

Cost-Per-Click (CPC) The cost the advertiser paid each time a person clicked through his PPC ad.

Coverage A variety of shots to give an editor plenty of material to work with. They usually include a mix of medium and close-up shots, but also wide shots for establishing a scene.

Crawler *See* Search Engine Spider

Crew The people involved in the shooting and production side of your video. That can include a camera operator, grip, audio, and gaffer.

Cut The end of the scene or the breaking up of shots in the editing process. It can also be what the director calls to end the shooting and is used to describe the completely edited version of a movie.

Cutaway A shot that cuts away from the action at hand and should be related to the scene.

Depth Of Field The range of distance between the nearest and farthest objects in a scene that appear sharp in an image. DOF for short.

Diffuser A white or pearlescent piece of material that diffuses or spreads out light, softening harsh shadows. It is also a type of camera filter used to create a soft focus effect.

Digital Single-Lens Reflex Camera (DSLR) A digital camera that combines the functionality of a single-lens reflex camera with a digital back.

Director The principal creative person whose job it is to communicate and direct the action during the shooting according to the script, storyboard, and shot lists.

Dissolve (Cross Dissolve) An editing technique used as a transition between two shots where the image of one shot is gradually replaced by the image of another.

Documentary A non-fiction video or film which is usually a journalistic record of an event, person, or place.

Domain Name The unique location or address of a website.

Dutch Tilt A shot composed at a diagonal to the horizon line.

ebook An electronic book.

eCommerce Buying and selling over the internet.

Editing (Film Editing) Constructing the sequence of events in a movie.

Editor The person who carries out the editing function.

Email Marketing Service An online service that allows you to send thousands of emails at one time, track and analyze email performance, and allows subscribers to easily unsubscribe.

Equipment The camera, lighting, and audio gear required to shoot a video.

Establishing Shot Usually the first shot of a new scene, designed to show the audience where the action will take place or to establish a concept.

Evergreen Meaning the information in the product will be relevant for a long time or more.

Exclusivity A contract term where one party grants another party the sole rights with regard to a particular business function such as between a distributor and a video producer.

Ezine An electronic magazine or newsletter that is usually syndicated.

Fade An editing technique showing the smooth, gradual transition from an image to complete blackness or vice versa.

FAQ (Frequently Asked Questions) A set of questions that are commonly asked on a given topic along with their answers.

Flat Rate Charging a single fixed fee.

Forum An online discussion site.

Frame In terms of composing a shot, a frame is the image that makes up the complete moving picture. In the recording process video consists of a number of frames or images per second.

Frame Rate (Frames per Second) The number of frames captured or projected per second. NTSC, the standard in the United States, is 29.97 frames per second.

Fulfillment The process of delivering the product to the customer, beginning when an order is placed and ending when the product is satisfactorily in the customer's hands.

Fullscreen A term used to describe the shape a film image is in order for it to fill a regular TV screen. Also called (4:3) which is the aspect ratio of 4 inches across by 3 inches high on older television sets.

Gaffer The crew member who is in charge of the lighting on a shoot. Also an electrician on the set.

Gaffer's Tape A flexible, tough, fabric-backed adhesive tape that can be ripped apart easily and removed from surfaces cleanly. It is used a lot for securing cables to surfaces.

Google AdSense Google's advertisement service which allows users to post ads from Google AdWords programs on their websites and YouTube videos.

Google AdWords Google's Pay-Per-Click advertising program.

Graphics The images and illustrations used in a video production, on a website, and in marketing materials.

Grip The crew member responsible for adjusting and maintaining all the production equipment on the shoot.

Hyperlink A graphic or piece of text on a web page or in an email that connects (links) to another spot on the page, a separate page, or another web page or site.

HyperText Markup Language (HTML) A computer language developed for website creation.

Inbound Links *See* Backlinks

Internet Service Provider (ISP) The company that provides you access to the Internet.

Jump Cut Two sequential shots, where the second image closely matches the image of the previous shot causing it to look like the camera "jumped" thus interrupting the continuity of the production.

Keyword A word used in performing a search online.

Keyword Research The search for and analysis of keywords related to your topic.

Keyword Stuffing Excessively and unnaturally using keywords on a page or in an article to enhance your SEO.

Landing Page (Capture Page, Lead Capture Page) A single web page that appears in response to clicking through a link with directed sales copy encouraging a call to action.

Lavalier Microphone Also known as a lapel mic. A small microphone that attaches to a person's clothing. It can be wired or wireless.

Lead Generating Video A video designed to attract new leads to your website or landing page.

Link Juice The search engine credibility and/or page rank one website link passes to another site. Backlinks from authority sites have good link juice.

Link Shortening A service that substantially shortens the length of a URL and still directs the person to the appropriate page.

Location Filming at a place different than a studio and not constructed specifically for the production.

Long Tail Keywords A keyphrase used in a search

Lower Third A text or graphic used mainly to introduce the person on camera and placed in the title safe lower area of the screen.

Marketing Mix The mix of product, price, promotion, place, and position in your marketing strategy. This is different than promotional mix.

Medium Shot A shot that usually shows the characters from the waist up.

Narration The information or story that is spoken aloud in a video.

News Feed (*See also* RSS) A data format used to provide users with frequently updated website content.

Niche In our usage of the word we are speaking of a group of people with a shared interest, like people who enjoy fly fishing.

Non-Linear Editing Editing video footage without needing to assemble it in linear sequence. Non-linear editing software allows you to cut, copy and paste footage as you would text with a word processor.

Offline Business activities, primarily related to marketing, that are not done over the internet.

On-Camera Everything, primarily the talent, that is shot in front of the camera. Also refers to equipment attached to the camera, such as an on-camera microphone or on-camera light.

On Consignment Product given to a business to sell whereby they do not pay for it until it sells.

On Spec Doing work without pay (speculative) work, done with the assumption that it will sell later.

Online Business activities, primarily related to marketing, that are done over the internet.

Open Source Software Software that is available free of charge. Users are permitted to make their own modifications.

Opt-In A person who by submitting an online form and giving their email address, i.e., opting in, has given their permission for a specific business to send them email.

Organic Listings (or Search) The websites that show up in a search engine results page that were found based on their contents' relevance to the keyword(s) searched on and not through a Pay-Per-Click ad.

Outsource To get work done by people outside of your organization.

Over the Shoulder Placing the camera to shoot over the one person's shoulder while capturing the person opposite him.

PageRank (R) The patented analysis algorithm that Google uses to measure the importance of a web page; and it's one of the ways used to determine which pages will appear in a search result.

Pan Rotating a camera horizontally (panning across) during the shot.

Pay-Per-Click (PPC) An online pay for performance advertising model used to direct traffic to websites and where payment is made to the PPC service provider only when the link is clicked through.

Permission Marketing A marketing strategy based on getting your customer's consent to receive information from you.

Pickup Shots Shots that are created after the main videography is completed.

Ping A computer utility used to test network connections. In relation to blogging, it means updates on your blog are sent out to crawlers so they can index your site and content much faster.

Podcast A series of audio, video, and document files that are syndicated and delivered over the internet.

Point Of View (POV) The angle in which the camera records the scene from a particular character's or object's viewpoint.

Pop Up (Pop Under) A form of online advertising you can place on your website to capture email addresses or drive traffic to another site.

Post A word for a single entry in your blog which is then stored in your blog's database. It is also used to describe the action of writing or adding images and video in your social media site feed.

Post-Production A term for everything done to the video after the shooting is finished through completion of the final editing process.

Pre-Production The process of making all the arrangements for the filming of a video production. It can include hiring cast and crew, location scouting, script editing, and set building.

Production The stage of the video project where the video is created and shot.

Production Schedule A detailed plan of how the production will be done over a given time frame, detailing not only the timing of activities but how the production budget will be spent.

Promotional Mix The combination of the marketing tools, i.e., direct marketing, advertising, video marketing, public relations, etc., you will use in your marketing campaign. Not to be confused with marketing mix.

Public Domain Creative works (video, images, books, etc.) whose intellectual property rights are ineligible for copyright protection or have expired or forfeited copyrights. They can be copied and used without permission.

Radio Microphone Also known as a wireless microphone. The mic connects to a transmitter and broadcasts wirelessly to a receiver.

Rate Card An informational document that details the prices for various advertising rates and placement options available for a media outlet.

Reaction Shot A shot that will be included in the final edit which shows the reaction of the person on camera to a scene. It is used as a cutaway from the scene to show the reaction of a character to the action in the scene.

Reflector A tool, usually made with reflective, metallic material that uses a light source to reflect or "bounce" light to where you want it in a scene.

Releases Documents that give written permission to the video producer to use a person's image, location, or creative property, etc., in a video production.

Room Tone A short recording of the "silence" or ambient sounds at a location or space when no one is talking. It is used in the editing process to mask digital silence.

Royalty Payment made to a contributor to a video project based upon sales of that item.

RSS A family of web or news feed formats used to publish frequently updated blog posts, video, and audio files or news stories in a standardized format.

Run and Gun A style of shooting that usually involves hand-held camera work with no particular shooting plan other than keeping things in frame and following the action.

Safe Area There are two types of Safe Area: Title Safe and Action Safe. Graphical and titling elements all need to fit within the Title Safe area to insure that nothing will get cut off on the viewer's screen. This is more of an issue with older TVs. Action Safe is a wider area that should show on most television sets, but does not go to the edge of the frame.

Sales Funnel (or called Marketing Funnel) A structured approach to selling a product that is designed to direct purchasers through the sales process, eventually leading them to buy.

Sales Page A page that features the product a person is interested in when they click on an ad, email, or other web page link.

Scene A shot (or series of shots) that together make up a single, complete, and cohesive action within your video.

Screen Capture Software that records the actions of a user on a computer screen, such as demonstrating software, running a PowerPoint slide show, etc.

Screencast Movie A short movie recording of the changes over time that a person sees on a computer screen, usually with a narration track included.

Script A document detailing the visual and auditory elements that will be recorded.

Search Engine Marketing (SEM) The process of using search engines to promote your business through utilizing search engine optimization. It could also include using pay-per-click and other paid search advertising.

Search Engine Optimization (SEO) Using targeted keyword phrases and website elements to maximize your website's position in the organic listings of search engine results.

Search Engine Results Page (SERP) A listing of web pages that show up when a keyword or keyphrase is searched on.

Search Engine Spider (also called crawler, bot, or webcrawler) A program that is automatically and continuously dispatched by search engines to find and obtain web pages to index. It's called a spider because it *crawls* over the Web.

Search Engine Submission The process of providing a URL to a search engine so that the search engine becomes aware of and indexes the site or page.

Set The environment where filming takes place.

Shooting Script The detailed script that is used during the filming of the video that contains numbered scenes and technical notes.

Shopping Cart A software program that makes your website's products available for online ordering. Customers may select, view, add/delete, and purchase the product.

Shot A continuous block of unedited footage that runs for an uninterrupted period of time.

Shot Composition The arranging of key visual elements within the frame so that they communicate your intended message clearly.

Shot List A production document that contains shot numbers, descriptions, everything required for a particular scene, and groups shots by scene, location, talent and time of day for efficiency.

Shotgun Microphone A highly directional microphone with a narrow range of sensitivity that must be pointed directly at its target sound source.

Slate See Clapboard.

SLR Single-lens reflex (camera).

Social Bookmarking A method for storing, organizing, managing, searching, and sharing the websites you bookmark.

Social Media The process of communicating and exchanging user-generated content to create, build, and nurture relationships online.

Social Networking Actively networking using social media platforms.

Sound Effects Artificially created or enhanced sounds that are added during post-production.

Special Interest Video (SIV) Videos that appeal to a special interest, are non-fiction in nature, and usually not made for broadcast.

Split Testing *See* A/B testing

Squeeze Page A single web page created with the sole purpose of capturing information for follow-up marketing.

Stock Music Music that is not written for the particular video. You can find and purchase stock music from music libraries.

Stock Video Footage (Stock Footage) Moving images that were not shot with any particular production in mind. You can find and buy stock footage from a film library.

Storyboard A sequence of drawings created to communicate the shots planned for a production and the desired general visual appearance on-camera of a scene.

Subtitle The textual translation or transcription of the dialog or narrative in a video program. It is usually displayed at the bottom of the screen.

Take A single continuous recording of a scene with no break in time.

Talent The people (cast) who will be featured in your video, either on-camera or as a voice-over narration.

Target Audience A specific group of prospects within your target market at which your marketing message is aimed.

Target Market A group of potential customers you have identified to receive your promotional effort because they have needs or problems that your products can fulfill.

Teleprompter A tool that provides the narrator with the correct lines from the script.

Text Ad An online advertisement that uses only text-based hyperlinks.

Tilt The action of rotating the camera either up or down.

Two-Shot A shot of two subjects, usually framed fairly close.

Uniform (or Universal) Resource Locator (URL) The address of a web page.

Unique Selling Proposition Outlining and communicating the qualities that are unique to your product and what differentiates it from your competitors' and in so doing, edifying why your customer will want to buy it from you.

Vertical Niche A very narrow segment of a group or niche. For example, bird owners are a large niche. Parrot owners are a more narrow niche. Breeders of Sulfur Crested Cockatoos are a vertical niche.

Video Blog (or Vlog) A form of blogging using mostly video.

Video Cassette Recorder (VCR) The household video player that records and plays VHS tapes.

Video Home System (VHS) Video Cassettes (or Tapes) An analog recording videocassette that is played on a VCR system.

Video Publishing The process of producing and disseminating information in video format to the general public. It includes the stages of the pre-production, production, editing, graphic design, and marketing, selling and distribution of the videos.

Viral Video A video that becomes popular through people sharing it over the internet, typically through video sharing websites, social media, and email.

Voice-Over Off-camera commentary or narration.

Voice-Over Artist The unseen narrator who does the speaking necessary to create a voice-over.

Web Directory A site that specializes in organizing, categorizing, and linking to other websites.

Web Hosting A type of internet hosting service that provides all the storage, connectivity, and services necessary to make a website accessible on the internet.

Webcrawler *See* Search Engine Spider

Webinar A seminar or meeting conducted over the web via special software.

Website Analytics A tool for collecting, analyzing, and measuring internet data for the purposes of understanding and optimizing web traffic, conducting business, market research, and assessing the effectiveness of a website.

White Balance A setting that allows the camera to adjust for lighting so that white objects in the shot appear white.

Wide Angle Shot A camera shot that shows the entire scene.

Widescreen An aspect ratio for video or movies that is wider than 4:3 standard definition. In HD videos the most common dimension is 16:9. Other aspect ratios exist but are generally not available on consumer and prosumer camcorders.

Wipe A type of video transition where one image travels across another to indicate a change of scene. The most common is a horizontal wipe but other examples include barn door wipe, iris wipe, clock wipe (to indicate passage of time).

Word-of-Mouth Marketing A marketing method that relies on unpaid promotion in which satisfied customers tell other people how much they like a product.

WordPress A popular, open-source (i.e., free) web publishing application that is often used for blogging. It is available as a hosted service (wordpress.com) and self-hosted platform (wordpress.org).

Work for Hire While in most cases the person who creates a copyrightable work holds all rights for that work, two exceptions to that rule are: (1) an employee who does the work within the scope of their employment or (2) independent contractors that are specially commissioned by the business and the two parties agree in a contract that it is a work made for hire.

Working Title The temporary name of your project used during development and production.

Wrap When the shooting is done, either for the day or the entire production.

Zoom A shot where you are adjusting the lens magnification of an object in a scene from a wide view to a close-up (zoom in) or vice versa (zoom out).

15 SHOOTING YOUR SPECIAL INTEREST VIDEO

1. Dexter, Ron. "Inside Search." 2 Feb. 2012. http://rondexter.com/intermediate/production/interview_techniques.htm

36 VIDEO MARKETING BASICS

1. *Trend Data.* 23 Mar. 2012. http://www.pewinternet.org/static-pages/trend-data-(adults)/online-activities-total.aspx
2. Ryan, Shaun. "Inside Search." *Internet Retailer* 31 Mar. 2010. http://www.internetretailer.com/2010/03/31/inside-search (accessed 1 Mar. 2012).

37 SOCIAL MEDIA MARKETING

1. It's a Social World: Top 10 Need-to-Knows about Social Networking and Where It's Headed. 21 Dec. 2011. http://www.comscore.com
2. *Facebook Shows Strong Growth over Past Five Years.* 1 Feb. 2012. http://www.comscore.com

Index

Note: Page numbers followed by "*t*" refer to tables.